STREET ATLAS
Hertfordshire

Contents

PHILIP'S

First edition published 1986
Fourth edition published 1994
First colour edition published 1996
Reprinted 1997, 1998, 1999 by

Ordnance Survey® and George Philip Ltd, a division of
Romsey Road   Octopus Publishing Group Ltd
Maybush   2-4 Heron Quays
Southampton   London
SO16 4GU   E14 4JP

ISBN 0-540-06174-3 (hardback)
ISBN 0-540-06175-1 (spiral)

To the best of the Publishers' knowledge, the information in this atlas was
correct at the time of going to press. No responsibility can be accepted
for any errors or their consequences.

The representation in this atlas of a road, track or path is no evidence
of the existence of a right of way.

**The mapping between pages 1 and 176 (inclusive) in this atlas is
derived from Ordnance Survey® OSCAR® and Land-Line® data, and
Landranger® mapping.**

Ordnance Survey, OSCAR, Land-Line and Landranger are registered trade
marks of Ordnance Survey, the national mapping agency of Great Britain.

Printed and bound in Spain by Cayfosa

Key to map symbols

▬▬	**Motorway**
▬▬	**Primary Routes** (Dual carriageway and single)
▬▬	**A Roads** (Dual carriageway and single)
▬▬	**B Roads** (Dual carriageway and single)
▬▬	**C Roads** (Dual carriageway and single)
──	**Minor Roads**
─ ─ ─	**Roads under construction**
─ · ─ · ─	**County boundaries**
──	**All Railways**
·······	**Track or private road**
──┼──	**Gate or obstruction to traffic** (restrictions may not apply at all times or to all vehicles)
─ ─ ─	**All paths, bridleways, BOAT's, RUPP's, dismantled railways, etc.**

> The representation in this atlas of a road, track or path is no evidence of the existence of a right of way

174	**Adjoining page indicator**

Acad	**Academy**	Mon	**Monument**
Cemy	**Cemetery**	Mus	**Museum**
C Ctr	**Civic Centre**	Obsy	**Observatory**
CH	**Club House**	Pal	**Royal Palace**
Coll	**College**	PH	**Public House**
Ex H	**Exhibition Hall**	Resr	**Reservoir**
Ind Est	**Industrial Estate**	Ret Pk	**Retail Park**
Inst	**Institute**	Sch	**School**
Ct	**Law Court**	Sh Ctr	**Shopping Centre**
L Ctr	**Leisure Centre**	Sta	**Station**
LC	**Level Crossing**	TH	**Town Hall/House**
Liby	**Library**	Trad Est	**Trading Estate**
Mkt	**Market**	Univ	**University**
Meml	**Memorial**	YH	**Youth Hostel**

⇌	**British Rail station**
🚂	**Private railway station**
●──	**Bus, coach station**
◆	**Ambulance station**
◆	**Coastguard station**
◆	**Fire station**
◆	**Police station**
✚	**Casualty entrance to hospital**
✛	**Churches, Place of worship**
H	**Hospital**
_i_	**Information Centre**
P	**Parking**
▢	**Post Office**
●	**Public Convenience**
▬	**Important buildings, schools, colleges, universities and hospitals**
River Soar	**Water Name**
·········	**Stream**
▬ ▬	**River or canal** (minor and major)
▬	**Water Fill**
▭	**Tidal Water**
▬	**Woods**
▬	**Houses**

0		¼		½		¾		1 mile

0		250 m		500 m		750 m		1 Kilometre

The scale of the maps is 5.52 cm to 1 km (3½ inches to 1 mile)

The small numbers around the edges of the maps identify the 1 kilometre National Grid lines

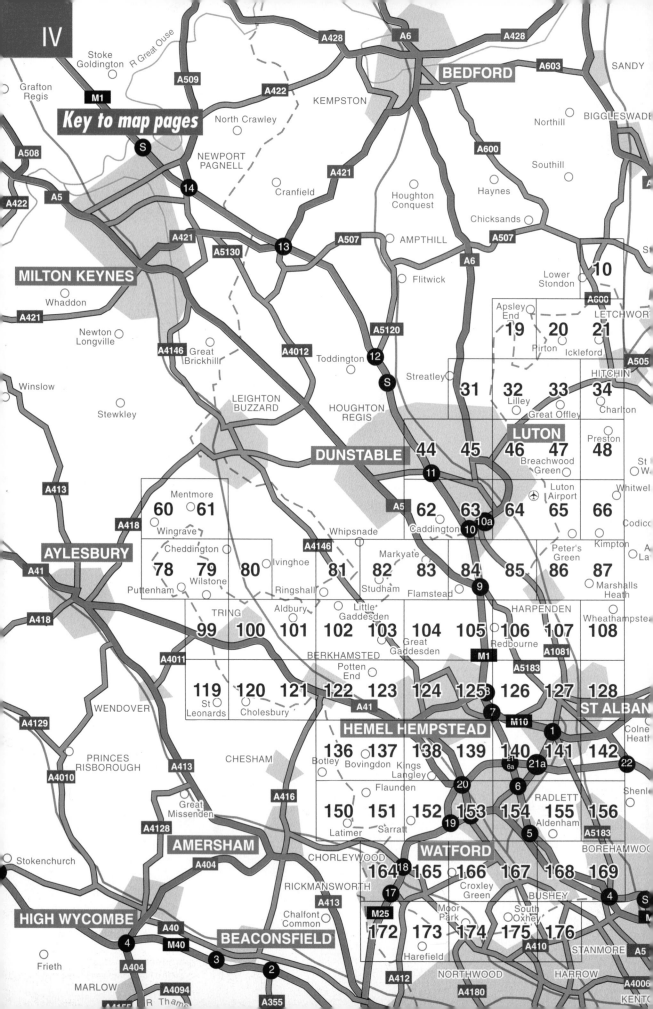

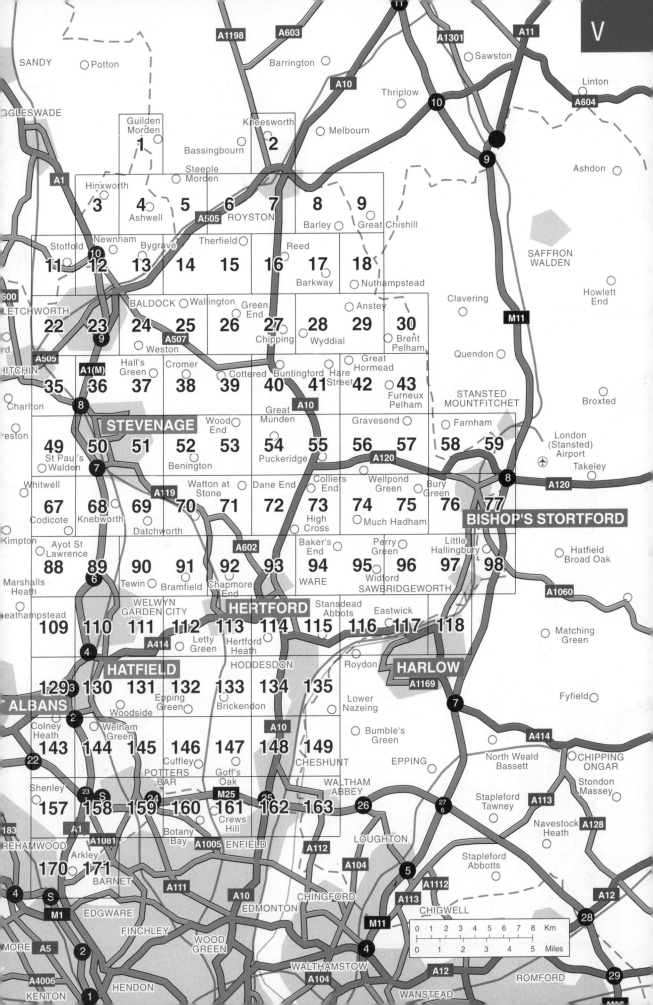

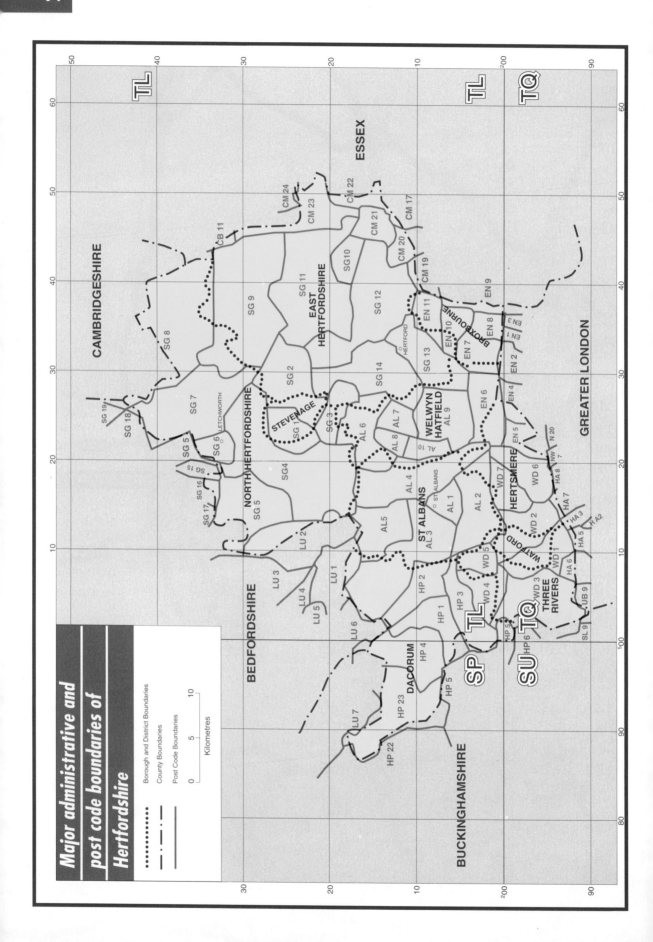

Major administrative and post code boundaries of Hertfordshire

Borough and District Boundaries
County Boundaries
Post Code Boundaries

Kilometres
0   5   10

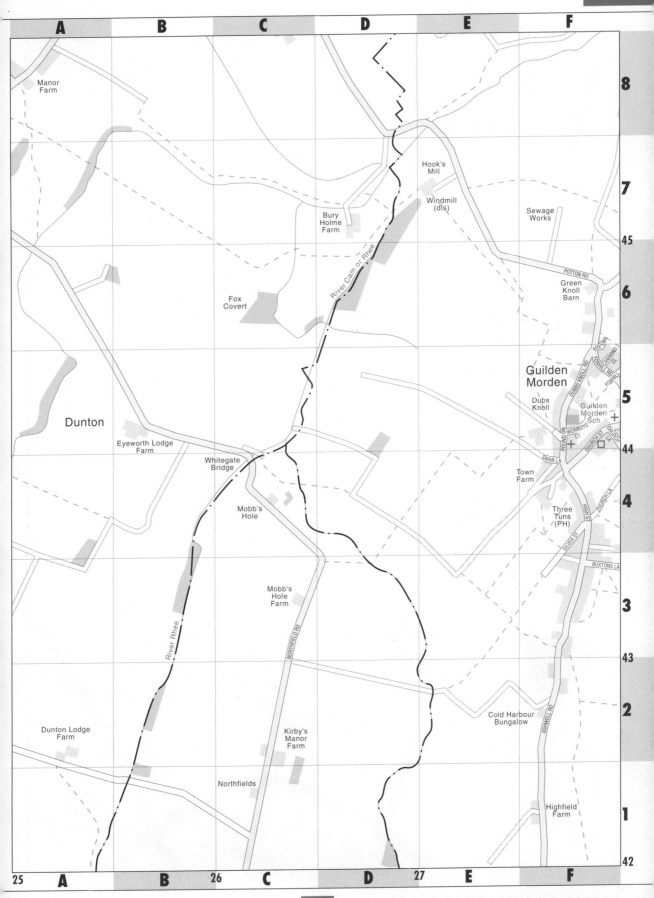

A B C D E F

8

7

45

6

5

44

4

3

43

2

1

42

Manor
Farm

Hook's
Mill

Windmill
(dis)

Bury
Holme
Farm

Sewage
Works

River Cam or Rhee

Potton Rd

Green
Knoll
Barn

Fox Covert

Dunton

Guilden
Morden

Dubs Knoll Rd

Fox Cnr

Cannons Cl

Foxhill Rd

Foxhill

Dubs
Knoll

Guilden
Morden
Sch

Eyeworth Lodge
Farm

Church St

Church La

Whitegate
Bridge

Pound Gn

Worboys
Ct

Swan La

Town
Farm

Mobb's
Hole

Three
Tuns
(PH)

High St

Church La

Silver St

Buxtons La

Mobb's
Hole
Farm

River Rhee

Northfield Rd

Ashwell Rd

Cold Harbour
Bungalow

Dunton Lodge
Farm

Kirby's
Manor
Farm

Northfields

Highfield
Farm

25 A B 26 C D 27 E F

4

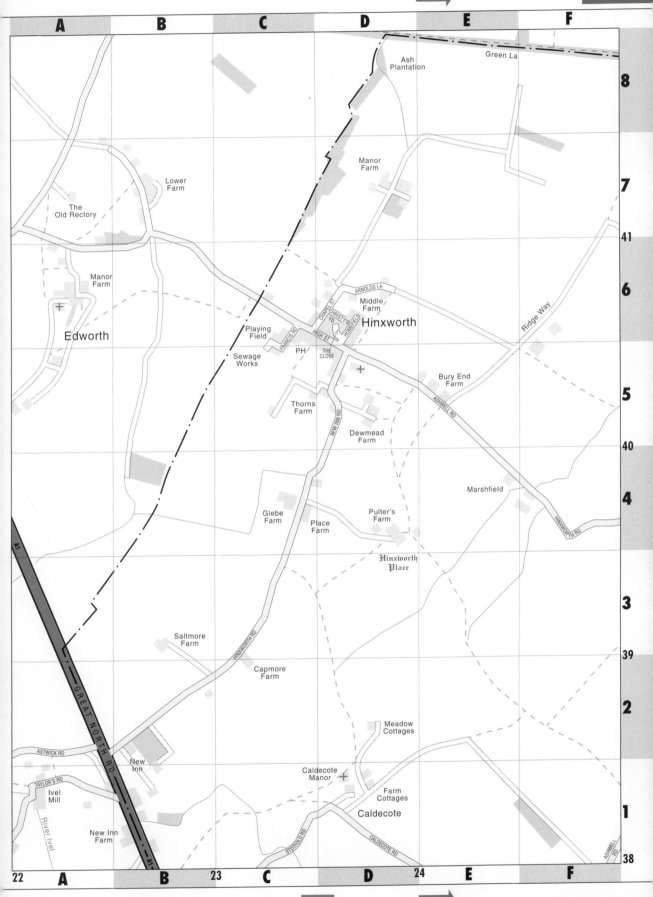

A B C D E F

8
7
41
6

5
40
4

3
39
2

1
38

Green La

Ash
Plantation

Manor
Farm

Lower
Farm

The
Old Rectory

Manor
Farm

Edworth

ARNOLDS LA

Middle
Farm

Hinxworth

Ridge Way

Playing
Field

Sewage
Works

PH

THE
CLOSE

HIGH ST

CHAPEL ST

CHRISTY'S YD

HOMEFIELD

FRANCIS RD

Thorns
Farm

NEW INN RD

Dewmead
Farm

Bury End
Farm

ASHWELL RD

Marshfield

HINXWORTH RD

Glebe
Farm

Place
Farm

Pulter's
Farm

Hinxworth
Place

Saltmore
Farm

HINXWORTH RD

Capmore
Farm

Meadow
Cottages

GREAT NORTH RD

A1

ASTWICK RD

New
Inn

TAYLOR'S RD

Ivel
Mill

River Ivel

New Inn
Farm

Caldecote
Manor

Farm
Cottages

Caldecote

STOTFOLD RD

CALDECOTE RD

ASHWELL RD

A B C D E F

8 Green La
Barrowsford
Bridge
Ridge Way
NORTHFIELD RD
ASHWELL RD

7
Cold
Harbour
ASHWELL RD

41
Sewage
Works
COMMON LA

6

Bluegates
Farm
River Rhee

Ashwell
End
Bluegates
Dairy
Elbrook
House

5
Baldwin's
Corner

Cemy
GREEN LA

40
Love's
Farm
LOVE LA
Ashwell
Bury
FORDHAM CL
MILL ST
ROLLYS LA
SPRINGHEAD
LUCAS LA

Ashridge
Farm

4 Quarry Hills
Farm
Whittington
Farm
GARDINERS LA
BACON'S
SWAN ST
ALMS LA
HODWELL
HIGH ST
Hotel
STATION RD

HINXWORTH RD
Farrow's
Farm
THE
RICKYARD
WILSTOCK LA
BACK ST
BEAR LA
SILVER ST
ANGEL'S NEY
KINGSLAND WAY
NEW ST
ASHWELL ST
WOODFORDE
CL

WEST END
DIXIES CL
CLAYBUSH RD
Ashwell Junior
Mixed Infants
Sch

3
PARTRIDGE HILL
Ashwell

39 Newnham Hill
NEWNHAM WAY
Claybush
Hill

2
Arbury
Banks

1 Ash Hill
ASHWELL RD

38
25 A B 26 C D 27 E F

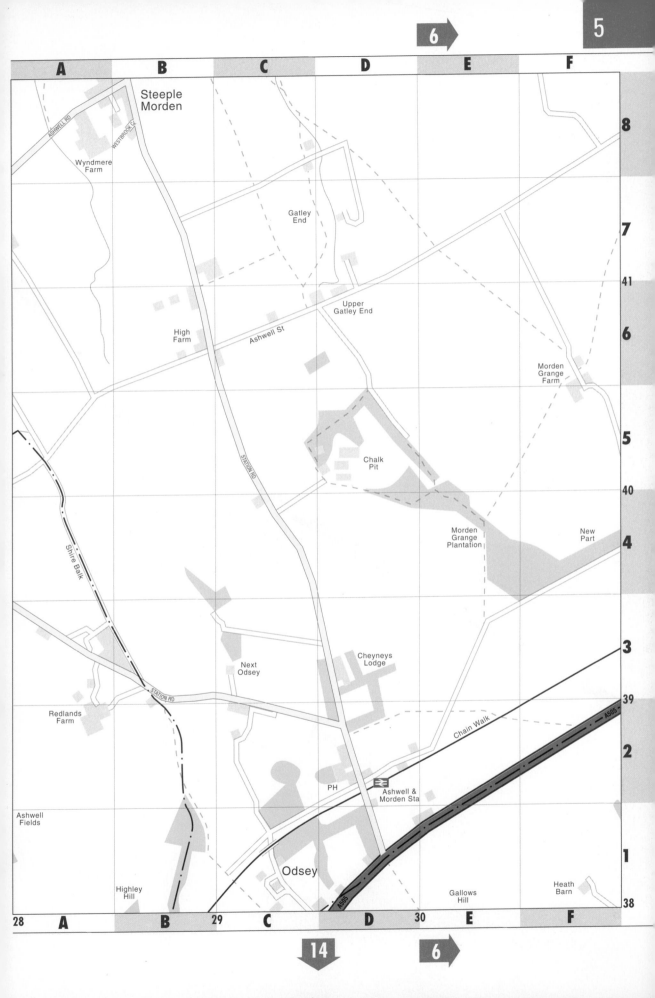

A   B   C   D   E   F

8

Steeple
Morden

Wyndmere
Farm

ASHWELL RD

WESTBROOK CL

Gatley
End

7

41

Upper
Gatley End

6

High
Farm

Ashwell St

Morden
Grange
Farm

5

STATION RD

Chalk
Pit

40

Shire Balk

Morden
Grange
Plantation

New
Part

4

Cheyneys
Lodge

3

39

Redlands
Farm

STATION RD

Next
Odsey

Chain Walk

A505

2

Ashwell
Fields

PH

Ashwell &
Morden Sta

1

Odsey

Highley
Hill

A505

Gallows
Hill

Heath
Barn

38

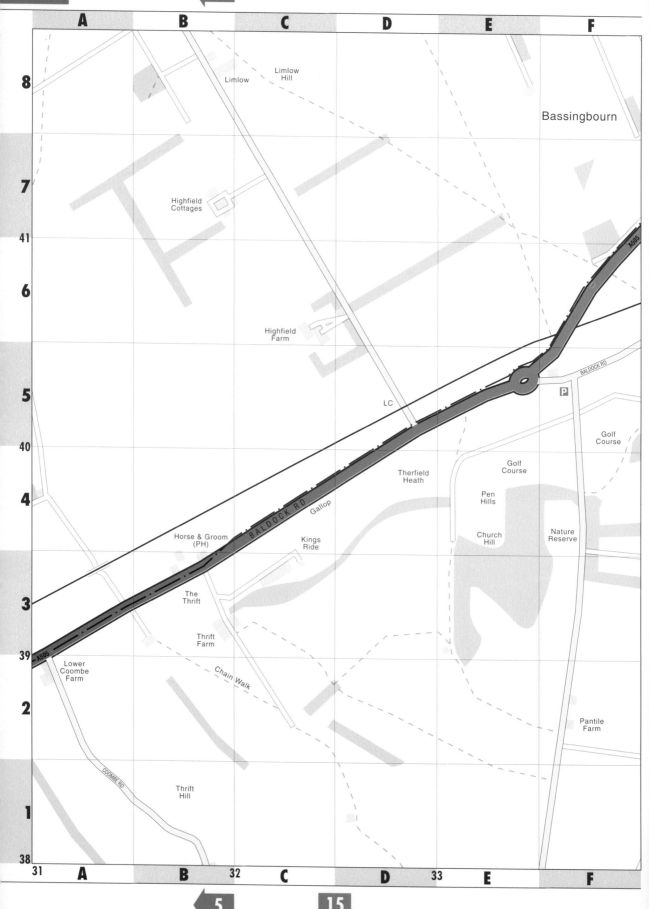

Bassingbourn

Limlow
Limlow
Hill

Highfield
Cottages

Highfield
Farm

LC

A505

BALDOCK RD

Therfield
Heath

Gallop

Golf
Course

Golf
Course

Pen
Hills

Church
Hill

Nature
Reserve

Horse & Groom
(PH)

Kings
Ride

The
Thrift

Thrift
Farm

Lower
Coombe
Farm

A505

Chain Walk

Pantile
Farm

COOMBE RD

Thrift
Hill

BALDOCK RD

P

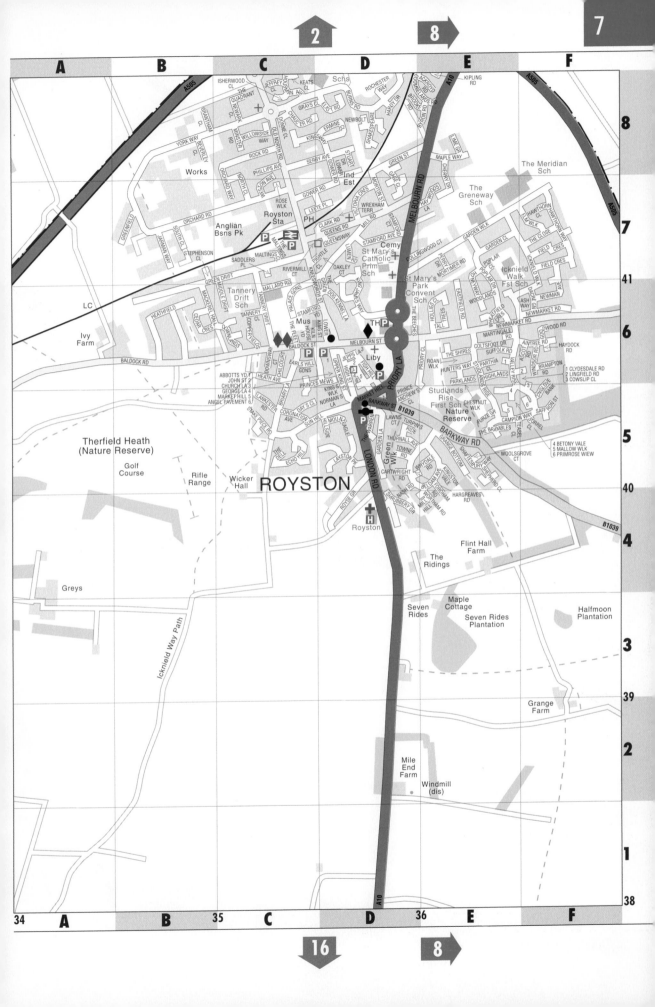

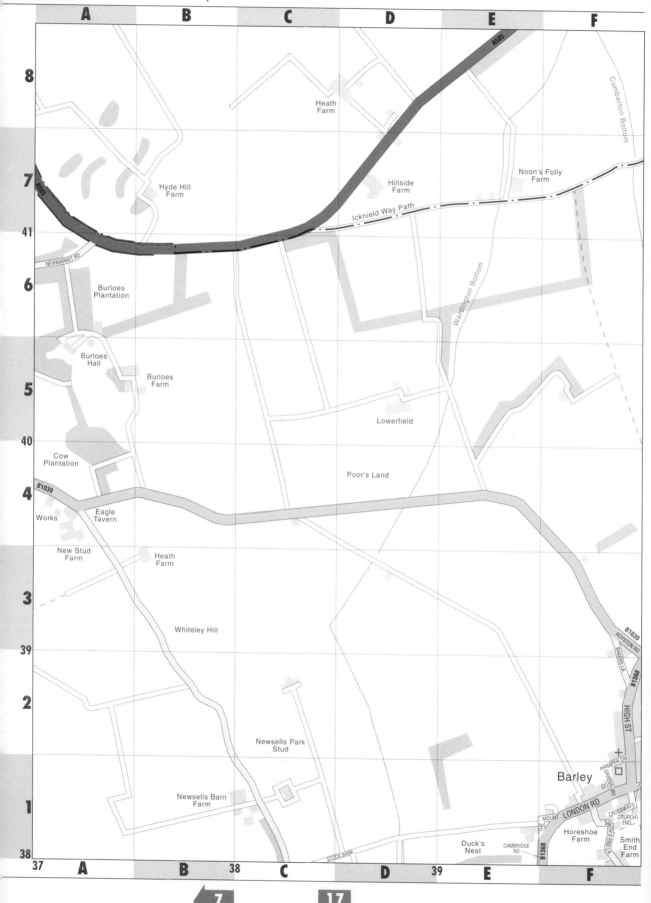

A B C D E F

North Hall
Farm

Harcamlow Way

Icknield Way Path

B1368

Sells Close
Farm

BARLEY RD

Harcamlow Way
Icknield Way Path

FOWLMERE RD

Green Ditch

Clay Hill

NEW RD

New Buildings
Farm

Rectory
Farm

Cumberton Bottom

CAMBRIDGE RD

New
Hill

Lynchets
Farm

CHISHILL RD

Lime
Farm

HAYDON RD

REEVES PIGHTLE

THE PUDGELL

Great Chishill

PICKNAGE RD

BARLEY RD

PLAISTOW WAY

PH

Chishill
Windmill

CHISHILL RD

B1039

Hill
Farm

MALTINGS LA

COLTS CROFT

HALL LA

MAY ST

WALLER LA

Barley
Voluntary
Primary
Sch

PICKNAGE
CNR

CHURCH END

SCHOOL LA

PUDDING LA

CHURCHFIELD

SHAFTENHOE END RD

Standard
Hill

May Street
Farm

The
Hall

B1039

BOGMOOR RD

LITTLE CHISHILL RD

40 A B 41 C D 42 E F 38

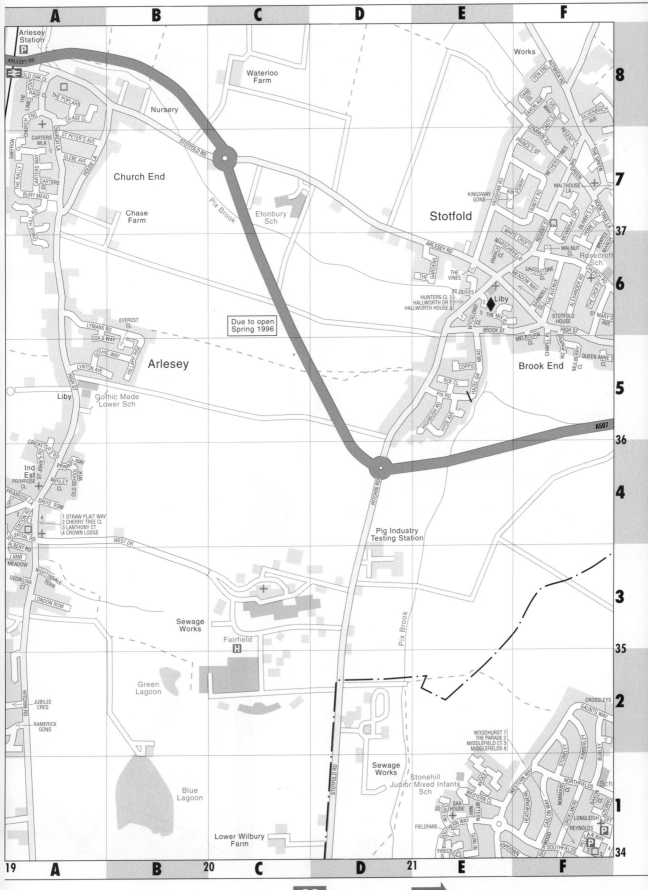

Arlesey Station

OLD OAK CL

Works

Waterloo Farm

Nursery

STOTFOLD RD

Church End

Chase Farm

Etonbury Sch

Stotfold

ARLESEY RD

Due to open Spring 1996

THE GARDENS

THE VINES

ST. OLIVES

Liby

HUNTERS CL 1
HALLWORTH DR 2
HALLWORTH HOUSE 3

THE MA...

STOTFOLD HOUSE

Arlesey

Brook End

Liby

Gothic Mede Lower Sch

PIX RD

A507

Ind Est

1 STRAW PLAIT WAY
2 CHERRY TREE CL
3 LANTHONY CT
4 CROWN LODGE

WEST DR

Pig Industry Testing Station

Sewage Works

Fairfield

Green Lagoon

PIX BROOK

CROSSLEYS

WOODHURST 1
THE PARADE 2
MIDDLEFIELDS CT 3
MIDDLEFIELDS 4

Sewage Works

Stonehill Junior Mixed Infants Sch

Blue Lagoon

STOTFOLD RD

SAX HOUSE

FIELDFARE

Lower Wilbury Farm

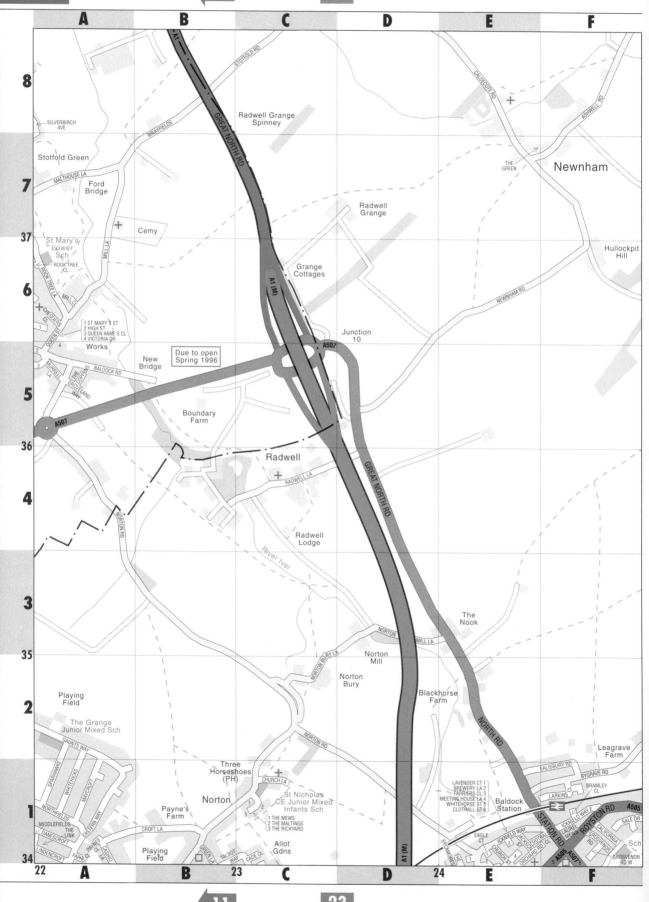

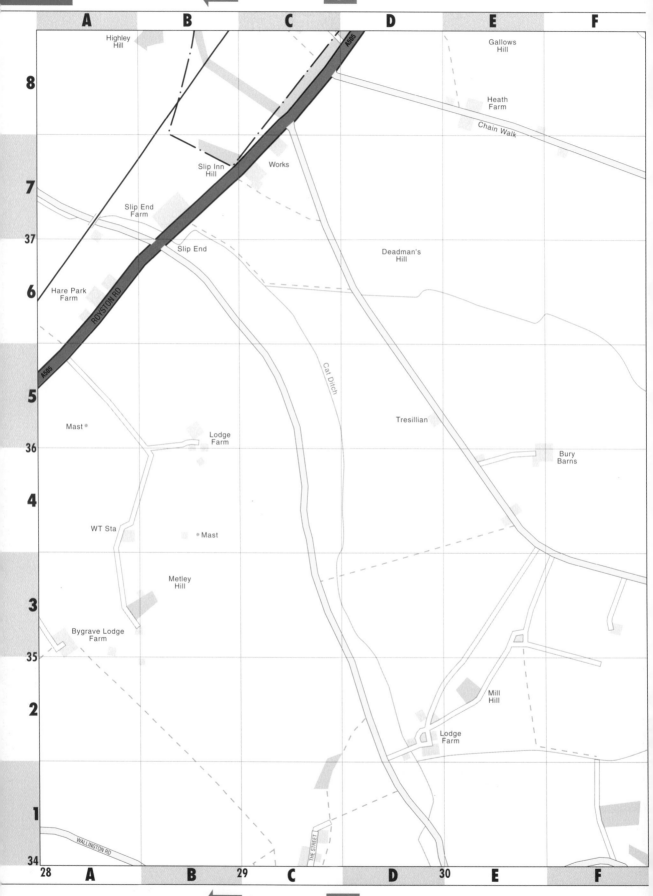

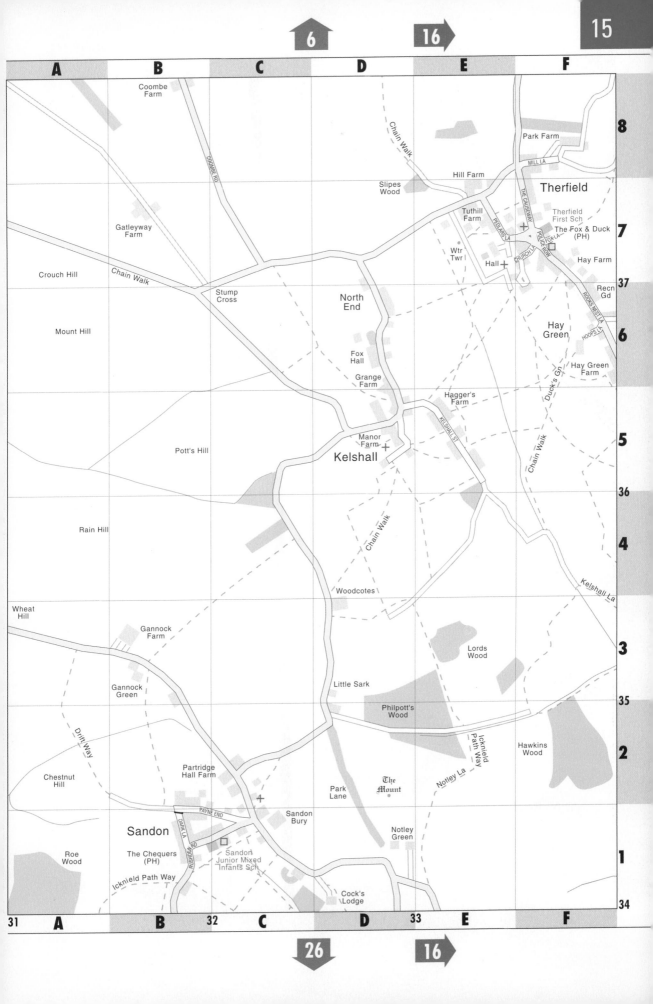

15
7

	A	B	C	D	E	F

8

Icknield Path Way

Hatchpen

A10

7

37

6

MEADOW WAY

Washingditch Green

HAYWOOD LA

River Rib

Mardleybury

Mast

THE JOINT

BRICKYARD LA

JACKSON'S LA

CROWN LA

Reed End

WILLOW CL

BLACKSMITH'S LA

Reed Junior Mixed Infants Sch

Wisbridge Farm

5

Holborn Farm

Southview

CHURCH LA

HIGH ST

The Cabinet (PH)

Reed

36

ROOKS NEST LA

Dane End

DRIFTWAY

Queenbury

4

Rooksnest Farm

Mast

+

Reed Hall

Gannock Grove

Keishall La

3

Chapel Green

Reed Wood

35

River Rib

Sewage Works

Hilly Wood

Southfield Grove

2

Brandish Wood

1

Slate Hall Farm

A10

34

34	A	35	B	C	36	D	E	F

15
27

17
9

A B C D E F

8

Hillside Farm

SHATTENHOE END RD

LITTLE CHISHILL RD

SMITH'S END LA

ROGMOOR RD

Old Manor Farm

Shattenhoe End

Pinner's Cross

7

Abbotsbury Farm

Rectory Farm

Little Chishill

Abbotsbury House

Manor Farm

Little Chishill Wood

37

Pondbottom Wood

6

Wigney Wood

5

Cross Leys

Gipsy Corner Farm

36

Trigg's Grove

Messop's Grove

New Lake

River Stort

Sheepwash Grove

4

Ash Grove

Oaks Bushes

3

Morrice Green Farm

Bury Farm

35

Bell Farm

Nuthampstead

Langley Lawn

2

Caylers Farm

PARK FARM LA

Langley

The Woodman (PH)

STOCKING LA

1

34

40 A B 41 C D 42 E F

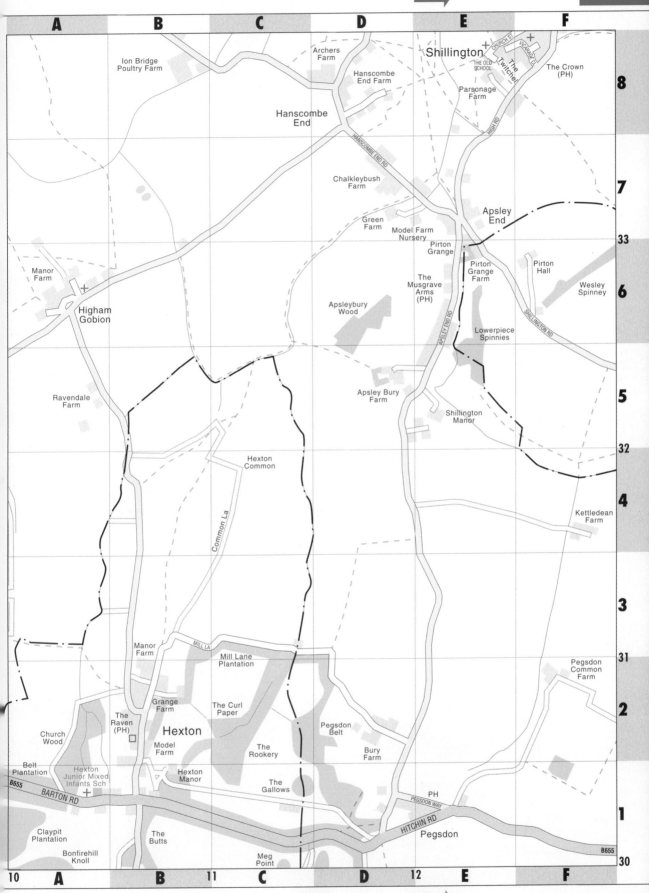

Ion Bridge
Poultry Farm

Archers
Farm

Shillington

Hanscombe
End Farm

CHURCH ST

THE OLD
SCHOOL

The
Twitchel

Parsonage
Farm

The Crown
(PH)

8

Hanscombe
End

HANSCOMBE END RD

HIGH RD

Chalkleybush
Farm

7

Green
Farm

Apsley
End

33

Model Farm
Nursery

Pirton
Grange

Manor
Farm

The Musgrave
Arms
(PH)

Pirton
Grange
Farm

Pirton
Hall

Higham
Gobion

Apsleybury
Wood

Wesley
Spinney

6

APSLEY END RD

SHILLINGTON RD

Lowerpiece
Spinnies

Ravendale
Farm

Apsley Bury
Farm

Shillington
Manor

5

32

Hexton
Common

Common La

4

Kettledean
Farm

3

31

Pegsdon
Common
Farm

Manor
Farm

MILL LA

Mill Lane
Plantation

2

Grange
Farm

The Curl
Paper

Pegsdon
Belt

The Raven
(PH)

Hexton

Church
Wood

Model
Farm

The
Rookery

Bury
Farm

Belt
Plantation

Hexton Junior Mixed
Infants Sch

Hexton
Manor

PH

B655

BARTON RD

The
Gallows

PEGSDON WAY

HITCHIN RD

Pegsdon

1

30

Claypit
Plantation

The
Butts

Bonfirehill
Knoll

Meg
Point

B655

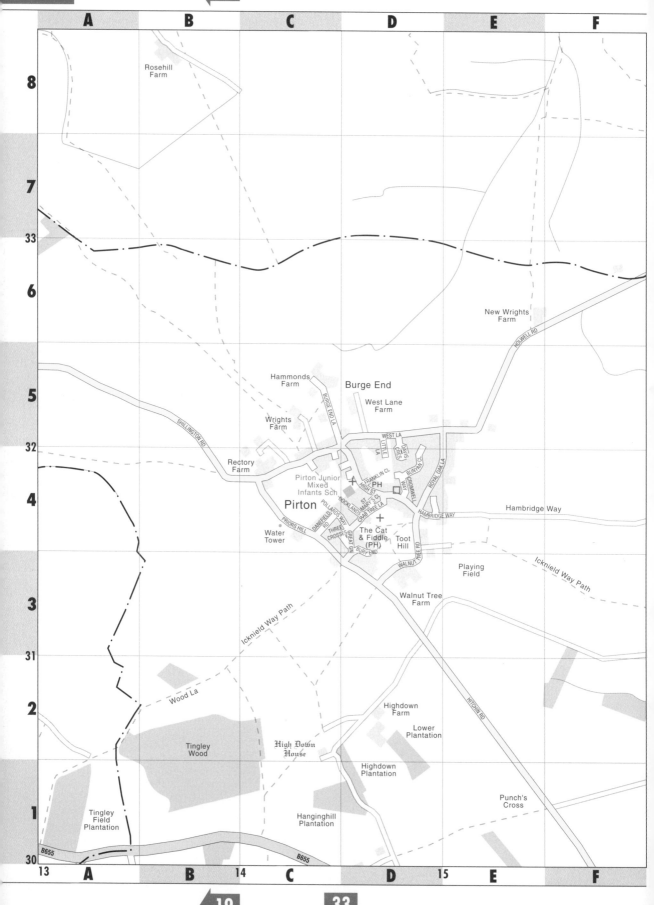

A B C D E F

8

Rosehill
Farm

7

33

6

New Wrights
Farm

HOLWELL RD

5

Hammonds
Farm

Burge End

West Lane
Farm

Wrights
Farm

BURGE END LA

SHILLINGTON RD

WEST LA

LITTLE
LA

DAVIS
CRES

32

Rectory
Farm

Pirton Junior
Mixed
Infants Sch

FRANKLIN CL

HIGH ST

ST
MARY'S CL

BUNYAN CL

CROMWELL

ROYAL OAK LA

PH

4

Pirton

PRIORS HILL

DANEFIELD
RD

POLLARDS WAY

THREE
CROSSES

BUCKLAND

CRAB TREE LA

GREAT GN

HAMBRIDGE WAY

Hambridge Way

Water
Tower

The Cat
& Fiddle
(PH)

Toot
Hill

Playing
Field

Icknield Way Path

WALNUT TREE RD

HITCHIN RD

3

Walnut Tree
Farm

Icknield Way Path

31

Wood La

Highdown
Farm

Lower
Plantation

2

Tingley
Wood

High Down
House

Highdown
Plantation

Punch's
Cross

1

Tingley
Field
Plantation

Hanginghill
Plantation

30

B655

B655

13 A 14 B C 15 D E F

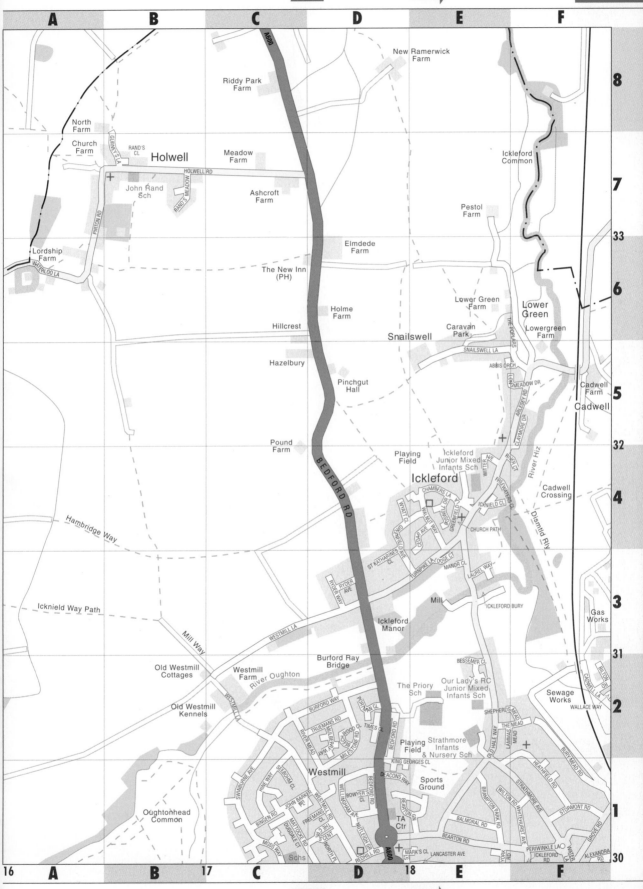

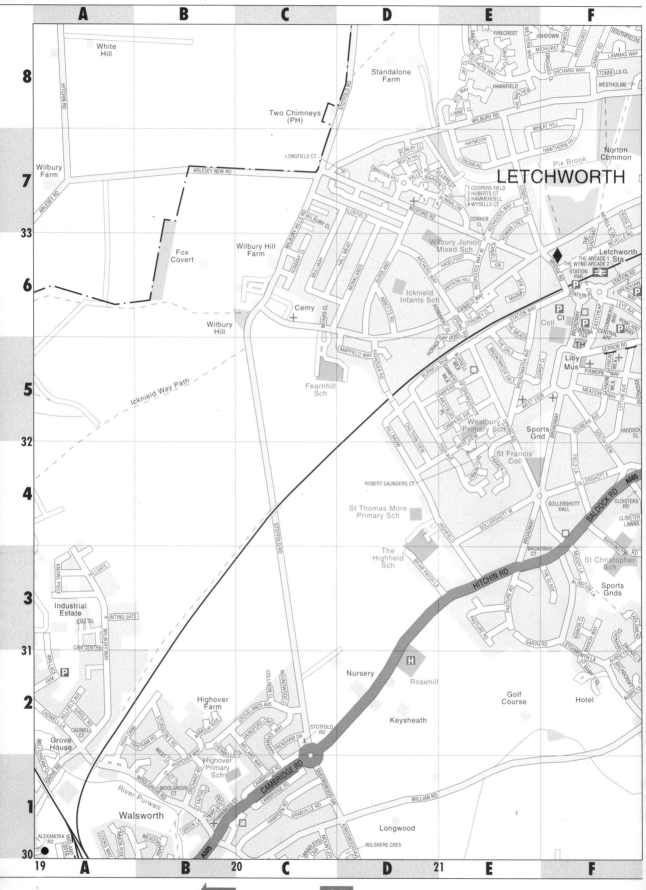

A B C D E F

8

White Hill

Standalone Farm

FIRECREST
ASHDOWN
SOUTHFIELDS
WESTERN WAY
MIDHURST
SHERWOOD
WOODHURST
ORCHARD WAY
GRANGE RD
LAMMAS WAY
STONNELLS CL
WESTHOLME

SANT
STERLING CL
SWIFT CL
SOUTHERN WAY
KITE WAY
HAWKFIELD
THE BACHES
WILBURY RD
HAYMOOR
LONGMEAD
WHEAT HILL
HAWTHORN HILL

HITCHIN RD

Wilbury Farm

ARLESEY RD

Two Chimneys (PH)

STOTFOLD RD

ARLESEY NEW RD

LONGFIELD CT

FINLAY CL
BEECH HILL
CHASTEN HILL
VALLEY RD
WARREN CT
FULLERS CT
BEDFORD RD
RUNNALOW

Pix Brook

Norton Common

LETCHWORTH

1 COOPERS FIELD
2 HUBERTS CT
3 HAMMERDELL
4 WYSELLS CT

7

33

Fox Covert

Wilbury Hill Farm

WILBURY HILLS RD
WILBURY CL
ELDEFIELD
ROMANY CL
MILLWAY
HALL MEAD
MONKLANDS
BURSLAND
ARCHERS WAY
HASELFOOT
SAFFRON HILL CT

CORNER CL

REDHOODS WAY E
ROWAN CRES
ICKNIELD
RIDGEWAY
NEVELLS RD
SPRING RD

Wilbury Junior Mixed Sch

THE QUADRANT
THE ARCADE 1
THE WYND ARCADE 2
STATION PAR
Letchworth Sta

NEVELLS RD
CROSS ST

6

Wilbury Hill

Cemy

MORRIS CL
HIGHOVER RD

Icknield Infants Sch

ICKNIELD WAY
ABBOTTS RD
ROSSMONT CL
CHAGNEY CL
SOUTH VIEW
STATION WAY

ICKNIELD GN

MARKET

CONVENT HILL
BRIDGE RD

STATION PL
STATION RD
STATION PL
P
OPENSHAW WAY
STATION RD
P

CAMPFIELD WAY

Fearnhill Sch

Icknield Way Path

HIGHOVER RD

BURNELL RISE
CAMPERS WLK
WESTBURY AVE
CAMPERS RD
CAMPERS PL
BROADWATER AVE
SPRINGSHOTT
BROADWATER DALE
GORST CL
THE DALE
THE MEADS

STATION WAY

Coll
Ct
EASTCHEAP
COMMERCE AVE
CENTRAL APP
BROADWAY

ROWLAND WAY

P

Liby Mus

PIXMORE WAY
GERNON RD
PIXMORE WLK
GERNON WLK
MEADOW GWAY
LYTTON AVE

5

HILLBROW
CHILTERN VIEW
HIGH AVE
CAMPERS RD
WEST VIEW
WEST VIEW

Westbury Primary Sch

BROADWAY

Sports Gnd

SOUVERINE AVE
SOUVERINE AVE
SOUTH VIEW
PADDOCK CL

32

St Francis' Coll

SOLLERSHOTT E

BALDOCK RD A505

4

ROBERT SAUNDERS CT

St Thomas More Primary Sch

HILLBROOK
UNWIN CL
PARKER CT
HIGHFIELD
SOLLERSHOTT W
SOLLERSHOTT

Sollershott Hall

SOLLERSHOTT RD

CLOISTERS RD
CLOISTER LAWNS

BARRINGTON RD

St Christopher Sch

Sports Gnds

STOTFOLD RD

The Highfield Sch

BRIAR PATCH LA

HITCHIN RD

BROADWAY CT
BROADWAY
PASTURE RD
THE GLADE
MUDDOTLA
ALINGTON LA

MANOR CL
MANOR RD
LETCHWORTH LA
ST MARY'S
EARLSMEAD
AUBREYS RD
BROADMEAD
CASHIO LA

3

HILLGATE
KNOWL PIECE
HILLFIELD AVE
HUNTING GATE

Industrial Estate

CAM SQ
CAM CENTRE

WILBURY WAY

PASTURE RD
GARTH RD

31

WALLACE AVE
P

WALLACE AVE

Nursery

H

Rosehill

Golf Course

Hotel

2

CADWELL RD
GIROLE RD
CADWELL CT

Grove House

Highover Farm

HIGH DANE
TRISTRAM RD
STURGEON'S RD
ARMOUR RISE
ORCHARDS RD
GROVELANDS AVE
GAINSFORD CRES
COLLISON CL
ROUNDWOOD CT
GROVELANDS WAY

ROUNDWOOD CL
MILLARD WAY
FRENSHAM DR

STOTFOLD RD

Keysheath

Longwood

1

MILLSTREAM RD
GROVE RD

River Purwell

Highover Primary Sch

WEST CL
EAST CL
WOOLGROVE RD

ORCHARDS RD
ST FAITHS
FRANKLIN CL
GREEN LA

CAMBRIDGE RD

CAMBRIDGE RD
HAMPDEN RD
GRANVILLE RD

WILLIAN RD

30

ALEXANDRA RD

COOK'S WAY

AVON RISE

MEADOWBANK

WALSWORTH

A505
HARKNESS CT

BRAMLEYS
MOUNT PLEASANT
KINGSWOOD AVE
WILSHERE CRES

QUEENSWOOD DR

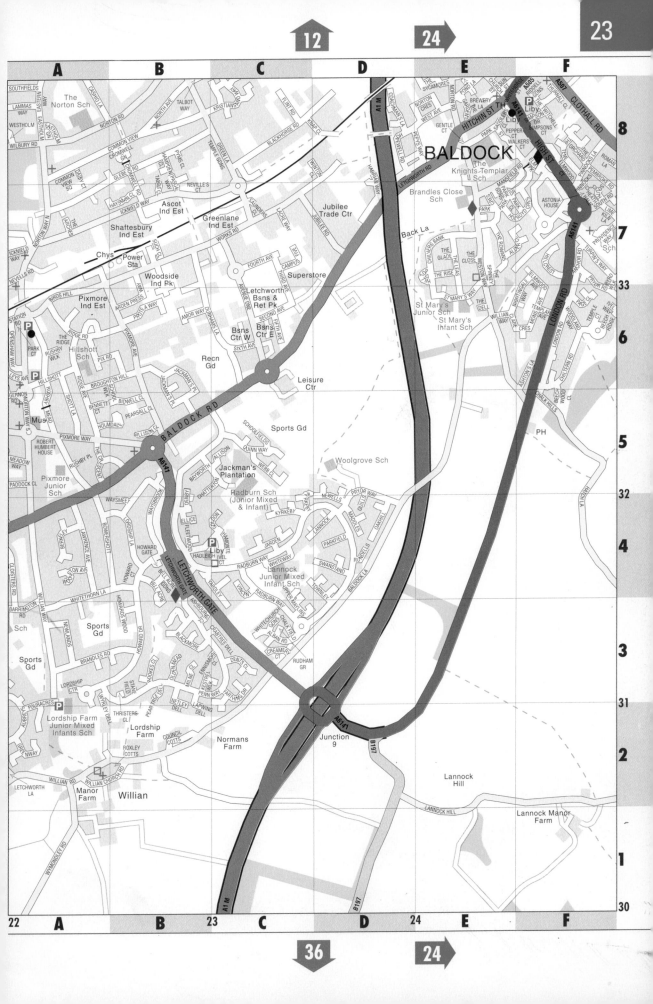

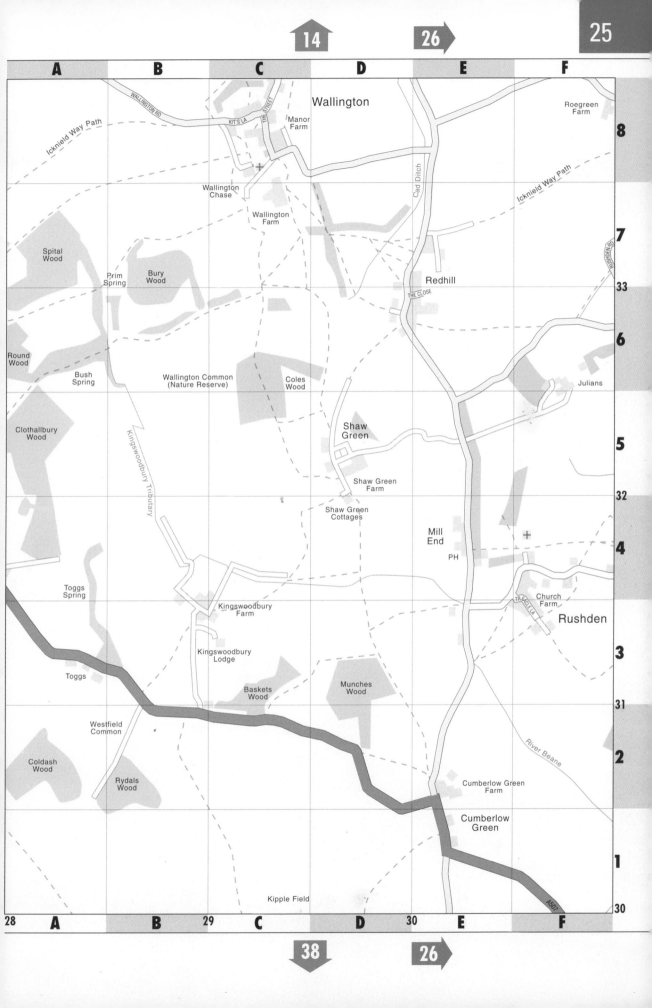

A   B   C   D   E   F

8

7

33

6

5

32

4

3

31

2

1

30

Wallington

Roegreen Farm

Manor Farm

WALLINGTON RD
KIT'S LA
THE STREET

Icknield Way Path

Wallington Chase

Wallington Farm

Cad Ditch

Icknield Way Path

Spital Wood

Prim Spring

Bury Wood

Redhill

THE CLOSE

RUSHDEN RD

Round Wood

Bush Spring

Wallington Common (Nature Reserve)

Coles Wood

Julians

Clothallbury Wood

Kingswoodbury Tributary

Shaw Green

Shaw Green Farm

Mill End

PH

Rushden

TRACTLE LA

Church Farm

Shaw Green Cottages

Toggs Spring

Kingswoodbury Farm

Toggs

Kingswoodbury Lodge

Baskets Wood

Munches Wood

River Beane

Westfield Common

Coldash Wood

Rydals Wood

Cumberlow Green Farm

Cumberlow Green

A507

Kipple Field

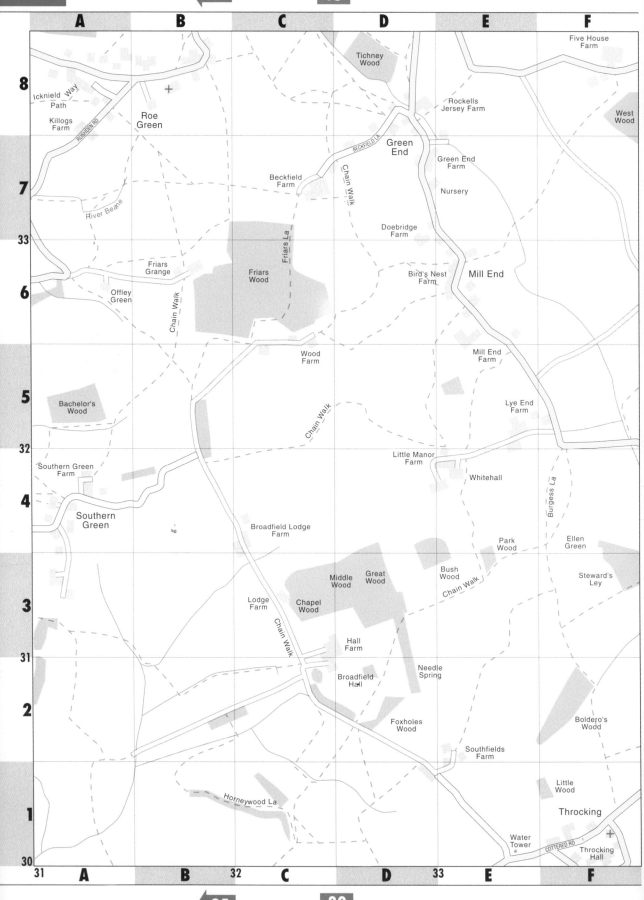

A **B** **C** **D** **E** **F**

8

Icknield Way
Path

Killogs
Farm

Roe
Green

RUSHDEN RD

Tichney
Wood

Rockells
Jersey Farm

West
Wood

Five House
Farm

Green
End

BECKFIELD LA

Green End
Farm

Nursery

7

River Beane

Beckfield
Farm

Chain Walk

Doebridge
Farm

33

Friars
Grange

Chain Walk

Friars
Wood

Friars La

Bird's Nest
Farm

Mill End

6

Offley
Green

5

Bachelor's
Wood

Wood
Farm

Chain Walk

Mill End
Farm

Lye End
Farm

32

Southern Green
Farm

Little Manor
Farm

Whitehall

Burgess La

4

Southern
Green

Broadfield Lodge
Farm

Park
Wood

Ellen
Green

Lodge
Farm

Chain Walk

Middle
Wood

Great
Wood

Bush
Wood

Chain Walk

Steward's
Ley

3

Chapel
Wood

Hall
Farm

Needle
Spring

31

Broadfield
Hall

2

Foxholes
Wood

Southfields
Farm

Boldero's
Wood

Horneywood La

Little
Wood

1

Throcking

Water
Tower

COTTERED RD

Throcking
Hall

30

27
17

A   B   C   D   E   F

8

7

33

6

5

32

4

3

31

2

1

30

B1368
LONDON RD

North End Farm

Biggin Bridge

Biggin Manor

Northey Wood

River Quin

BIGGIN HILL

Cave Gate

Cave Bridge

Stapleton Bridge

Lincoln Hill

Forty Acre Plantation

Cavehall Plantation

Cherry Orchard Plantation

New Barns

Wyddial Hall

Peartree Field Wood

Bushleys Grove

Fox Hill

ROSE COTTS
SOUTHSIDE

Wyddial

Home Farm

Beauchamps

Flint Cottages

MOLES LA

Silkmead Farm

River Quin

Moles Farm

Beauchamp's Plantation

Beauchamp's Wood

Bradbury Farm

Works

B1368

37   A   B   38   C   D   39   E   F

27
41

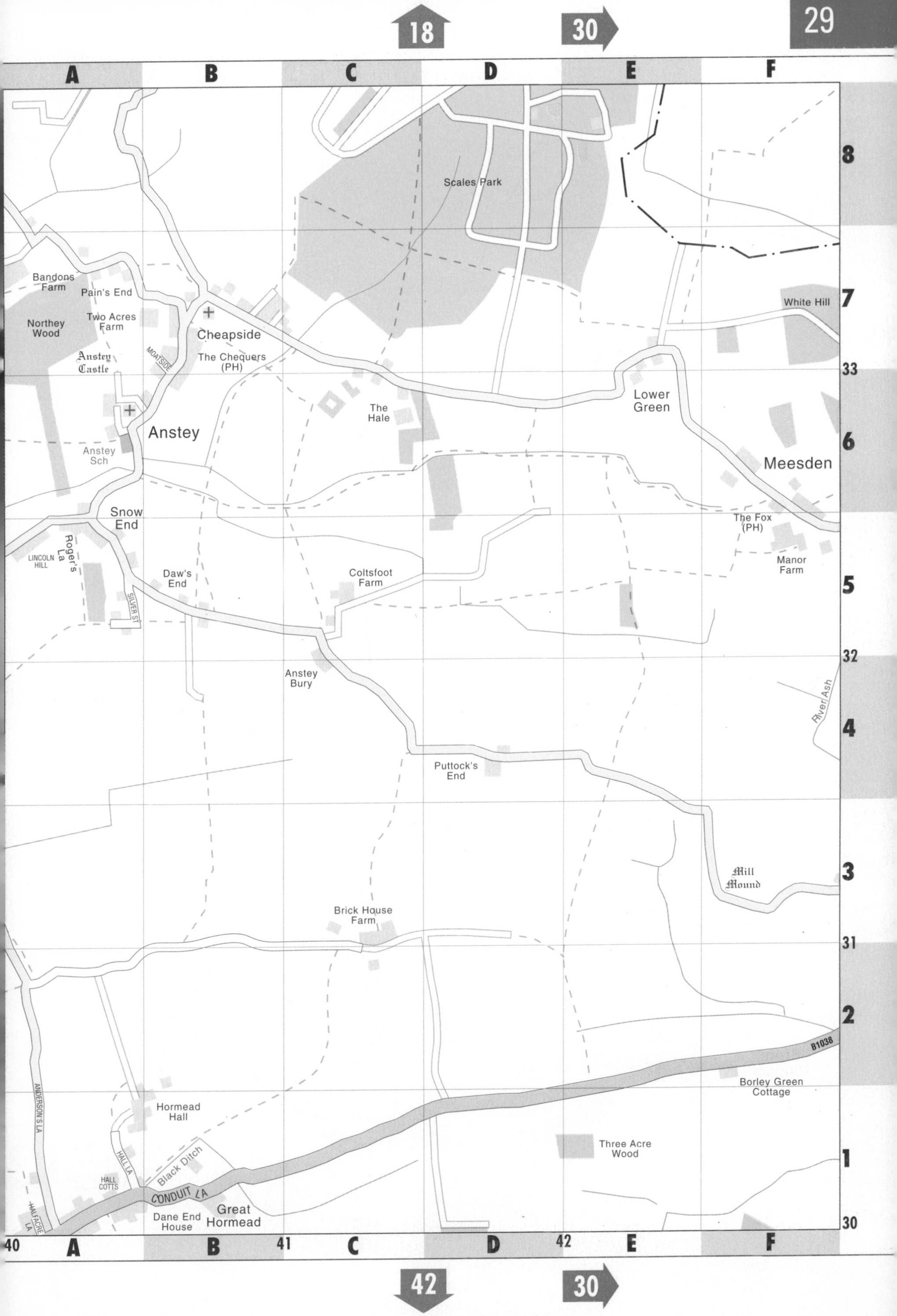
18
30
A
B
C
D
E
F
8
7
33
6
5
32
4
3
31
2
1
30
40
41
42
42
Scales Park
White Hill
Bandons
Farm
Pain's End
Northey
Wood
Two Acres
Farm
Cheapside
The Chequers
(PH)
Anstey
Castle
MOATSIDE
Anstey
Anstey
Sch
Lower
Green
The
Hale
Meesden
Snow
End
The Fox
(PH)
Manor
Farm
LINCOLN
HILL
Roger's
La
Daw's
End
Coltsfoot
Farm
SILVER ST
Anstey
Bury
River Ash
Puttock's
End
Mill
Mound
Brick House
Farm
B1038
Borley Green
Cottage
ANDERSON'S LA
Hormead
Hall
HALL LA
Black Ditch
Three Acre
Wood
HALL
COTTS
CONDUIT LA
HALFACRE
LA
Dane End
House
Great
Hormead

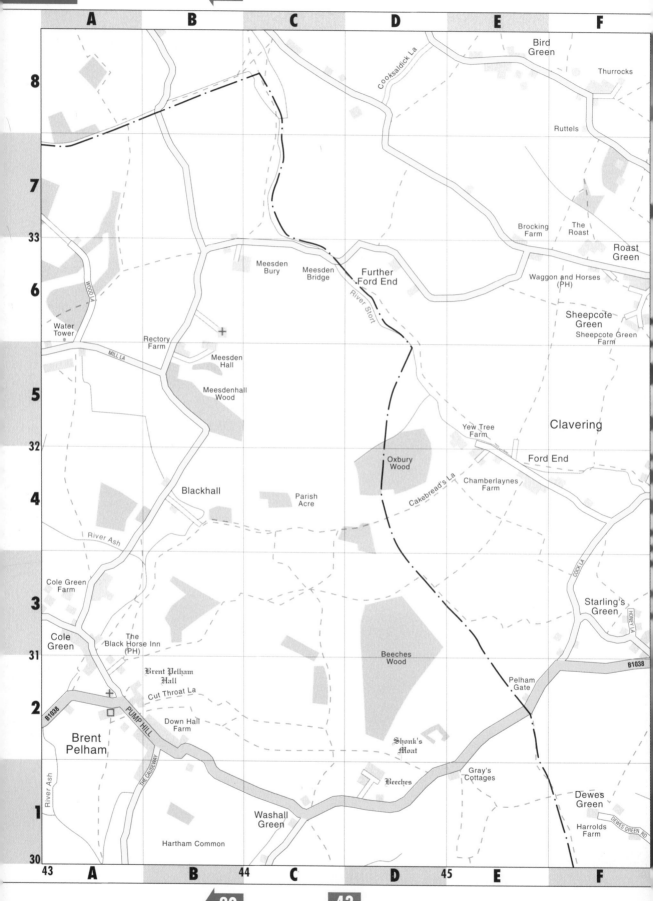

29

A B C D E F

8

Bird
Green

Thurrocks

Cooksaldick La

Ruttels

7

33

Brocking
Farm

The
Roast

Roast
Green

Meesden
Bury

Meesden
Bridge

Further
Ford End

Waggon and Horses
(PH)

6

WOOD LA

River Stort

Sheepcote
Green

Water
Tower

Rectory
Farm

MILL LA

Meesden
Hall

Sheepcote Green
Farm

5

Meesdenhall
Wood

Yew Tree
Farm

Clavering

32

Oxbury
Wood

Ford End

Blackhall

Parish
Acre

Chamberlaynes
Farm

4

Cakebread's La

River Ash

COCK LA

Cole Green
Farm

3

Starling's
Green

Cole
Green

HONEY LA

The
Black Horse Inn
(PH)

31

Beeches
Wood

Pelham
Gate

B1038

Brent Pelham
Hall

Cut Throat La

2

B1038

PUMP HILL

Down Hall
Farm

Shonk's
Moat

Brent
Pelham

THE CAUSEWAY

Gray's
Cottages

Beeches

Dewes
Green

River Ash

1

Washall
Green

Harrolds
Farm

DEWES GREEN RD

Hartham Common

30

43 A B 44 C D 45 E F

29
43

32 ▶

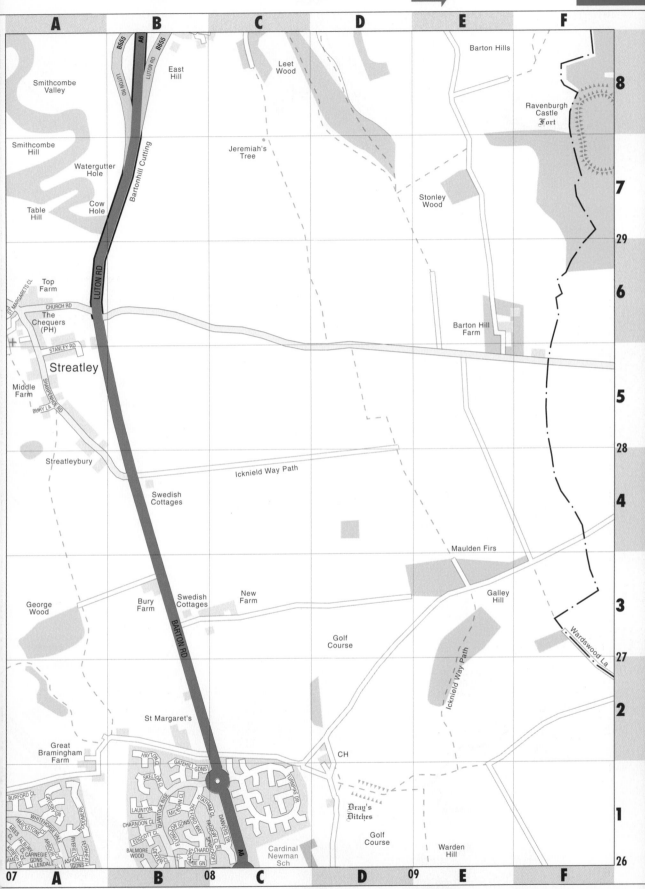

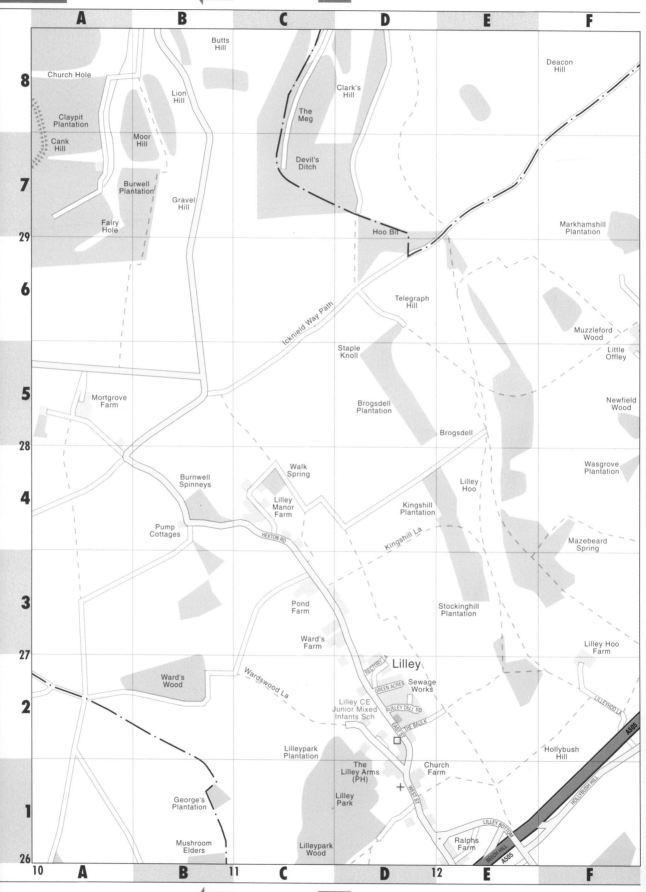

Church Hole

Claypit
Plantation

Cank
Hill

Fairy
Hole

Moor
Hill

Burwell
Plantation

Lion
Hill

Butts
Hill

Gravel
Hill

The
Meg

Clark's
Hill

Devil's
Ditch

Hoo Bit

Deacon
Hill

Markhamshill
Plantation

Icknield Way Path

Telegraph
Hill

Staple
Knoll

Brogsdell
Plantation

Brogsdell

Muzzleford
Wood

Little
Offley

Newfield
Wood

Mortgrove
Farm

Burnwell
Spinneys

Walk
Spring

Lilley
Manor
Farm

Pump
Cottages

HEXTON RD

Kingshill
Plantation

Lilley
Hoo

Kingshill La

Wasgrove
Plantation

Mazebeard
Spring

Pond
Farm

Ward's
Farm

Ward's
Wood

Wardswood La

Stockinghill
Plantation

RECTORY LA

Lilley

GREEN ACRES

Sewage
Works

Lilley Hoo
Farm

LILLEYHOO LA

Lilley CE
Junior Mixed
Infants Sch

RUELEY DELL RD

EAST ST THE BAULK

Lilleypark
Plantation

The
Lilley Arms
(PH)

Lilley
Park

WEST ST

Church
Farm

Hollybush
Hill

George's
Plantation

Ralphs
Farm

LILLEY BOTTOM

BEECH HILL

HOLLYBUSH HILL

A505

A505

Mushroom
Elders

Lilleypark
Wood

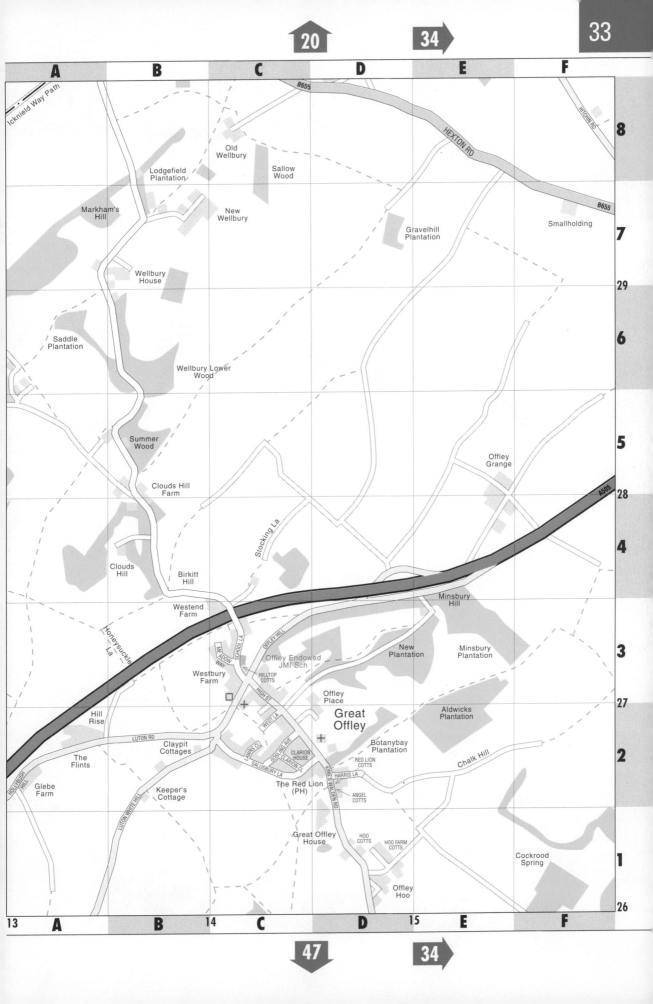

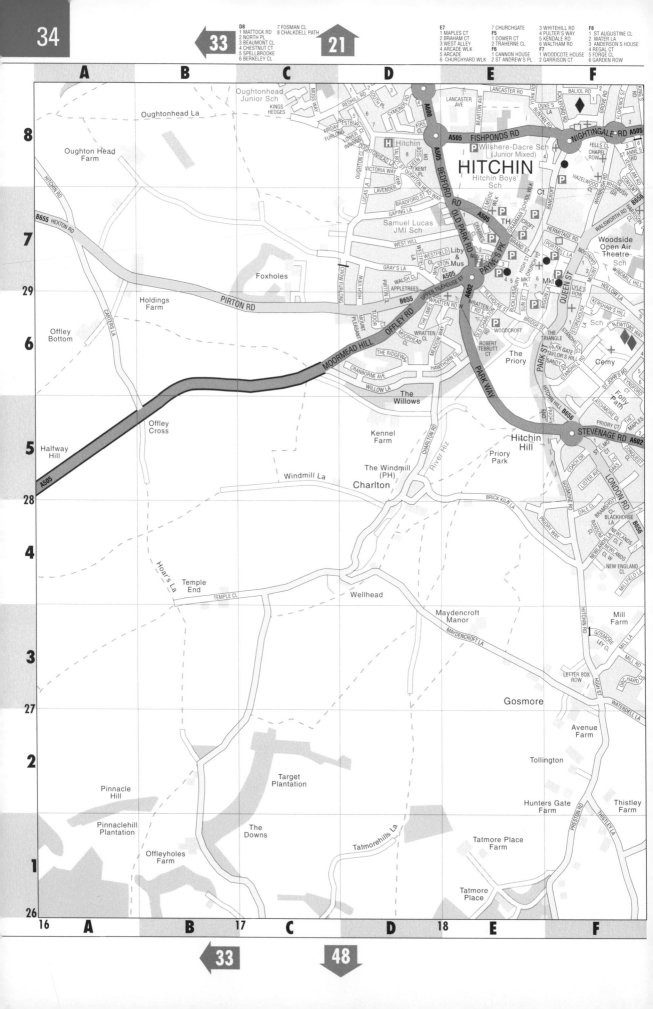

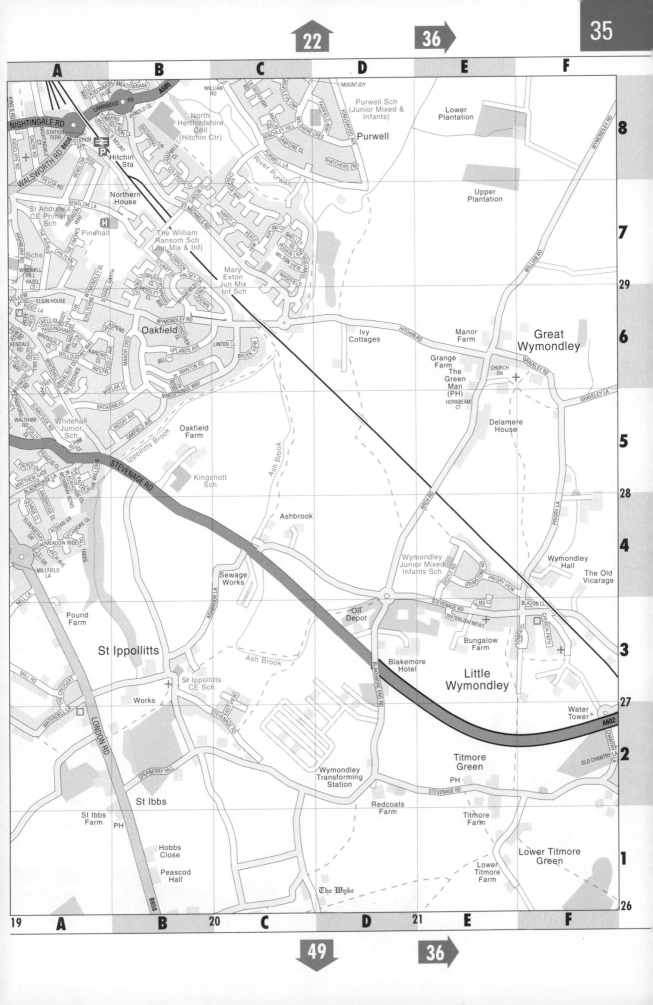

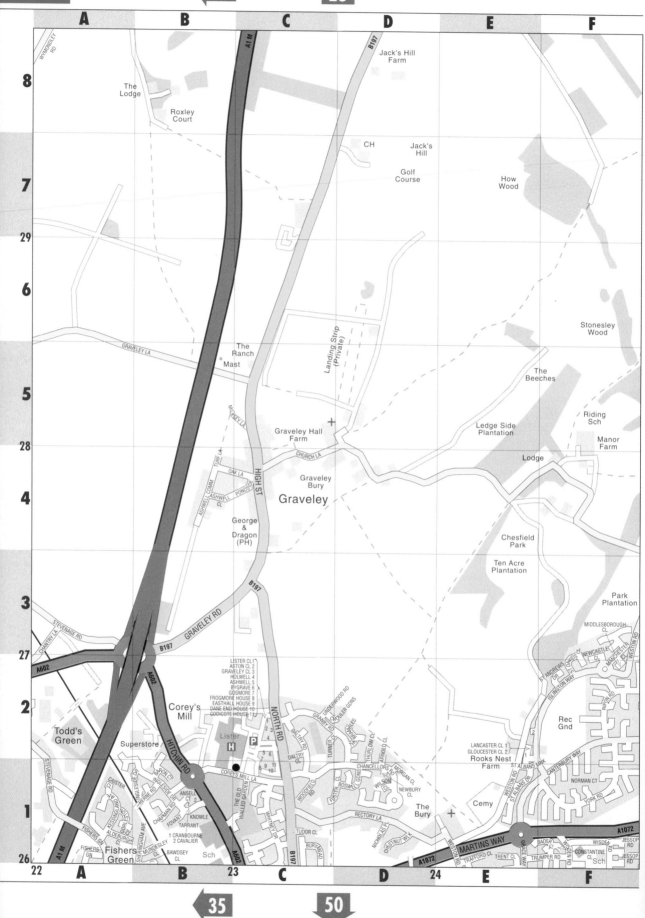

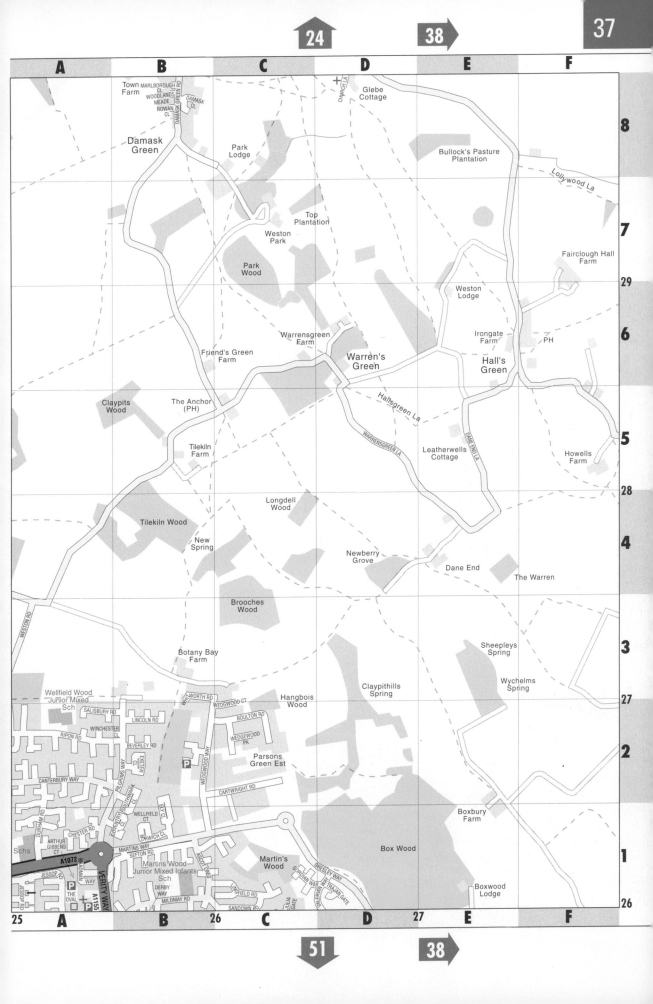

37
25

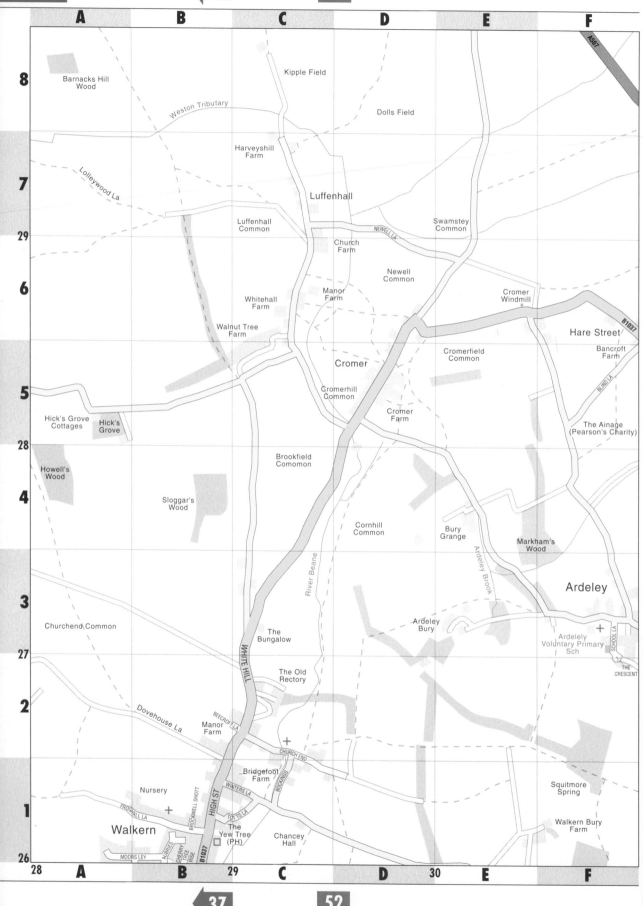

37
52

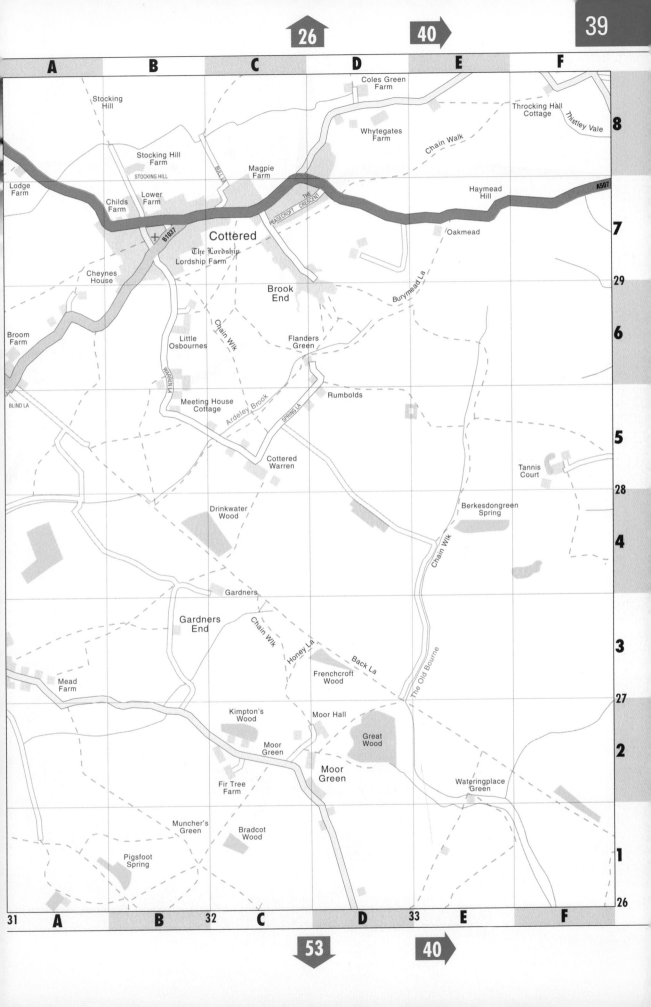

A B C D E F

Coles Green
Farm

Stocking
Hill

Throcking Hall
Cottage

Thistley Vale

8

Stocking Hill
Farm

Whytegates
Farm

Chain Walk

STOCKING HILL

Magpie
Farm

Lodge
Farm

Haymead
Hill

A507

Childs
Farm

Lower
Farm

BULL LA

PEASECROFT

THE CRESCENT

B1037

7

Cottered

Oakmead

29

The Lordship
Lordship Farm

Cheynes
House

Brook
End

Burymead La

Broom
Farm

Little
Osbournes

Chain Wlk

Flanders
Green

6

WARREN LA

Meeting House
Cottage

Ardeley Brook

SPRING LA

Rumbolds

BLIND LA

Cottered
Warren

5

Tannis
Court

28

Drinkwater
Wood

Berkesdongreen
Spring

Chain Wlk

4

Gardners

Gardners
End

Chain Wlk

Honey La

Back La

The Old Bourne

3

Mead
Farm

Frenchcroft
Wood

27

Kimpton's
Wood

Moor Hall

Great
Wood

2

Moor
Green

Fir Tree
Farm

Moor
Green

Wateringplace
Green

Muncher's
Green

Bradcot
Wood

1

Pigsfoot
Spring

26

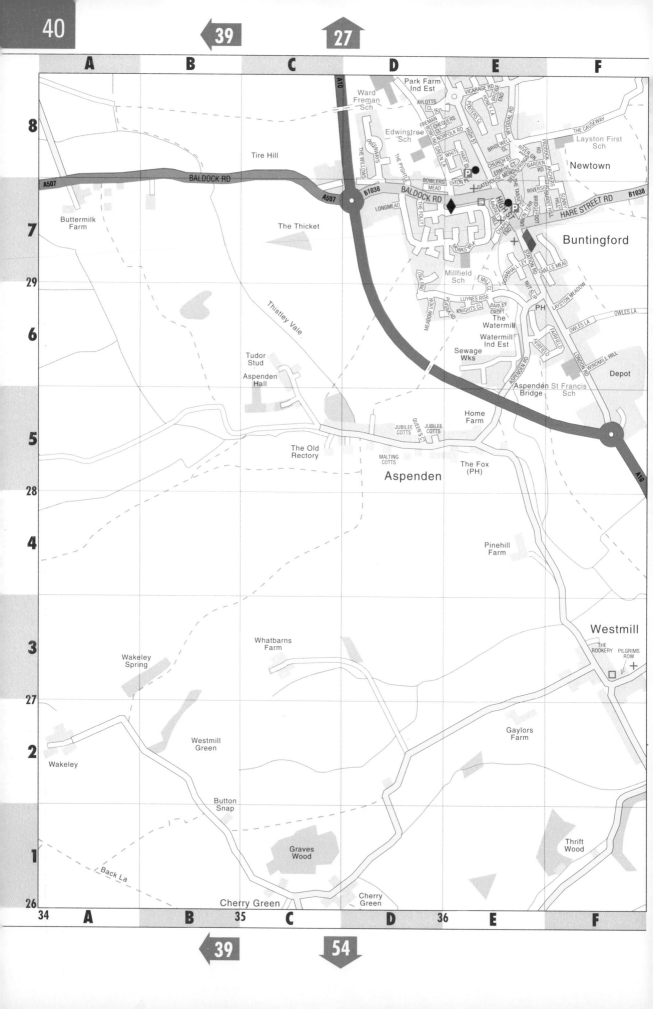

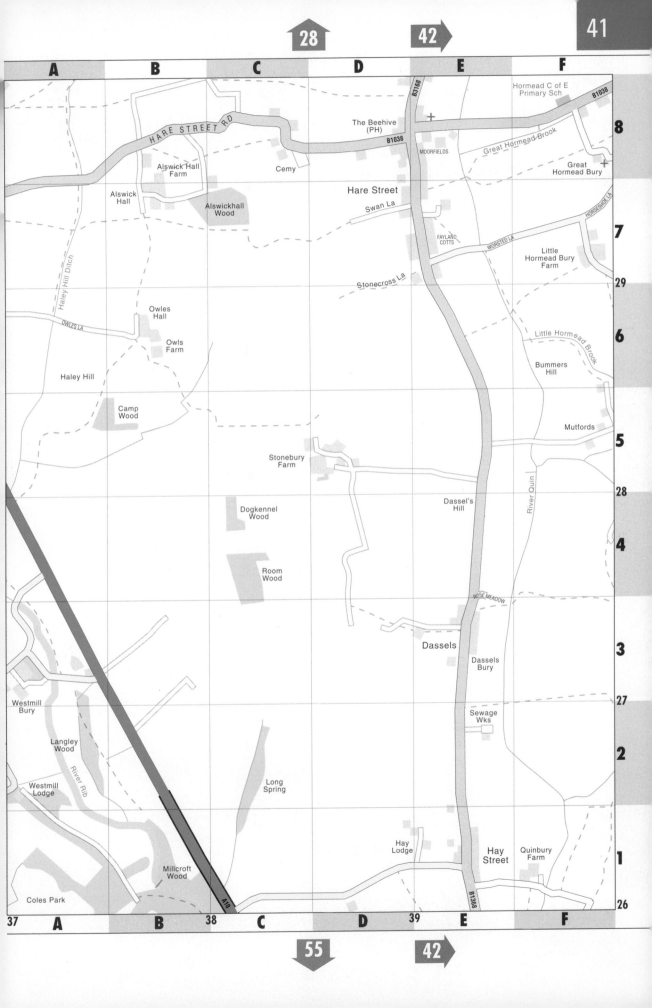

A B C D E F

8

7

29

6

5

28

4

3

27

2

1

26

HARE STREET RD

Alswick Hall Farm

Cemy

The Beehive (PH)

Hormead C of E Primary Sch

B1038

B3168

B1038

Moorfields

Great Hormead Brook

Great Hormead Bury

Alswick Hall

Alswickhall Wood

Hare Street

Swan La

Worsted La

Horseshoe La

Fayland Cotts

Little Hormead Bury Farm

Haley Hill Ditch

Owles La

Stonecross La

Owles Hall

Owls Farm

Little Hormead Brook

Haley Hill

Bummers Hill

Camp Wood

Mutfords

Stonebury Farm

Dassel's Hill

River Quin

Dogkennel Wood

Room Wood

Rose Meadow

Dassels

Dassels Bury

Westmill Bury

Sewage Wks

Langley Wood

River Rib

Long Spring

Westmill Lodge

Hay Lodge

Hay Street

Quinbury Farm

Millcroft Wood

A10

B1368

Coles Park

37 A B 38 C D 39 E F

A   B   C   D   E   F

8

B1038
Three Tuns (PH)
Great Hormead
HORSESHOE HILL
WILLOW CL
St Patrick's Wood
Church End Cott
HORSESHOE LA

Sparksfield

7

The Thrift
Great Hormead Park

29

Park View
Glebe Ho
Little Hormead Brook
Balons Farm
Little Hormead
Bulls Farm
Fair Lady Wood

6

The Willows
Lady Wood

Mutfords
Mutton Hall
Duck Street Cott

5

28

Furneux Pelham Hall
THE STREET

Shirley

4

Bradley Spring

High Wood
Patient End Farm

3

Hoare's La
Bozengreen Farm
Rotten Row
Patient End

27

Bozen Green

2

THE CAUSEWAY
Hole Farm Cott

1

Hole Farm

26

40   A   B   41   C   D   42   E   F

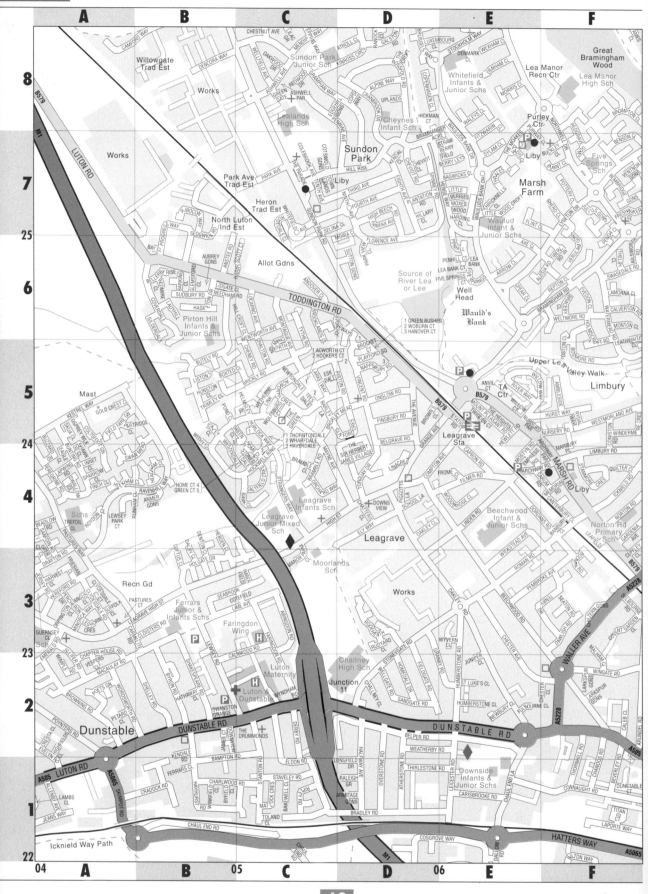

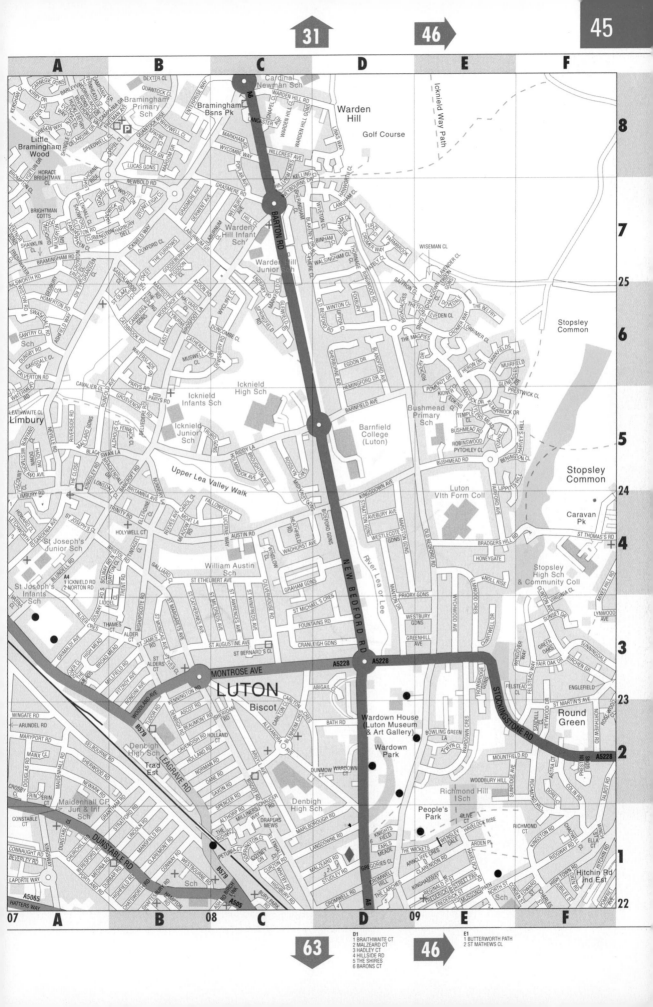

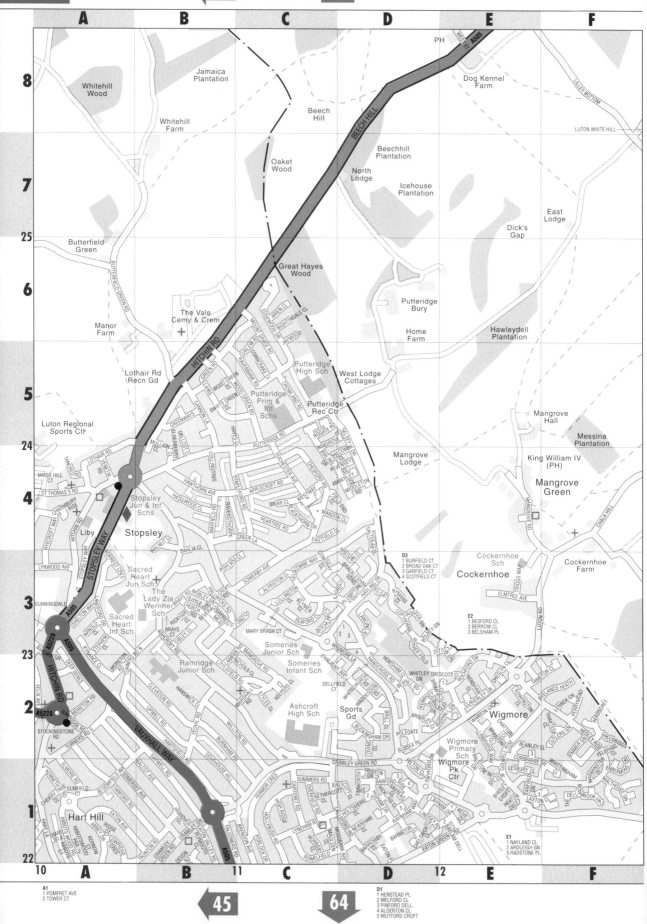

A
B
C
D
E
F

8
7
25
6
5
24
4
3
23
2
1
22

10
A
11
B
C
D
12
E
F

A1
1 POMFRET AVE
2 TOWER CT

D1
1 HENSTEAD PL
2 MELFORD CL
3 PINFORD DELL
4 ALDERTON CL
5 MUTFORD CROFT

D3
1 BURFIELD CT
2 BROAD OAK CT
3 GARFIELD CT
4 SCOTFIELD CT

E2
1 BESFORD CL
2 BERROW CL
3 BELSHAM PL

E1
1 NAYLAND CL
2 ARDLEIGH GN
3 RADSTONE PL

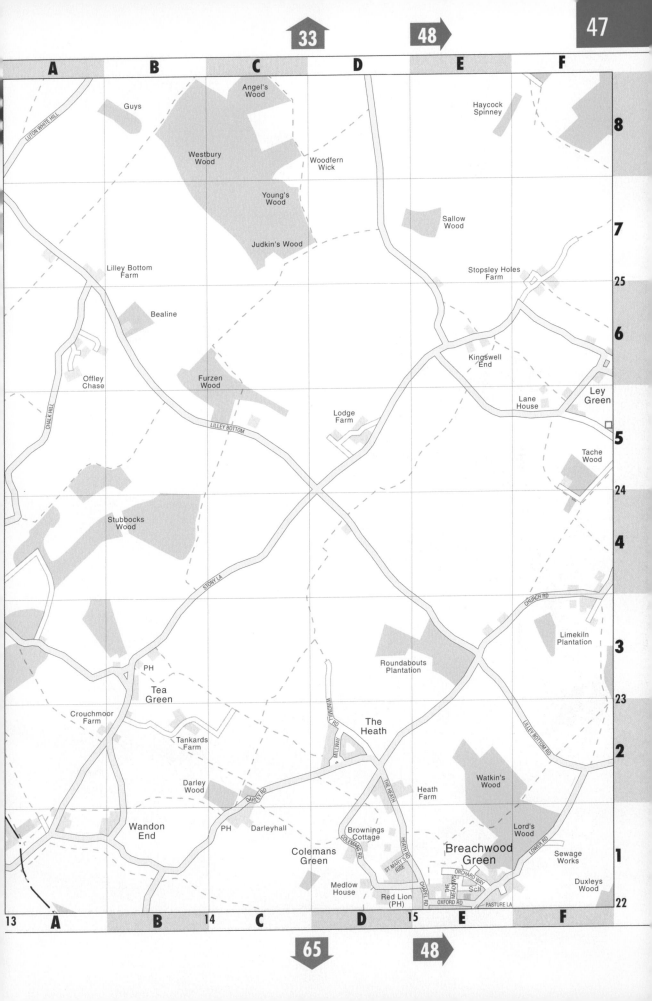

A B C D E F

8
7
25
6
Ley Green
5
24
4
3
23
2
1
22

13 A B 14 C D 15 E F

Luton White Hill
Guys
Angel's Wood
Haycock Spinney
Westbury Wood
Woodfern Wick
Young's Wood
Sallow Wood
Judkin's Wood
Lilley Bottom Farm
Stopsley Holes Farm
Bealine
Kingswell End
Offley Chase
Furzen Wood
Lane House
Chalk Hill
Lilley Bottom
Lodge Farm
Tache Wood
Stubbocks Wood
Limekiln Plantation
Stony La
Church Rd
Roundabouts Plantation
PH
Tea Green
The Heath
Lilley Bottom Rd
Crouchmoor Farm
Windmill Rd
Watkin's Wood
Tankards Farm
The Hillway
Darley Wood
Darley Rd
The Heath
Heath Farm
Wandon End
PH
Darleyhall
Lord's Wood
Brownings Cottage
Breachwood Green
Lower Rd
Colemans Green
Colemans Rd
St Mary's Rise
Sewage Works
Medlow House
Heath Rd
Chapel Rd
Orchard Way
Sch
The Meadows
Duxleys Wood
Red Lion (PH)
Oxford Rd
Pasture La

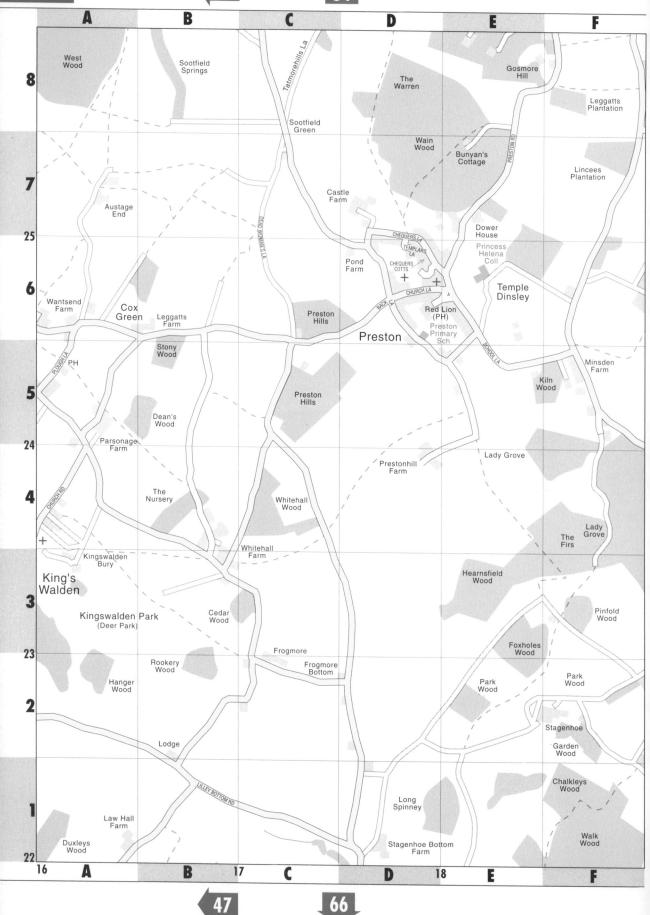

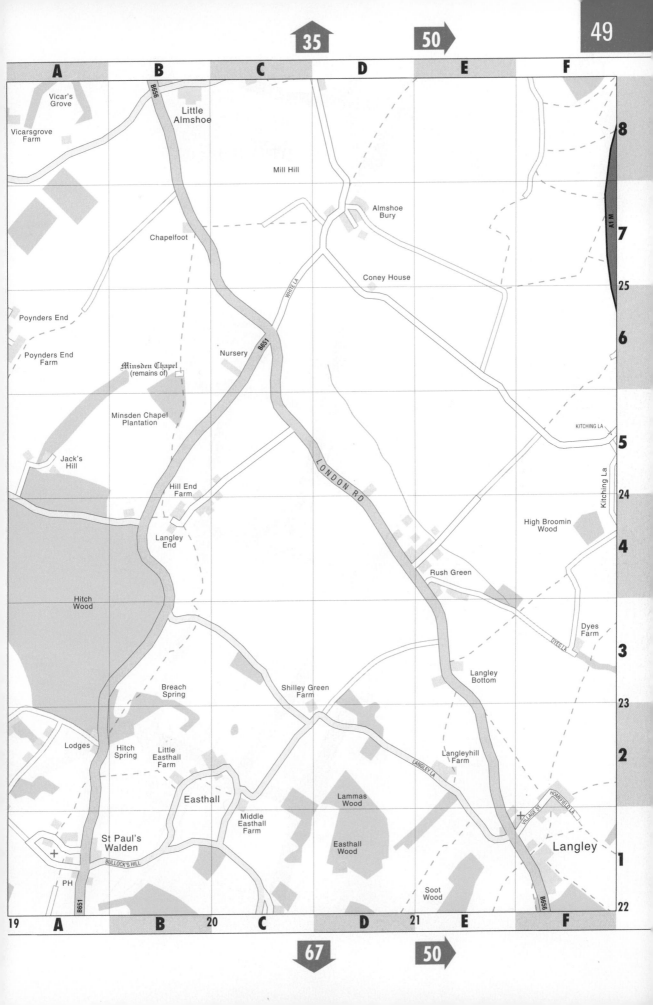

35
50
67
50

A   B   C   D   E   F

8

7

25

6

5

24

4

3

23

2

1

22

Vicar's
Grove

Vicarsgrove
Farm

B656

Little
Almshoe

Mill Hill

Almshoe
Bury

Chapelfoot

Coney House

White LA

Poynders End

B651

Nursery

Minsden Chapel
(remains of)

Minsden Chapel
Plantation

Jack's
Hill

Hill End
Farm

Langley
End

LONDON RD

KITCHING LA

Kitching La

High Broomin
Wood

Rush Green

Hitch
Wood

Langley
Bottom

Dyes
Farm

DYES LA

Breach
Spring

Shilley Green
Farm

Langleyhill
Farm

Lodges

Hitch
Spring

Little
Easthall
Farm

LANGLEY LA

HOMEFIELD LA

Easthall

Middle
Easthall
Farm

Lammas
Wood

VILLAGE ST

Langley

St Paul's
Walden

Easthall
Wood

Soot
Wood

+

B656

BULLOCK'S HILL

PH

B651

19   A   B   20   C   D   21   E   F

A1 M

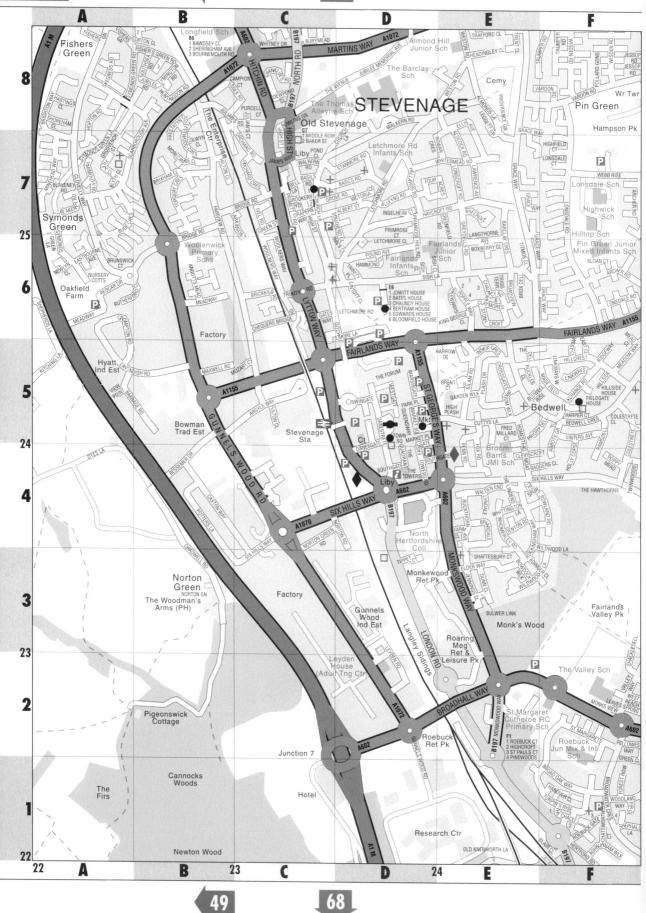

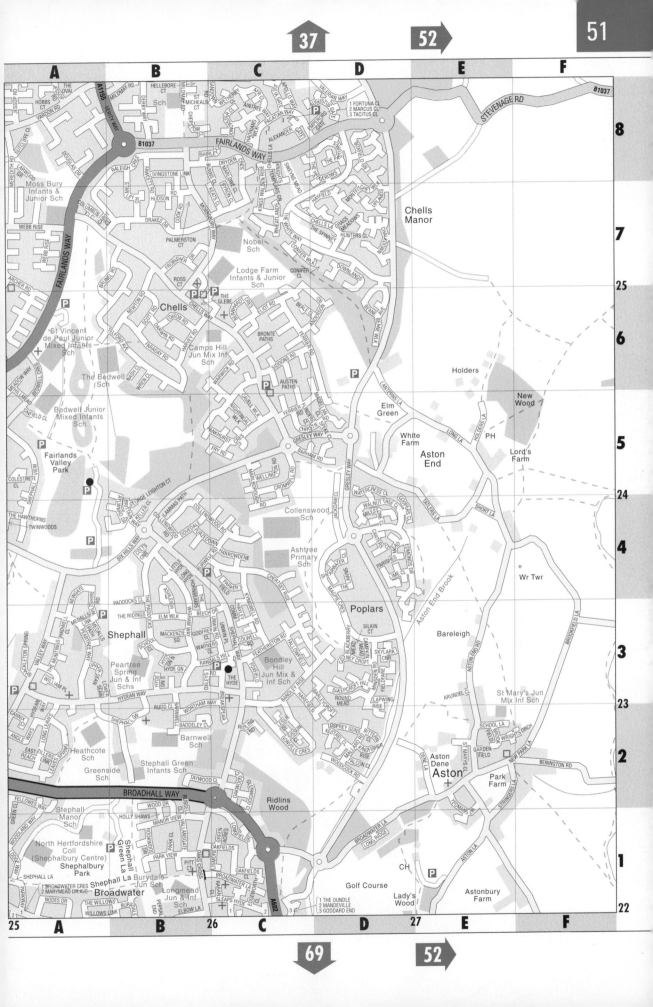

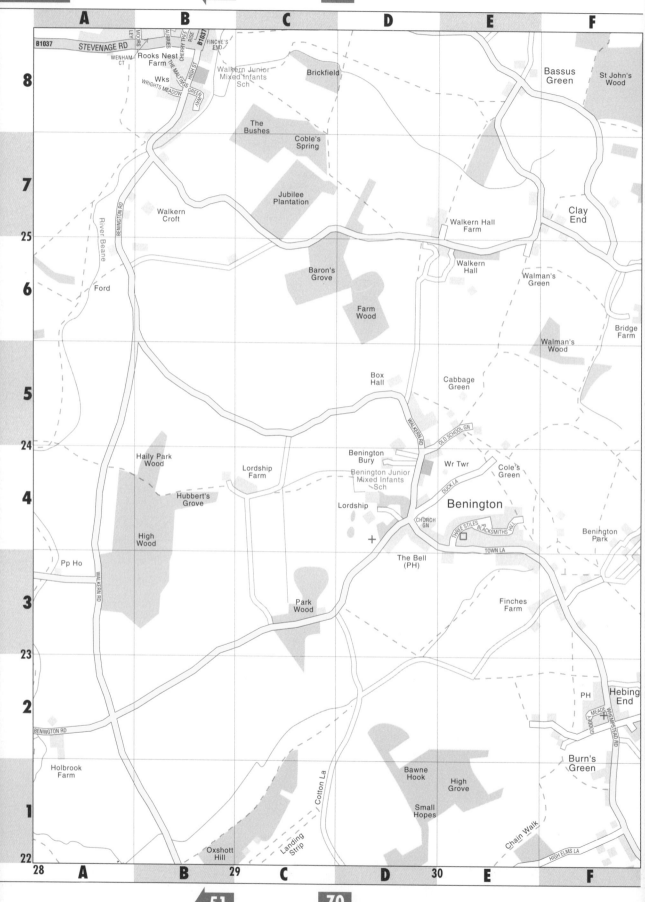

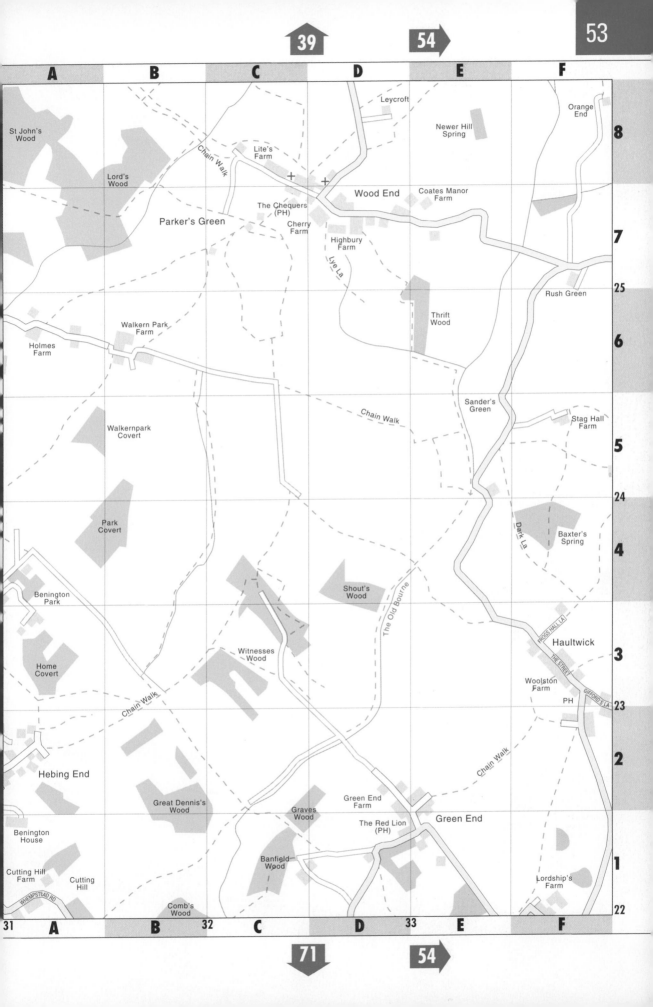

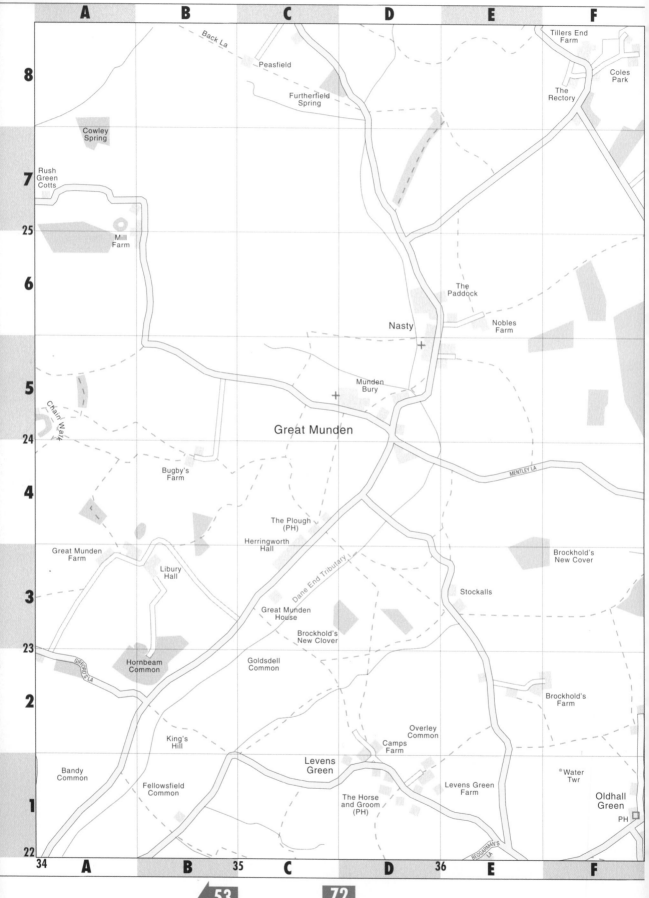

A B C D E F

8
7
25
6
5
24
4
3
23
2
1
22

Back La

Peasfield

Furtherfield
Spring

Tillers End
Farm

Coles
Park

The
Rectory

Cowley
Spring

Rush
Green
Cotts

Mill
Farm

The
Paddock

Nasty

Nobles
Farm

Munden
Bury

Chant Walk

Great Munden

Bugby's
Farm

MENTLEY LA

The Plough
(PH)

Herringworth
Hall

Dane End Tributary

Brockhold's
New Cover

Great Munden
Farm

Libury
Hall

Great Munden
House

Stockalls

Brockhold's
New Clover

GIFFORD'S LA

Hornbeam
Common

Goldsdell
Common

Brockhold's
Farm

King's
Hill

Overley
Common

Camps
Farm

Bandy
Common

Fellowsfield
Common

Levens
Green

Levens Green
Farm

Water
Twr

Oldhall
Green

The Horse
and Groom
(PH)

BEGGARMAN'S LA

PH

34 A 35 B C 36 D E F

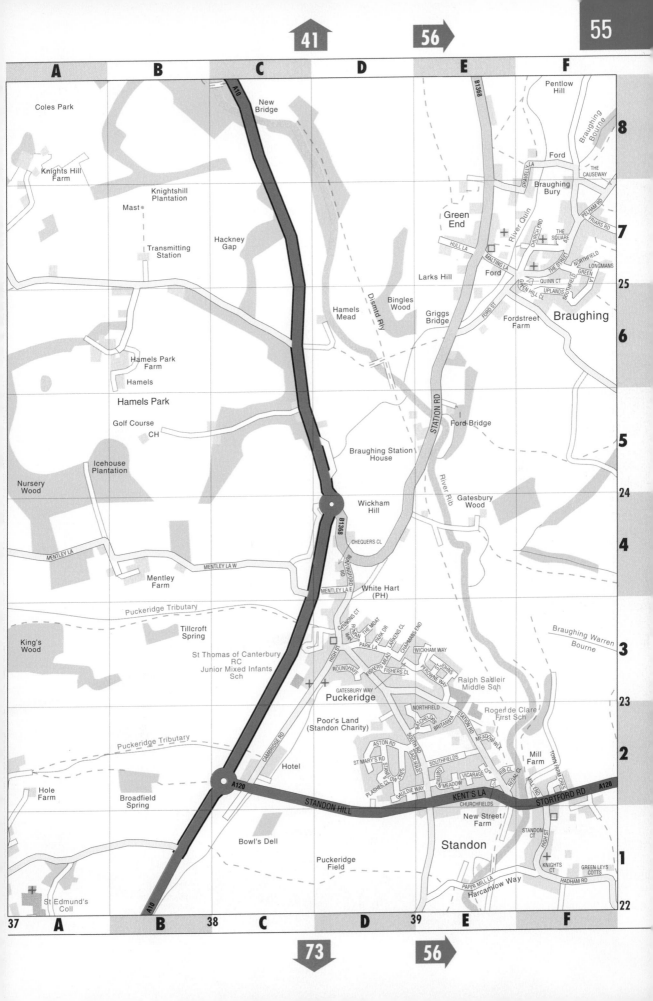

55
42

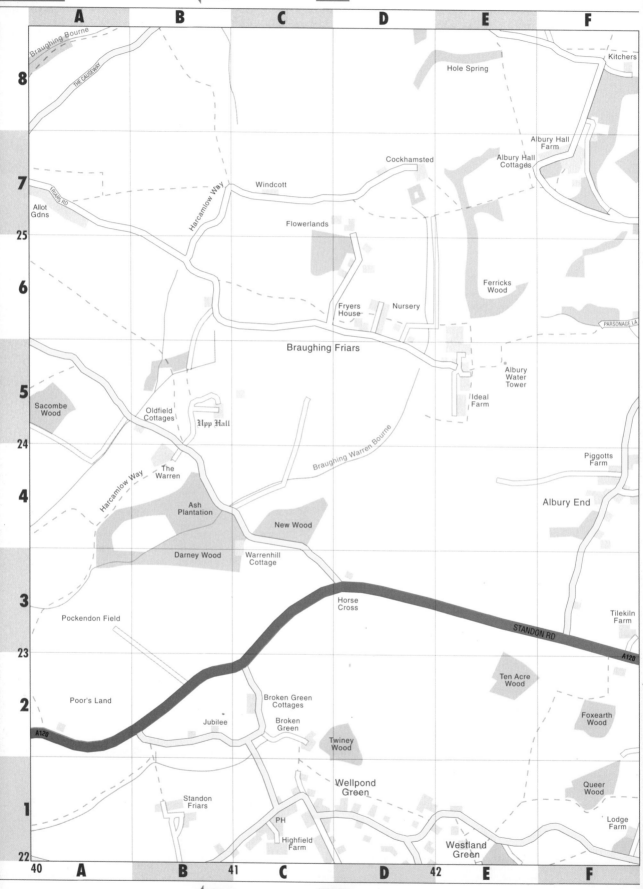

A | B | C | D | E | F

8

7

25

6

5

24

4

3

23

2

1

22

Braughing Bourne

THE CAUSEWAY

Hole Spring

Kitchers

Albury Hall Farm

Cockhamsted

Albury Hall Cottages

Windcott

Harcamlow Way

FRIARS RD

Allot Gdns

Flowerlands

Ferricks Wood

PARSONAGE LA

Fryers House

Nursery

Braughing Friars

Albury Water Tower

Ideal Farm

Sacombe Wood

Oldfield Cottages

Upp Hall

Braughing Warren Bourne

Piggotts Farm

The Warren

Harcamlow Way

Albury End

Ash Plantation

New Wood

Darney Wood

Warrenhill Cottage

Horse Cross

STANDON RD

Tilekiln Farm

Pockendon Field

A120

Ten Acre Wood

Poor's Land

Broken Green Cottages

Broken Green

Foxearth Wood

A120

Jubilee

Twiney Wood

Queer Wood

Wellpond Green

Standon Friars

Lodge Farm

PH

Highfield Farm

Westland Green

40 | A | | B | 41 | C | | D | 42 | E | | F

55
74

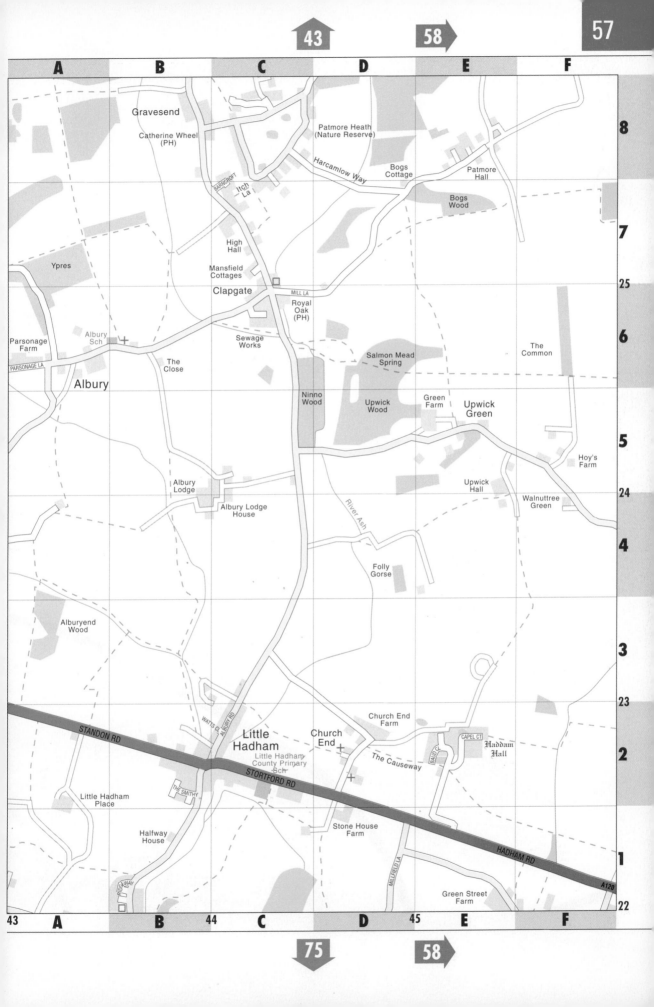

A B C D E F

8

Gravesend

Catherine Wheel
(PH)

Patmore Heath
(Nature Reserve)

BARNCROFT

Itch
La

Harcamlow Way

Bogs
Cottage

Patmore
Hall

7

Bogs
Wood

High
Hall

25

Ypres

Mansfield
Cottages

Clapgate

MILL LA

6

Parsonage
Farm

Albury
Sch

Royal
Oak
(PH)

Salmon Mead
Spring

The
Common

PARSONAGE LA

The
Close

Sewage
Works

Albury

Ninno
Wood

Upwick
Wood

Green
Farm

Upwick
Green

5

Albury
Lodge

Hoy's
Farm

24

Albury Lodge
House

Upwick
Hall

Walnuttree
Green

River Ash

4

Folly
Gorse

Alburyend
Wood

3

23

STANDON RD

WATTS CL

ALBURY RD

Little
Hadham

Church End
Farm

CAPEL CT

Haddam
Hall

2

Little Hadham
County Primary
Sch

Church
End

BAUD CL

The Causeway

STORTFORD RD

Little Hadham
Place

THE SMITHY

HADHAM RD

1

Halfway
House

Stone House
Farm

MILLFIELD LA

RIDGEWAY

Green Street
Farm

A120

22

57

57
76

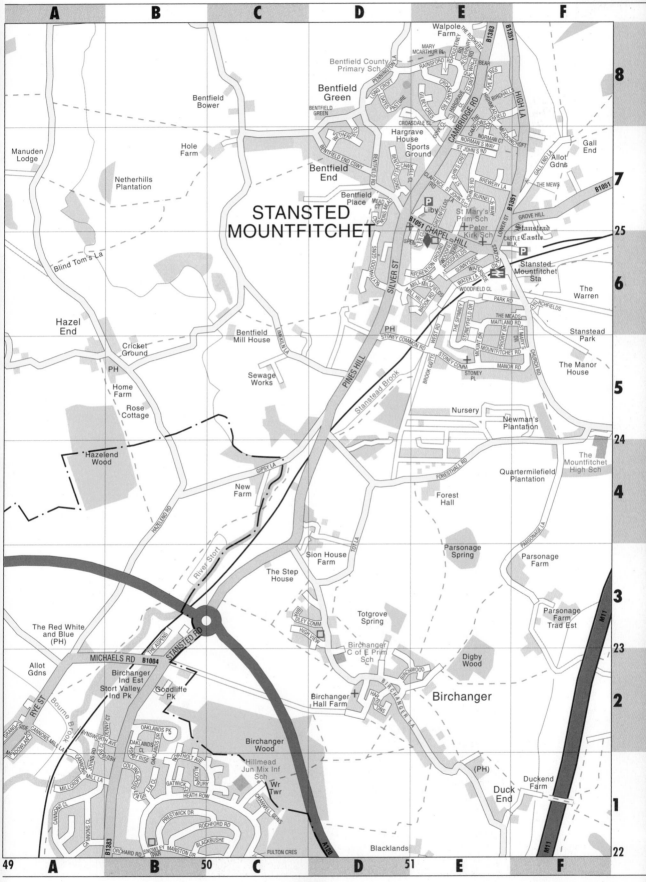

STANSTED
MOUNTFITCHET

Walpole Farm
Bentfield County Primary Sch
Bentfield Green
Bentfield Bower
Hole Farm
Manuden Lodge
Netherhills Plantation
Blind Tom's La
Hazel End
Cricket Ground
PH
Home Farm
Rose Cottage
Hazelend Wood
New Farm
Bentfield End
Bentfield Place
Bentfield Mill House
Sewage Works
Hargrave House Sports Ground
Gall End
Allot Gdns
The Warren
Stanstead Park
The Manor House
St Mary's Prim Sch
Peter Kirk Sch
Stanstead Castle
Stansted Mountfitchet Sta
Liby
Nursery
Newman's Plantation
The Mountfitchet High Sch
Quartermilefield Plantation
Forest Hall
Parsonage Spring
Parsonage Farm
Sion House Farm
The Step House
Totgrove Spring
Parsonage Farm Trad Est
The Red White and Blue (PH)
Allot Gdns
Michaels Rd
B1004
Birchanger Ind Est
Stort Valley Ind Pk
Goodliffe Pk
Birchanger C of E Prim Sch
Digby Wood
Birchanger
Birchanger Hall Farm
Birchanger Wood
Hillmead Jun Mix Inf Sch
Wr Twr
Duck End
Duckend Farm
Blacklands
Stansted Rd

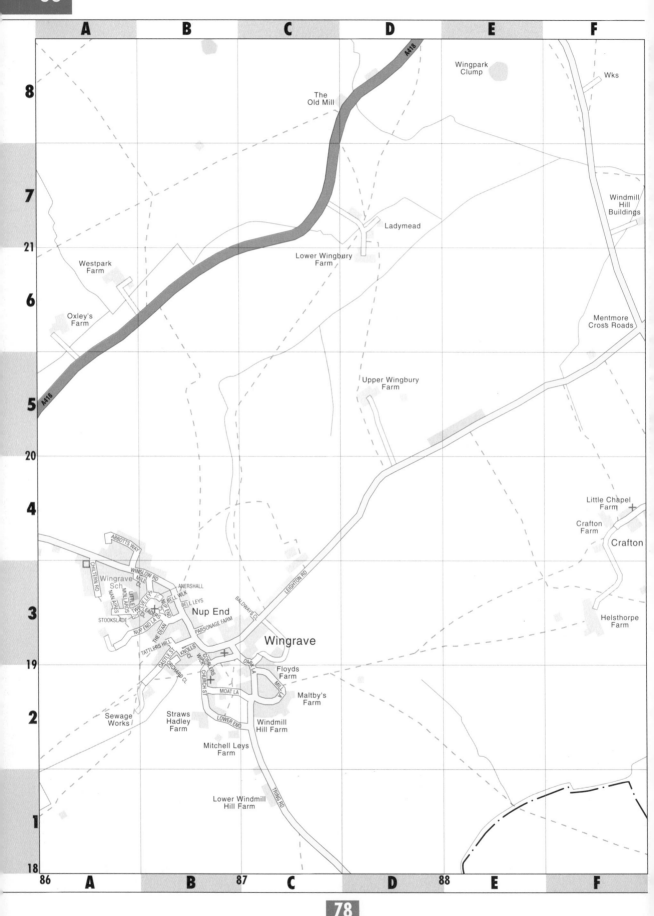

A B C D E F

8

7

21

6

5

20

4

3

19

2

1

18

86 A B 87 C D 88 E F

Wingpark Clump

Wks

The Old Mill

A418

Ladymead

Windmill Hill Buildings

Westpark Farm

Lower Wingbury Farm

Oxley's Farm

Mentmore Cross Roads

A418

Upper Wingbury Farm

Little Chapel Farm

Crafton Farm

Crafton

Abbotts Way

Chiltern Rd

Winslow Rd

Wingrave Sch

Mill Cl

Mollards

Twelve Leys

Nup End La

Nam Aires

Little Cl

Leaders

Stookslade

Nup End La

Anershall Wlk

Bell Wlk

Bell Leys

Nup End

Baloways Cl

Leighton Rd

The Dean

Parsonage Farm

Tattlers Hill

Castle St

Knolls Cl

Orchard Cl

Cobblers Wick

Church St

Wingrave

Helsthorpe Farm

Dovia La

Floyds Farm

Moat La

Mill La

Maltby's Farm

Sewage Works

Straws Hadley Farm

Lower End

Windmill Hill Farm

Mitchell Leys Farm

Lower Windmill Hill Farm

Tring Rd

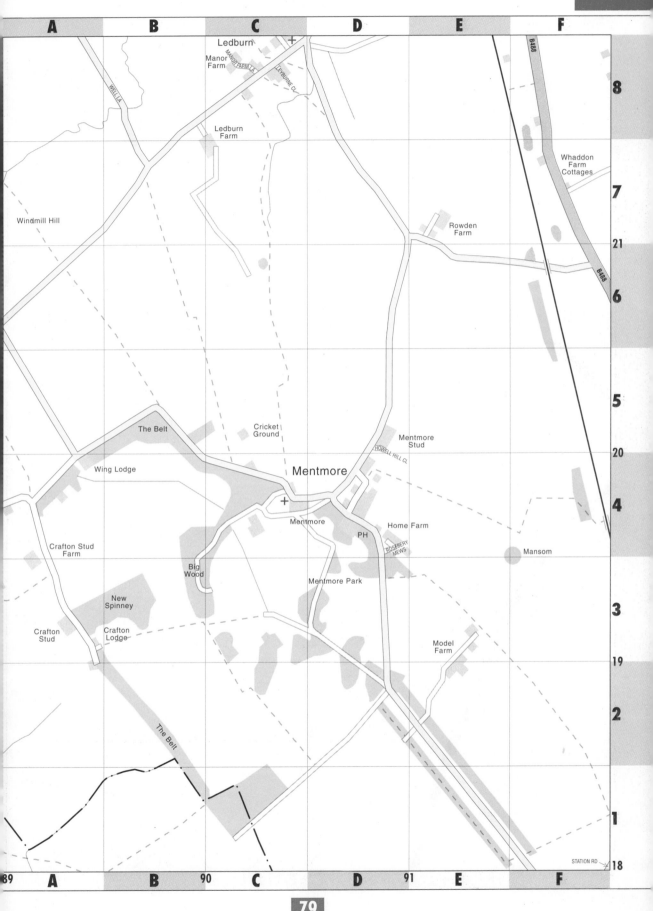

A B C D E F

8

Skimpot Wood

Stanner's Wood

Foxdell Junior Sch

COSGROVE WAY

COULSON CT

BILTON WAY

BILTON WAY

Works

DALLOW RD

EASTINGWOLD GDNS

WARREN RD

KENT RD

HAREFIELD RD

HAREFIELD CT

SUMMERFIELD RD

HAREFIELD RD

FINWAY

RUNLEY RD

Chaul End Farm

7

Zouches Farm

Chaul End

Vehicle Test Circuit

Round Wood

HIGH WOOD CL

BLUEBELL WOOD CL

M1

21

Twentynine Wood

Bush Wood

Badgerdell Wood

MORTIMER CL

Golf Course

6

Dame Ellen's Wood

Thirty Wood

Blossom Spring

Little John's Wood

Brickkiln Farm

Castlecroft Wood

5

Folly Wood

Manor Farm

RUSHMORE CL

COLLINGS WELLS CL

Meadow Croft

20

Bury Farm

FOLLY LA

MANOR CT

LUTON RD

CADIA

MEADOW WAY

HEATHFIELD CL

4

A5

Turnpike Farm

Cradle Spinney

Caddington

Heathfield Lower Sch

DELFIELD CL

HYDE RD

Willowfield Sch

THE OAKS

Lodge Farm

Gatehouse

HOLLY FARM CL

HAWTHORN CRES

THE DELL

THE CRESCENT

FIVE OAKS

Five Oaks Sch

3

Buncer's Wood

DUNSTABLE RD

Garden Centre

CULWORTH CL

EDGECOTE CL

ELM AVE

LEDWELL

ADSTONE RD

FAIRGREEN RD

Jockey Farm

CROSSLANDS

THE GLEN

TAG LA

ENSLOW CL

19

MILLFIELD WAY

LITTLEGREEN LA

MANOR RD

Tipplehill Farm

2

Kensworth House

Horse and Jockey (PH)

Cotswold Bsns Pk

MILLFIELD LA

MANCROFT RD

Piper's Farm

Aley Green

Millfield Farm

1

Corner Farm

Kensworth Lynch

Lynch Farm

Nurseries

PIPERS LA

Cemy

18

A5

04 A B 05 C D 06 E F

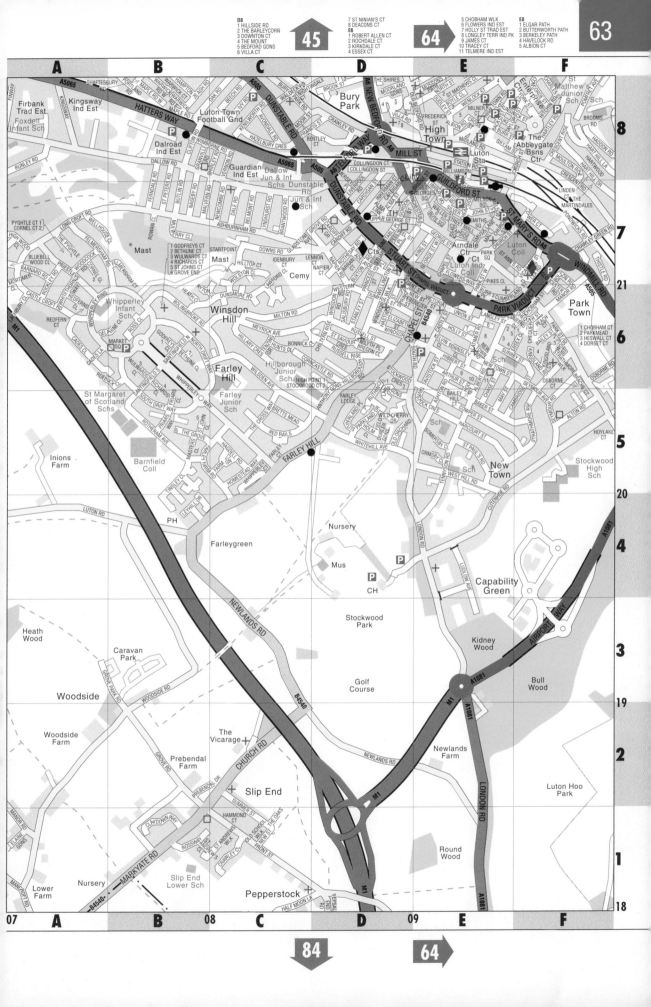

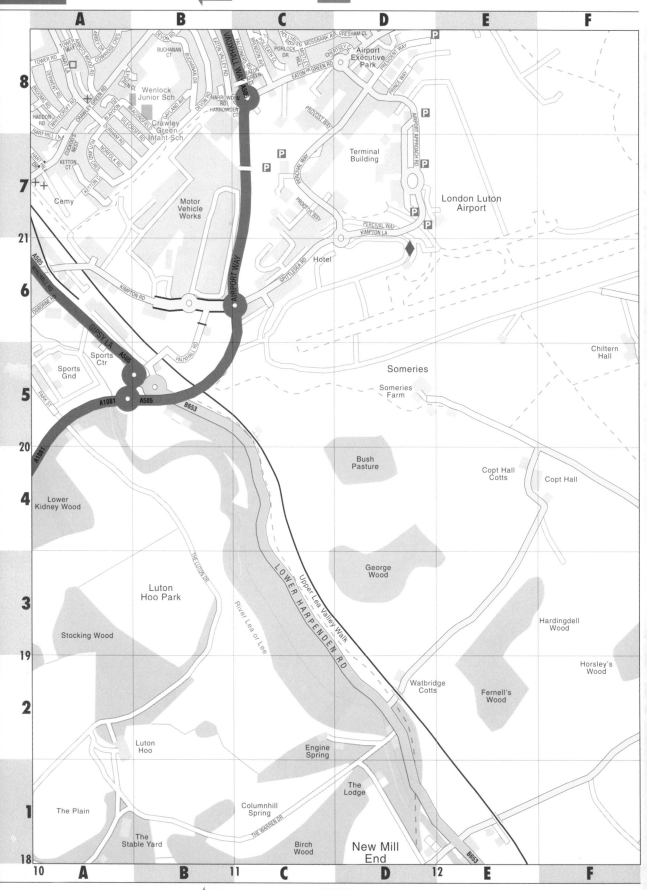

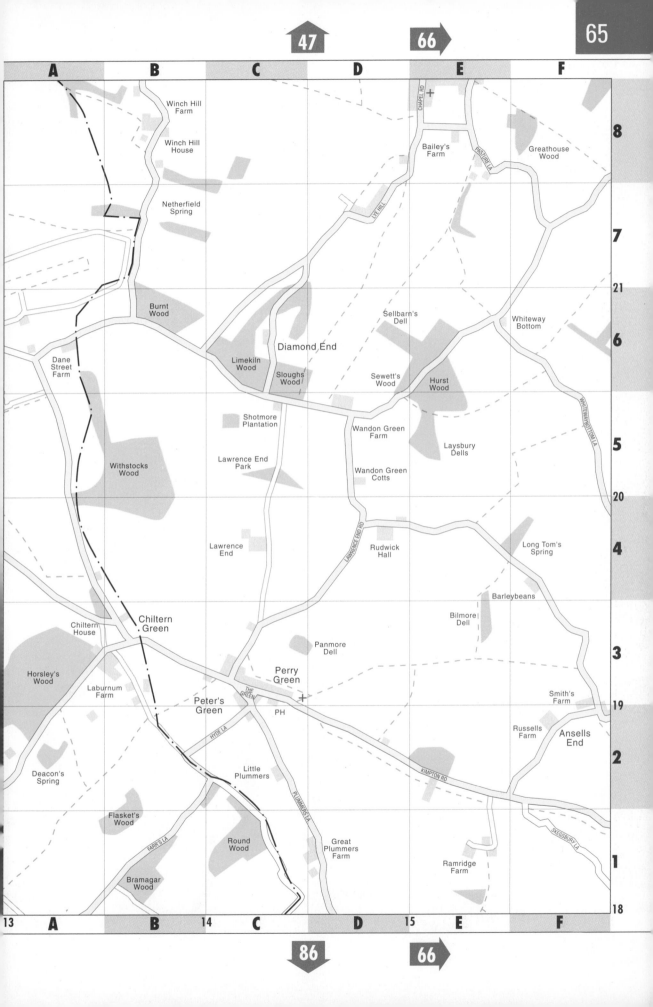

47
66

A   B   C   D   E   F

8

7

21

6

5

20

4

3

19

2

1

18

Winch Hill Farm
Winch Hill House
Netherfield Spring
Burnt Wood
Dane Street Farm
Limekiln Wood
Sloughs Wood
Diamond End
Shotmore Plantation
Withstocks Wood
Lawrence End Park
Lawrence End
Chiltern House
Chiltern Green
Horsley's Wood
Laburnum Farm
Peter's Green
Deacon's Spring
Flasket's Wood
Bramagar Wood
Round Wood
Little Plummers
Great Plummers Farm
Perry Green
PH
Panmore Dell
Rudwick Hall
Wandon Green Cotts
Wandon Green Farm
Sewett's Wood
Sellbarn's Dell
Bailey's Farm
Greathouse Wood
Hurst Wood
Whiteway Bottom
Laysbury Dells
Long Tom's Spring
Barleybeans
Bilmore Dell
Smith's Farm
Russells Farm
Ansells End
Ramridge Farm

CHAPEL RD
LYE HILL
PASTURE LA
WHITEWAYBOTTOM LA
LAWRENCE END RD
THE GREEN
HYDE LA
PLUMMERS LA
FARR'S LA
KIMPTON RD
SKEGSBURY LA

86
66

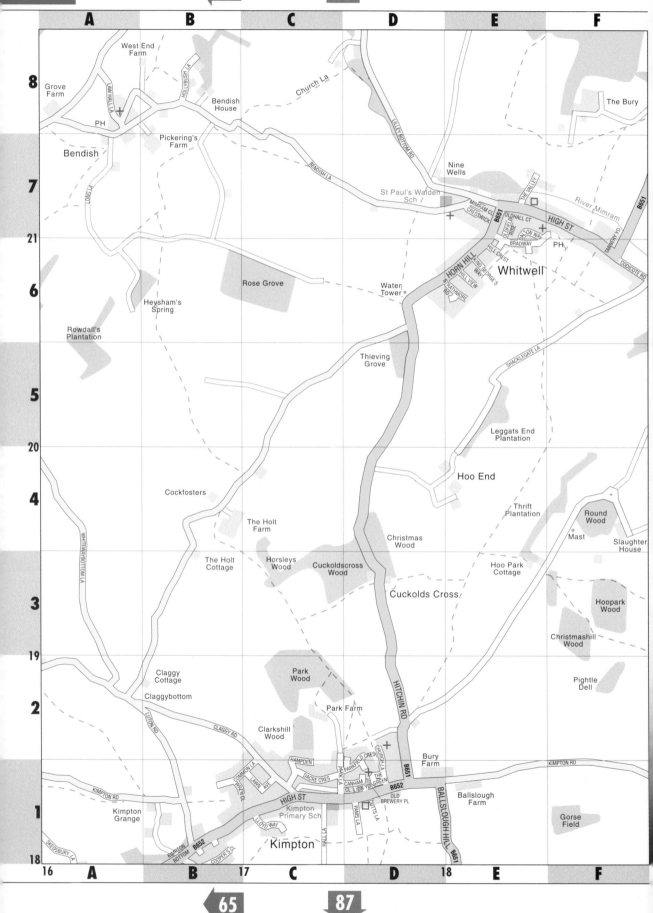

A B C D E F

Grove Farm
West End Farm
Church La
The Bury
Bendish House
Pickering's Farm
PH
Bendish
Nine Wells
St Paul's Walden Sch
River Mimram
LAW HALL LA
WHITBITTOM LA
BENDISH LA
LILLEY BOTTOM RD
THE VALLEY
MIMRAM CL
CRESSWICK
OLDHALL CT
HIGH ST
B651
OLDFIELD RISE
DAL ON WAY
BRADWAY
PH
TANBURY YD
CODICOTE RD
LONG LA
Rose Grove
Heysham's Spring
Water Tower
HORN HILL
HILL CREST
KING GEORGE'S WAY
HILL VIEW
STRATHMORE RD
Whitwell
Rowdall's Plantation
Thieving Grove
SHACKLEGATE LA
Leggats End Plantation
Hoo End
Thrift Plantation
Round Wood
Mast
Slaughter House
Cockfosters
The Holt Farm
Christmas Wood
Hoo Park Cottage
Hoopark Wood
WHITEWAYBOTTOM LA
The Holt Cottage
Horsleys Wood
Cuckoldscross Wood
Cuckolds Cross
Christmashill Wood
Claggy Cottage
Claggybottom
Park Wood
Park Farm
Bury Farm
Pightle Dell
LUTON RD
CLAGGY RD
Clarkshill Wood
HITCHIN RD
KIMPTON RD
KIMPTON RD
Kimpton Grange
HAMPDEN
COMMON LA
WREN CL
LAWN AVE
DACRE CRES
PARK LA
PARRETTS D CRES
CANHAM CL
LION YD
THE GREEN
BUTTS LA
OLD BREWERY PL
B652
Ballslough Farm
Gorse Field
SKEGSBURY LA
HIGH ST
Kimpton Primary Sch
LLOYD WAY
HALL LA
PINKS LA
B651
BALLSLOUGH HILL
KIMPTON BOTTOM
B652
COOPER'S CL
Kimpton

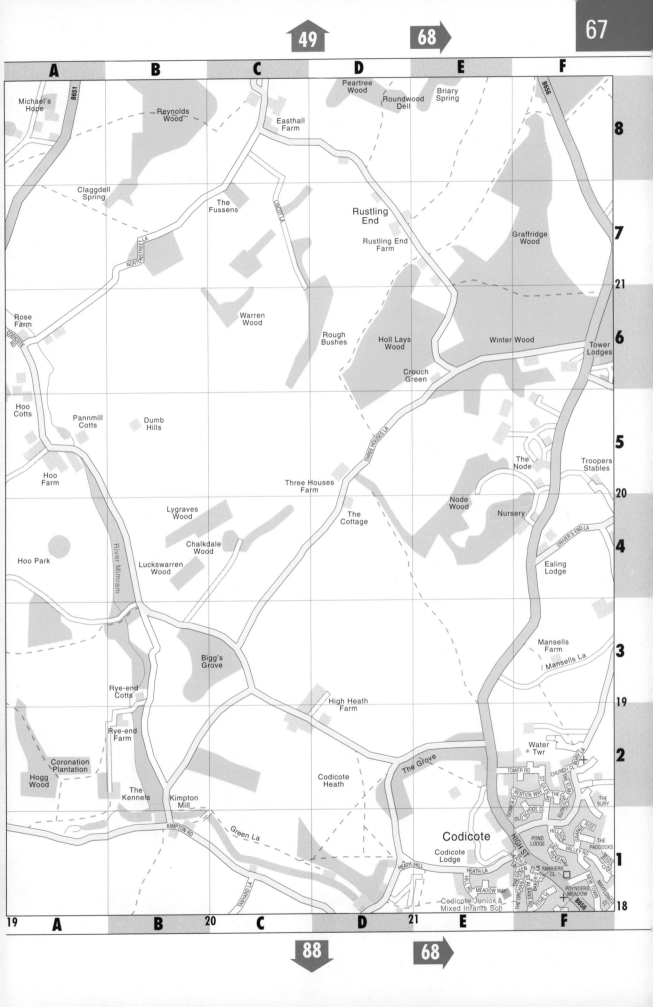

A B C D E F

8

7

21

6

5

20

4

3

19

2

1

18

Michael's Hope

B651

Reynolds Wood

Easthall Farm

Peartree Wood

Roundwood Dell

Briary Spring

Claggdell Spring

The Fussens

Rustling End

Rustling End Farm

Graffridge Wood

NORTON STREET LA

LINCOTT LA

Rose Farm

CODICOTE RD

Warren Wood

Rough Bushes

Holl Lays Wood

Winter Wood

Tower Lodges

Crouch Green

Hoo Cotts

Pannmill Cotts

Dumb Hills

THREE HOUSES LA

The Node

Troopers Stables

Hoo Farm

Lygraves Wood

Three Houses Farm

Node Wood

Nursery

DRIVER'S END LA

Hoo Park

River Mimram

Chalkdale Wood

Luckswarren Wood

The Cottage

Ealing Lodge

Mansells Farm

Mansells La

Bigg's Grove

High Heath Farm

Rye-end Cotts

Rye-end Farm

Water Twr

TOWER RD

BURY LA

CHURCH CL

THE ELMS

Coronation Plantation

The Grove

Codicote Heath

BENTICK WAY

OLD SCHOOL CL

THE CHESTNUTS

THE BURY

Hogg Wood

The Kennels

Kimpton Mill

KIMPTON RD

Green La

TANYARD LA

Codicote Lodge

Codicote

HIGH ST

POND LODGE

HILL SIDE

GRANGE RISE

THE PADDOCKS

VALLEY RD

HEATH HILL

HILL RD

MEADOW WAY

Heath La

THE GREEN

ST ALBANS RD

BAKER ST

FARRIERS CL

RIDGEWAY

THE CL

POYNDERS MEADOW

B656

NEW TOWN CL

MAYFLOWER CL

Codicote Junior & Mixed Infants Sch

GOMER CL

B656

A B C D E F

8 Burleigh Grove
Cowley's Corner Wood
North Lodges

Burleigh Farm

7 Wintergreen Wood
B656
Knebworth Country Park
A1 M
LONDON RD
B197
HAZELMERE RD
SKIPTON CL
HERTFORD RD
BROXHILL
STON CRES

Mausoleum
Golf Course
STEVENAGE RD

21 +

6 Knebworth Ho
Miniature Rly
CH
DEARD'S END LA
STIBARTS CL
B197
BADGER CL
PETERS WAY
NEW CL

Manor Farm
Old Knebworth
Lodge Farm
PARK LA
Martlets
WESTLAND RD
KEITHS WOOD
DEARD'S WOOD
COTE
KENT CL

5 Lytton Arms (PH)
THE GLEN
Knebworth Sta
MUIRHEAD WAY
LYTTON FIELDS
DEANCROFT
BROOM GR
STATION RD
GIBBONS WAY

20 DRIVER'S END LA
Park Wood
STOCKENS DELL
CHASE
HORNBEAM
GUN LA

4 Driver's End
Nup End
SUP LA
Homewood
GYPSY LA
STOCKENS GN
STOCKENS GN
CHERRY
GUN ROAD GDNS
CRAB TREE RD

The Bothy
Hogsnorton
New Wood
WOODSTOCK
WADNAL

3 BURY LA
Thickney Wood
SALLY DEARDS LA
Plummer's Farm
Robin Hood & Little John (PH)
Hornbeam Spring

Deard's Wood
DEARD'S LA
Rableyheath
Water Twr
DARBY DR
WYCH ELM LA
The Iron House

19 SPINNEY LA

2 Tagmore Green
Rableyheath Farm
NINNING'S LA
NORMAN'S LA
Ninning's Wood
A1 M

Ashley Grove
RIPLEY HEATH RD
Arnold's Farm

Pottersheath
POTTERSHEATH RD
HEATH RD
Heath Field

1 1 THE BIRCHES
2 THE PADDOCKS
3 MAYFLOWER CL
Little Wood
Nursery
Mardley Heath
MARDLEY DELL
MARDLEY HILL
Welwyn Heath
HEATHLANDS

Ridge Farm
CODICOTE HEIGHTS
Little Bury Farm
Arnold's Spring
DANESBURY PARK RD
CANONSFIELD RD
MARDLEY WOOD

18

22 A 23 B C 24 D E F

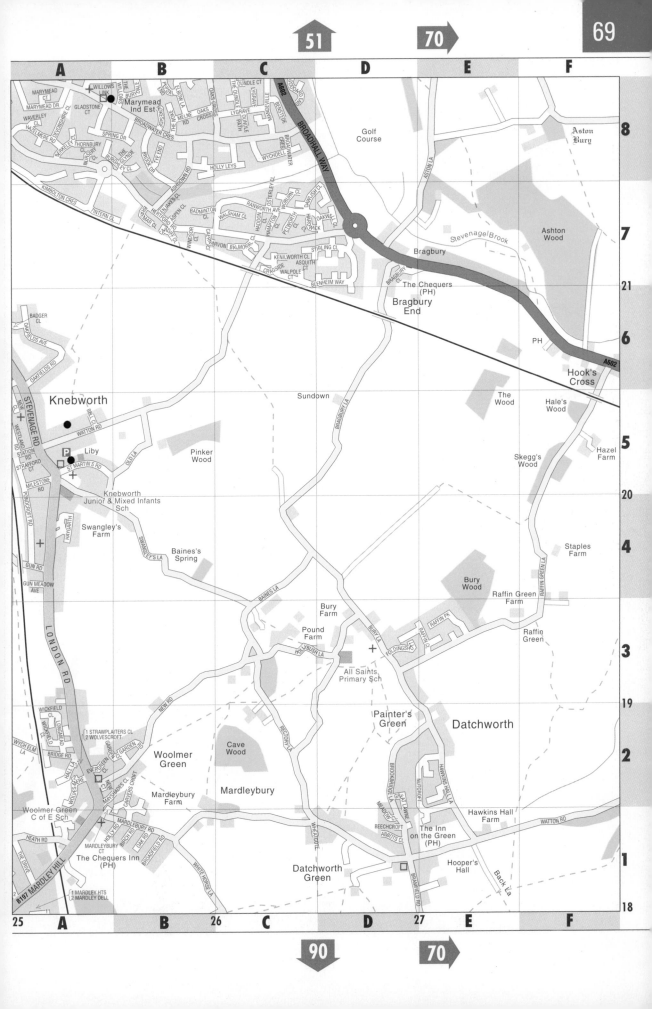

53
72

A **B** **C** **D** **E** **F**

Chain Walk

Comb's Wood

Apsley Common

Customs Wood

Easington Common

Little Munden Junior Mixed & Infants Sch

Short Whiteley Common

8

Dane End

CHURCH LA
WINDMILLS
GLADSTON
KINGSFIELD RD
WHITTLEY
COUNCELEY AVE

Chapel Farm

Long Spring

The Old Bourne

EASTFIELD RD
MUNDEN RD
KENNEDY RD
WHITTLEY CL
WIN WAY
RISE

PAGET COTTS

Whempstead Green

PEARMAN DR

Dane End House

WHEMPSTEAD RD

7

Home Farm

Whempstead

Cottonborough Common

Claypits Wood

21

MILL LA

Whempstead Gate Farm

Whempstead Farm

Hog's Wood

Lodge Farm

6

WHEMPSTEAD LA

Wicks Wood

Brookfield Common

Smart's Hill

Bromley Common

Bushy Leys Spring

Longcroft Wood

5

Willeycotes Wood

Dane End Tributary

20

Bardolphspark Wood

Sacombe Hill Farm

Sacombe Hill

4

SACOMBE GREEN RD

Bardolphs

Sacombe

3

SACOMBE POUND

19

WARE RD

Heath Mount Sch

Sacombebury Farm

Sacombe House

The Springs

Sacombe Park

2

Woodhall Park

The Clumps

Broad Water

River Beane

Home Farm

Sacombe Lake

The Cuts

Ware Lodge

1

A119

A602

King Edward's Gorse

18

31 **A** **B** **32** **C** **D** **33** **E** **F**

71
54

A B C D E F

8
7
21
6
5
20
4
19
2
1
18

Fullars Common

Moorfield Common

High Trees Farm

Hatchett Farm

BEGGARMAN'S LA

Hatchett Poultry Farm

Beggarman's Wood

Hill Farm

Trenchern Hills

Whitehill Farm

Langton's La

Shelly's Wood

Roughground Wood

Cock's Wood

Rigery Farm

RIGERY LA

Potter's Green

Potter's Hall Farm

Labdens Farm

ROWNEY LA

Rowney Priory

Black Grove

Standon Green End Farm

Willowtree Farm

Rowney Wood

LOWGATE LA

Knoll Farm

LOWGATE LA

Secombe Green

Standon Green End

Church Wood

Dilly Wood

Mott's Wood

The Bourne

Barwick Tributary

Low Wood

Salmonsley Wood

DARE END RD

Home Wood

Home Farm

MARSHALL'S LA

Sutes

CAMBRIDGE COTTS

Gages Wood

Marshall's Farm

Pullar Memorial Junior Mixed & Infants Sch

High Cross

Furzeground Wood

Marshall's

NORTH DR

POPLAR CL

PH

PASSFIELD COTTS

Rennesley Garden Wood

Hazelwood Farm

Mark's Wood

Highcross Hill

A10

Gravelpit Wood

71
93

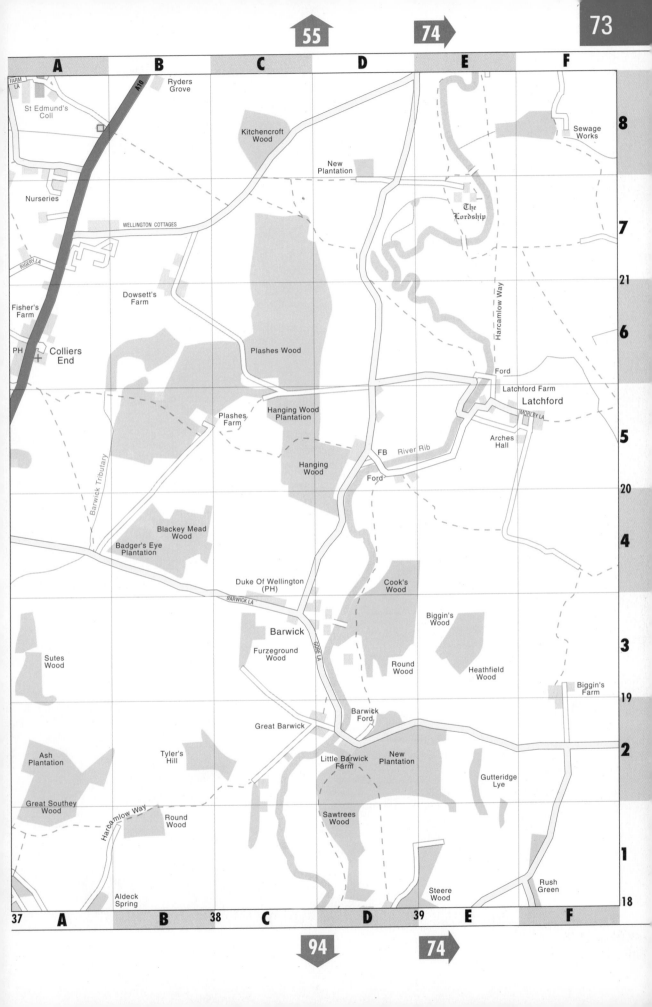

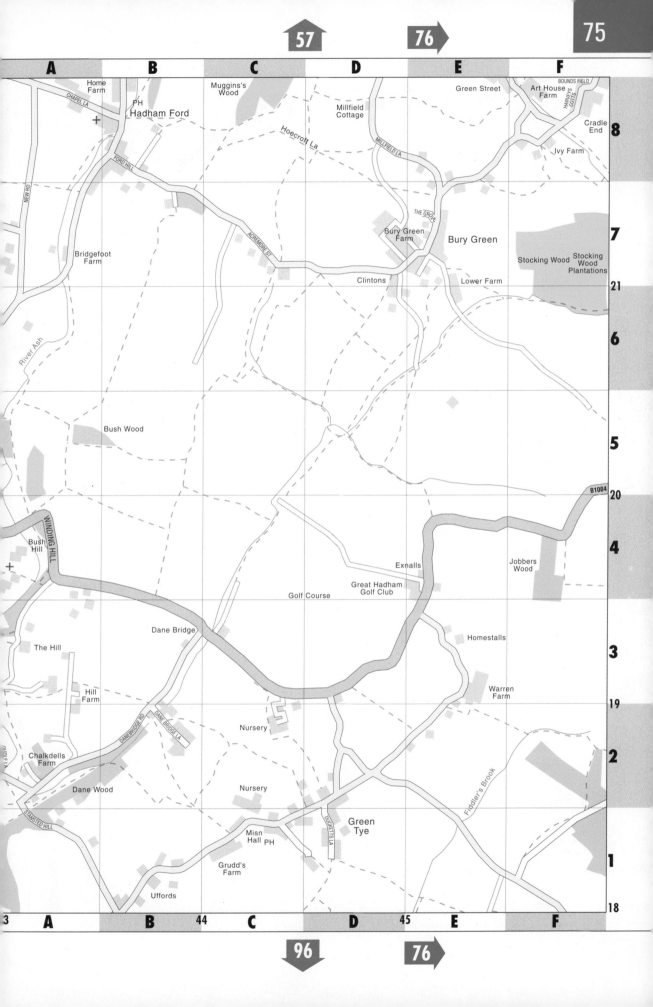

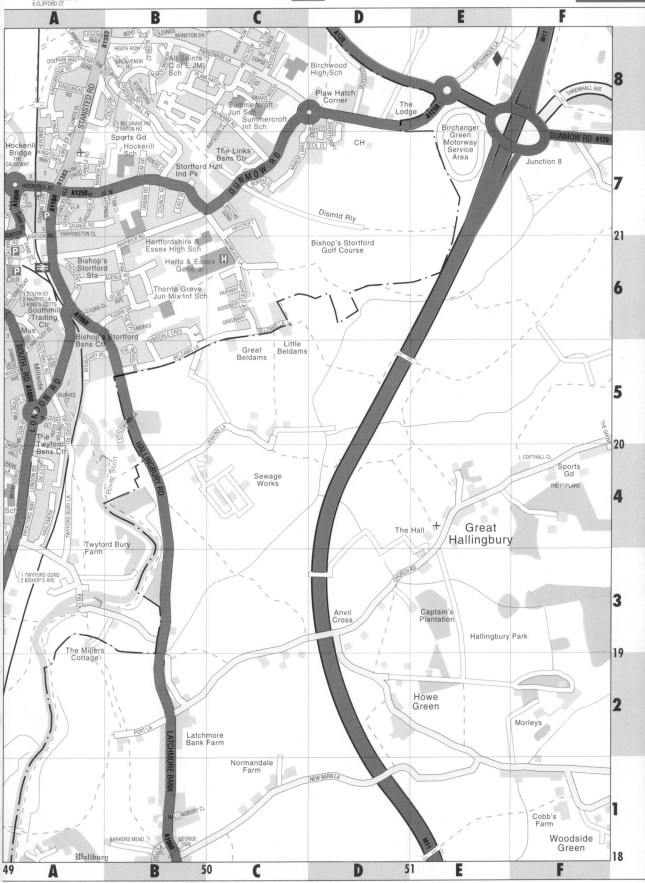

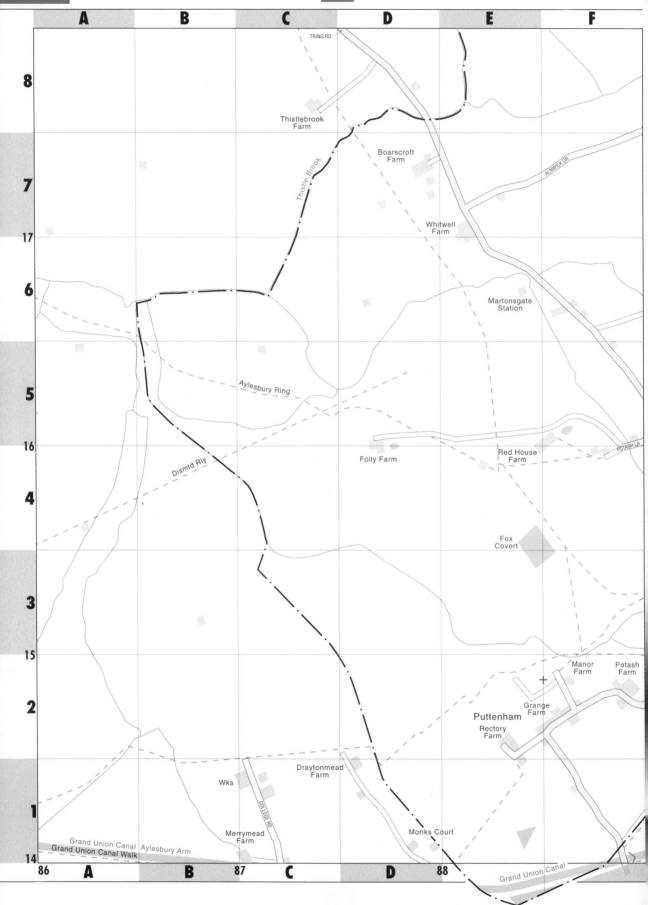

A B C D E F

8

TRING RD

Thistlebrook
Farm

Boarscroft
Farm

ALNWICK DR

Thistle Brook

7

Whitwell
Farm

17

6

Martonsgate
Station

Aylesbury Ring

5

Dismtd Rly

16

Folly Farm

Red House
Farm

POTASH LA

4

Fox
Covert

3

15

Manor
Farm

Potash
Farm

Grange
Farm

Puttenham

2

Rectory
Farm

Draytonmead
Farm

COLLEGE RD

Wks

1

Merrymead
Farm

Monks Court

14

Grand Union Canal Aylesbury Arm
Grand Union Canal Walk

Grand Union Canal

86 A B 87 C D 88

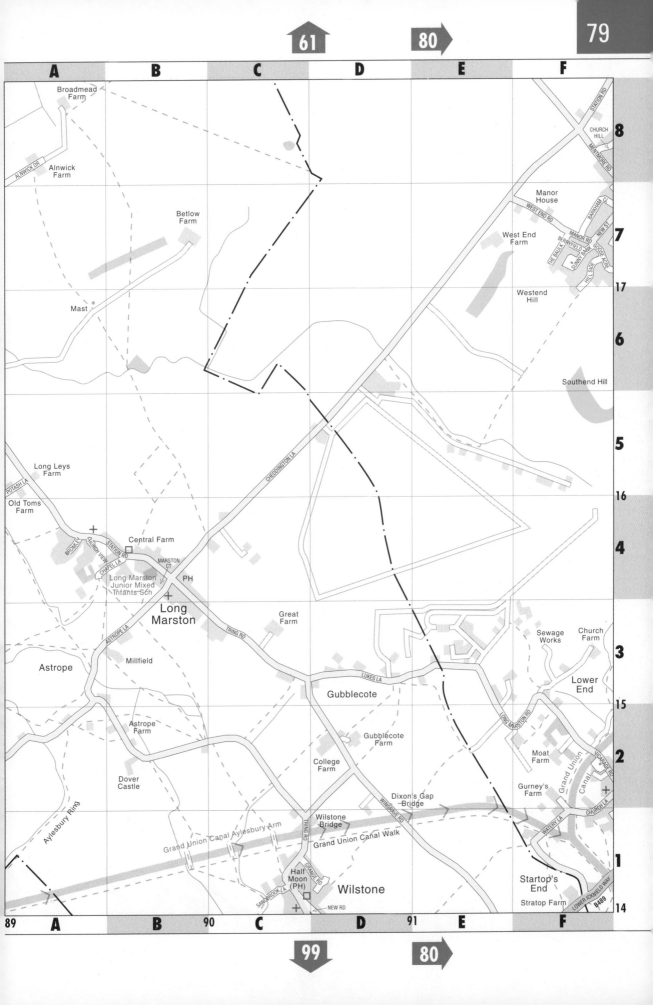

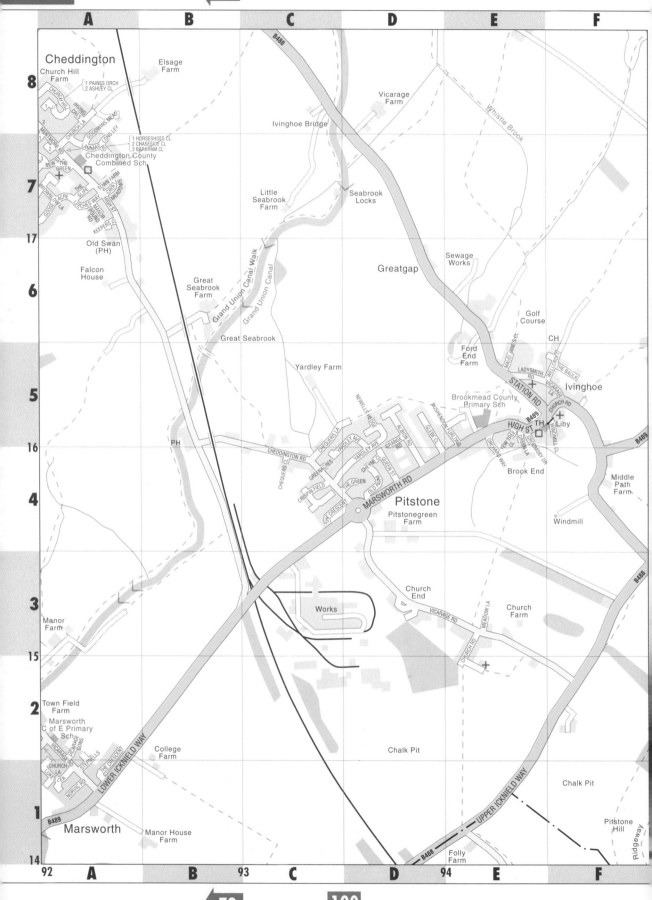

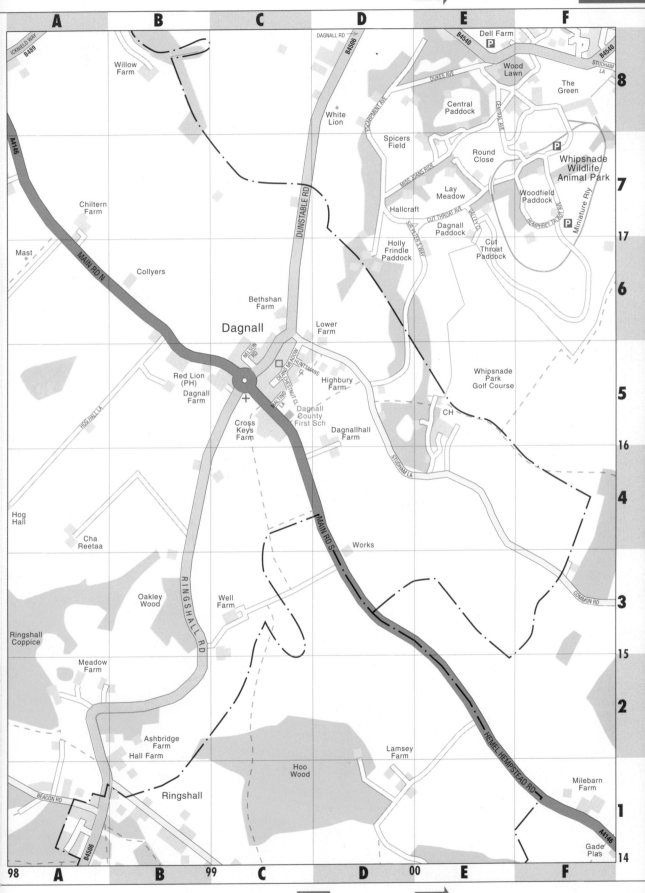

81

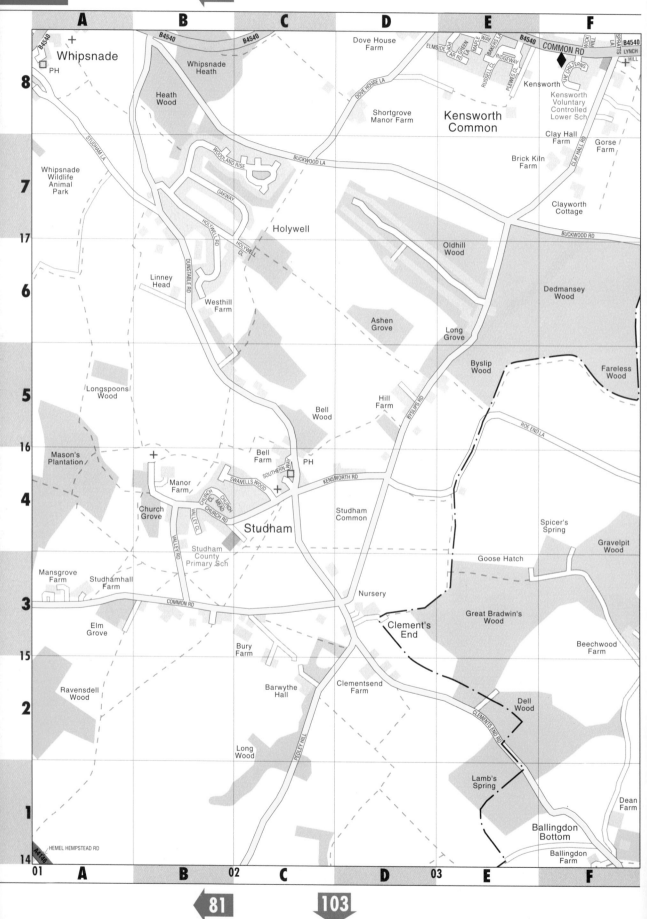

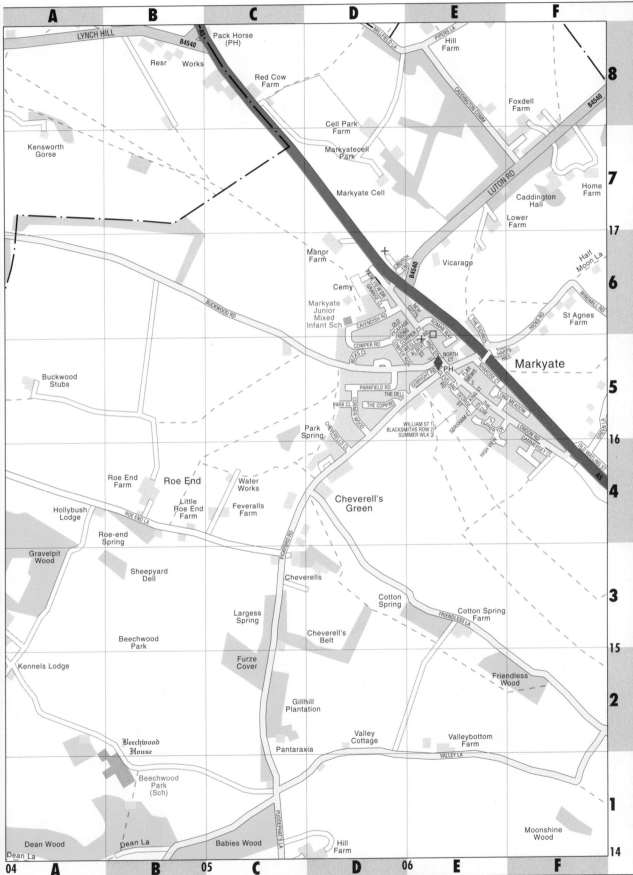

A   B   C   D   E   F

8

Wild Fowl Park

MARKYATE RD   B4540

Grove Farm

Birchin Grove

Half Moon La

Pepsal End

PEPSAL END RD

Chalk Wood

M1

The New Lodge

LONDON RD   A1081

Gibraltar Cottages

7

Top Spring

Limekiln Plantation

Middle Spring

Half Moon La

Pepsalend Farm

Heavens Wood

Gibraltar Farm

A1081

17

Stable Spring

Sewage Works

WINDMILL RD

6

Broomhill Leys Wood

Bonners Farm

Ivy Farm

Doone Brae Farm

Smallgrove Farm

Cockrums

Lady Bray Farm

Green La

5

Rainbow Hall Farm

CHAD LA

Hogtrough Wood

Whitewalls

16

School House Farm

Brickfield Farm

Eight Acre Spring

ANNABLES LA

4

A5

Hotel

Highfield Farm

Hill and Coles Farm

Turner's Hall Farm

Sewage Works

OLD WATLING ST

River Hall

Chad Lane Farm

WATERY LA

3

River Ver

Friar's Wash

P

Junction 9

HOLLYBUSH LA

Wagon & Horses (PH)

CHEQUERS HILL

15

Hollybush Farm

RIVER HILL

A5

2

FRIENDLESS LA

CHAPEL RD

PRIORY CHURCH LA

HIGH ST

SINGLETS LA

Cemy

Sunny Ridge

Verlam End

Millfield Cottage

MILL LA

Pound Farm

CHURCH RD

CHURCH END

PIE CNR

A5183

DUNSTABLE RD

Flamstead

VICARAGE GDNS

COLLEGE CL

YE GARDEN

Delmerend Farm

DELMEREND LA

1

PRETLEY HILL

PARSON'S CL

TROWLEY HILL RD

Flamstead Junior Mixed Infant Sch

Norringtonend Farm

REDDING LA

Showground

A5183

14

M1

07   A   B   08   C   D   09   E   F

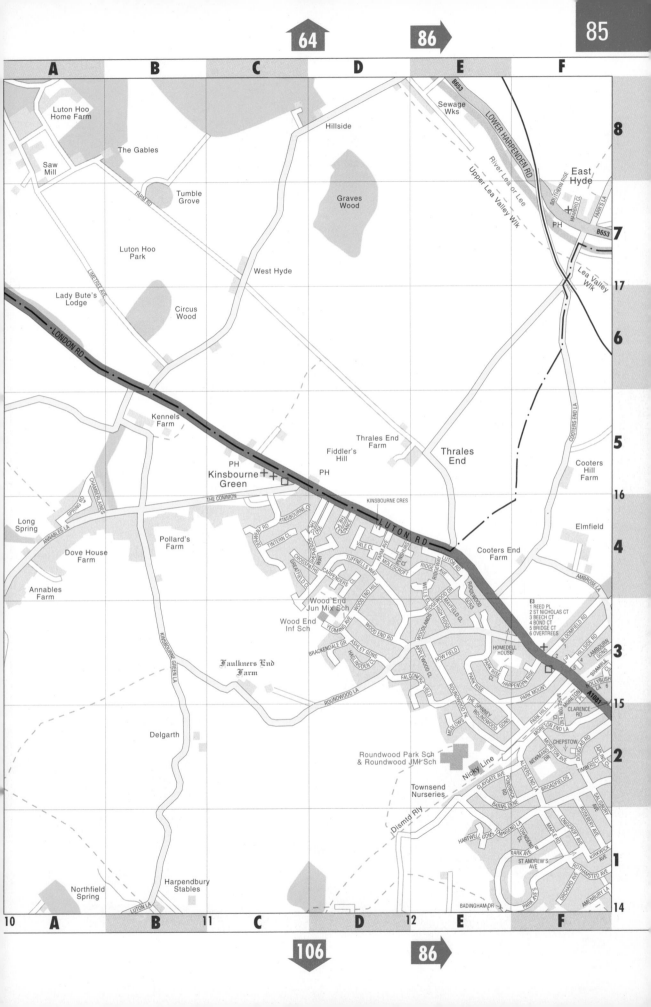

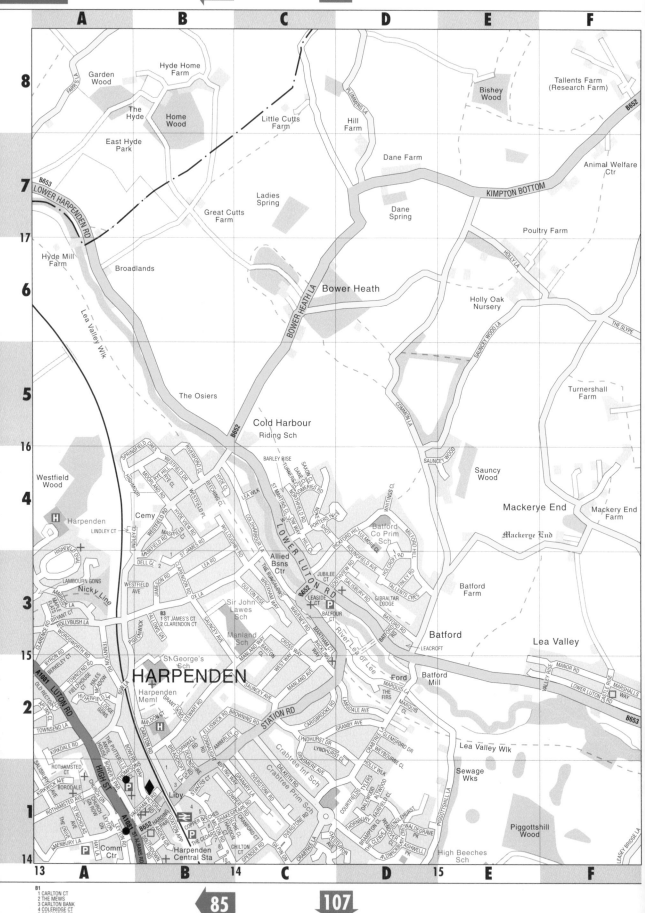

HARPENDEN

B1
1 CARLTON CT
2 THE MEWS
3 CARLTON BANK
4 COLERIDGE CT
5 BEAUMONT CT
6 MILTON CT
7 YARDLEY CT
8 SHELLEY CT
9 AVON CT
10 FURZEDOWN CT

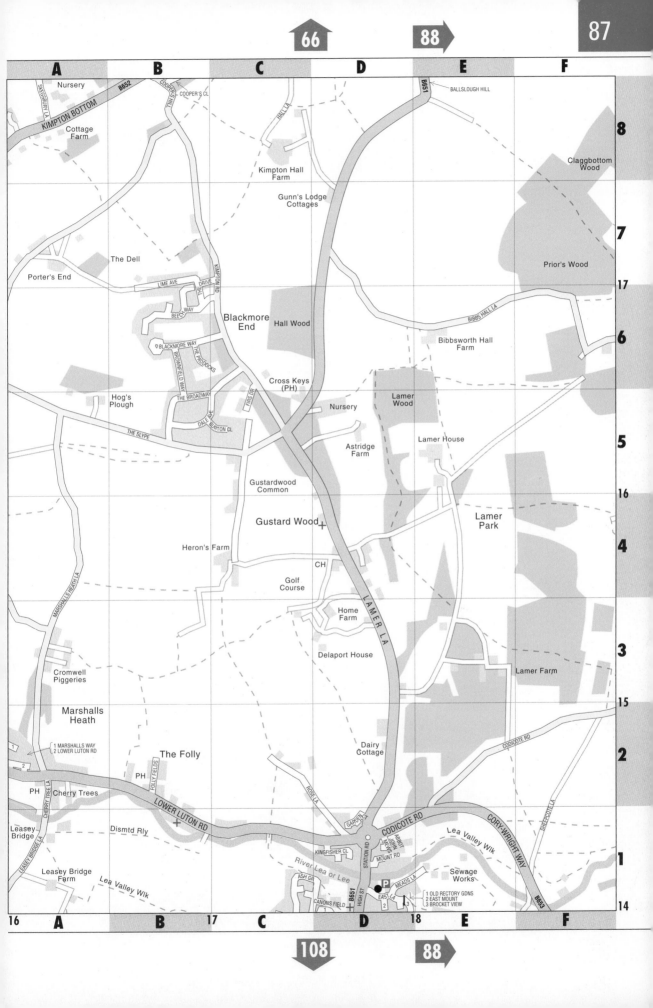

A B C D E F

8

Codicote
Bottom

Three
Hills

POYNDERS MEADOW 1
THE OPENING 2
NEW TOWN 3

HIGH ST

COWARDS LA

WINCH CL

THE RIDDY

B656

Bottom
Farm

Ayot
Lodge

Hollowdane
Spring

TANYARD LA

Long
Valley

ST ALBANS RD

Abbotshay

Brimstone
Wood

7

Ayot Park

LORD MEAD LA

Chalk
Pit

17

Ayot House

River Mimram

KIMPTON RD

6

BIBBS HALL LA

PH

Pulmer
Water

Ayot
Farm

Shaw's
Corner

Ayot
St Lawrence

Harepark
Spring

Ryefield
Farm

5

Norfolk
Cottages

BRIDE HALL LA

HILL FARM LA

Hill Farm

Linces
Spring

16

Bride
Hall

Hurstling's
Wood

4

Round
Spring

Little Norfolk
Wood

Stocking
Springs

Dowdell's
Wood

CODICOTE RD

Ayot
Bury

Great Norfolk
Wood

AYOT ST PETER RD

3

Fish
Wood

Ayot
St Peter

15

Scratching
Grove

Threegroves
Wood

Warren
Wood

War
Meml

Cherrytree
Spring

Ayot
Place

Saul's
Wood

2

Coneydell
Spring

Bladder
Wood

Ayot Greenway

Robinson's Wood

Hunter's
Bridge

Manor
Farm

AYOT LITTLE GREEN LA

1

River Lea or Lee

Sparrowhall
Bridge

WATEREND LA

Bowle's
Wood

Ayot
Little
Green

Lea Valley Wlk

Sparrowhall
Farm
James's Wood

14

19 A B 20 C 21 D E F

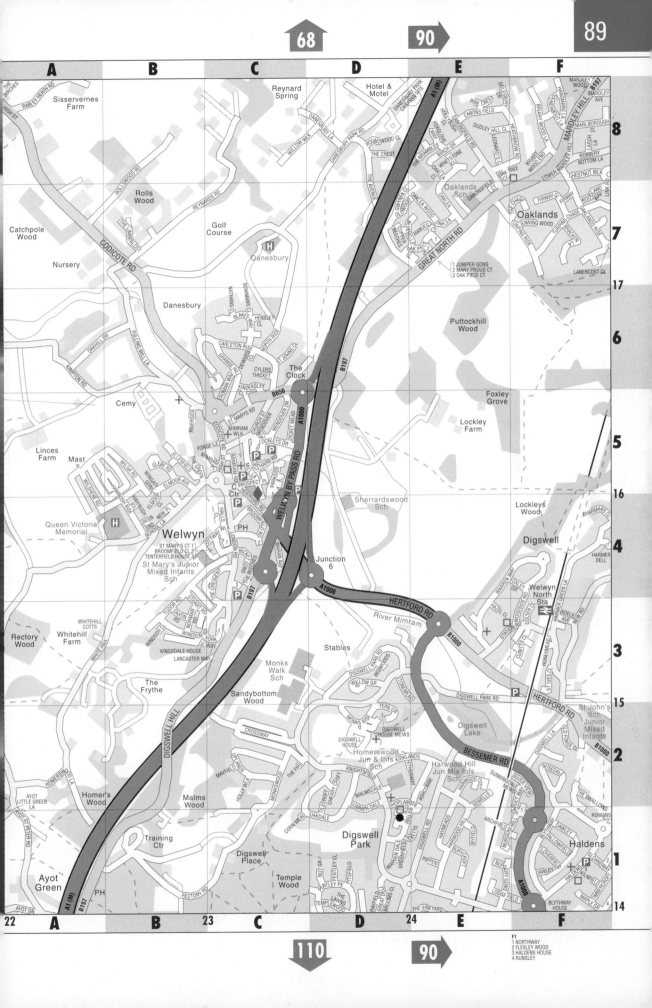

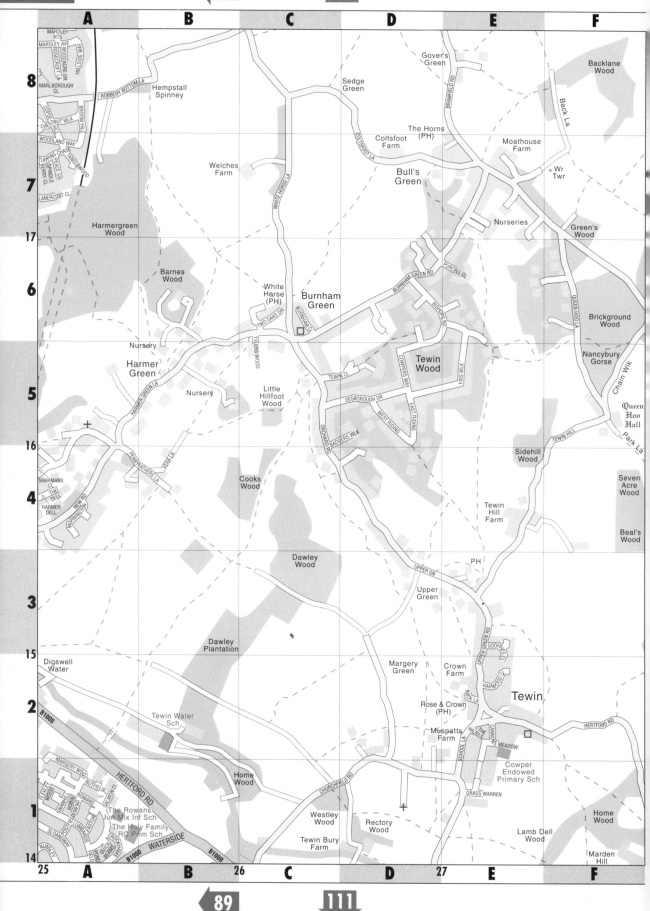

A **B** **C** **D** **E** **F**

8
MARDLEY HTS
MARDLEY AVE
WOODACRE DR
ROSECROFT LA
Hempstall Spinney
Gover's Green
Backlane Wood

MARLBOROUGH CL
CHESTNUT WLK
WOODLAND WAY
TAPPING CHASE
TANGLEWOOD
PEACE DR
SPINDLE
BERRY CL
LANERCOST CL

The Horns (PH)
Coltsfoot Farm
Coltsfoot LA
Moathouse Farm
Wr Twr
Back La

7
Welches Farm
WHITE HORSE LA
Bull's Green
Nurseries
Green's Wood

17
Harmergreen Wood
BRAMFIELD RD

6
Barnes Wood
White Horse (PH)
Burnham Green
BURNHAM GREEN RD
PURCELL CL
BISHOPS RD
Queen Hoo La
Brickground Wood

Nursery
TWO OAKS DR
BURNHAM CL
TEWIN CL
Tewin Wood
COWPERS WAY
FIRS WLK
Nancybury Gorse
Chain Wlk

5
Harmer Green
HARMER GREEN LA
Nursery
Little Hillfoot Wood
DESBOROUGH DR
WEST RIDING
EAST RIDING
TEWIN HILL
Sidehill Wood
Queen Hoo Hall

16
PENN-RATHERS LA
YEW LA
ORCHARD RD
BADGERS WLK
Seven Acre Wood

4
SHARMANS CL
THE DELL
HARMER DELL
NEW RD
McFARRINGTON
Cooks Wood
Tewin Hill Farm
Beal's Wood

Dawley Wood
PH
UPPER GN

3
Upper Green
UPPER GREEN RD
GODFRIES CL

15
Digswell Water
Dawley Plantation
Margery Green
Crown Farm
HARWOOD CL

2
B1000
Tewin Water Sch
Rose & Crown (PH)
BACK LA
THE HAZELS
SCHOOL LA
CANNONS MEADOW
Tewin
HERTFORD RD

Home Wood
Muspatts Farm
Cowper Endowed Primary Sch

1
MARGERY WOOD
MUTFIELD
SALMON WY
FLEXLEY WOOD
SWANHILL
ROBINFIELD
PASTOR
ROWANS
LUMBARDS
POSTFIELD
CRACKNELL BEAMS
FINCHFIELD
HERTFORD RD
The Rowans Jun Mix Inf Sch
The Holy Family RC Prim Sch
CHURCHFIELD RD
Westley Wood
Rectory Wood
GRASS WARREN
Lamb Dell Wood
Home Wood

14
BURNSLEY
SLOANSWAY
WATERSIDE
B1000
B1000
Tewin Bury Farm
Marden Hill

25 **A** **B** 26 **C** **D** 27 **E** **F**

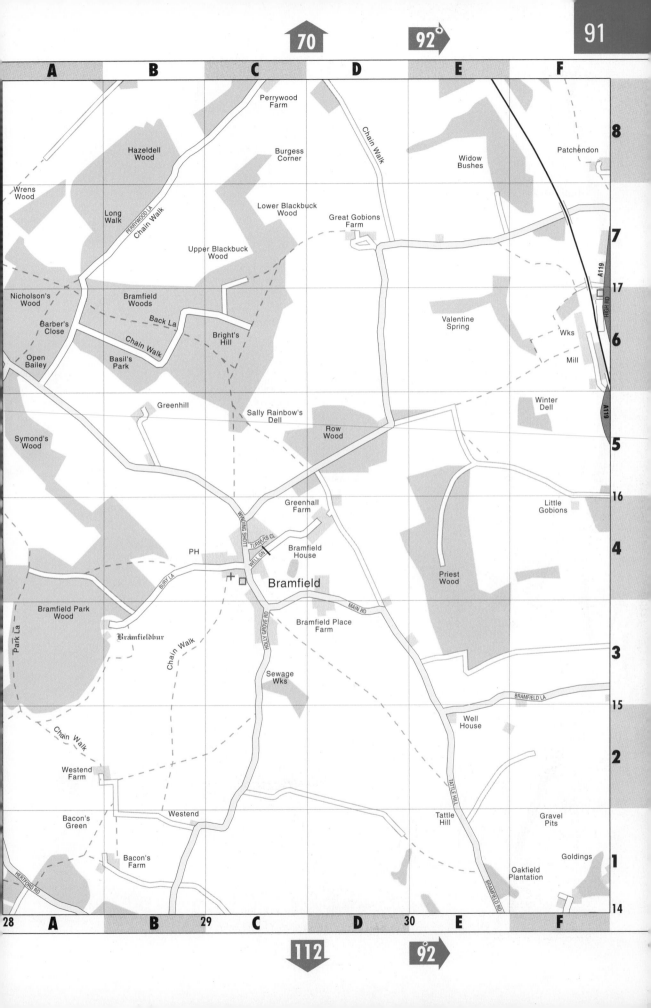

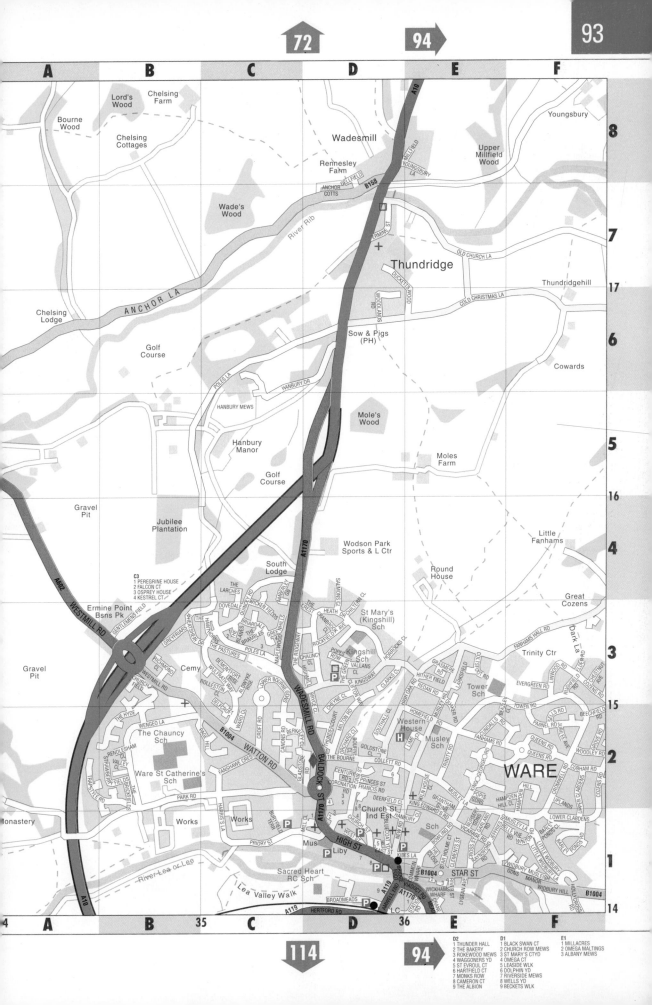

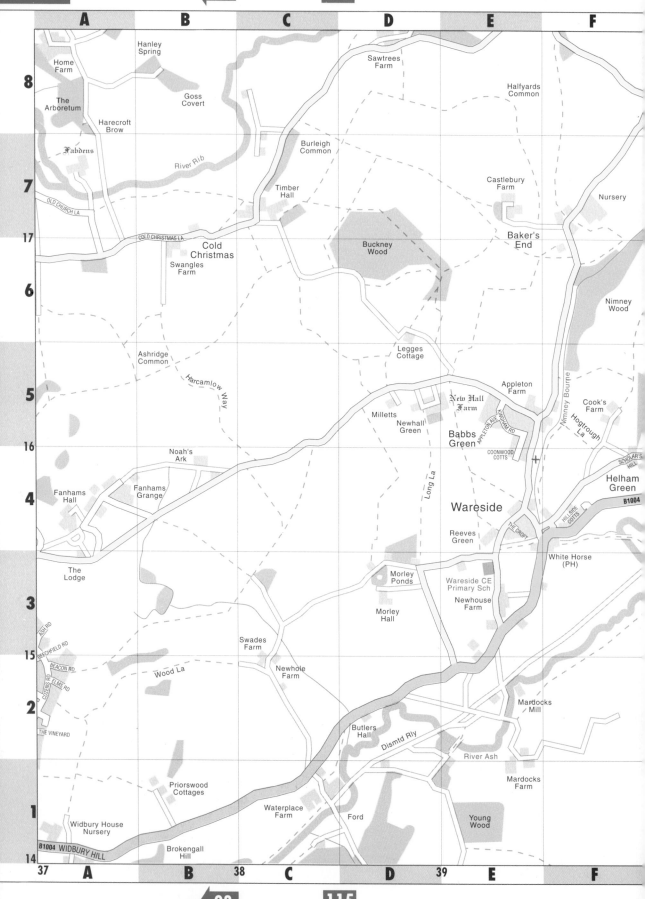

A B C D E F

8 Home Farm
The Arboretum
Hanley Spring
Goss Covert
Harecroft Brow
Sawtrees Farm
Halfyards Common

Fabdens
River Rib
Burleigh Common
Castlebury Farm
Nursery

7 OLD CHURCH LA
Timber Hall
Baker's End

17 COLD CHRISTMAS LA
Cold Christmas
Buckney Wood

Swangles Farm

6 Nimney Wood

Ashridge Common
Harcamlow Way
Legges Cottage

5 New Hall Farm
Appleton Farm
Cook's Farm
Hogtrough La

Milletts
Newhall Green
Babbs Green
KINGHAM RD
APPLETON AVE
COONWOOD COTTS
SCHOLAR'S HILL

16 Noah's Ark
Helham Green

4 Fanhams Hall
Fanhams Grange
Wareside
Reeves Green
THE CROFT
HILLSIDE COTTS
HILL SIDE COTTS
B1004

The Lodge
White Horse (PH)

3 Morley Ponds
Wareside CE Primary Sch
Newhouse Farm
Morley Hall

ASH RD
BEECHFIELD RD
Swades Farm
15 BEACON RD
Newhole Farm
COLENS RD
ELMS RD
Wood La
Mardocks Mill

2 THE VINEYARD

Butlers Hall
Dismtd Rly
River Ash
Mardocks Farm

Priorswood Cottages

1 Widbury House Nursery
Waterplace Farm
Ford
Young Wood

14 B1004 WIDBURY HILL
Brokengall Hill

37 A B 38 C D 39 E F

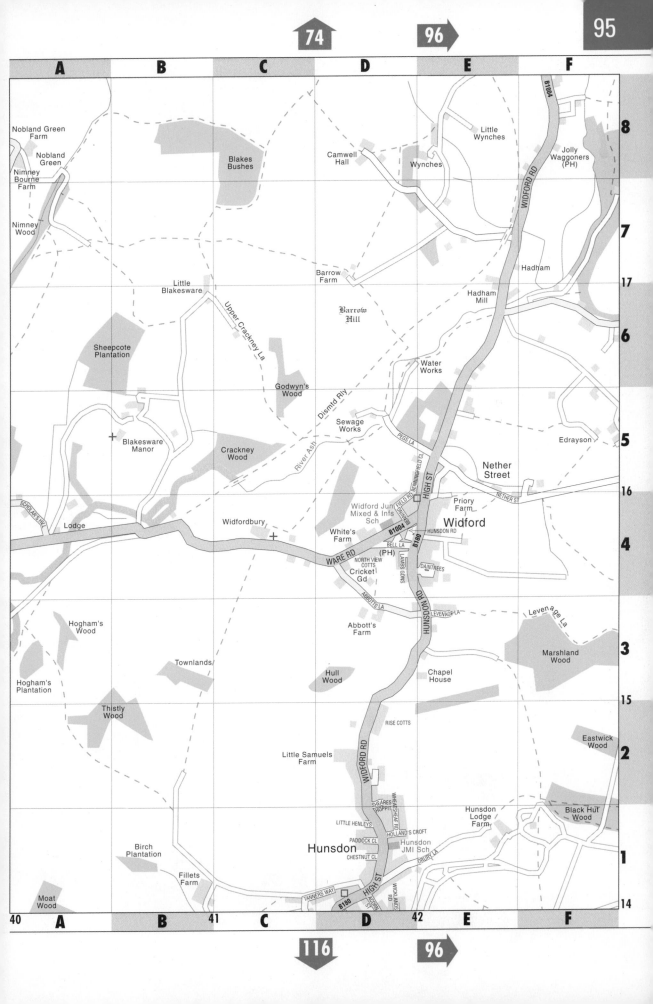

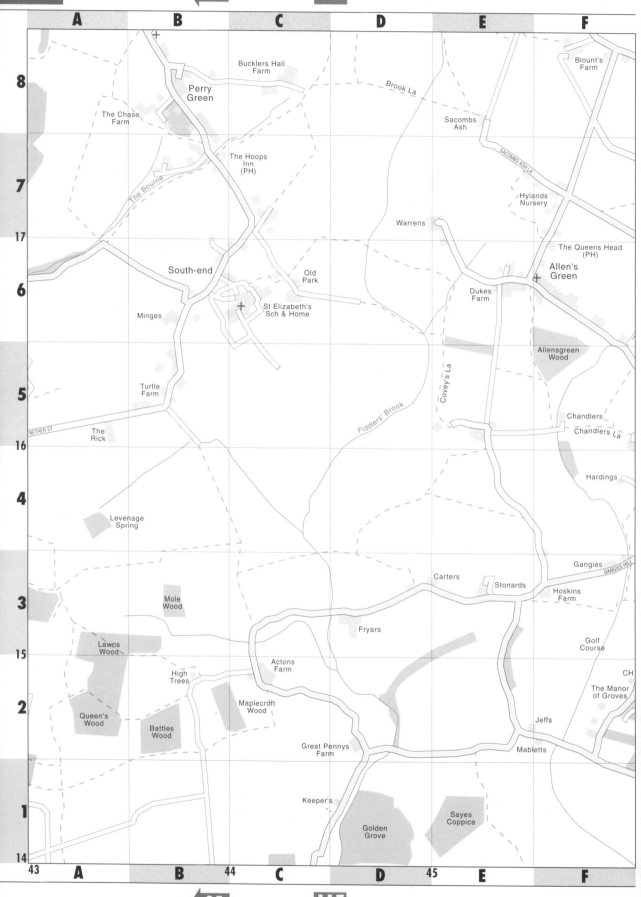

Blount's Farm

Bucklers Hall Farm

Brook La

8

Perry Green

Sacombs Ash

The Chase Farm

SACOMBS ASH LA

The Hoops Inn (PH)

7

Hylands Nursery

The Bourne

17

Warrens

The Queens Head (PH)

Allen's Green

South-end

Old Park

6

Dukes Farm

St Elizabeth's Sch & Home

Minges

Allensgreen Wood

Covey's La

Turtle Farm

5

Chandlers

NETHER ST

The Rick

Chandlers La

Fiddlers' Brook

16

Hardings

4

Levenage Spring

Gangies

GANGIES HILL

Carters

Stonards

3

Mole Wood

Hoskins Farm

Fryars

Golf Course

Lawns Wood

15

CH

High Trees

Actons Farm

The Manor of Groves

Maplecroft Wood

2

Queen's Wood

Jeffs

Battles Wood

Great Pennys Farm

Mabletts

Keeper's

1

Sayes Coppice

Golden Grove

14

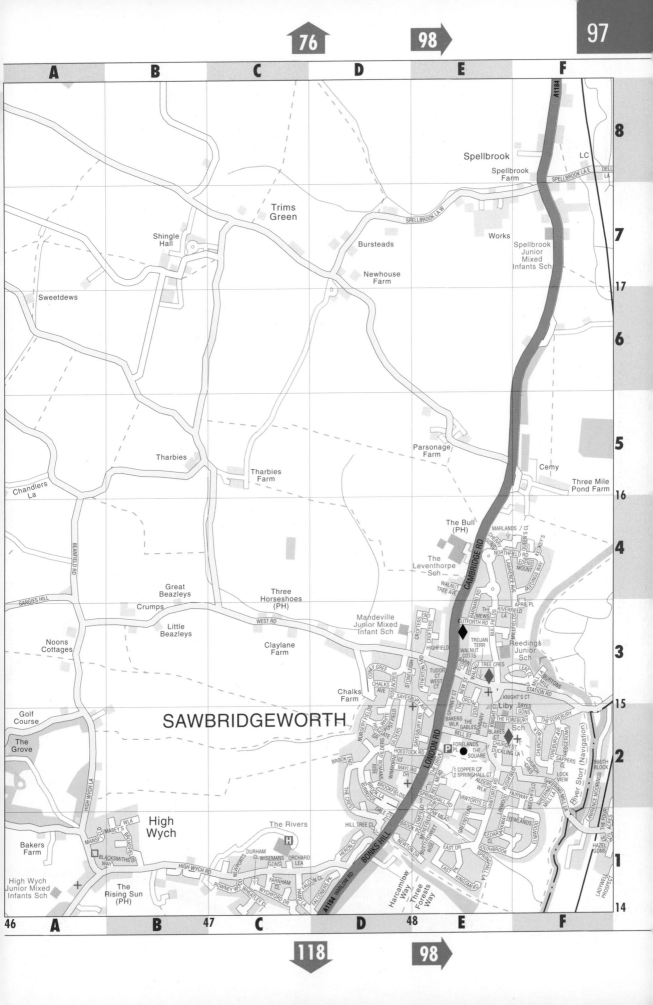

A B C D E F

8
7
17
6
5
16
4
3
15
2
1
14

Spellbrook
Spellbrook
Farm
LC
DELL LA
Spellbrook La E

Trims
Green
Spellbrook La W
Works
Spellbrook
Junior
Mixed
Infants Sch

Shingle
Hall
Bursteads

Newhouse
Farm

Sweetdews

A1184

Parsonage
Farm
Cemy
Three Mile
Pond Farm

Tharbies

Chandlers
La
Tharbies
Farm

The Bull
(PH)

MARLANDS / CL
CHERRY
GRNS
QUEEN'S CL
KEENSY'S
NORTHFIELD RD
EDENS
MOUNT
REEDINGS WAY
LAWRENCE AVE

The
Leventhorpe
Sch

Great
Beazleys

Three
Horseshoes
(PH)

WALNUT
TREE AVE
APRIL PL

CAMBRIDGE RD

Crumps

Little
Beazleys

WEST RD

Claylane
Farm

Mandeville
Junior Mixed
Infant Sch

CROFTERS
END
CROFTERS
HIGHFIELD

BARNARD RD
THE
MEWS
RIVERFIELD
MILLFIELD
BULL FIELDS
CUTFORTH RD

Reedings
Junior
Sch

Noons
Cottages

Golf
Course

Chalks
Farm

CONEY GREE
ATHERTON END
STONELEIGH
ROSEACRES
CHALKS
AVE
SAYESBURY AVE
NURSERY FIELDS
HUCKATE GR
WHYTE
GILDERS
SAYESBURY RD
HOESTOCK RD
LONDON RD
BROOK LA
ROMANS
MAYLINS
DR
BIRNSIDE

TUDOR
CT
WEST
END
BARN
SPINNEY CT
ORCH
THE NEWTS
BELL ST
FORELANDS
PL
THE
SQUARE
THE GABLES
BLAKES
GRANARY CT
KNIGHTS
THE FOREBURY
Sch
CHURCH ST
DUCKLING LA
FOREBURY AVE
WYMAN
HEDGEROWS
SAPPERS
CL
LOCK
VIEW

WALNUT
COTTS
TROJAN
TERR
T TREE CRES
WALNUT
LEA CT
BURTONS
MILL
STATION RD
Knight's CT
Liby
SAYES
GDNS
THE FOREBURY

River Stort (Navigation)
SOUTH
BLOCK

SAWBRIDGEWORTH

GANGIES HILL

BEANFIELD RD

The
Grove

The Rivers
H

High
Wych

Bakers
Farm

High Wych
Junior Mixed
Infants Sch

The Rising Sun
(PH)

HIGH WYCH LA

MANSF
MABEY'S
WLK
BRADFIELD
BLACKSMITHS
WAY

HIGH WYCH RD

DURHAM
CL
NEXPORTS
ROWNEY WOOD
WHEATLEY CL
WYCHFORD CL
WISEMANS
GDNS
ORCHARD
LEA
FARNHAM
CL
HAVIL CL
FALCON CL
FALCONERS PK

HEROL CL
HARLOW RD
HILL TREE CL
NEWTON DR
LONGCROFT
LOWKING
MEREFIELD
BUTTERSWEET
RISE
EAST DR
CEDARS
SOUTHBROOK
SPRINGHALL LA
EAST
KINGSMEAD
ELMWOOD

BONKS HILL

A1184

Three
Forests
Way

Harcamlow
Way

COPPER CT
SPRINGHALL CT
ALDERS
WLK
VANTORTS CL
VANTORTS RD
RUSHFIELD
FAIRWAY
LINWOOD
GREENSTEAD
BEECH FLD
CHURCH CL
MILL LA
SHERING MILL LA
SOUTHBROOK
THE CREST
BROOK LA
BROOKFIELDS
DALE CT
SPRINGHALL RD
LOW MEAD
YEWLANDS
FAIRWAY
LADYWELL PROSPECT
LAWRENCE MOORINGS
HAZEL GDNS
THE FOUR ACRES

46 A 47 B C 48 D E F

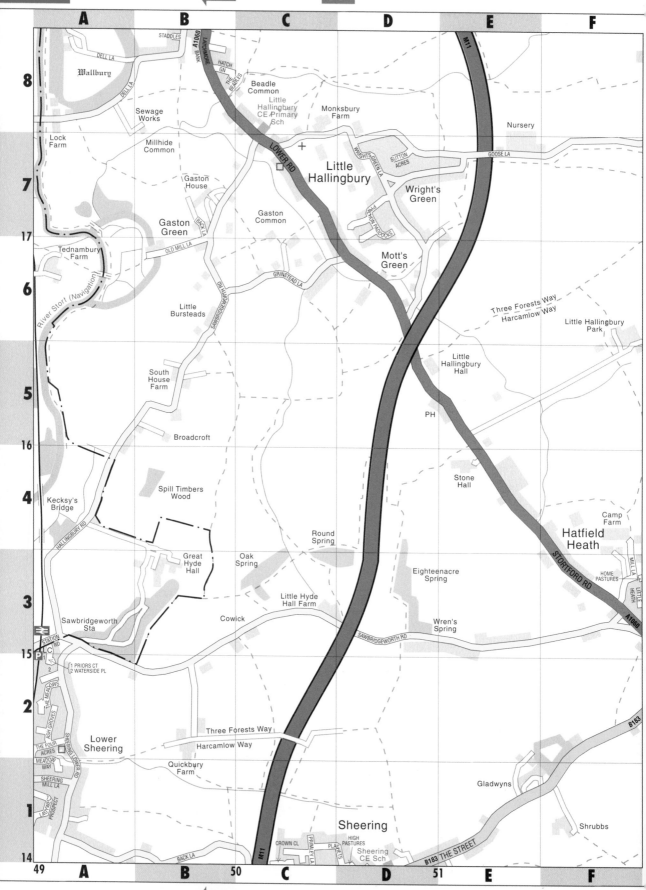

8

Wallbury

DELL LA

STADDLES

A1060 LADYMORE BANK

HATCH GN

THE BEADLES

Beadle Common

Little Hallingbury CE Primary Sch

Monksbury Farm

M11

Nursery

Sewage Works

Lock Farm

Millhide Common

7

Gaston House

LOWER RD

Little Hallingbury

WRIGHTS GREEN LA

SUTTON ACRES

GOOSE LA

17

Gaston Green

BACK LA

OLD MILL LA

Gaston Common

Wright's Green

DICKON PADDOCKS

Tednambury Farm

Mott's Green

6

River Stort (Navigation)

SAWBRIDGEWORTH RD

GRINSTEAD LA

Little Bursteads

Three Forests Way

Harcamlow Way

Little Hallingbury Park

Little Hallingbury Hall

5

South House Farm

PH

16

Broadcroft

Stone Hall

4

Kecksy's Bridge

HALLINGBURY RD

Spill Timbers Wood

Camp Farm

Hatfield Heath

STORTFORD RD

MILL LA

LITTLE HEATH

HOME PASTURES

Round Spring

Great Hyde Hall

Oak Spring

Eighteenacre Spring

3

Little Hyde Hall Farm

Cowick

Wren's Spring

A1060

Sawbridgeworth Sta

STATION RD

SAWBRIDGEWORTH RD

15

P

1 PRIORS CT
2 WATERSIDE PL

2

THE MEADOWS

ASH GROVES

SHEERING LOWER RD

Lower Sheering

Three Forests Way

Harcamlow Way

B183

THE FOUR ACRES

MEADOW WAY

Quickbury Farm

Gladwyns

1

SHEERING MILL LA

LADYWELL PROSPECT

Shrubbs

M11

BACK LA

Sheering

CROWN CL

PRIMLEY LA

HIGH PASTURES

Sheering CE Sch

B183 THE STREET

14

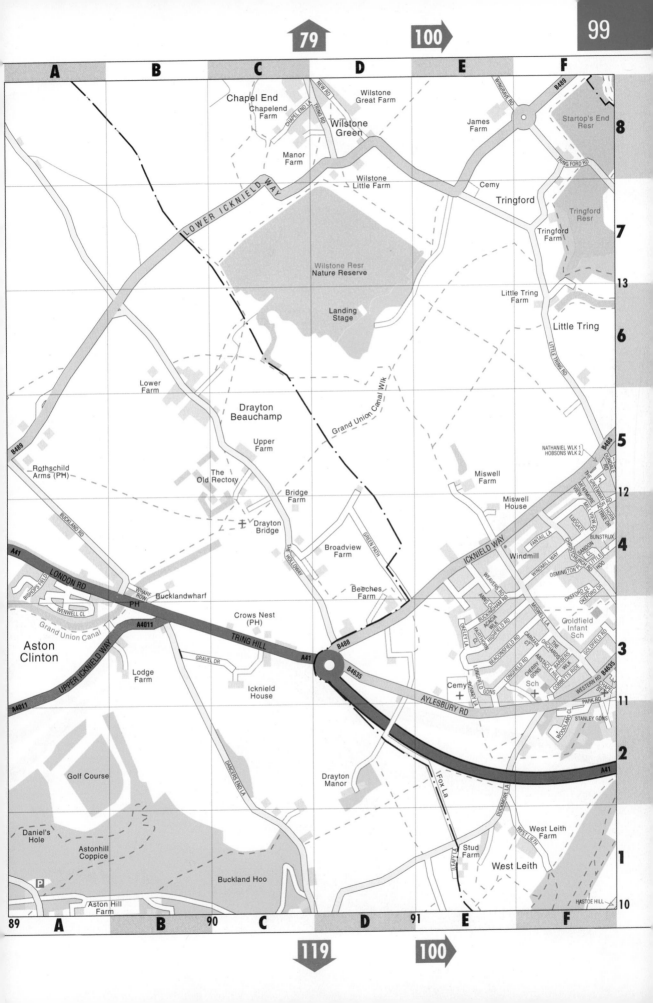

A   B   C   D   E   F

Chapel End
Chapelend
Farm

Wilstone
Great Farm

James
Farm

Startop's End
Resr

8

Wilstone
Green

Manor
Farm

Cemy

Tringford

Tringford
Resr

7

Wilstone
Little Farm

Tringford
Farm

LOWER ICKNIELD WAY

13

Wilstone Resr
Nature Reserve

Little Tring
Farm

Little Tring

6

Landing
Stage

LITTLE TRING RD

Lower
Farm

Drayton
Beauchamp

Grand Union Canal Wlk

NATHANIEL WLK 1
HOBSONS WLK 2

5

B489

Upper
Farm

Miswell
Farm

Rothschild
Arms (PH)

The
Old Rectory

Miswell
House

12

BUCKLAND RD

Bridge
Farm

ICKNIELD WAY

Windmill

4

Drayton
Bridge

Broadview
Farm

GREEN PATH

THE HOLLOWAY

A41

Beeches
Farm

Goldfield Infant
Sch

LONDON RD

Bucklandwharf

Crows Nest
(PH)

B488

3

WHARF
ROW
PH

TRING HILL

A41

B4635

Sch

Aston
Clinton

A4011

Lodge
Farm

Icknield
House

B4635

WESTERN RD

11

UPPER ICKNIELD WAY

Grand Union Canal

GRAVEL DR

AYLESBURY RD

Cemy

PARK RD

STANLEY GDNS

A4011

2

Golf Course

DANCERS END LA

Drayton
Manor

A41

Fox La

West Leith
Farm

Daniel's
Hole

WEST LEITH

1

Astonhill
Coppice

Stud
Farm

West Leith

P

Buckland Hoo

HASTOE HILL

10

Aston Hill
Farm

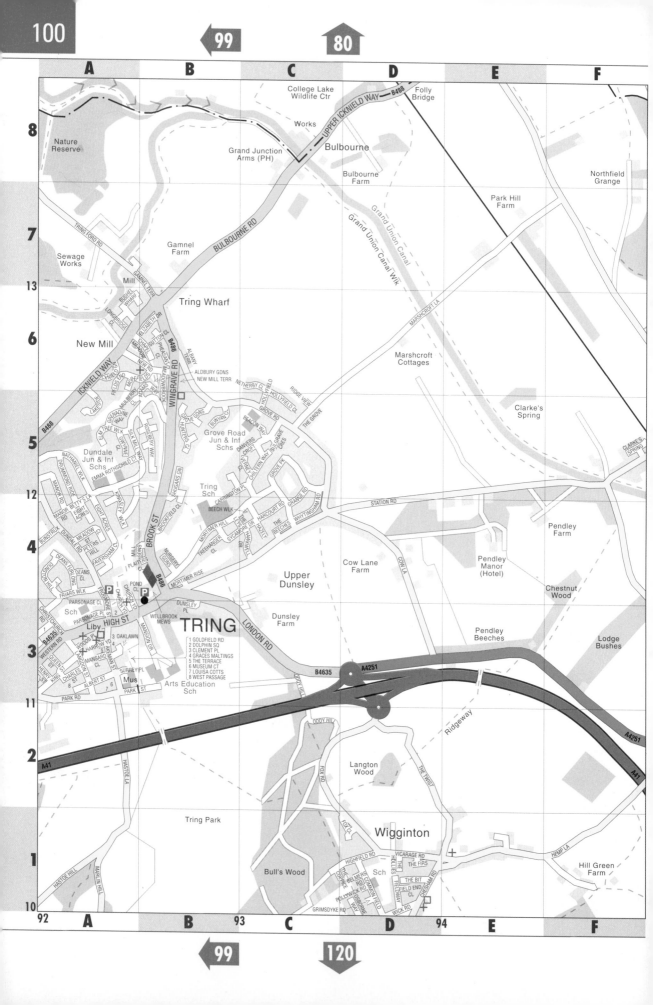

Nature Reserve

College Lake Wildlife Ctr

Works

UPPER ICKNIELD WAY

B488

Folly Bridge

Bulbourne

Grand Junction Arms (PH)

Bulbourne Farm

Northfield Grange

Park Hill Farm

Sewage Works

Tring Ford Rd

Gamnel Farm

BULBOURNE RD

Grand Union Canal

Grand Union Canal Wlk

Mill

BUSHEL WHARF

LONGBRIDGE CL

ELIZABETH DR

GAMNEL TERR

Tring Wharf

MARSHCROFT LA

New Mill

ICKNIELD WAY

SUTTON CL

NEW MILL

PHEASANT CL

WINGRAVE RD

B486

Marshcroft Cottages

ALBANY TERR

ALDBURY GDNS

NEW MILL TERR

B488

CHARLWOOD

MEADWAY

MEADWAY

WAYSIDE

WOODBRIDGE

NORTHFIELDS

NETHERBY CL

HOLLYFIELD

RIDGE VIEW

HOLLYFIELD CL

Clarke's Spring

FIELDS END

MULBERRY

ADAMS WAY

GROVE GDNS

BUNYANS

BEACON WAY

THE GROVE

Clarke's Spring

Dundale Jun & Inf Schs

GRENADINE WAY

SILK MILL WAY

GWYNNE

ROSEBERY WAY

SHUGARS GN

Grove Road Jun & Inf Schs

DANVERS

CHILTERN WAY

HALE CROFT

SILGRAVE

THE SPIRES

GROVE PK

GROVE RD

BRAMBLE WLK

NATHANIEL WLK

DRUMMOND RIDE

EMMA ROTHSCHILD CT

KINGSLEY WAY

Tring Sch

CARRINGTON PL

GRANGE RD

WHYTTINGHAM RD

MANOR RD

BETTY'S LA

EIGHT ACRES

EIGHT ACRES

BEECH WLK

MORTIMER HILL

HARCOURT RD

THE BEECHES

STATION RD

Pendley Farm

BUNSTRUX

DUNDALE RD

MEADOW

ST PETERS HILL

FAVERSHAM CL

MILL LA

PLAITERS

SYCAMORE DR

TREEHANGER CL

Cow Lane Farm

COW LA

Pendley Manor (Hotel)

DEANS FURLONG

DEANS CL

FRIARS WLK

BROOK ST

BROOKFIELD CL

B486

MORTIMER RISE

Upper Dunsley

Chestnut Wood

CHRISTCHURCH RD

PARSONAGE CL

CHURCH YD

POND CL

DUNSLEY PL

WELLBROOK MEWS

Dunsley Farm

Pendley Beeches

Sch

PARSONAGE PL

Liby

HIGH ST

3 OAKLAWN

TRING

LONDON RD

Lodge Bushes

WESTERN RD

WOODS YD

HARROW YD

MANSION DR

SURREY PL

1 GOLDFIELD RD
2 DOLPHIN SQ
3 CLEMENT PL
4 GRACES MALTINGS
5 THE TERRACE
6 MUSEUM CT
7 LOUISA COTTS
8 WEST PASSAGE

B4635

A4251

B4635

KING

HENRY

CHARLES ST

MARSH CL

MANSARD CL

ALBERT ST

Mus

PARK ST

Arts Education Sch

ODDY HILL

Ridgeway

A4251

PARK RD

HASTOE LA

A41

ODDY HILL

FOX RD

A41

Langton Wood

THE TWIST

A4251

Tring Park

THE HOLLIES

FOX CL

Wigginton

HEMP LA

Hill Green Farm

Bull's Wood

HIGHFIELD RD

VICARAGE RD

THE FIRS

Sch

BELMERS RD

THE BIT

POLLYWICK RD

COMMON FIELD

THE FIELDWAY

FIELD END

CHESHAM RD

MARLIN HILL

HASTOE HILL

GRIMSDYKE RD

WICK RD

92

93

94

101
81

A B C D E F

8

7

13

6

5

12

4

3

11

2

1

10

B4506

ALDERTON DR

GATESDENE CL

RINGSHALL DR

BRIDGEWATER CT

Bridgewater Arms (PH)

BERE CT

CHURCH RD

Church Farm

Badger Wood

Little Gaddesden C of E Sch

Little Gaddesden

Hudnall Common Plantation

Hudnall Common

HUDNALL LA

Hudnall

Hudnall Farm

B4506

Pitstone Park Copse

Ashridge

CH

Old Park Lodge

Golf Course

Ashridge Park

Prince's Riding

Golden Valley

The Rookery

CHAPEL CL

Robin Hood Farm

Little Brownlow Farm

Little Gaddesden House

Home Farm

Lady Grove

Thunderdell Wood

Ashridge Management Coll

Cromer Wood

CROMER CL

CROMER CL

NETTLEDEN RD

Harding's Rookery

Woodyard Cottage

Berkhamstead Common

Little Coldharbour Farm

Coldharbour Spring

Coldharbour Farm

Pulridge Wood

Golden Valley Farm

Nettleden Lodge

Furzefield Wood

Ashridge

Webb's Copse

Bluebell Spring

Brickkiln Cottage

Frithsden Beeches

Frithsden Gardens

Golf Course

98 A B 99 C D 00 E F

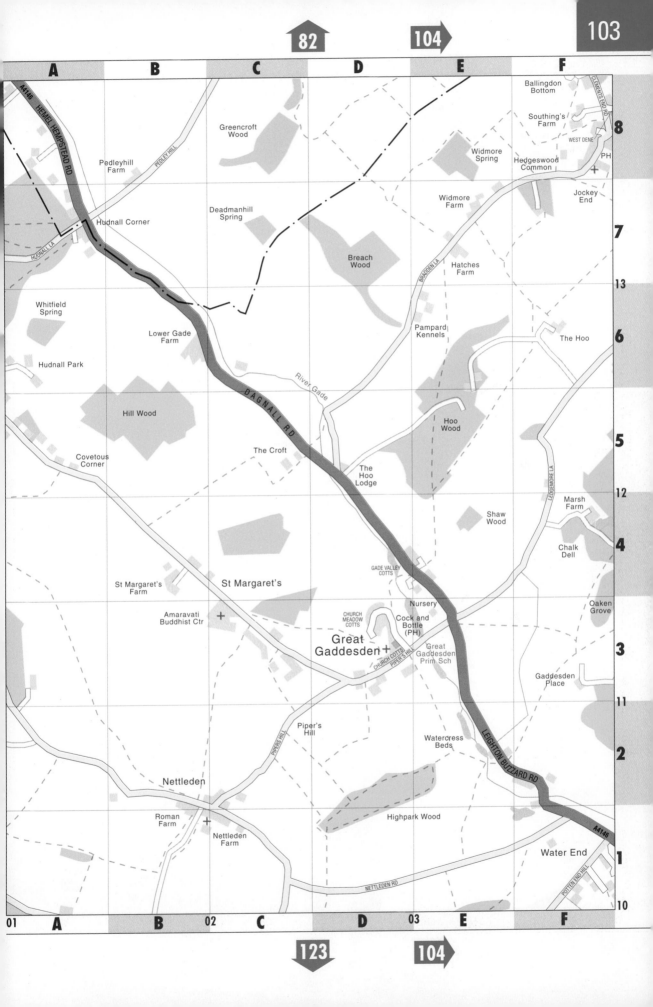

A B C D E F

8
7
13
6
5
12
4
3
11
2
1
10

Ballingdon
Bottom

Southing's
Farm

WEST DENE

PH

Hedgeswood
Common

Jockey
End

Widmore
Spring

Widmore
Farm

Greencroft
Wood

Pedleyhill
Farm

Deadmanhill
Spring

Breach
Wood

Hatches
Farm

Hudnall Corner

Whitfield
Spring

Lower Gade
Farm

River Gade

Pampard
Kennels

The Hoo

Hudnall Park

Hill Wood

The Croft

Hoo
Wood

Covetous
Corner

The Hoo
Lodge

Shaw
Wood

Marsh
Farm

Chalk
Dell

St Margaret's
Farm

St Margaret's

Gade Valley
Cotts

Oaken
Grove

Amaravati
Buddhist Ctr

Church
Meadow
Cotts

Nursery

Cock and
Bottle
(PH)

Great
Gaddesden

Great
Gaddesden
Prim Sch

Gaddesden
Place

Piper's
Hill

Watercress
Beds

Nettleden

Roman
Farm

Nettleden
Farm

Highpark Wood

Water End

HEMEL HEMPSTEAD RD
A4146
HUDNALL LA
PEDLEY HILL
DAGNALL RD
BRADDEN LA
LEDGEMORE LA
PIPER'S HILL
CHURCH COTTS
PIPER'S HILL
LEIGHTON BUZZARD RD
NETTLEDEN RD
A4146
POTTEN END HILL
CLEMENTS END RD

103
83

103
124

A   B   C   D   E   F

8

AS183

LUTON LA

CH

Golf
Course

New
Cottages

Harpendenbury
Farm

Nicky Way

Rothamsted
Experimental Farm

Scout Spring

7

Bylands
House

LUTON LA

Knott
Wood

Rothamsted
Experimental Station

Hillbury
Farm

DUNSTABLE RD

Rothamsted

13

St Luke's
Sch

BLACKHORSE LA
PRIERS CL
LUSSEY CT
LINDEN RD

Redbourn

6

COOPERS MEADOW
BUTTS SPOL
MEADOWS
AYSGARTH RD
CRECY GDNS
CAVAN RD

Scout
Farm

HARPENDEN LA

B487

REDBOURN LA

B487

LONG CUT
CROUCH HALL
GDNS

Schs

Liby

BEECHFIELD CL

Nursery

VER RD

APPLE TREE
GR
CUMBERLAND
DR

FLINT CROSSE

Golf
Course

OAKHURST
AVE

ROSEDOWN
SNATCHUP
FINGCS
DOWN
EDGE

CROUCH HALL RD
LORDS MEADOW

TOTTON MEWS
THE RUINS

SHEPHERD'S ROW
CROWN'S
BASSET
WADSLEY

CH

5

RICKYARD
MEADOW
WHEATLOCK
MEAD

NORTH
COMM

MONKS CL
ARCHERS
CL
FISH ST

WATEREND LA
PONDSMEADE

Nursery

Redbourn
Ind Est

Hammondsend
Farm

WHEATFIELD
RD
OAKFIELD

ST MARY'S
BRACHE CL
LEYBURY LA
STEPHEN'S
WAY
LAMSTEADBURY

Redbourn
Common

FISH ST
FISY FARM ST

Redbourn
Ind Est

PROSPECT LA

12

THE
TERRACE
WOOLLAMS

THE PARK

THE PARK

4

BEN
AUSTINS
WEST
COMM
CHURCH END

HEMEL HEMPSTEAD RD
NORTH COMMON RD
EAST
COMM
CHEQUER LA

Park
Estate

B487

CHEQUER LA
PH

Hammondsend
Wood

Nicky Way

B487

ST ALBANS RD

The
Elms

3

River Ver

Ver-Colne Valley Wlk

BEESONEND LA

Flowers
Farm

11

BEAUMONT HALL LA

Baeumont
Hall

Redbournbury

REDBOURNBURY LA

Mill

2

Dane-End
Farm

REDBOURN RD

1

HILL FARM LA

Punch Bowl
(PH)

PUNCH BOWL LA

AS185

Works

10

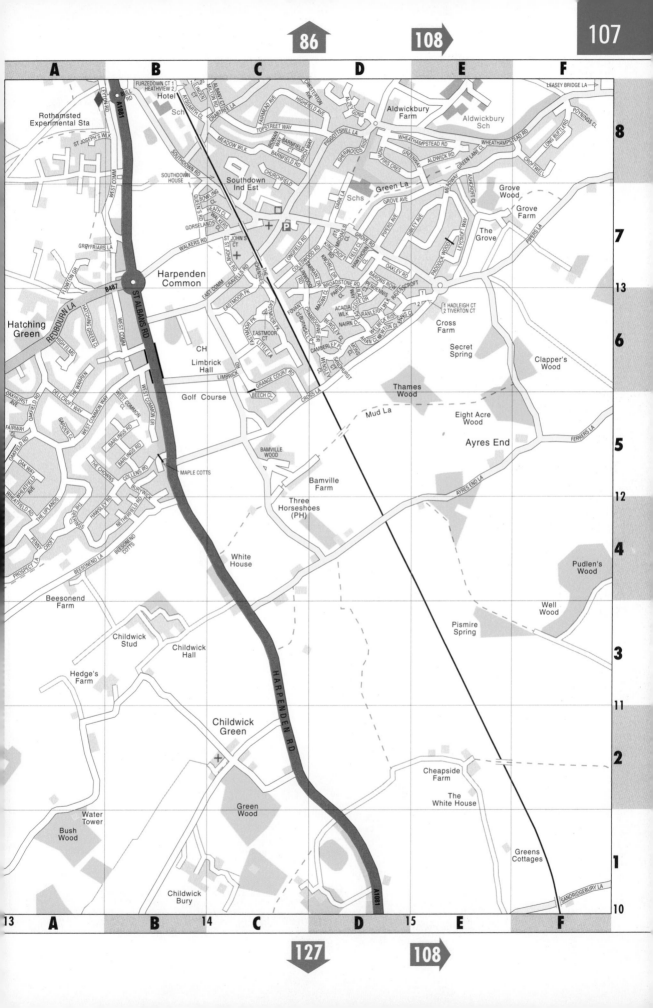

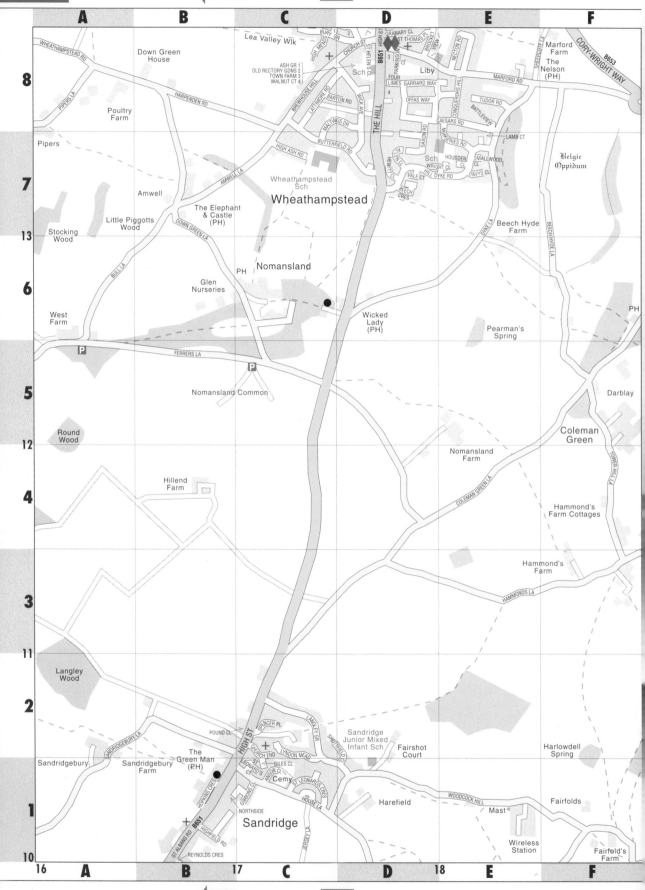

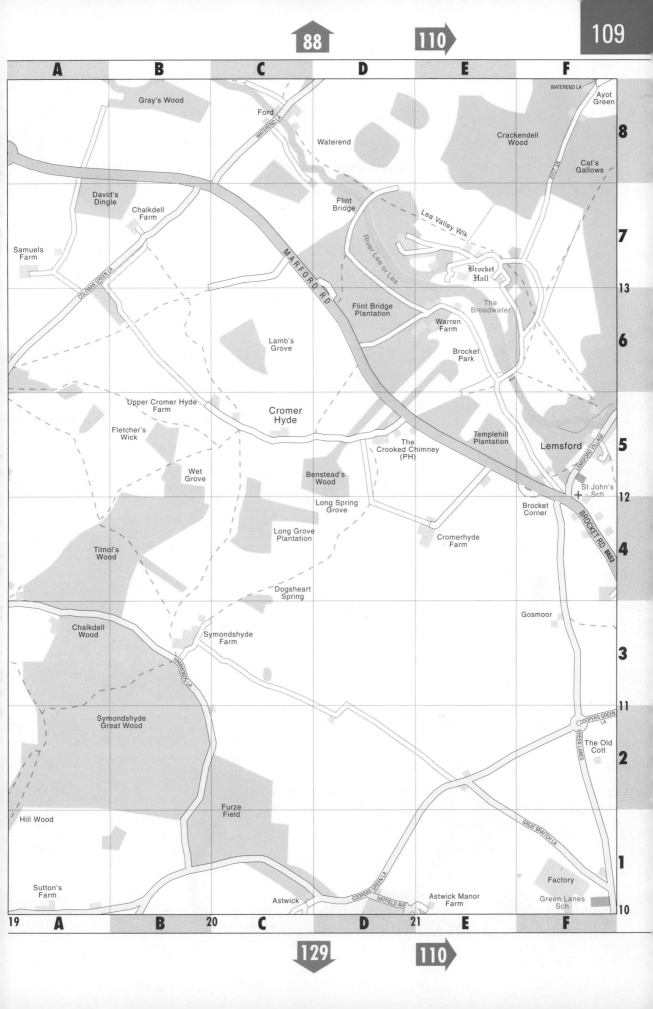

A   B   C   D   E   F

WATEREND LA

Ayot Green

Gray's Wood

Ford

WATEREND LA

Waterend

Crackendell Wood

Cat's Gallows

8

AYOT LN

David's Dingle

Chalkdell Farm

Flint Bridge

Lea Valley Wlk

7

Samuels Farm

MARFORD RD

River Lee or Lea

Brocket Hall

13

COLEMAN GREEN LA

Flint Bridge Plantation

The Broadwater

Warren Farm

6

Lamb's Grove

Brocket Park

Upper Cromer Hyde Farm

Cromer Hyde

Templehill Plantation

Lemsford

5

Fletcher's Wick

The Crooked Chimney (PH)

LEMSFORD VILLAGE

Wet Grove

Benstead's Wood

St John's Sch

Long Spring Grove

Brocket Corner

12

BROCKET RD

Long Grove Plantation

Cromerhyde Farm

B653

Titnol's Wood

4

Dogsheart Spring

Gosmoor

Chalkdell Wood

Symondshyde Farm

3

HAMMONDS LA

COOPERS GREEN LA

11

Symondshyde Great Wood

GREEN LANES

The Old Cott

2

Hill Wood

Furze Field

GREAT BRAITCH LA

1

Factory

Sutton's Farm

COOPERS GREEN LA

Astwick

HATFIELD AVE

Astwick Manor Farm

Green Lanes Sch

10

109
89

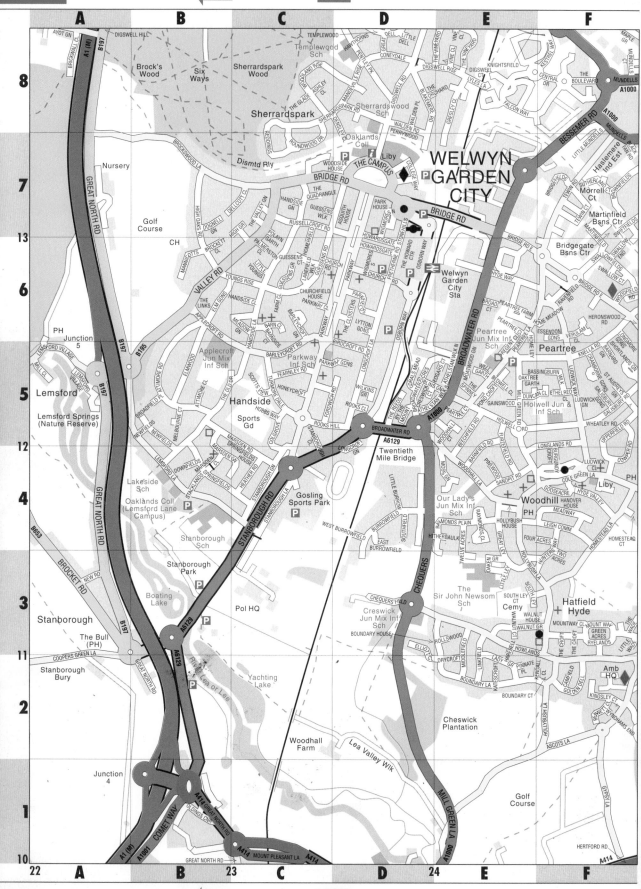

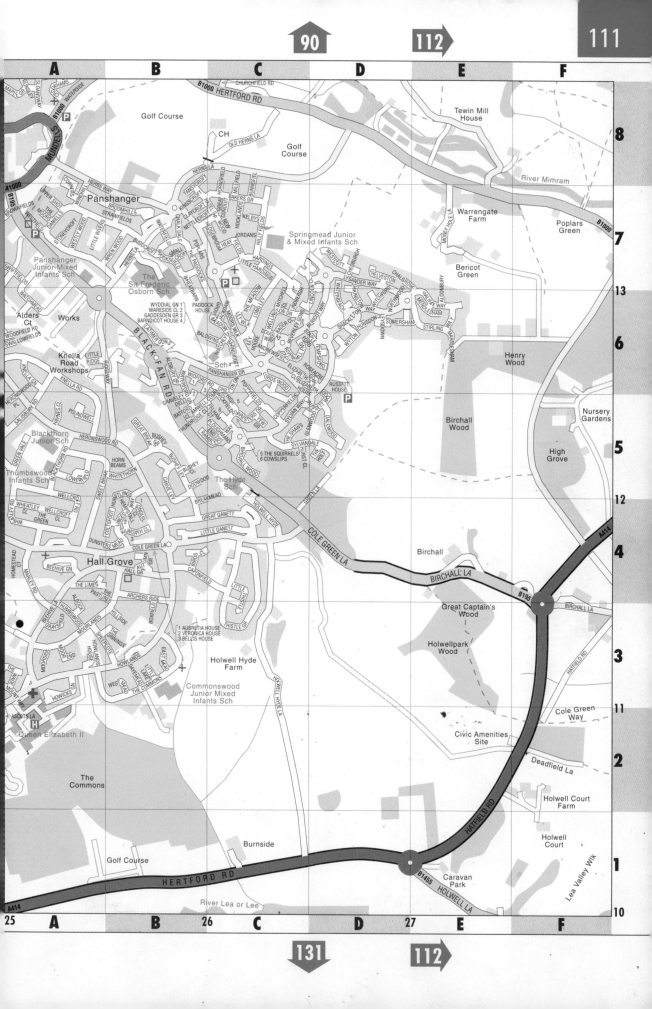

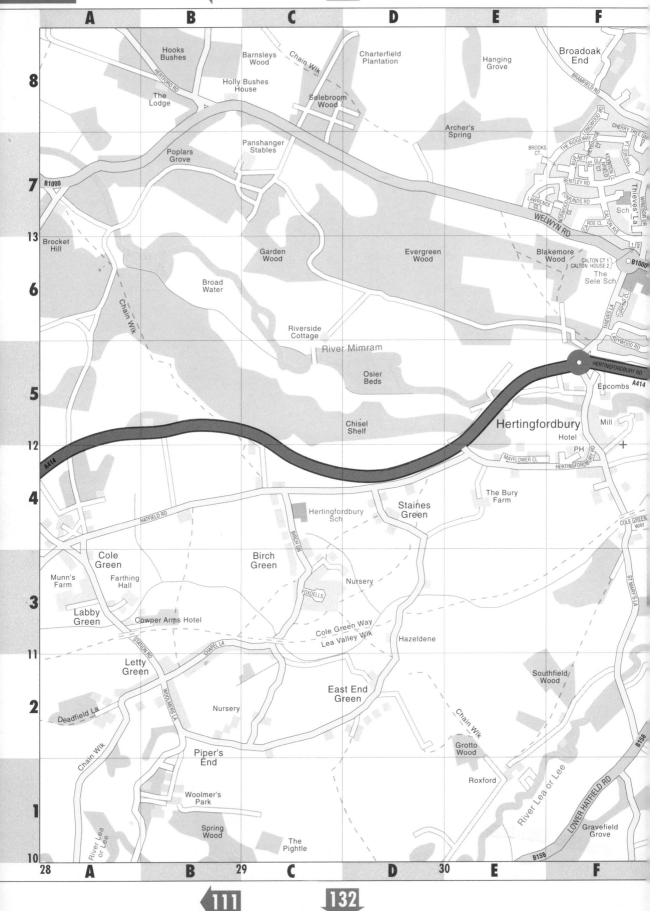

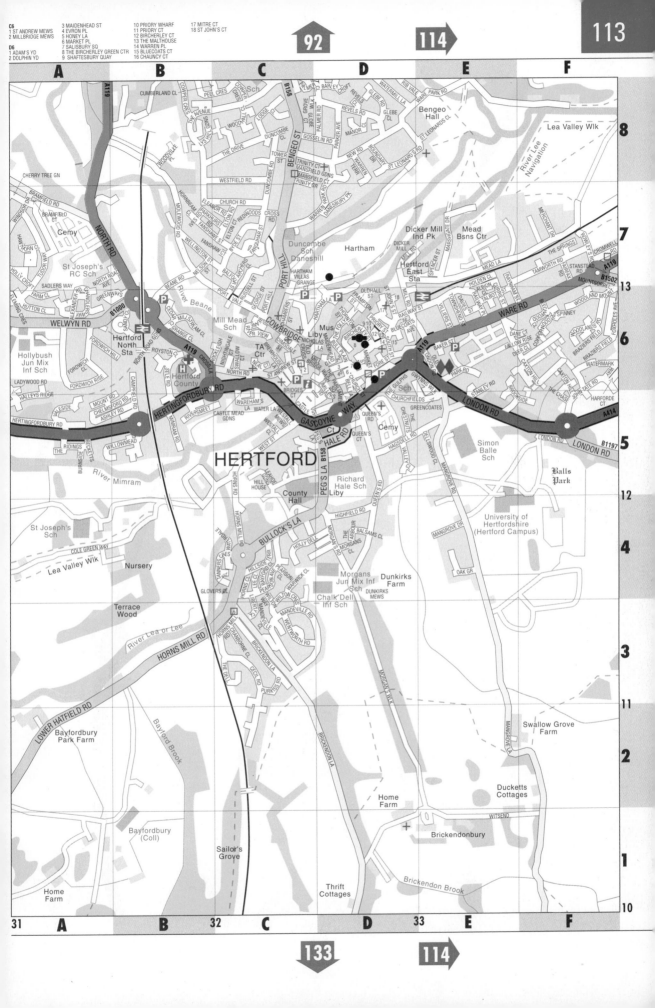

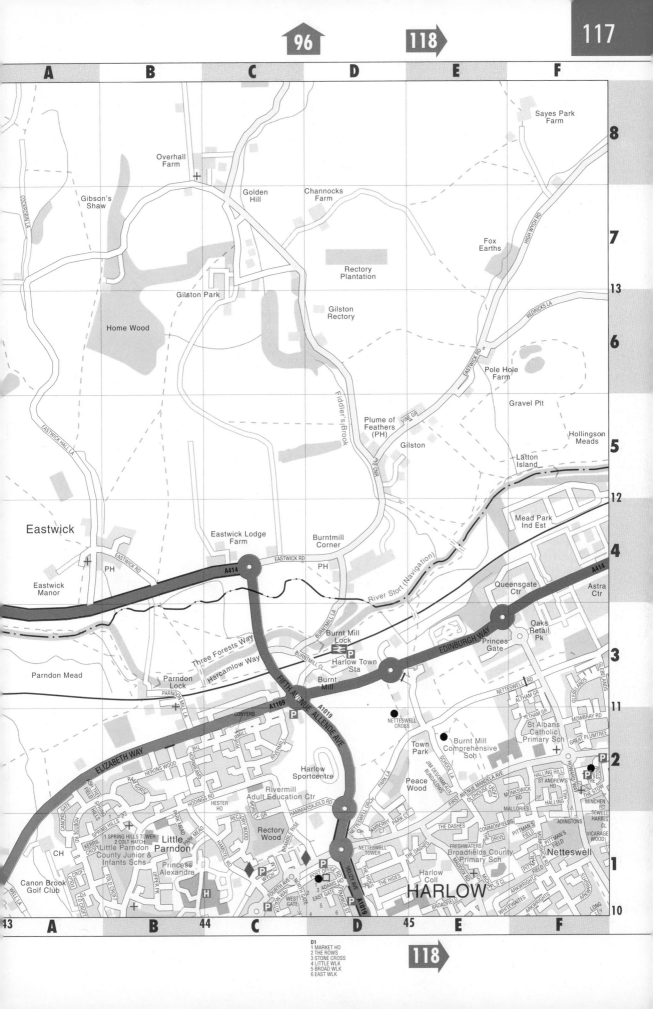

D1
1 MARKET HO
2 THE ROWS
3 STONE CROSS
4 LITTLE WLK
5 BROAD WLK
6 EAST WLK

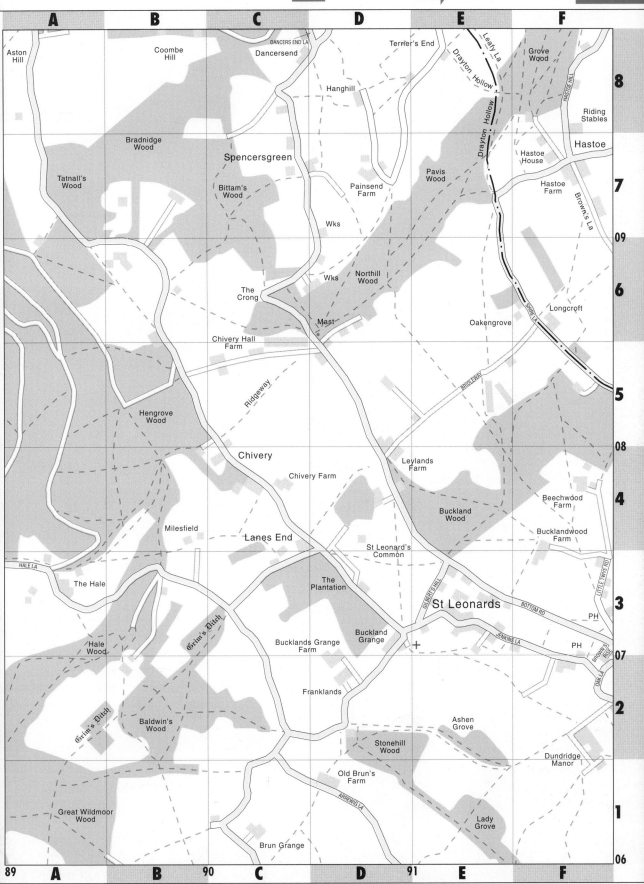

Aston Hill

Coombe Hill

DANCERS END LA

Dancersend

Terrier's End

Leafy La

Drayton Hollow

Grove Wood

HASTOE HILL

8

Hanghill

Drayton Hollow

Riding Stables

Bradnidge Wood

Spencersgreen

Hastoe

Tatnall's Wood

Bittam's Wood

Painsend Farm

Pavis Wood

Hastoe House

Hastoe Farm

Brown's La

7

Wks

09

Wks

Northill Wood

SHIRE LA

6

The Crong

Oakengrove

Longcroft

Mast

Chivery Hall Farm

BRIDLEWAY

5

Ridgeway

Hengrove Wood

08

Chivery

Leylands Farm

Chivery Farm

Beechwood Farm

4

Buckland Wood

Milesfield

Bucklandwood Farm

Lanes End

St Leonard's Common

LITTLE TWYE RD

The Hale

HALE LA

The Plantation

GILBERT'S HILL

St Leonards

BOTTOM RD

PH

3

Hale Wood

Grim's Ditch

Buckland Grange

JENKINS LA

PH

BROWN'S RISE

07

Bucklands Grange Farm

OAK LA

Franklands

Ashen Grove

2

Grim's Ditch

Baldwin's Wood

Dundridge Manor

Stonehill Wood

Old Brun's Farm

Great Wildmoor Wood

ARREWIG LA

Lady Grove

1

Brun Grange

06

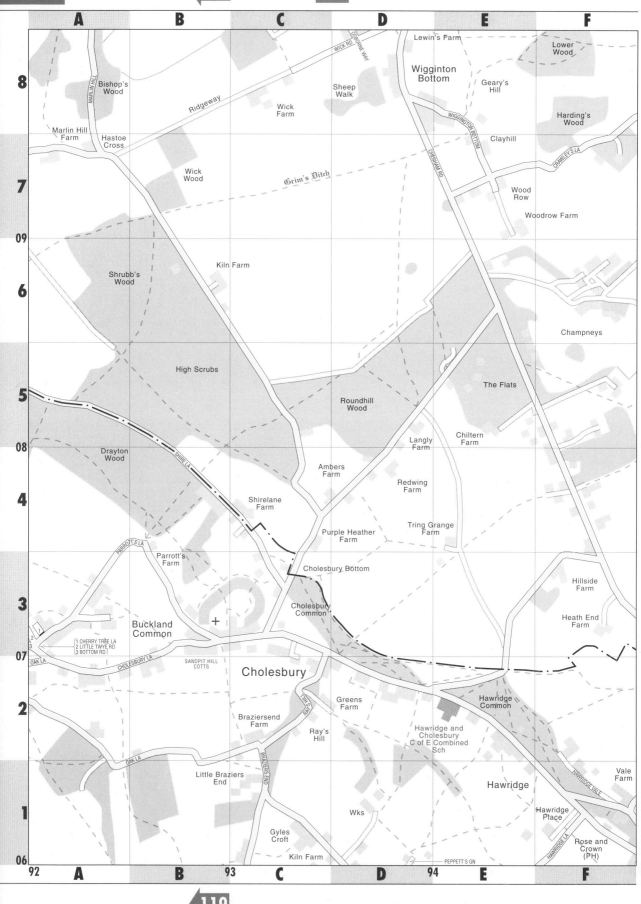

A   B   C   D   E   F

8

7

09

6

5

08

4

3

07

2

1

06

92   A   B   93   C   D   94   E   F

Marlin Hill Farm
Bishop's Wood
Marlin Hill
Hastoe Cross
Ridgeway
Wick Farm
Wick Rd
Osborne Way
Sheep Walk
Wigginton Bottom
Lewin's Farm
Lower Wood
Geary's Hill
Harding's Wood
Chesham Rd
Wigginton Bottom
Clayhill
Crawley's La
Wood Row
Woodrow Farm

Wick Wood
Grim's Ditch

Shrubb's Wood
Kiln Farm

Champneys

High Scrubs
The Flats
Roundhill Wood
Chiltern Farm
Langly Farm

Drayton Wood
Shire La
Ambers Farm
Redwing Farm
Tring Grange Farm

Shirelane Farm
Purple Heather Farm

Parrott's La
Parrott's Farm
Cholesbury Bottom
Hillside Farm
Heath End Farm

Buckland Common
1 CHERRY TREE LA
2 LITTLE TWYE RD
3 BOTTOM RD
Cholesbury Common

Oak La
Cholesbury La
Sandpit Hill Cotts
Cholesbury
Greens Farm
Hawridge Common

Braziersend Farm
Braziers End
Tring Rd
Ray's Hill
Hawridge and Cholesbury C of E Combined Sch

Oak La
Little Braziers End
Hawridge Vale
Vale Farm
Hawridge

Gyles Croft
Wks
Hawridge Place
Hawridge La
Rose and Crown (PH)
Kiln Farm
Peppett's Gn

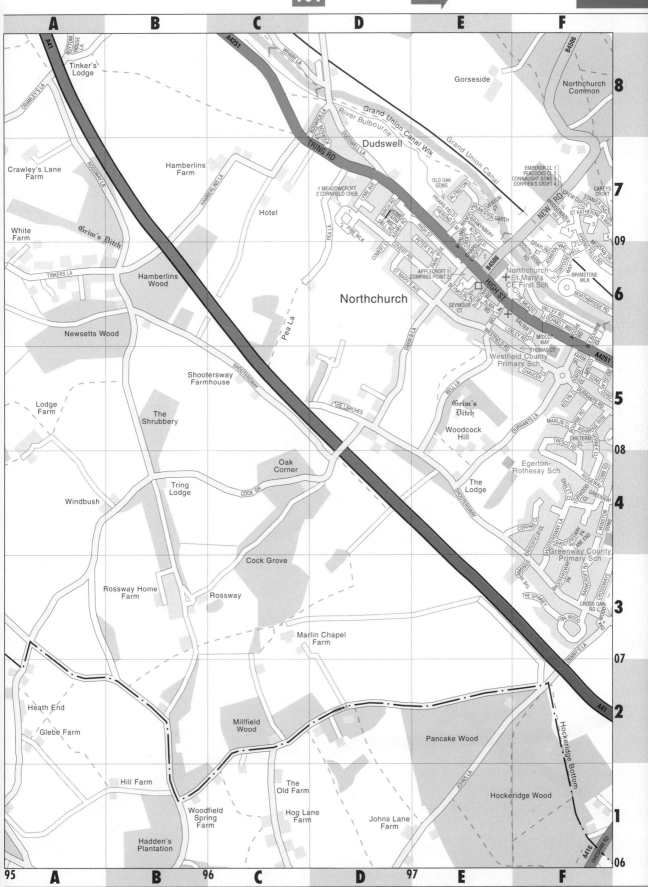

A B C D E F

8

Northchurch Farm

Berkhamsted Common

Well Farm

7

Golf Course

CAREYS CROFT

1 ST KATHERINE'S WAY
2 MORTAIN DR
3 MONTGOMERIE CL
4 BECKETS SQ

HILL VIEW

Bridgewater Sch

CH

NETTLEDEN RD

FRITHSDEN COPSE

09

SAYERS GDNS
HAINES MEAD
PARGES
BRIDLE WAY
LONG VIEW
SPRING FIELD RD
CHILTERN PARK AVE

Castle Hill Farm

THE COMMON

NORTHBRIDGE RD
BILLET LA

EGERTON RD
MEADOW ROAD CL
MEADOW RD
DELANY RISE
BRIDGEWATER RD
TREVELYAN WAY

GALVESTON RD

CASTLE HILL

BERKHAMSTED

6

River Park Ind Est

BELTON LA
RIVERSIDE GDNS
SOUTH PARK GDNS

CASTLE HILL AVE

BROWNLOW RD

THE COMMON

BYWAYS

GUTTERIDGE FARM

5

VICTORY RD
GOSSOMS END
DOUGLAS GDNS
DURRANTS RD

STAG LA
TWEED
PARK HO
WELL CT

Berkhamsted Sta

CRANSTONE HILL
HUNTERS PK
GRAVEL PATH

GILPIN'S RIDE

MEADWAY

08

CHILTERN GREEN
THE HAWTHORNS
LARCH RISE
WHITEWOOD RD
SHRUBLANDS RD

QUEENS RD
WEST RD

HIGH ST

NIGHTINGALE LODGE

KINGS RD
LOWER KINGS RD

Berkhamsted Sch

STATION RD
WHITEHILL
WHITEHILL CT
BEECH

MILLFIELD

CAMBRIDGE TERR

IVY HOUSE LA

4

St Thomas More Primary Sch

ORCHARD AVE
GREENWAY
KITSBURY RD
HAMILTON RD
CHARLES ST
MONTAGUE RD
ANGLEFIELD RD
THE OAKS

1 KILFILLAN PK
2 RAGLAN HO

ILEX CT

BAY CT

LINCOLN

Victoria C of E Sch
1 PRINCE EDWARD ST
2 CAVALIER CT
3 PRIORY CT

TH
Liby
CLARENCE RD
C Ctr

BRIDGE CT
CHAPEL ST
MANOR CL

CASTLE MEWS
RAVENS WHARF
ELLESMERE RD
GEORGE ST

3

Greenway County Primary Sch
GREYS CL
MARLIN COPSE
RED LION GDNS
GRAEMESDYKE RD

SHOOTERSWAY
LOWER CL
OXFORD CL
KINGSDALE RD

KINGS RD

BALLINGER CT

UPPER ASHLYNS RD

ASHLYNS RD

Berkhamsted School for Girls

ALDERLEY RD
HILLTOP RD

LOW RIDGE

CURLEW CL
KESTREL
PHEASANT
WOODLANDS AVE
HAZEL RD
SYCAMORE RISE
ST MARGARET'S
HILLSIDE GDNS

Swing Gate Sch
CURTIS WAY
GREENE WLK
CAPTAINS WLK
HOLLY DR

LOMBARDY DR
CEDAR DR
CEDAR

LONDON RD

River Bulbourne

Bankmill Bridge

BULLBEGGARS LA

07

Kingshill

KINGSHILL WAY
MEADOW CL
A416

CORAM CL

Ashlyns Sch

BRIAR WAY
CHESTNUT DR
SWING GATE LA

ST MARGARET'S RD

HALL PK
HALL PARK HILL
UPPER HALL PK
TALL PARK GATE
FIELDWAY
GARDEN FIELD LA

A4251

2

National Film Archive

Cemy

KINGSHILL WAY

Ashlyn's Hall

The Augustus Smith Sch

Long Green

A41

1

A416 CHESHAM RD

Haresfoot

Haresfoot Farm

Sandpit Green

Bottom Farm

A41

06

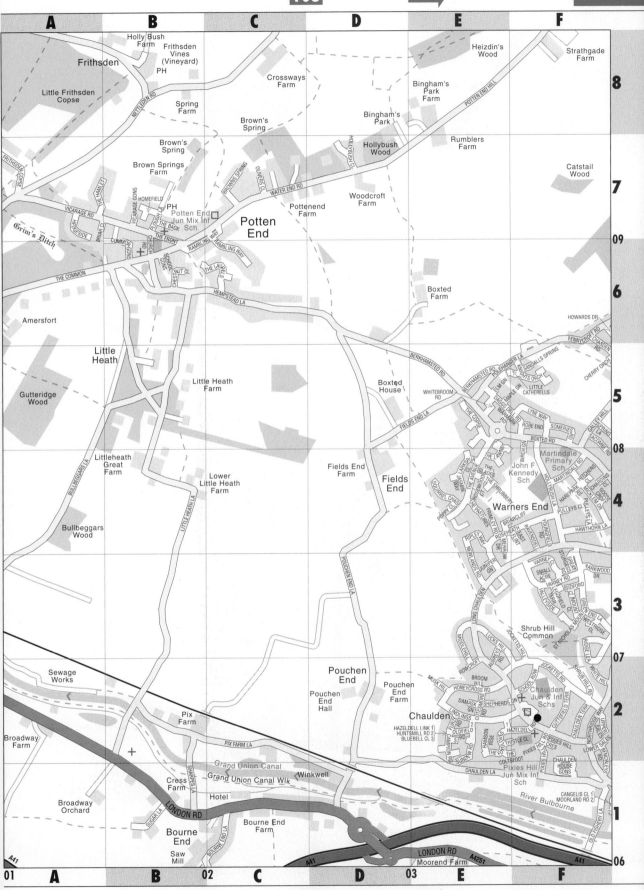

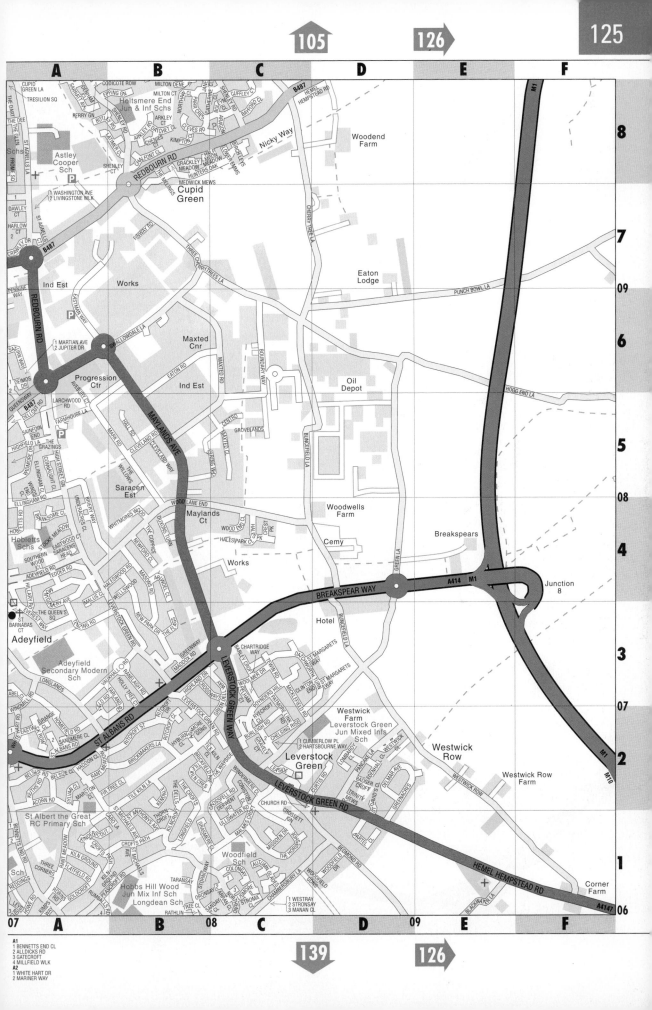

A B C D E F

8

Hill Farm La

Hill Farm

Punch Bowl La

New Jerome Cottage

A5183

Ver-Colne Valley Wlk

7

Baker's Farm

Shafford Farm

Southend Farm

Hogg End

Whitehedge Spring

09

Beech Hyde

Hogg End La

Redbourn Rd

Bow Bridge

6

Old Jeromes

Butlers Farm

River Ver

A5183

Kettlewell's Farm

Maynes Farm

5

Kentish Wood

Windmillhill Wood

08

The Vistas

Gorhambury

Shepherds Cottages

4

Bruce's Plantation

Gorhambury (remains of)

Brickkiln Wood

Cypress Wood

Lord Bacon's Mount

3

Temple Cottage

Temple Wood

Prae Wood House

07

Stud Cottages

Praewood Farm

Prae Wood

2

Westwick Hall

Bechtre La

Square Wood

A4147

Bermond La

Indial

Maynes Av

Gleum Cl

Apeline Cl

Caban Cl

Habiram Cl

Meautys

1

Junction 7

M10

Hill End Farm

Hemel Hempstead Rd

Ickenild Cl

Potterscrouch La

06

A4147

M1

Akeman Cl

Meautys 2

10 A 11 B C 12 D E F

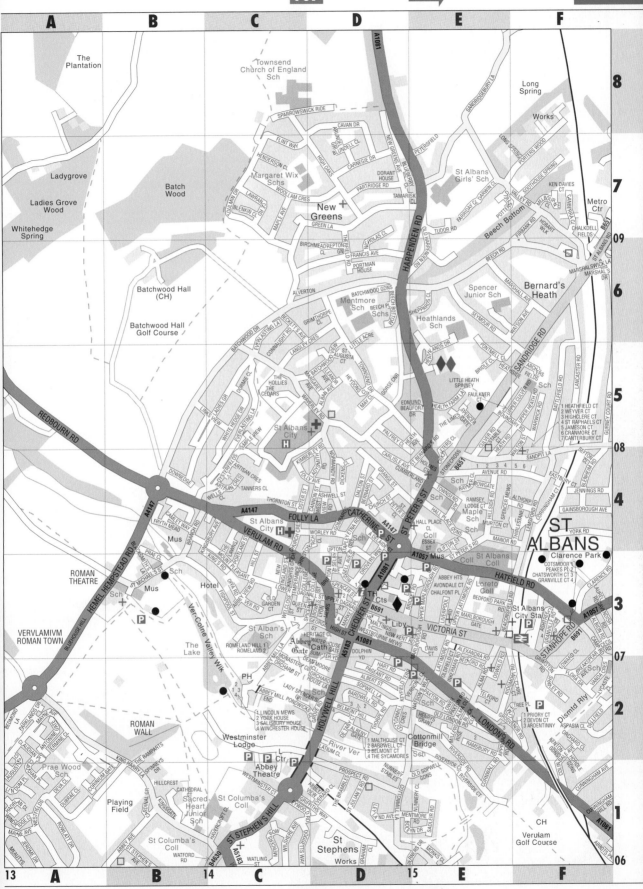

141 | 128 →

D3
1 WADDINGTON RD
2 CROSS ST
3 CHRISTOPHER PL
4 FRENCH ROW
5 HALF MOON MEWS

127
108

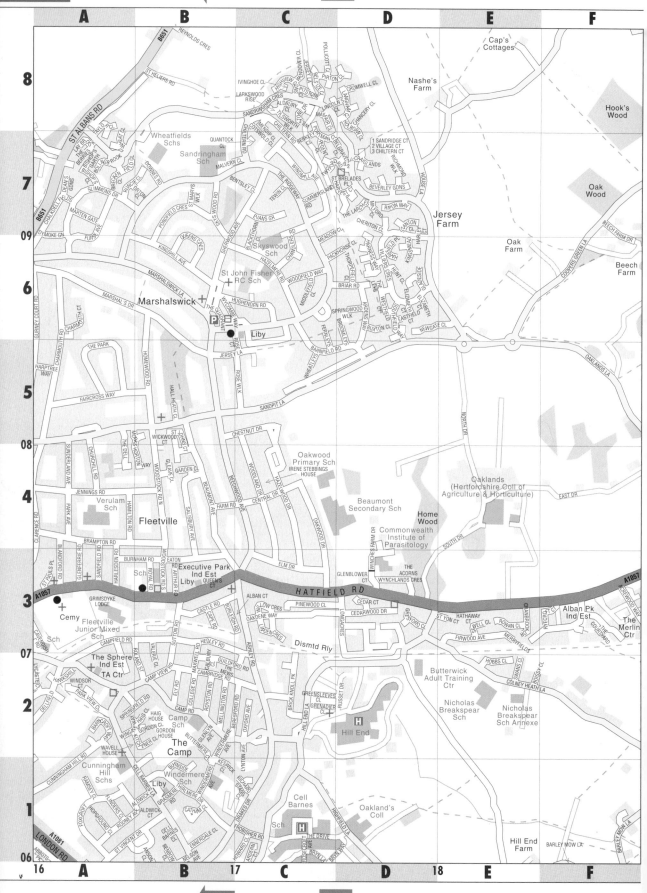

127
142

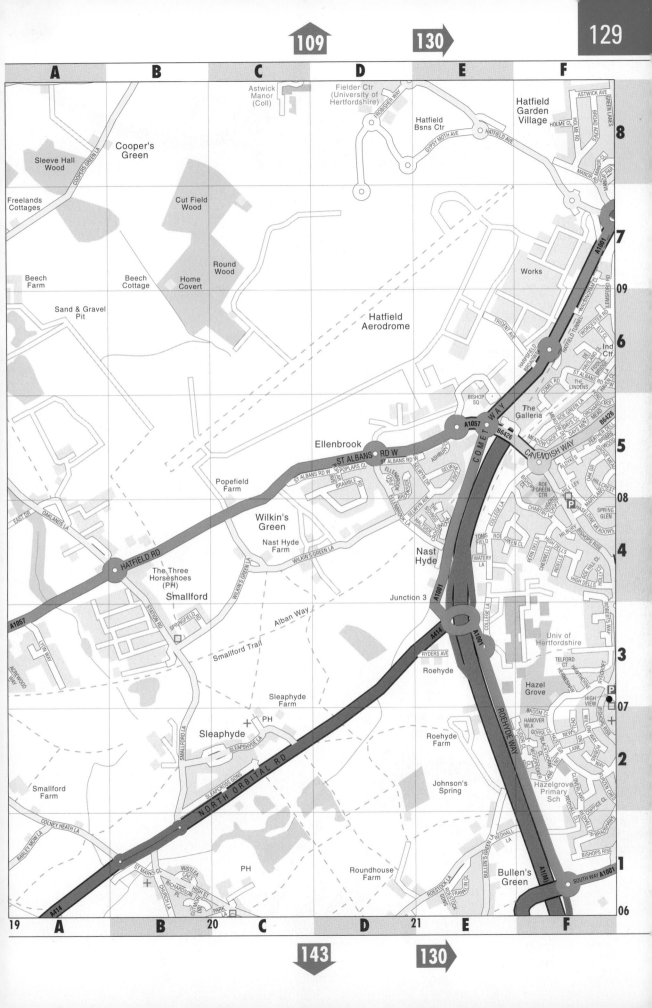

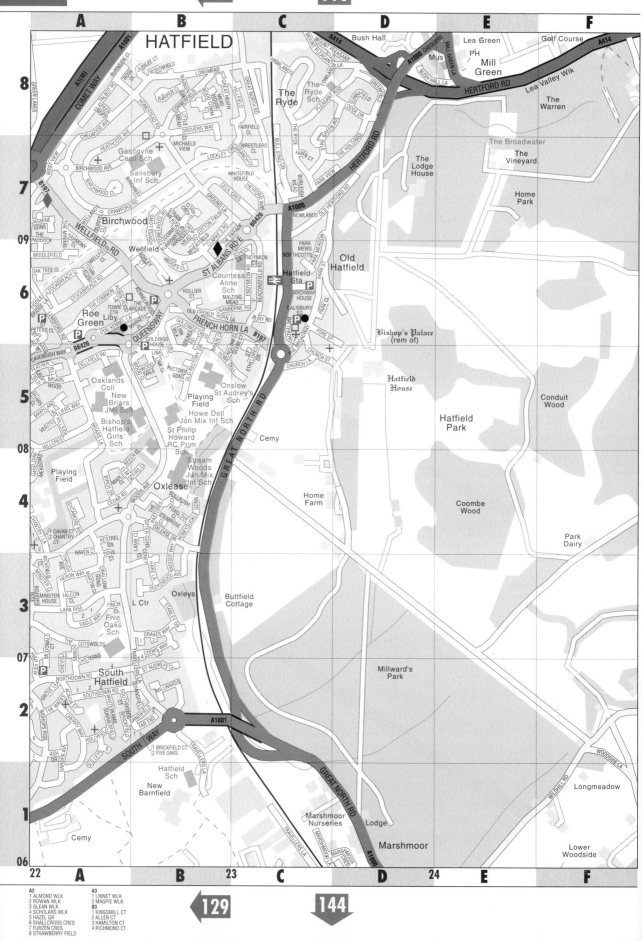

HATFIELD

A2
1 ALMOND WLK
2 ROWAN WLK
3 GLEAN WLK
4 SCHOLARS WLK
5 HAZEL GR
6 SHALLCROSS CRES
7 FURZEN CRES
8 STRAWBERRY FIELD

A3
1 LINNET WLK
2 MAGPIE WLK
B3
1 KINGSMILL CT
2 ALLEN CT
3 HAMILTON CT
4 RICHMOND CT

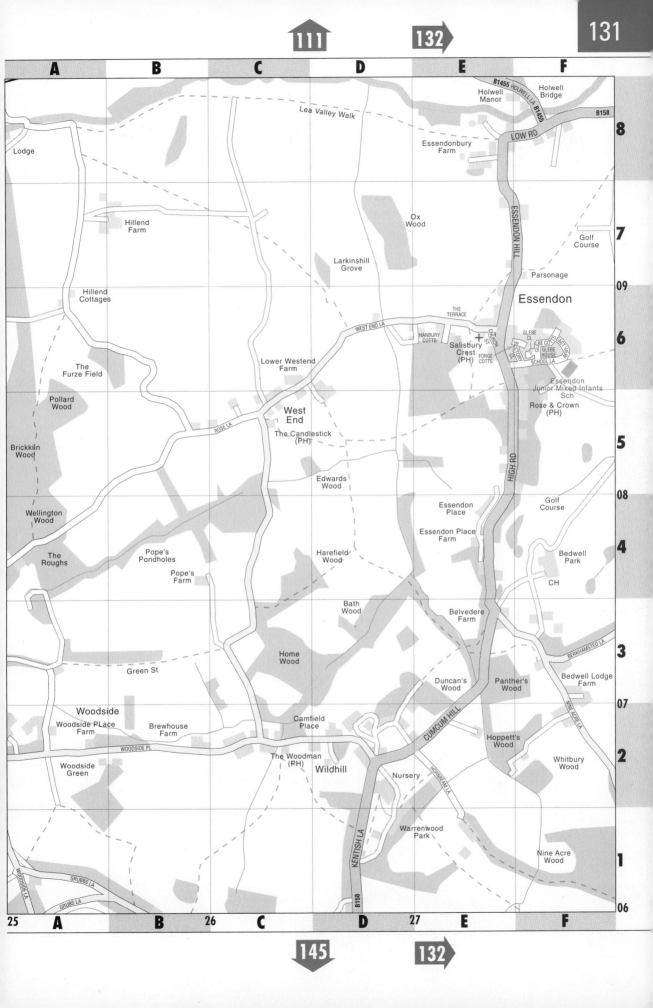

A B C D E F

8
7
09
6
5
08
4
3
07
2
1
06

B1455 HOLWELL LA B1455
Holwell Manor
Holwell Bridge
B158
LOW RD
ESSENDON HILL

Lea Valley Walk

Lodge

Essendonbury Farm

Hillend Farm

Ox Wood

Golf Course

Larkinshill Grove

Parsonage

Hillend Cottages

Essendon

THE TERRACE

WEST END LA

HANBURY COTTS
Salisbury Crest (PH)
CHURCH ST
FORGE COTTS
SCHOOL LA
GLEBE CL
RECTORY CL
BE CUT
GLEBE HOUSE
EAST VIEW

The Furze Field

Lower Westend Farm

Essendon Junior Mixed Infants Sch
Rose & Crown (PH)

Pollard Wood

West End

ROSE LA

The Candlestick (PH)

HIGH RD

Brickkiln Wood

Golf Course

Edwards Wood

Wellington Wood

Essendon Place

Essendon Place Farm

The Roughs

Pope's Pondholes

Harefield Wood

Bedwell Park

CH

Pope's Farm

Bath Wood

Belvedere Farm

BERKHAMSTED LA

Home Wood

Green St

Duncan's Wood

Panther's Wood

Bedwell Lodge Farm

NINE ACRE LA

CUMCUM HILL

Woodside
Woodside PLace Farm
Brewhouse Farm

Camfield Place

Hoppett's Wood

WOODSIDE PL

The Woodman (PH)
Wildhill

Whitbury Wood

Woodside Green

Nursery

HORNBEAM LA

Warrenwood Park

KENTISH LA

Nine Acre Wood

WOODSIDE LA
GRUBBS LA
GRUBS LA

B158

25 A B 26 C D 27 E F

131 112

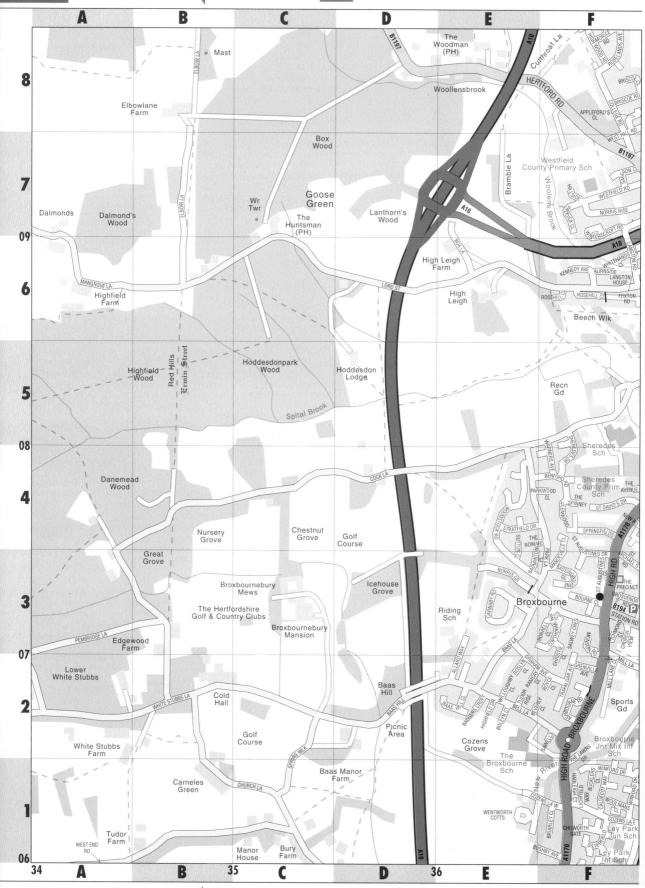
8

Elbowlane
Farm

Box
Wood

The
Woodman
(PH)

Woollensbrook

HERTFORD RD

Cutthroat La

B1197

Westfield
County Primary Sch

Bramble La

Woolens Brook

Appleford's
Cl

West End
Rd

7

Wr
Twr

Goose
Green

Lanthorn's
Wood

A10

High Leigh
Farm

High
Leigh

Box La

Norris Rise

Rosehill Cl

Foxton
Rd

Beech Wlk

09

Dalmonds

Dalmond's
Wood

Elbow La

Mast

The Huntsman
(PH)

Mangrove La

Lord St

Kennedy Ave

Burnside

Langton
House

Rosehill

6

Highfield
Farm

5

Highfield
Wood

Red Hills
Ermin Street

Hoddesdonpark
Wood

Hoddesdon
Lodga

Spital Brook

Recn
Gd

Sheredes
Sch

08

Danemead
Wood

Cock La

Warners Ave

Benford Rd

Parkwood
Cl

Glenwood

Sheredes
County Prim
Sch

The
Spinney

St David's Dr

The
Avenue

St Augustines Dr

The Rowans

Springfields

A1170

New Rd

St Michael's

4

Nursery
Grove

Chestnut
Grove

Golf
Course

Norris Gr

Stratfield Dr

Hollins

Badminton
Cl

Mandel Cl

Park La

Bassinge

High Rd

The Precinct

3

Great
Grove

Broxbournebury
Mews

The Hertfordshire
Golf & Country Clubs

Broxbournebury
Mansion

Icehouse
Grove

Riding
Sch

Carnaby Rd

Broxbourne

Bourne Cl

Bournell

Copthorne

Sawey Cres

Grovenor
Rd

B194
Station Rd

Church
Cl

Mill La

07

Pembridge La

Edgewood
Farm

Allard Way

Baas Hill

Graham Ave

Royce

Grenville
Ave

Redmond

Acremore

2

Lower
White Stubbs

White Stubbs La

Cold
Hall

Baas
Hill

Picnic
Area

Baas Hill Cl

Badgers Croft

Highfield Dr

Bolenn Cl

Bell La

Beverley

Cozens
Grove

The
Broxbourne Sch

Sports
Gd

Broxbourne
Jnr Mix Inf
Sch

HIGH ROAD BROXBOURNE

1

White Stubbs
Farm

Golf
Course

Spring Wlk

Carneles
Green

Church La

Baas Manor
Farm

Bury
Farm

A10

Cozens
Grove

New River

Wentworth
Cotts

Cozens La W

Cozens La E

Brierley Cl

Bushby Ave

Chilworth
Gate

Silverfield

Winford Dr

Caldecote Way

Woolmans

Ley Park
Jun Sch

Ley Park
Inf Sch

06

West End
Rd

Tudor
Farm

Manor
House

Bury
Farm

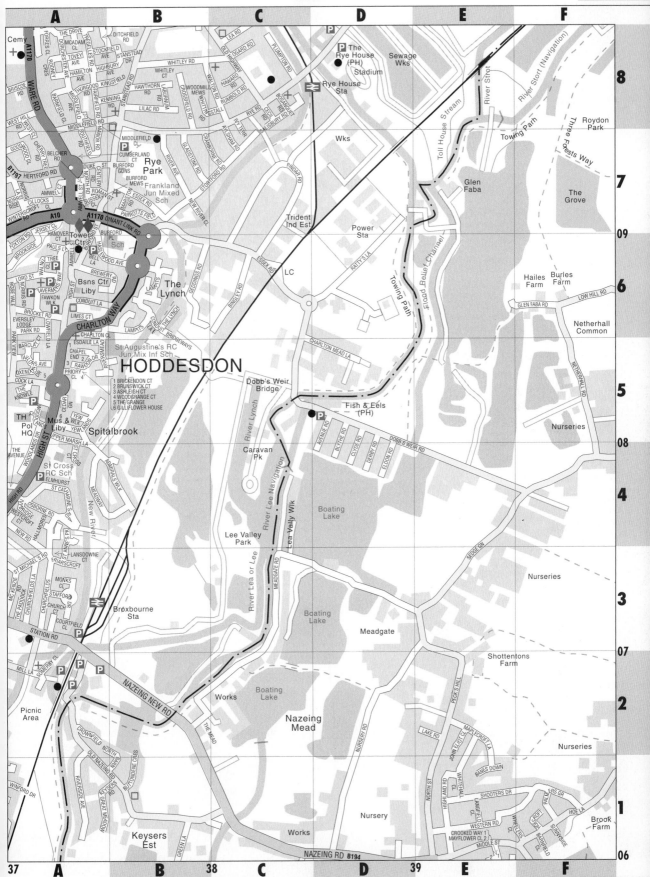

HODDESDON

1 BRICKENDON CT
2 BRUNSWICK CT
3 ASHLEIGH CT
4 WOODGRANGE CT
5 THE GRANGE
6 GILLIFLOWER HOUSE

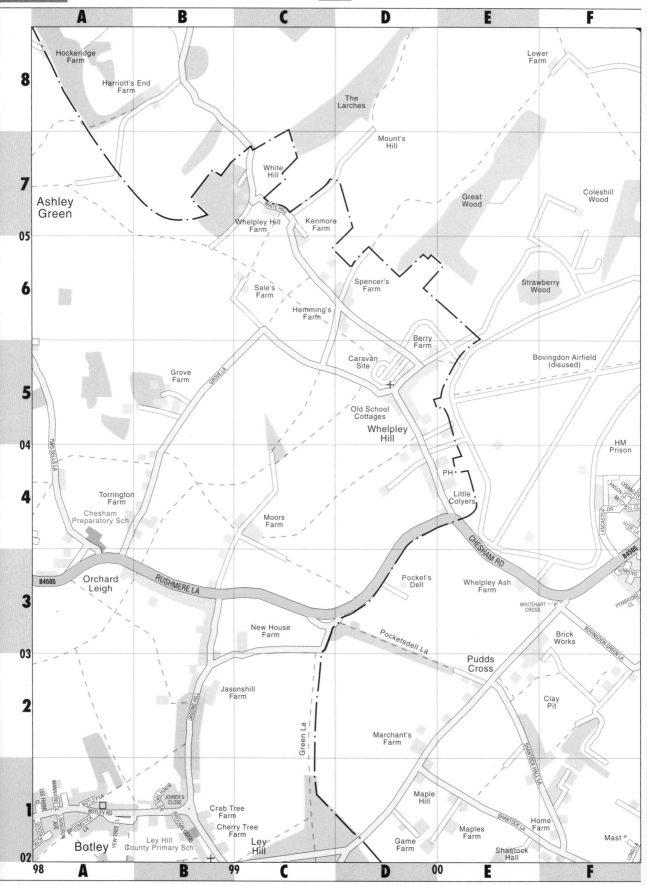

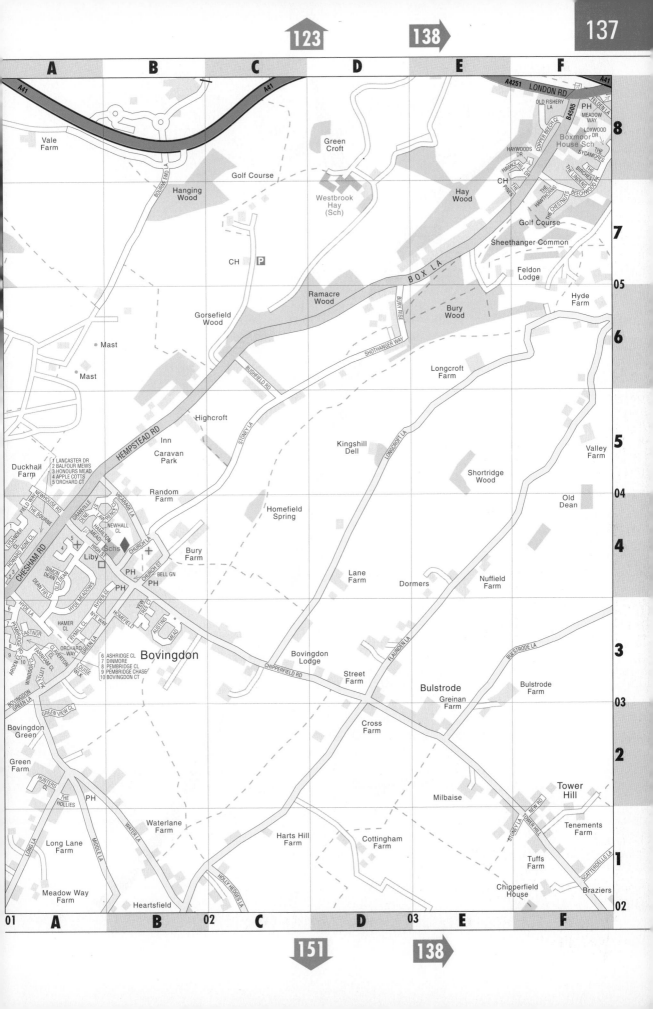

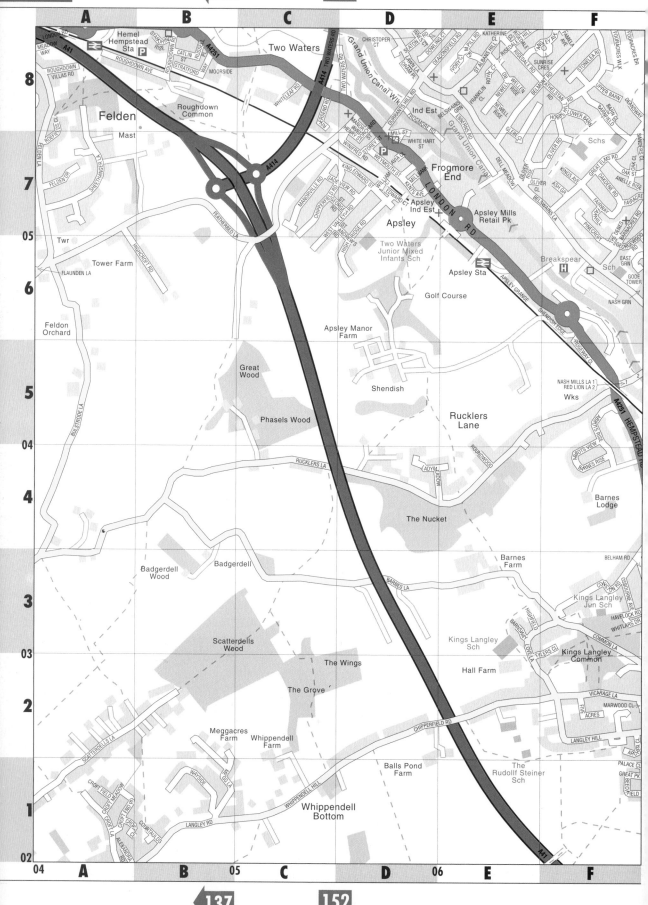

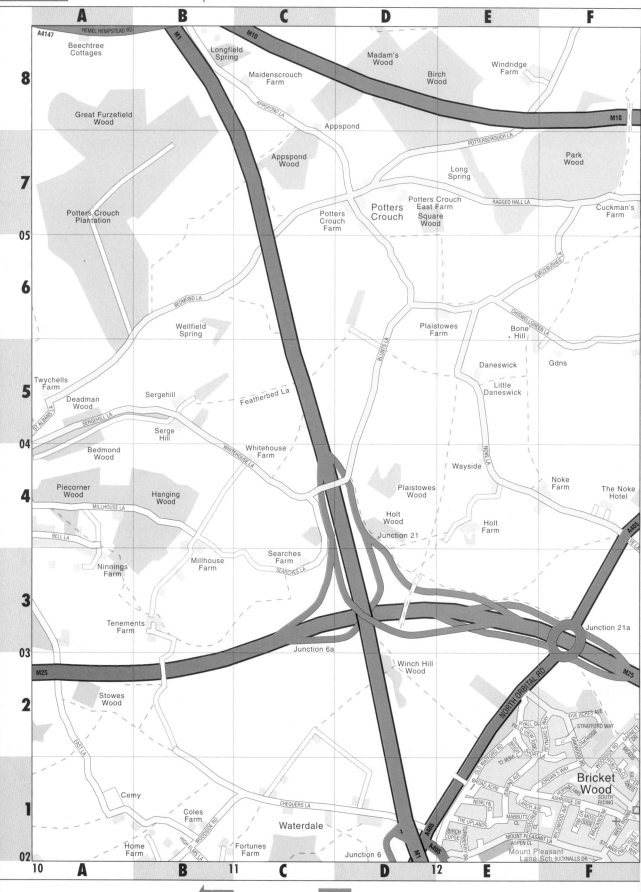

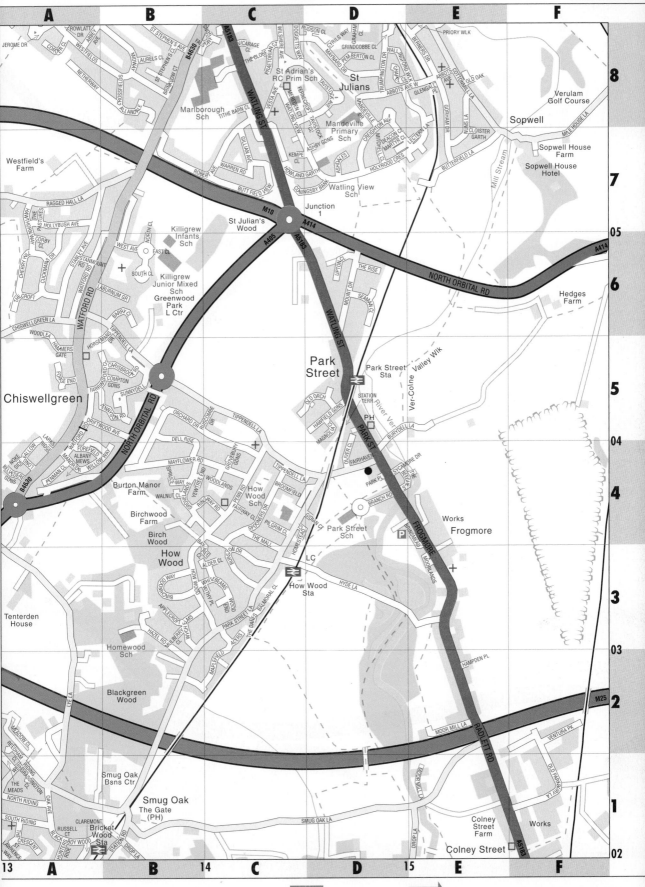

141
128

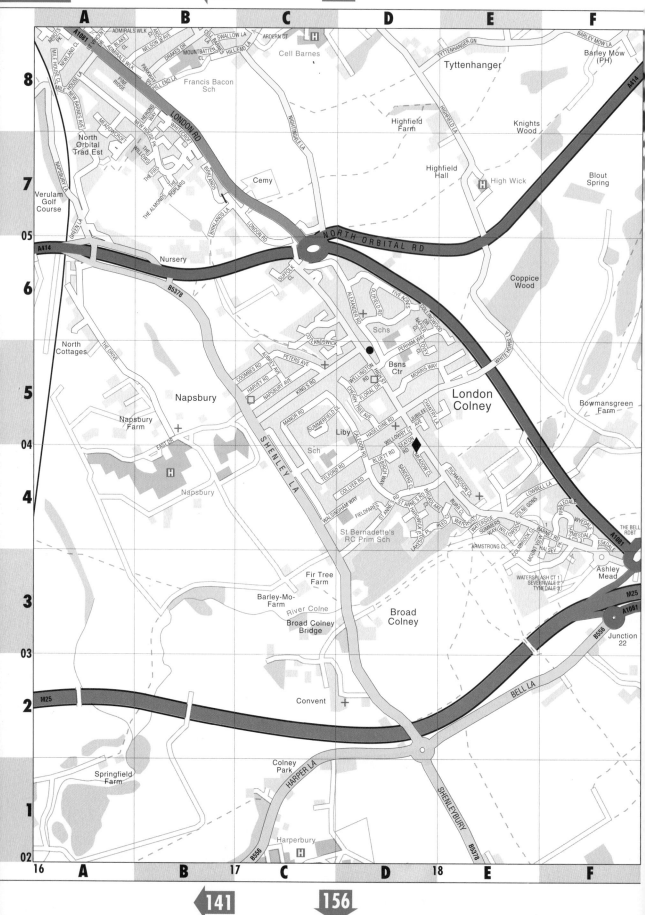

A   B   C   D   E   F

NORTH ORBITAL RD
A414

Park Corner

River Colne

Water
Works

CHURCH LA
HEATH SIDE
PARK LA

SCHOLARS CT

HIGH ST

Colney
Heath

ROESTOCK LA
HALL CONS
MEADWAY

Roestock

HALL CONS

ADMIRALS CL

BILLERN'S GREEN LA

DELLSOME LA

Junction
2

DELLSOME LA

A1 (M)

8

PH

Colney Heath
Farm

DENNETTS
CL

FELLOWES LA

Windmill

Warren
Farm

Frederick's
Wood

Tollgate
Farm

Tollgate
Wood

TOLLGATE RD

Park
Cottage

The
Osierbeds

A1 (M)

7

05

Tyttenhanger
Farm

The New
Plantation

COURSERS RD

Coursers
Farm

North Mymms
Park

6

Garden Wood

Tyttenhanger
Park

Red Lodge

Walsingham
Wood

North Mymms
Park

5

Lodge
Plantation

04

4

The Bell
(PH)

A1081

B556

Junction
22

Cobs Ash

Cangsley
Grove

3

Round
Wood

Potwells

03

Salisbury
Hall

Redwell Wood
Farm

Oak Lodge

Hawkshead
Wood

2

Salisbury Hall
Farm

Mus

Ridgehill Stud

Shenley Lodge
Cottage

Manor Lodge
Sch

RECTORY LA

Ridgehill

PACKHORSE LA

Redwell Wood

1

Shenley Lodge
Farm

M25

BLACKHORSE LA

B556 RD

Woodhill
Farm

02

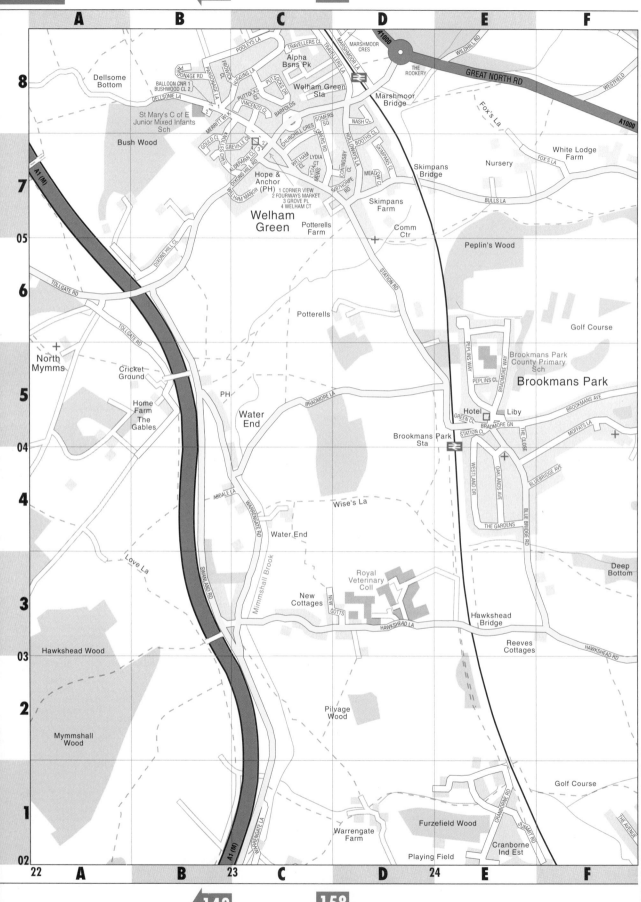

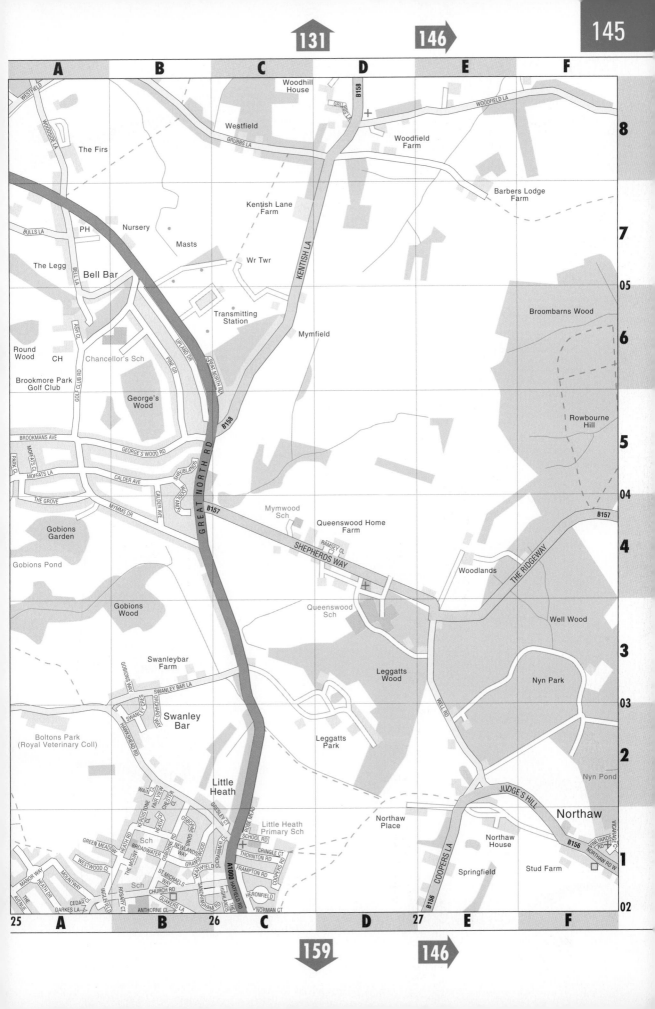

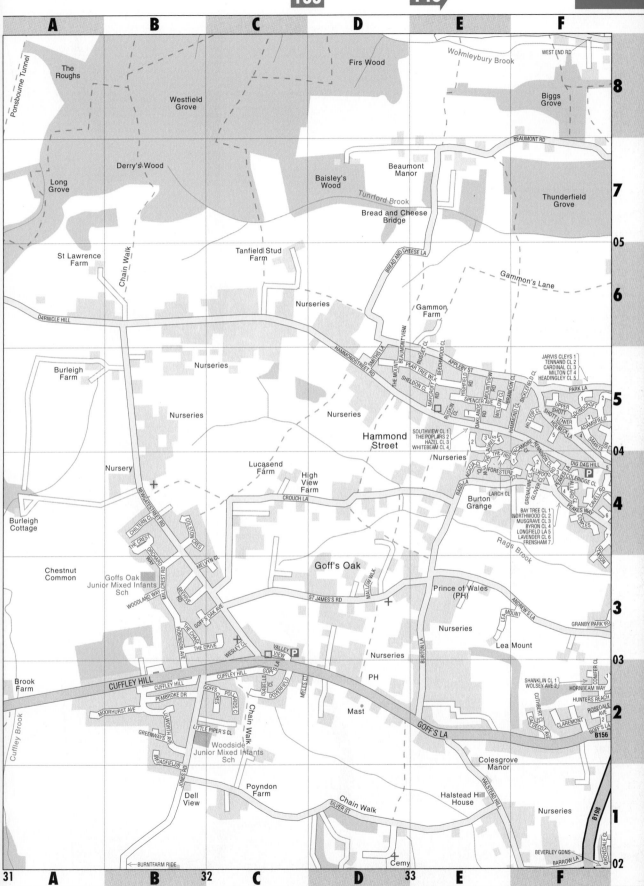

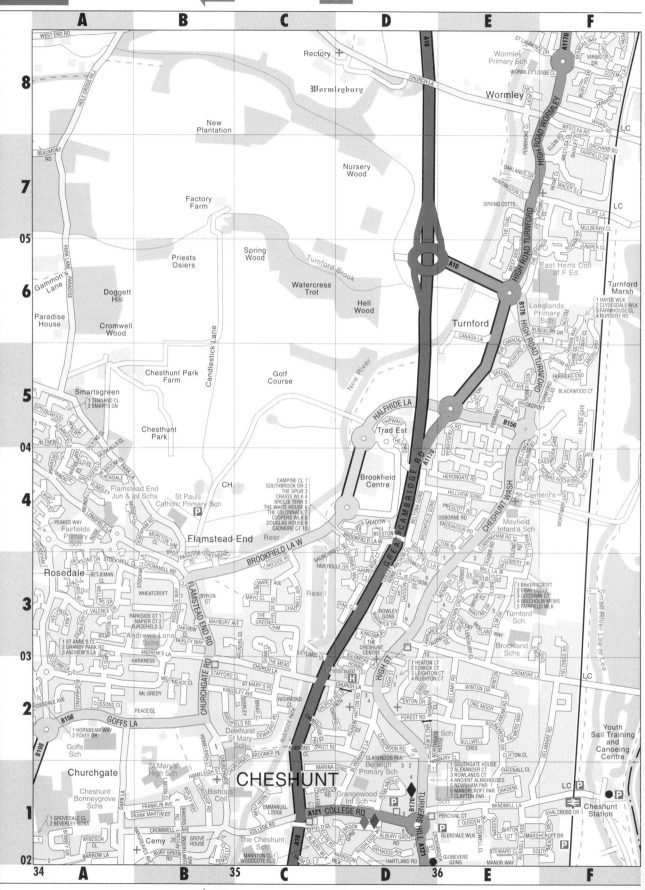

147
134

A B C D E F

8

7

05

6

5

04

4

3

03

2

1

02

34 A B 35 C D 36 E F

Wormley

Turnford

Turnford Marsh

New Plantation

Wormleybury

Nursery Wood

Factory Farm

Spring Wood

Priests Osiers

Watercress Trot

Hell Wood

Gammon's Lane

Doggett Hill

Paradise House

Cromwell Wood

Chesthunt Park Farm

Chesthunt Park

Golf Course

New River

Smartsgreen

Flamstead End Jun & Inf Schs

St Pauls Catholic Primary Sch

Flamstead End

Rosedale

Churchgate

CHESHUNT

Brookfield Centre

Halfhide La

Trad Est

Cheshunt Station

Youth Sail Training and Canoeing Centre

East Herts Coll of F Ed

Longlands Primary Sch

Wormley Primary Sch

St Clement's Sch

Mayfield Infant's Sch

Turnford Sch

Brookland Schs

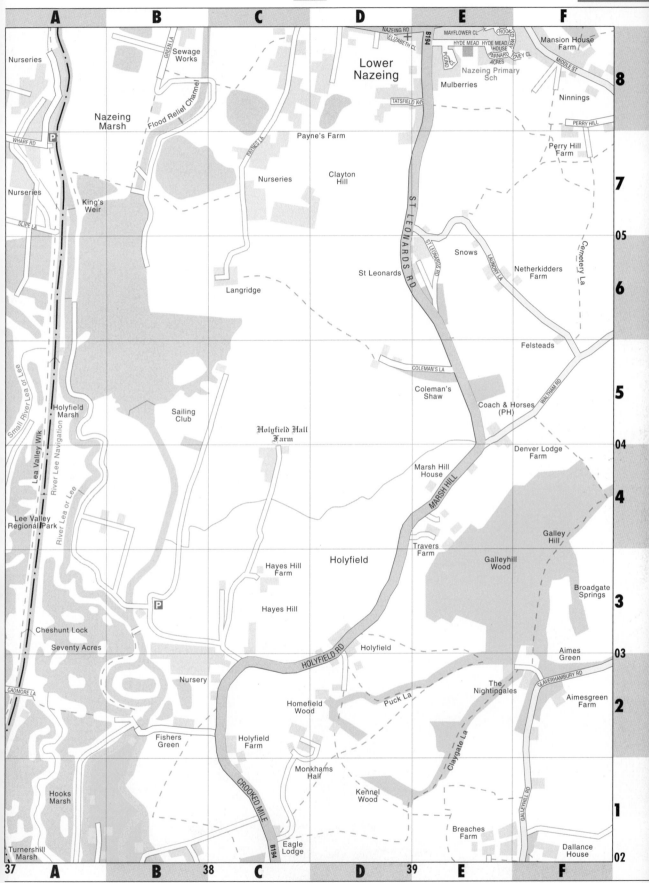

A B C D E F

Nurseries

Nazeing Marsh

Sewage Works

GREEN LA

Flood Relief Channel

WHARF RD

P

King's Weir

Nurseries

SLIPE LA

PAYNES LA

Nurseries

Clayton Hill

Payne's Farm

Lower Nazeing

NAZEING RD

ELIZABETH CL

B194

MAYFLOWER CL

HYDE MEAD
HOUSE

HYDE MEAD

ARNARO

COVEY CL

4 ACRES

POUND

Nazeing Primary Sch

Mulberries

Mansion House Farm /

MIDDLE ST

Ninnings

PERRY HILL

Perry Hill Farm

8

7

05

TATSFIELD AVE

ST LEONARDS RD

ST LEONARDS RD

St Leonards

Snows

LAUNDRY LA

Netherkidders Farm

Cemetery La

6

Langridge

Small River Lea or Lee

Lea Valley Wlk

River Lee Navigation

Holyfield Marsh

Sailing Club

Holyfield Hall Farm

COLEMAN'S LA

Coleman's Shaw

Coach & Horses (PH)

WALTHAM RD

Felsteads

Denver Lodge Farm

5

04

River Lea or Lee

Lee Valley Regional Park

Marsh Hill House

MARSH HILL

Holyfield

Hayes Hill Farm

Travers Farm

Galleyhill Wood

Galley Hill

4

Broadgate Springs

3

Cheshunt Lock

Seventy Acres

P

Hayes Hill

Nursery

HOLYFIELD RD

Holyfield

Holyfield

Puck La

The Nightingales

CLAVERHAMBURY RD

Aimes Green

Aimesgreen Farm

03

2

CADMORE LA

Fishers Green

Holyfield Farm

Homefield Wood

CLAYGATE LA

GALLEYHILL RD

CROOKED MILE

Monkhams Hall

Kennel Wood

Breaches Farm

Dallance House

1

Hooks Marsh

Turnershill Marsh

B194

Eagle Lodge

02

37 **A** 38 **B** **C** 39 **D** **E** **F**

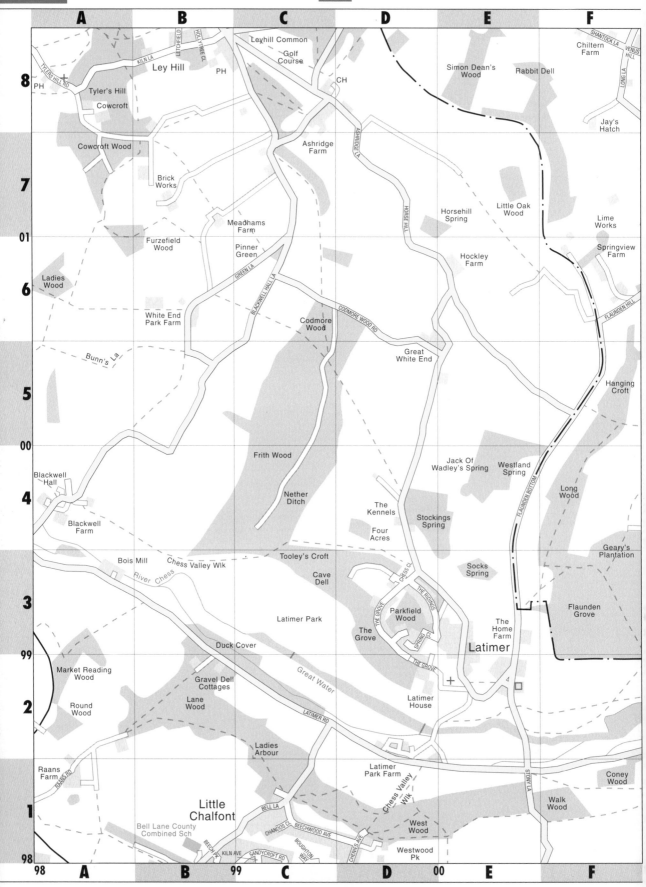

A B C D E F

8

7

01

6

00

5

00

4

3

99

2

98

98 A B 99 C D 00 E F

Ley Hill
Leyhill Common
Golf Course
CH
Tyler's Hill
Cowcroft
PH
PH
Cowcroft Wood
Brick Works
Ashridge Farm
Simon Dean's Wood
Rabbit Dell
Chiltern Farm
Jay's Hatch
Meadhams Farm
Furzefield Wood
Pinner Green
Horsehill Spring
Little Oak Wood
Lime Works
Springview Farm
Ladies Wood
White End Park Farm
Hockley Farm
Codmore Wood
Great White End
Hanging Croft
Bunn's La
Frith Wood
Nether Ditch
Jack Of Wadley's Spring
Westland Spring
Long Wood
Blackwell Hall
The Kennels
Stockings Spring
Geary's Plantation
Blackwell Farm
Four Acres
Socks Spring
Bois Mill
Chess Valley Wlk
Tooley's Croft
Flaunden Grove
River Chess
Cave Dell
Parkfield Wood
The Ridings
The Home Farm
Latimer Park
The Grove
Latimer
Duck Cover
Market Reading Wood
Gravel Dell Cottages
Great Water
Latimer House
Round Wood
Lane Wood
Latimer Rd
Ladies Arbour
Raans Farm
Latimer Park Farm
Chess Valley Wlk
Coney Wood
Walk Wood
Little Chalfont
Bell La
West Wood
Bell Lane County Combined Sch
Chandos Cl
Beechwood Ave
Westwood Pk
Kiln Ave
Sandycroft Rd
Boughton Way

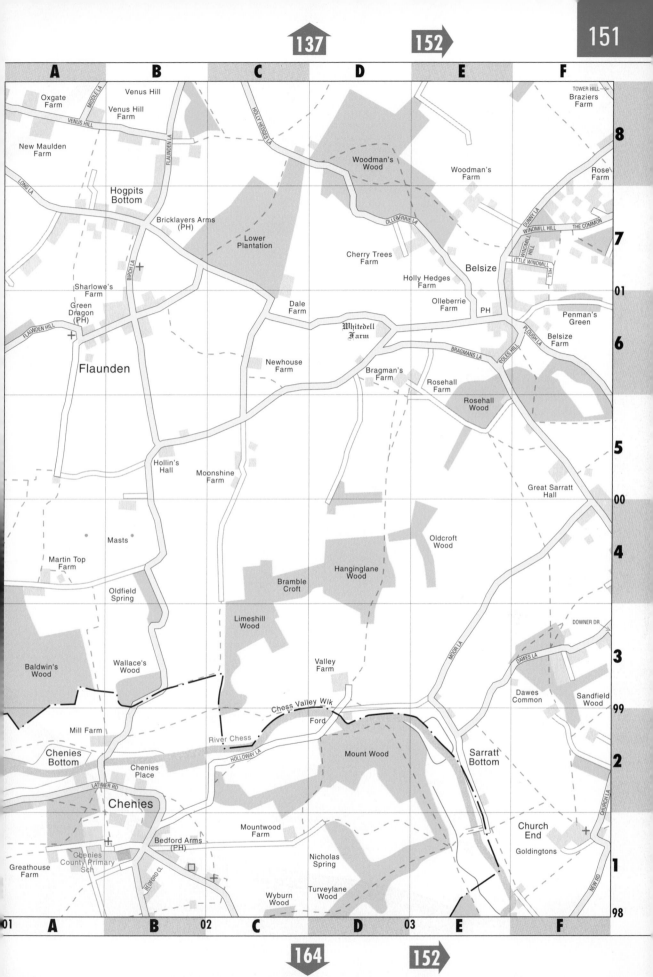

A B C D E F

8

7

01

6

5

00

4

3

99

2

1

98

Oxgate Farm

Venus Hill

Venus Hill Farm

MIDDLE LA

New Maulden Farm

VENUS HILL

FLAUNDEN LA

LONG LA

Hogpits Bottom

Bricklayers Arms (PH)

HOLLY HEDGES LA

Woodman's Wood

Woodman's Farm

TOWER HILL
Braziers Farm

Rose Farm

OLLEBERRIE LA

Cherry Trees Farm

Belsize

QUINRY LA

Windmill Hill

THE COMMON

LITTLE WINDMILL HILL

WINDMILL HILL

Lower Plantation

Holly Hedges Farm

Olleberrie Farm

PH

Penman's Green

BIRCH LA

Sharlowe's Farm

Dale Farm

Whitedell Farm

Belsize Farm

POLES HILL

PLOUGH LA

FLAUNDEN HILL

Green Dragon (PH)

Flaunden

Newhouse Farm

Bragman's Farm

BRAGMANS LA

Rosehall Farm

Rosehall Wood

Hollin's Hall

Moonshine Farm

Great Sarratt Hall

Masts

Martin Top Farm

Oldfield Spring

Oldcroft Wood

Hanginglane Wood

Bramble Croft

Limeshill Wood

DOWNER DR

Baldwin's Wood

Wallace's Wood

Valley Farm

MOOR LA

DAWES LA

Dawes Common

Sandfield Wood

Chess Valley Wlk

Ford

Mill Farm

River Chess

HOLLOWAY LA

Mount Wood

Sarratt Bottom

Chenies Bottom

LATIMER RD

Chenies Place

Chenies

Mountwood Farm

Nicholas Spring

Church End

Goldingtons

CHURCH LA

Bedford Arms (PH)

BEDFORD CL

Chenies County Primary Sch

Greathouse Farm

Wyburn Wood

Turveylane Wood

NEW RD

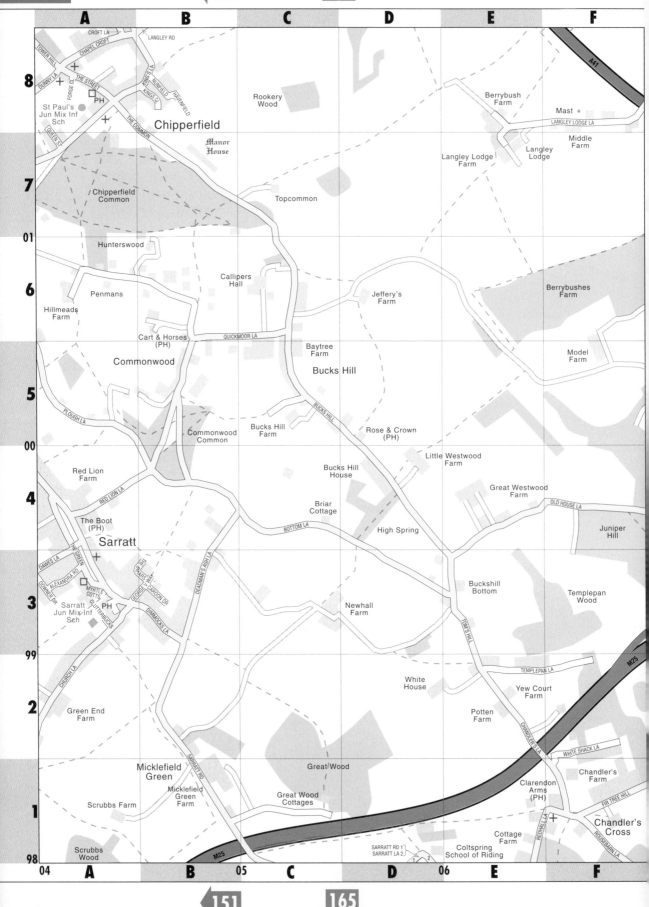

A B C D E F

8

7

01

6

5

00

4

00

3

99

2

98

04 A B 05 C D 06 E F

CROFT LA
LANGLEY RD
TOWER HILL
CHAPEL CROFT
DUNNY LA
KING'S LA
NUNFIELD
HAVENFIELD
FORGE CL
THE STREET
KINGS CL
PH
St Paul's Jun Mix Inf Sch
QUEEN ST
THE COMMON
Chipperfield
Rookery Wood
Berrybush Farm
Mast
Middle Farm
LANGLEY LODGE LA
Langley Lodge Farm
Langley Lodge
Manor House
Chipperfield Common
Topcommon
Hunterswood
Callipers Hall
Jeffery's Farm
Berrybushes Farm
Penmans
Hillmeads Farm
Cart & Horses (PH)
QUICKMOOR LA
Baytree Farm
Model Farm
Commonwood
Bucks Hill
PLOUGH LA
BUCKS HILL
Commonwood Common
Bucks Hill Farm
Rose & Crown (PH)
Little Westwood Farm
Red Lion Farm
Bucks Hill House
Great Westwood Farm
OLD HOUSE LA
RED LION LA
Briar Cottage
High Spring
Juniper Hill
The Boot (PH)
BOTTOM LA
Sarratt
THE GREEN
DAWES LA
DONKEY DR
ALEXANDRA RD
MYRTLE COTTS
PH
GEORGE
CARDON DR
DEADMAN'S ASH LA
Buckshill Bottom
Templepan Wood
Sarratt Jun Mix Inf Sch
CLUTTERBUCKS
DIMMOCKS LA
Newhall Farm
TOM'S HILL
CHURCH LA
White House
TEMPLEPAN LA
Yew Court Farm
M25
Green End Farm
Potten Farm
CHANDLER'S LA
Micklefield Green
SARRATT RD
Great Wood
WHITE SHACK LA
Chandler's Farm
Micklefield Green Farm
Great Wood Cottages
Clarendon Arms (PH)
REDHALL LA
FIR TREE HILL
ROUSEBARN LA
Scrubbs Farm
Cottage Farm
Chandler's Cross
Scrubbs Wood
M25
SARRATT RD 1
SARRATT LA 2
Coltspring School of Riding
A41

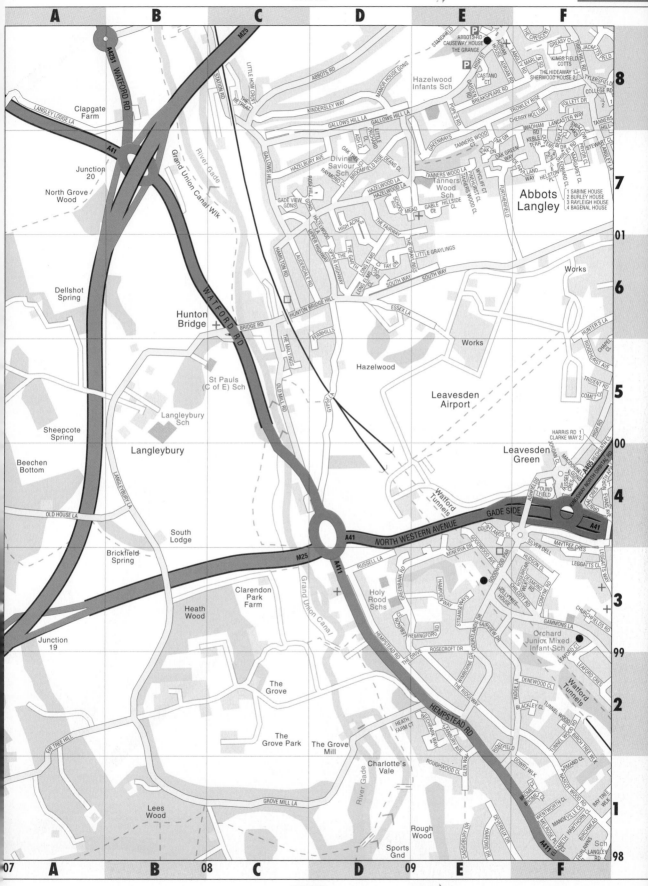

◀ 153
▲ 140

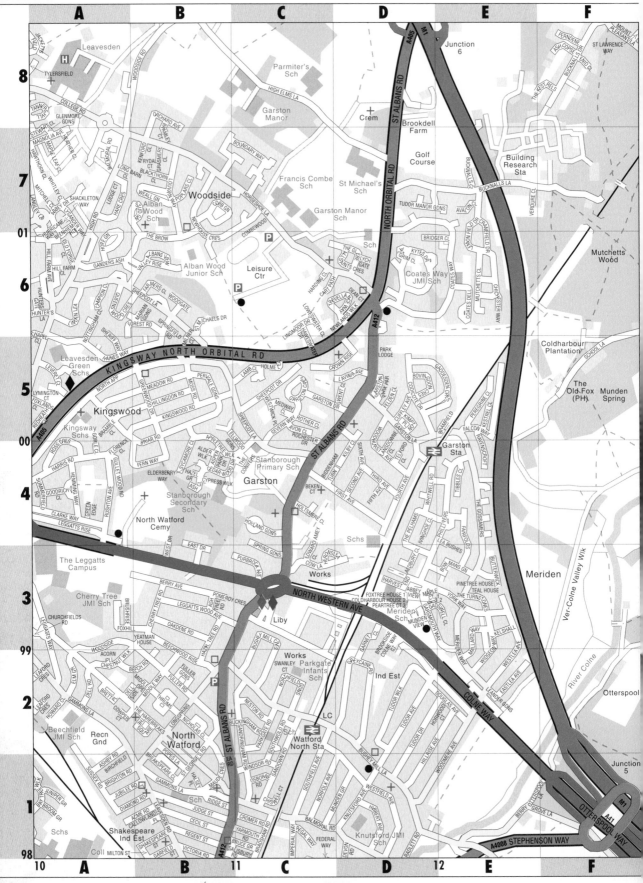

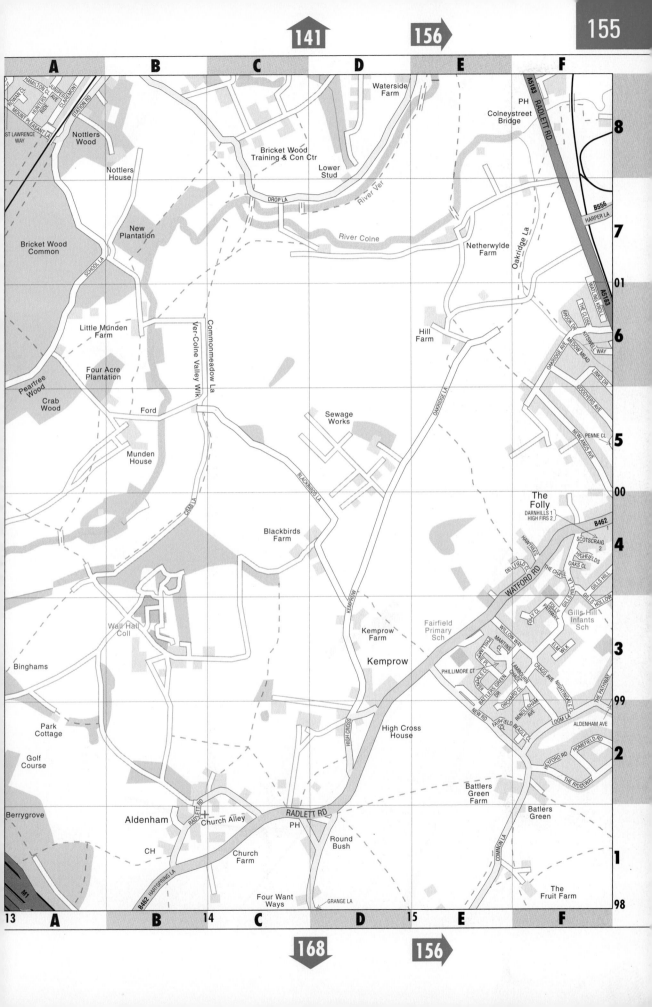

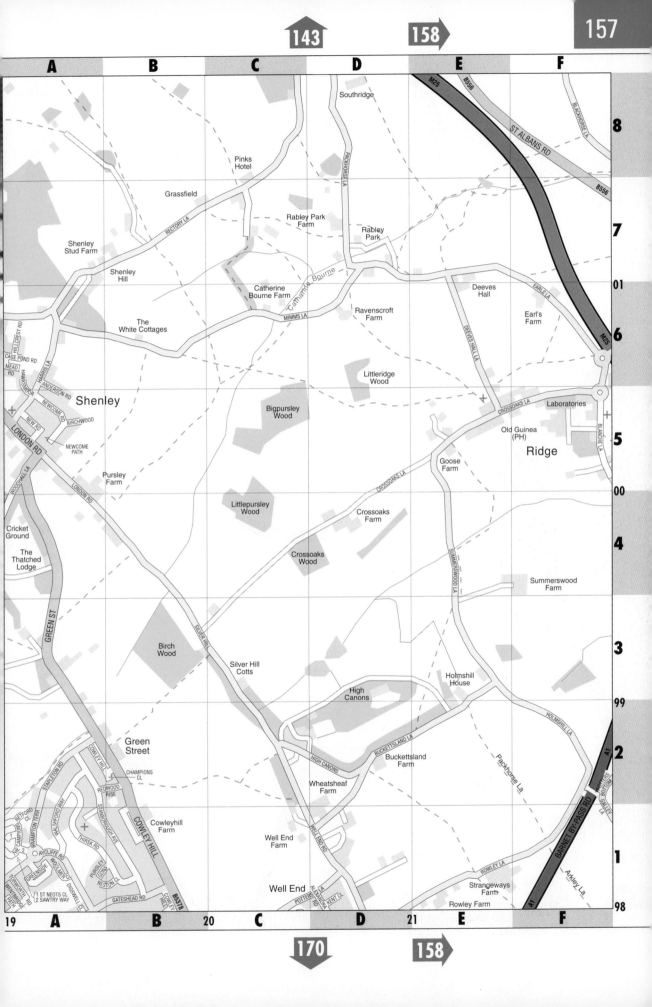

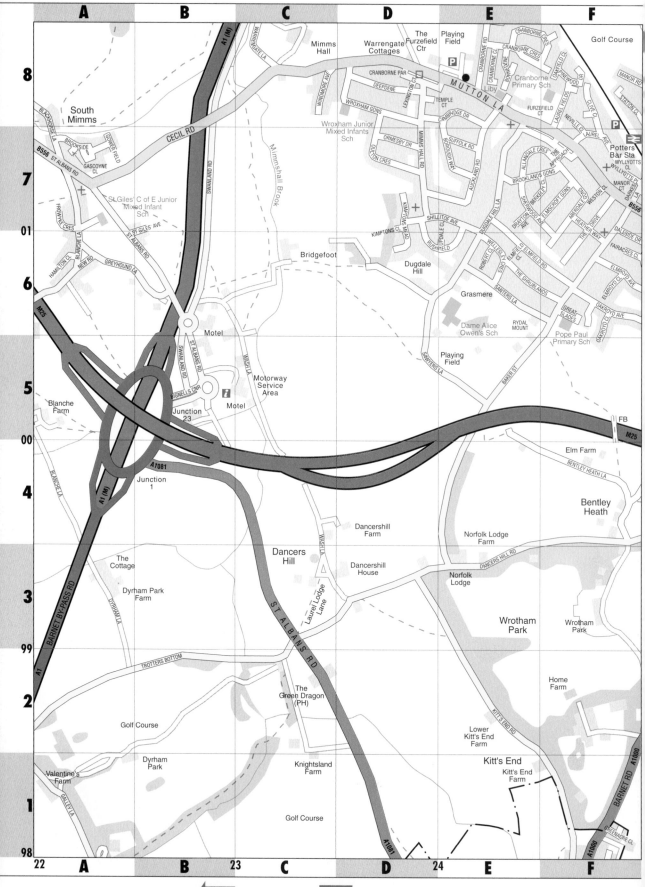

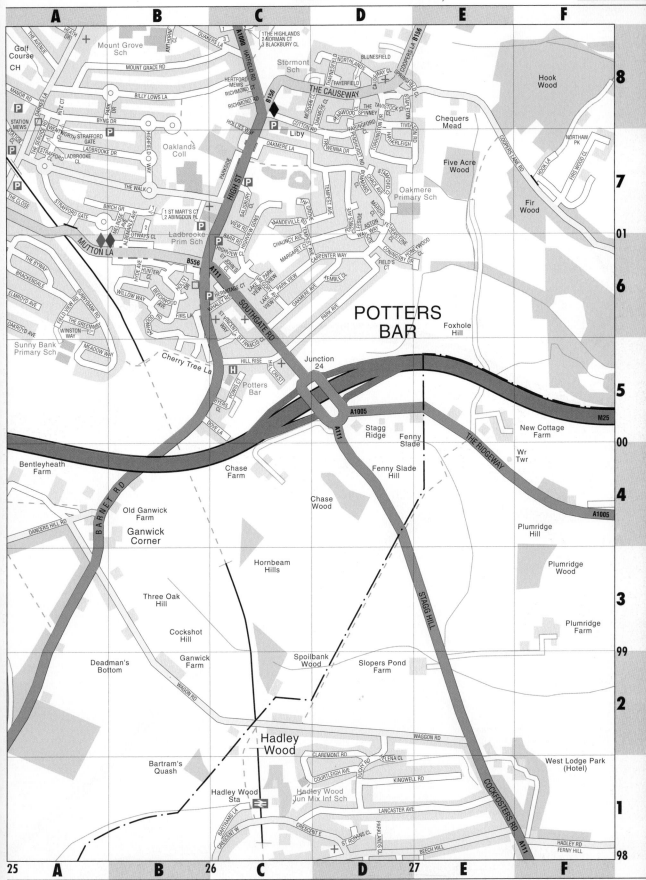

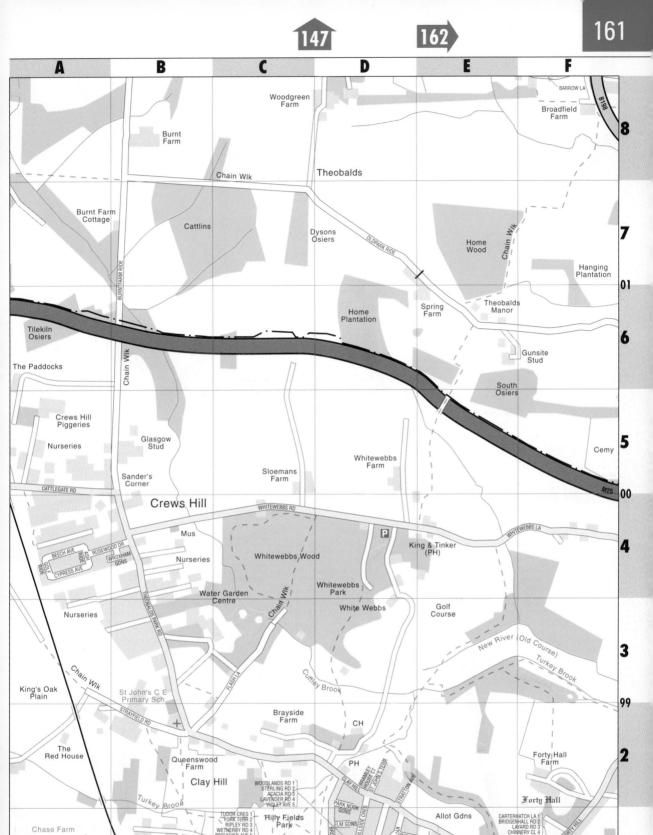

BARROW LA

B198

8

Woodgreen
Farm

Broadfield
Farm

Burnt
Farm

Chain Wlk

Theobalds

7

Burnt Farm
Cottage

Cattlins

Dysons
Osiers

OLDPARK RIDE

Home
Wood

Chain Wlk

Hanging
Plantation

01

BURNT FARM RIDE

Tilekiln
Osiers

Home
Plantation

Spring
Farm

Theobalds
Manor

6

The Paddocks

Chain Wlk

Gunsite
Stud

Crews Hill
Piggeries

Glasgow
Stud

South
Osiers

Nurseries

Sander's
Corner

Sloemans
Farm

Whitewebbs
Farm

Cemy

5

00

CATTLEGATE RD

Crews Hill

WHITEWEBBS RD

M25

Mus

WHITEWEBBS LA

Nurseries

BEECH AVE
ASH RIDE
ROSEWOOD DR
WROXHAM GDNS
CYPRESS AVE
GOLF RIDE

Whitewebbs Wood

P

King & Tinker
(PH)

4

Nurseries

THEOBALDS PARK RD

Water Garden
Centre

Chain Wlk

Whitewebbs
Park

White Webbs

Golf
Course

New River (Old Course)

Turkey Brook

3

FLASH LA

King's Oak
Plain

Chain Wlk

Cuffley Brook

99

STRAYFIELD RD

St John's C E
Primary Sch

Brayside
Farm

CH

The
Red House

Queenswood
Farm

PH

Forty Hall
Farm

2

Clay Hill

WOODLANDS RD 1
STERLING RD 2
ACACIA RD 3
LAVENDER RD 4
VIOLET AVE 5

PARK NOOK
GDNS

CLAY HILL
BRAMLEY HOUSE CT
ST JOHN'S TERR

STRATTON AVE

Allot Gdns

Forty Hall

CARTERHATCH LA 1
BRIDGENHALL RD 2
LAYARD RD 3
CHINNERY CL 4
DOWLAND HOUSE 5

FORTY HILL

Turkey Brook

ELM GDNS

HILLSIDE CRES

BROWNING RD

KENILWORTH CRES

Worcesters
Primary Sch

GOAT LA

Chase Farm

TUDOR CRES 1
YORK TERR 2
RIPLEY RD 3
WETHERBY RD 4
BRIGADIER AVE 5

Hilly Fields
Park

COOK'S HOLE RD

PHIPPS HATCH LA

ST LUKE'S AVE

MORLEY HILL

BIRKBECK RD

MYRTLE GR

CONWAY GDNS

HENRY
BURNHAM CL
PORTLAND DR

PH

ST GEORGE'S RD

RUSSELL RD

1

SPRING COURT RD

H

THE RIDGEWAY

Cemy

RENDLESHAM RD

LAKESIDE GDNS

LIME TREE WLK

CEDAR RD

BLOSSOM

CHANTRY

CEDAR RD

BRIGADIER HILL

GLOUCESTER RD

GREEN

PARK RD

BRODIE RD

GLENVILLE AVE

MERTON RD

HAWTHORN GR

Lavender
Sch

Enfield Chase
Lower Sch

BAKER'S

RIDLER RD

MYDDELTON
ADELAIDE CL

HALLSIDE RD
OLD FORGE

CARMULT RD

98

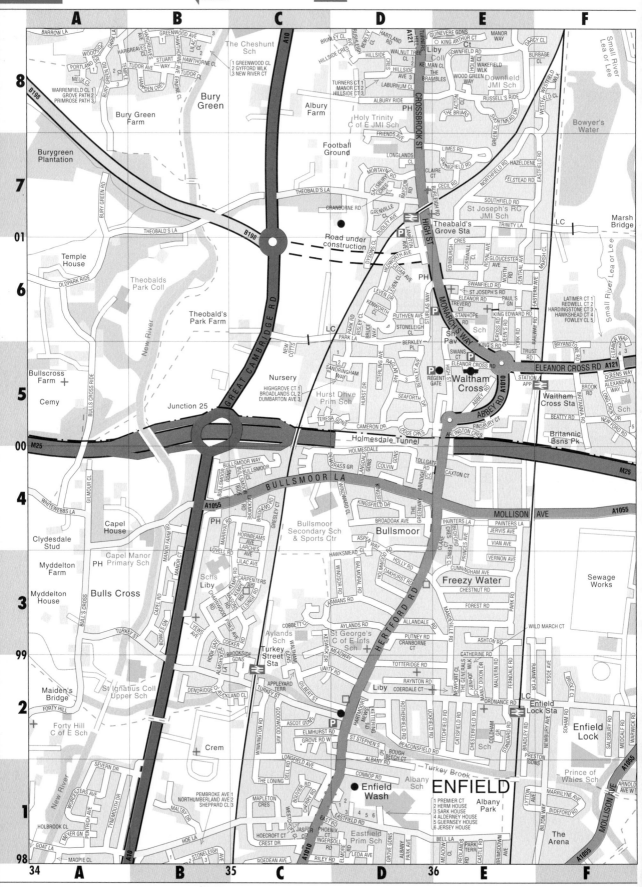

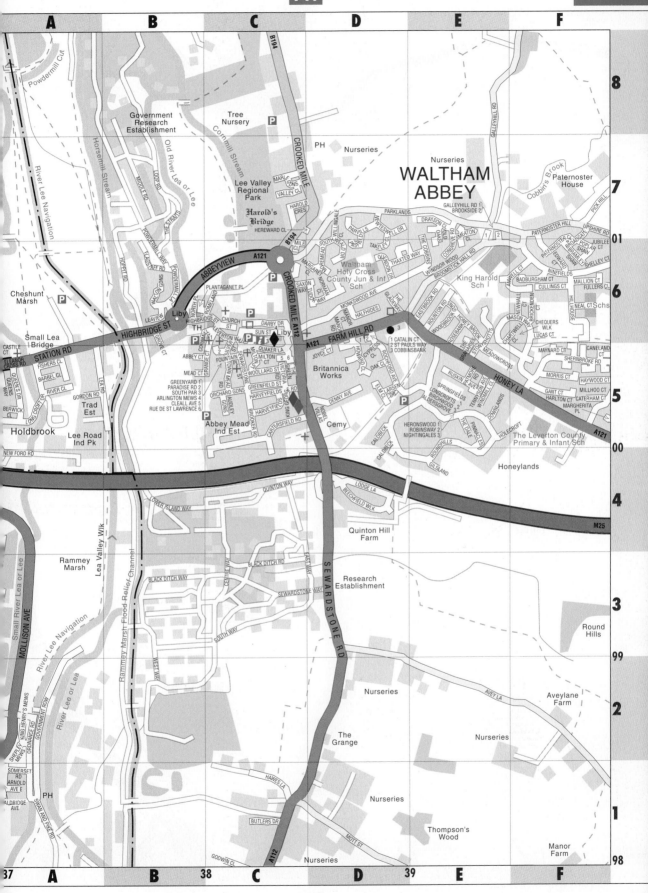

WALTHAM ABBEY

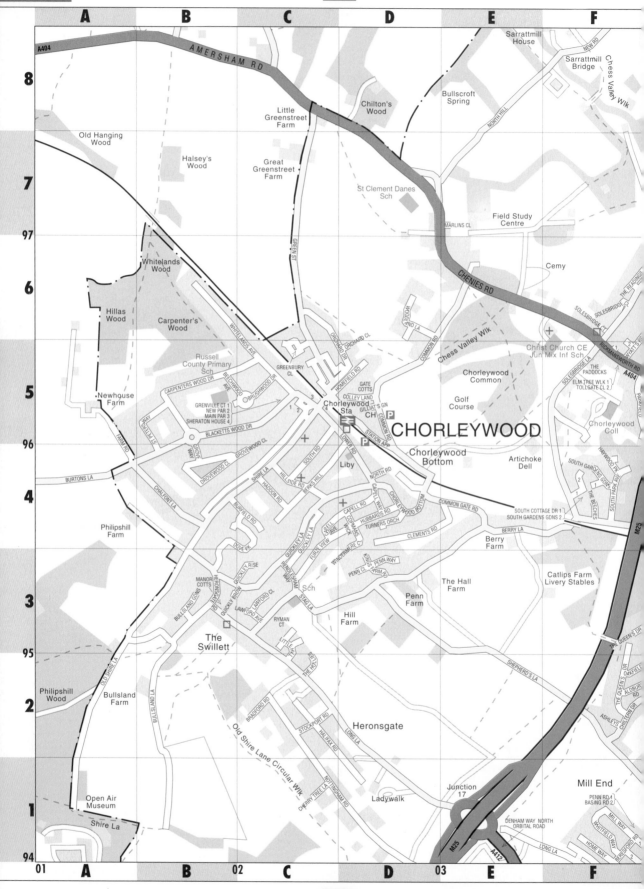

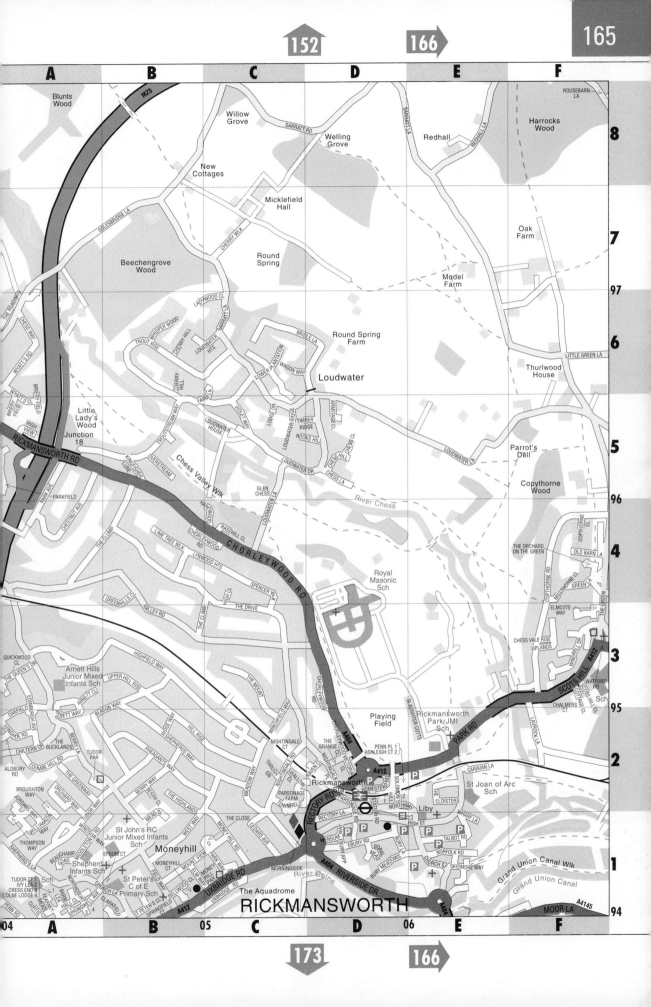

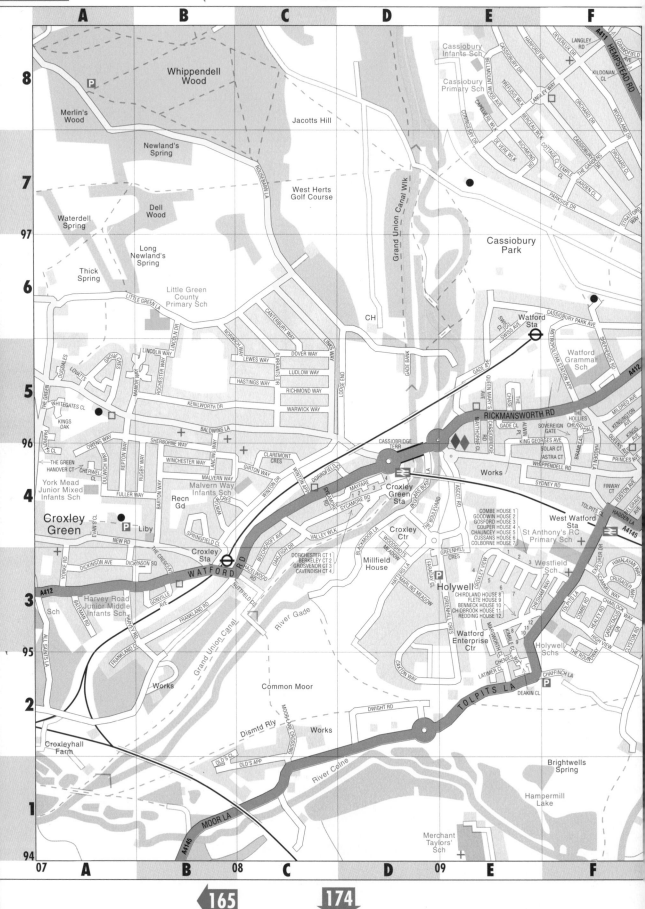

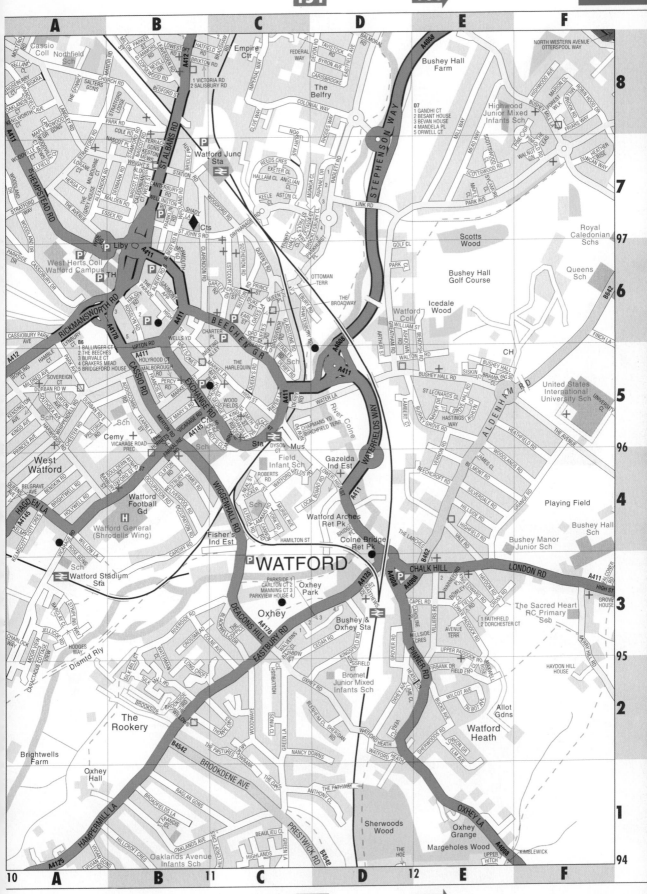

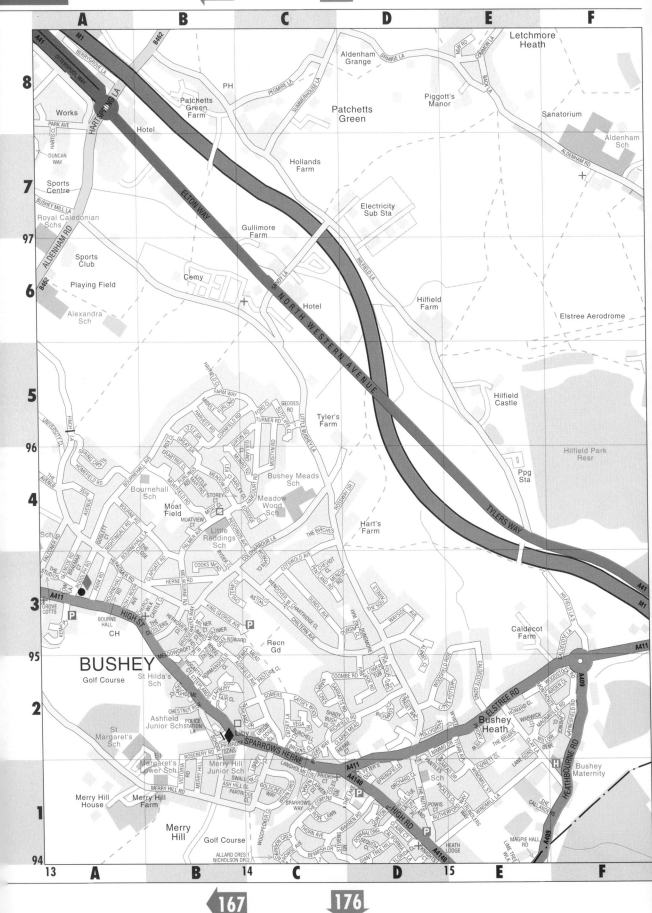

169
157

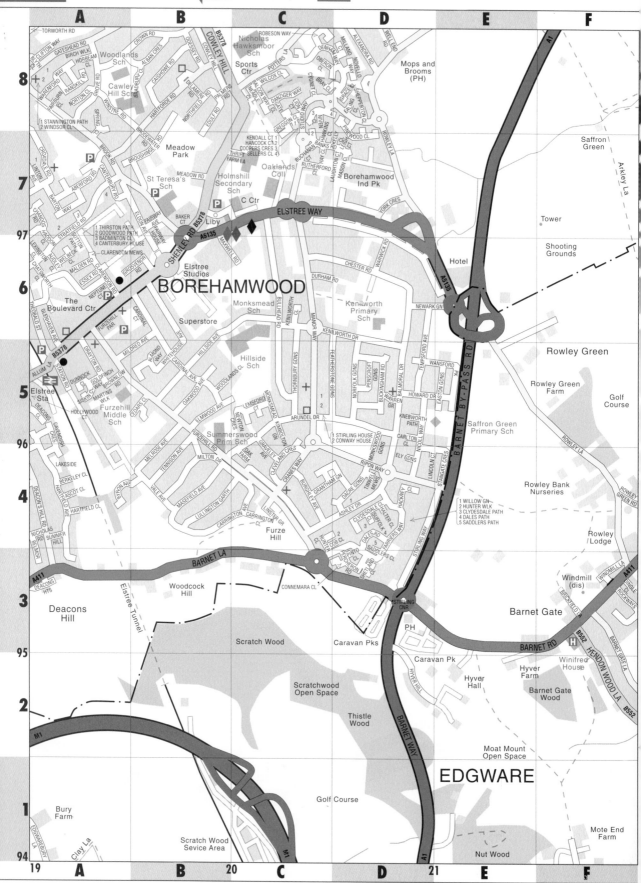

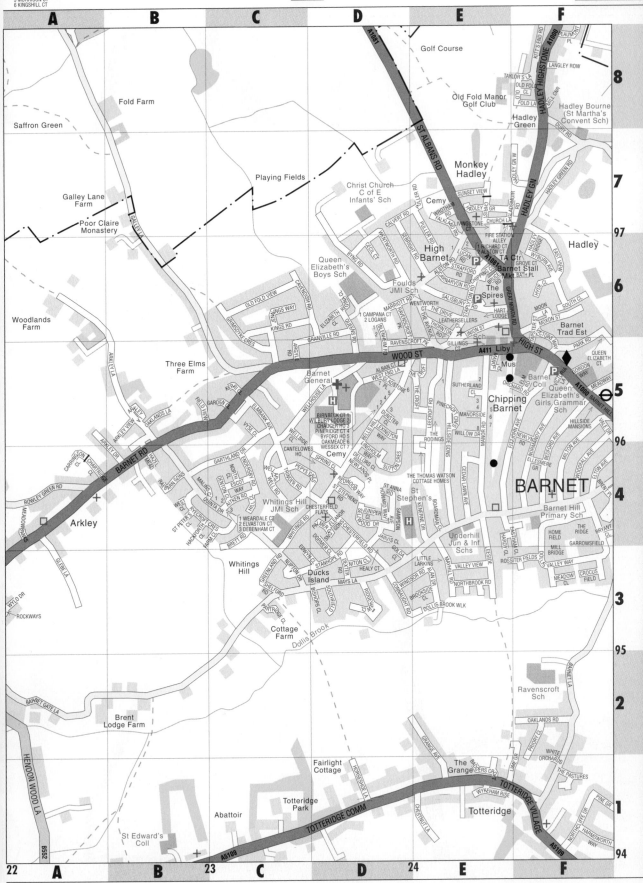

E5
1 HERTSWOOD CT   7 BARONSMERE CT
2 SUNBURY CT   8 CHARTWELL CT
3 MERIDEN HO
4 NORFOLK CT
5 MORRISON CT
6 KINGSHILL CT

Map labels (reading across the map):

Golf Course

Old Fold Manor Golf Club

Hadley Bourne (St Martha's Convent Sch)

Langley Row

Fold Farm

Saffron Green

Monkey Hadley

Hadley Green

Hadley

Playing Fields

Christ Church C of E Infants' Sch

Cemy

High Barnet

Fire Station Alley

TA Ctr

Barnet Stall Mkt

Galley Lane Farm

Poor Claire Monastery

Queen Elizabeth's Boys Sch

Foulds JMI Sch

The Spires

Barnet Trad Est

Woodlands Farm

Old Fold View

Kings Way

Kings Rd

1 CAMPANA CT
2 LOGANS

Leathersellers

Barnet Coll

Queen Elizabeth Ct

Three Elms Farm

Granville Rd

WOOD ST

Barnet General

Chipping Barnet

Queen Elizabeth's Girls Grammar Sch

Hillside Mansions

BARNET

Barnet RD

Arkley

BIRNBECK CT 1
WILBURY LODGE 2
CHAUCER HO 3
PINERIDGE CT 4
BYFORD HO 5
OAKMEADE 6
WESSEX CT 7

Cemy

The Thomas Watson Cottage Homes

St Stephen's

Barnet Hill Primary Sch

Whitings Hill JMI Sch

1 WEARDALE CT
2 ELVASTON CT
3 DEBENHAM CT

Chesterfield Flats

Underhill Jun & Inf Schs

Home Field

The Ridge

Garrowsfield

Mill Bridge

Whitings Hill

Ducks Island

Little Larkins

Valley View

Rossiter Fields

Valley Way

Meadow Cl

Crocus Field

Cottage Farm

Dollis Brook

Dollis Brook Wlk

Ravenscroft Sch

Rockways

Brent Lodge Farm

Oaklands Rd

White Orchard

The Pastures

Fairlight Cottage

The Grange

Totteridge

Totteridge Village

Hendon Wood La

Abattoir

Totteridge Park

Totteridge Comm

Wykeham Rise

St Edward's Coll

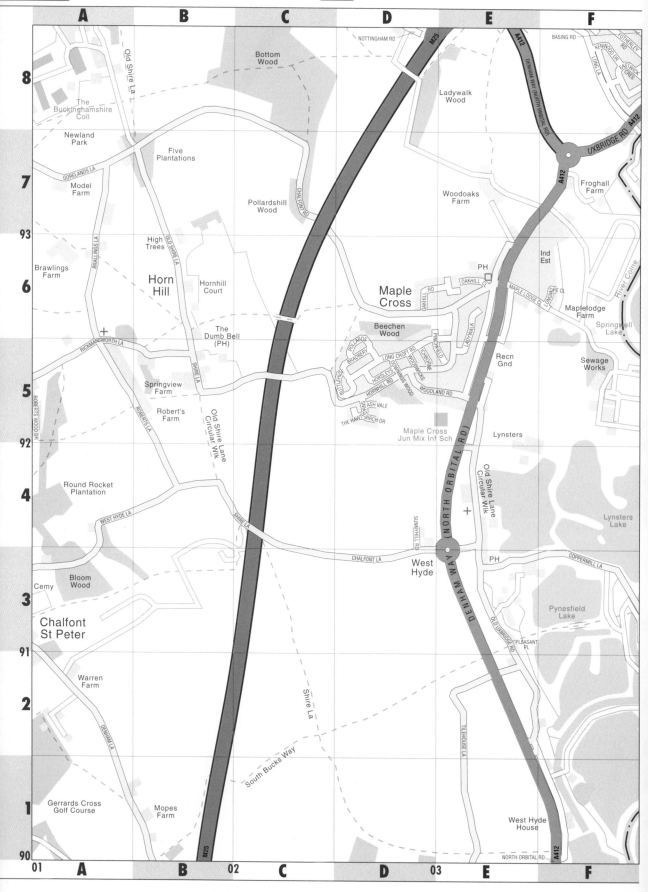

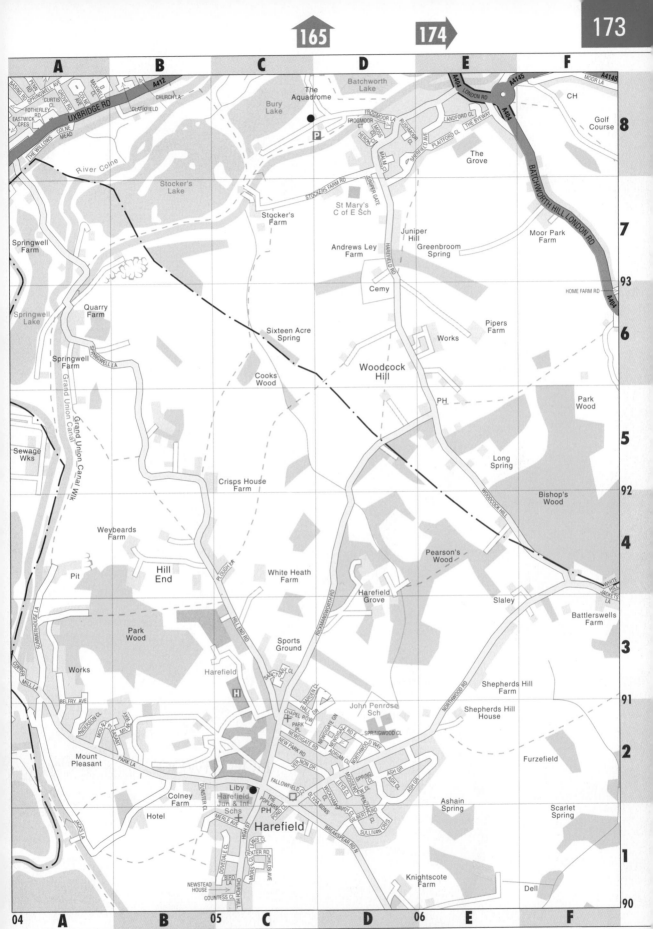

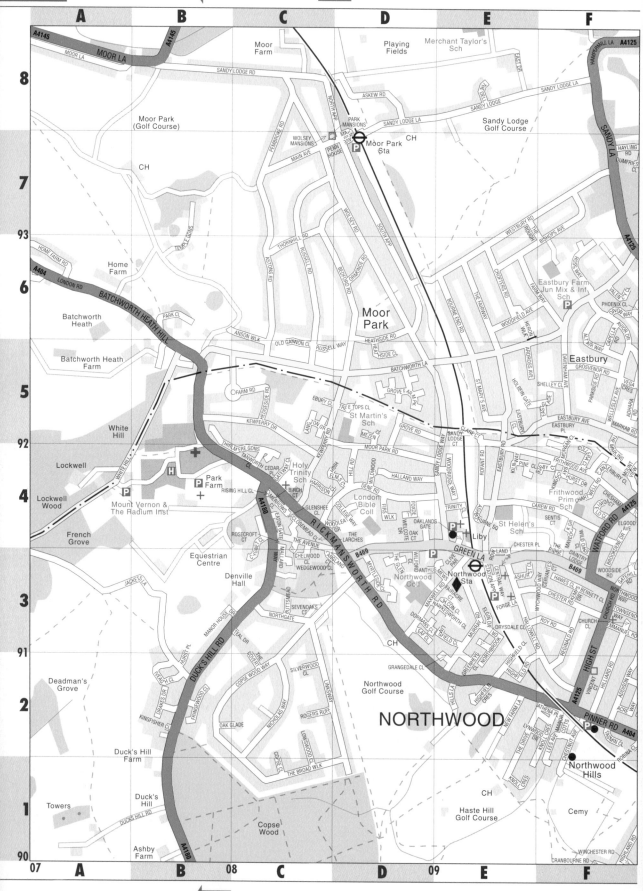

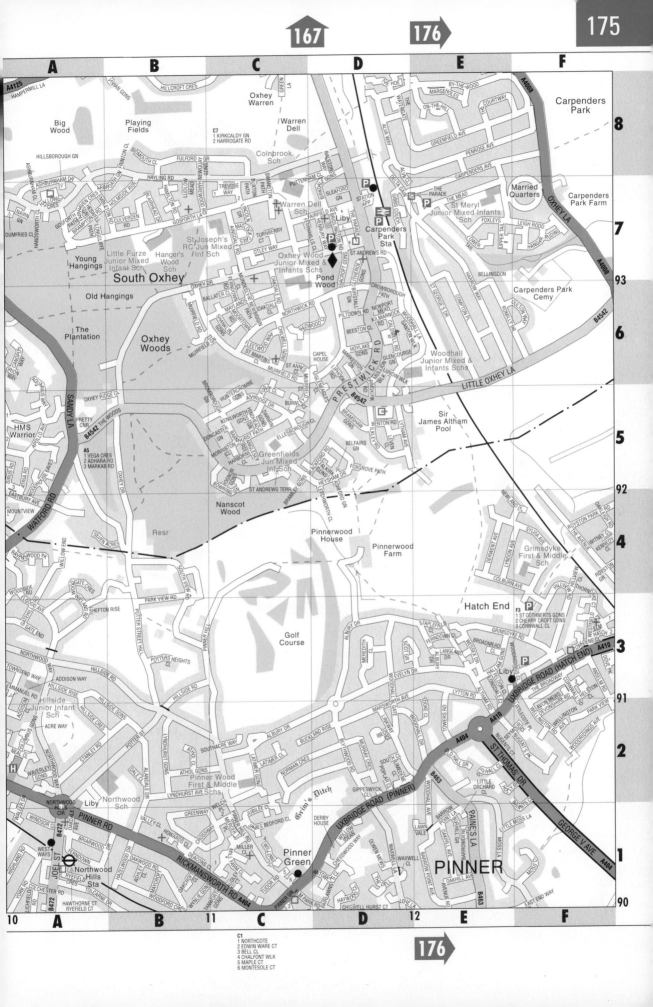

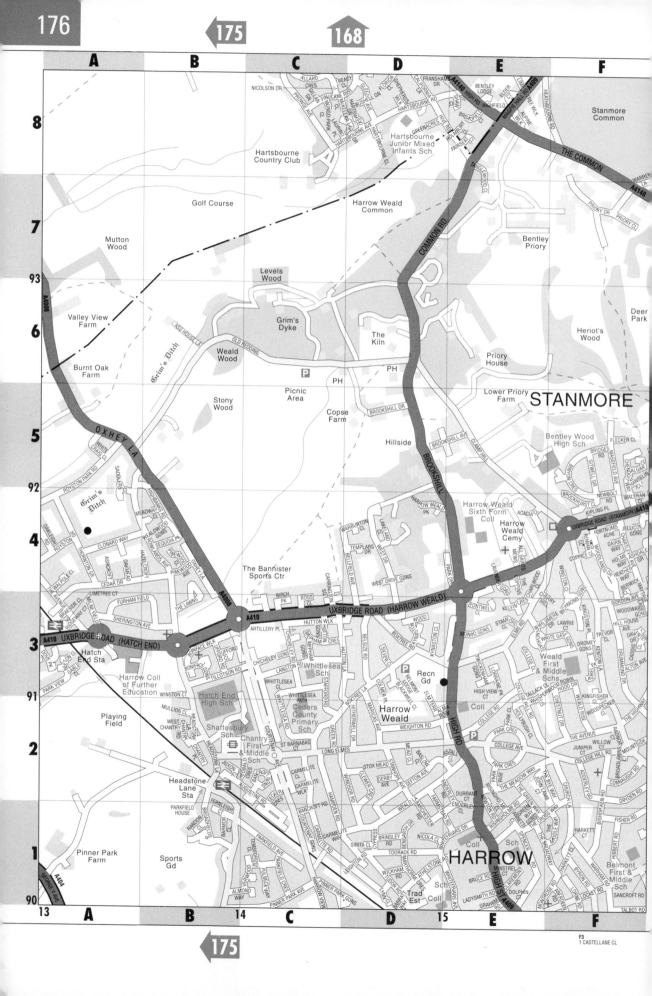

A · B · C · D · E · F

8
7
93
6
5
92
4
3
91
2
1
90

NICOLSON DR
ALLARO CRES
TREACY
GLEESON AV
FLORIDA GDNS
SHEPHERDS LA
FRANSHAMS DR
BENTLEY LODGE
ELDER CL
HIGHFIELD
Stanmore Common

HUCKLEBERRY
HOUSEHILL
MAXFELDA
HARTSBOURNE AVE
HARTSBOURNE RD
MAPPLE HALL RD
TREE WLK
ALPINE WLK
WARREN LA

Hartsbourne Country Club
Hartsbourne Junior Mixed Infants Sch
FAIRSEAT CL
MOLESWORTH

Golf Course
Harrow Weald Common
THE COMMON
A4140

PRIORY DR
PRIORY CL

Mutton Wood
Bentley Priory
Deer Park
Heriot's Wood

Levels Wood
Valley View Farm
Grim's Dyke
The Kiln
PH
Priory House
Lower Priory Farm
STANMORE

Burnt Oak Farm
Weald Wood
OLD REDDING
PH
P
Picnic Area
Copse Farm
BROOKSHILL DR

OXHEY LA
Stony Wood
Hillside
Bentley Wood High Sch
FLECKER CL

WHITE CRAIG CL
ROYSTON PARK RD
SADDLERS
Grim's Ditch
HIGHBANKS RD
WEALDWOOD GDNS
SEQUOIA CL
PINEWOOD AVE
CLONARD WAY
HARROW WEALD PK
Harrow Weald Sixth Form Coll
ACACIA
BROOKSHILL
BROOKSHILL AVE
CLAMP HILL
Harrow Weald Cemy
UXBRIDGE ROAD (STANMORE) A409

The Bannister Sports Ctr
WARBURTON CL
LAKE LAND
TEMPLARS DR
WEST DR
BELLFIELD AVE
WEST DRIVE GDNS
CARRINGTON SQ
BIRCH PK
ROSS CL
UXBRIDGE ROAD (HARROW WEALD)

A4008
A410

UXBRIDGE ROAD (HATCH END)
Hatch End Sta
Harrow Coll of Further Education
ARTILLERY PL
HUTTON WLK
Whittlesea Sch
Recn Gd
P
Weald First Middle Schs

Playing Field
Hatch End High Sch
Shaftesbury Sch
Chantry First & Middle Sch
Cedars County Primary Sch
Harrow Weald
Coll
P
College Ave

Headstone Lane Sta
Parkfield House
Carmelite Wlk

Pinner Park Farm
Sports Gd
HIGH ST A409
HARROW
Belmont First & Middle Sch

A404
GEORGE V AVE

13 · 14 · 15

A · B · C · D · E · F

175

F3
1 CASTELLANE CL

EXPLANATION OF THE STREET INDEX REFERENCE SYSTEM

Street names are listed alphabetically and show the locality, the Post Office Postcode District, the page number and a reference to the square in which the name falls on the map page.

Example: Peterlee Ct. Heml H HP2....................................124 F7 2

Peterlee Ct   This is the full street name, which may have been abbreviated on the map.

Heml H   This is the abbreviation for the town, village or locality in which the street falls.

HP2   This is the Post Office Postcode District for the street name.

124   This is the page number of the map on which the street name appears.

F7   The letter and figure indicate the square on the map in which the centre of the street falls. The square can be found at the junction of the vertical column carrying the appropriate letter and the horizontal row carrying the appropriate figure.

2   In congested areas numbers may have been used to indicate the location of a street. In certain circumstances, the number used to represent a street will follow the reference in the gazetteer entry.

ABBREVIATIONS USED IN THE INDEX
Road Names

Approach .... App	Corner .... Cnr	Grove .... Gr	Promenade .... Prom
Arcade .... Arc	Cottages .... Cotts	Heights .... Hts	Retail Park .... Ret Pk
Avenue .... Ave	Court .... Ct	Industrial Estate .... Ind Est	Road .... Rd
Boulevard .... Bvd	Courtyard .... Ctyd	Interchange .... Intc	Roundabout .... Rdbt
Buildings .... Bldgs	Crescent .... Cres	Junction .... Junc	South .... S
Business Park .... Bsns Pk	Drive .... Dr	Lane .... La	Square .... Sq
Business Centre .... Bsns Ctr	Drove .... Dro	North .... N	Stairs .... Strs
Bungalows .... Bglws	East .... E	Orchard .... Orch	Steps .... Stps
Causeway .... Cswy	Embankment .... Emb	Parade .... Par	Street,Saint .... St
Centre .... Ctr	Esplanade .... Espl	Park .... Pk	Terrace .... Terr
Circle .... Circ	Estate .... Est	Passage .... Pas	Trading Estate .... Trad Est
Circus .... Cir	Gardens .... Gdns	Place .... Pl	Walk .... Wlk
Close Cl	Green .... Gn	Precinct .... Prec	West .... W
Common .... Comm			Yard .... Yd

Key to abbreviations of Town, Village and Rural locality names used in the index of street names.

Abbots Langley	Abb L	153	F7	Crews Hill	Cre H	161	B4	Kensworth Common . Ken Co	82	E8	Rushden	Rus	25	F3
Albury	Alb	57	A6	Croxley Green	Cro Gr	166	A4	Kimpton	Kim	66	C1	Sacombe	Sac	71	E3
Aldbury	Ald	101	C5	Cuffley	Cuf	146	E3	Kings Langley	Kin L	139	A1	Sandon	San	15	B1
Anstey	Ans	29	B6	Dagnall	Dagn	81	C6	Kings Walden	Kin Wd	48	A3	Sandridge	Sand	108	C1
Ardeley	Ard	38	F3	Dane End	Dan En	71	F8	Knebworth	Kneb	69	A5	Sarratt	Sar	152	A4
Arlesey	Arl	11	B5	Datchworth	Dat	69	E2	Kneesworth	Knee	2	A5	Sawbridgeworth	Saw	97	C2
Ashley Green	Ash Gr	136	A7	Dunstable	Dun	44	A2	Langley	Lan	49	F1	Sheering	Sheer	98	D1
Ashwell	Ashw	4	D3	Dunton	Dunt	1	A5	Langley (Essex)	Lang	18	F2	Shenley	Shen	157	A5
Aspenden	Asp	40	D5	Eastwick	East	117	A4	Latimer	Lat	150	E3	Shillington	Shill	19	E8
Aston	Ast	51	E2	Edgware	Edg	170	E1	Letchworth	Letw	22	F7	South Oxhey	Sth Ox	175	B7
Aston Clinton	Ast Cl	99	A3	Edworth	Edw	3	A6	Lilley	Lily	32	D2	St Albans	St Alb	127	F4
Ayot St Lawrence	A St L	88	B6	Elstree	Elst	169	E3	Little Berkhamsted .. L Berk	132	C4	St Ippolitts	St Ipp	35	B3
Ayot St Peter	A St P	88	F3	Enfield	Enf	162	E1	Little Chalfont	L Chal	150	B1	St Leonards	St Le	119	E3
Baldock	Bal	23	E8	Essendon	Ess	131	F6	Little Gaddesden	L Gad	102	D7	Standon	Stand	55	E1
Barkway	Bark	17	D4	Farnham	Far	58	D6	Little Hadham	L Had	57	C2	Stanmore	Stan	176	F5
Barley	Bar	8	F1	Felden	Fel	138	A8	Little Hallingbury	L Hal	98	D7	Stanstead Abbotts ..... Sta Ab	115	F4
Barnet	Barn	171	F4	Flamstead	Fla	84	B1	Little Wymondley	L Wym	35	E3	Stanstead Mountfitchet. Sta M	59	C7
Bassingbourn	Bas	6	F8	Flaunden	Flau	151	A6	London Colney	Lon C	142	E5	Stapleford	Stap	92	A7
Bayford	Bay	132	F6	Furneux Pelham	Fur P	43	A5	Long Marston	Lon M	79	B3	Steeple Morden	Ste Mo	5	B8
Benington	Ben	52	E4	Goff's Oak	Gofs O	147	D3	Lower Nazeing	Lo Naz	149	D8	Stevenage	Stev	50	D8
Berden	Berd	43	F7	Graveley	Gra	36	C4	Lower Stondon	L Ston	10	A3	Stocking Pelham	Sto P	43	E7
Berkhamsted	Berk	122	C6	Great Amwell	Gt Am	114	F5	Luton	Luton	45	C3	Stotfold	Stot	11	E7
Birchanger	Birhr	59	E2	Great Chishill	Gt Ch	9	F2	Maple Cross	Map Cr	172	D6	Streatley	Str	31	A5
Bishop's Stortford	Bis St	76	D7	Great Gaddesden	Gt Gd	103	D3	Markyate	Mark	83	F5	Studham	Stu	82	C4
Borehamwood	Bor	170	B6	Great Hallingbury	Gt Ha	77	E4	Marsworth	Mars	80	A1	Tewin	Tewin	90	E2
Botley	Bot	136	A1	Great Hormead	Gt Ho	42	B8	Meesden	Mee	29	F6	Therfield	Ther	15	F7
Bovingdon	Bov	137	B3	Great Munden	Gt Mu	54	C5	Melbourn	Melb	2	F7	Thundridge	Thun	93	E7
Bramfield	Bram	91	C4	Great Offley	Gt Of	33	D2	Mentmore	Men	61	D4	Tonwell	Ton	92	F7
Braughing	Brag	55	F6	Great Wymondley	Gt Wy	35	F6	Moor Park	Mo Pk	174	D6	Tring	Tri	100	D3
Breachwood Green .... Bre Gr	47	E1	Guilden Morden	Gu M	1	F5	Much Hadham	Muc H	74	F3	Walkern	Walk	38	B1
Brent Pelham	Bre P	30	A2	Hadley Wood	Had W	159	C2	New Mill End	Nwml E	64	D1	Wallington	Wal	25	D8
Brickendon	Bric	133	C4	Hammond Street ..... Ham St	147	D5	Newgate Street	New St	146	C7	Waltham Abbey	Wa Aby	163	E7
Bricket Wood	Bri Wd	140	F1	Harefield	Hare	173	C1	Newnham	Newn	12	F1	Ware	Ware	93	F2
Brookmans Park	Bro Pk	144	F5	Harlow	Harl	117	E1	Northaw	Nort	145	F1	Wareside	Wars	94	E4
Buckland	Buck	27	C3	Harpenden	Harp	86	B2	Northchurch	Nthch	121	D6	Watford	Watf	167	C3
Buntingford	Bun	40	F7	Harrow	Har	176	E1	Northwood	Norwd	174	E2	Watton at Stone	Wat St	70	D4
Bushey	Bus	168	A2	Hatfield	Hat	130	B8	Nuthampstead	Nut	18	B2	Welham Green	Wel Gr	144	C2
Bygrave	Byg	13	C5	Hatfield Heath	Hatf H	98	F4	Odsey	Odsey	5	C1	Welwyn	Welw	89	B4
Caddington	Cad	62	E4	Hemel Hempstead .... Heml H	124	E1	Park Street	Pk St	141	D5	Welwyn Garden City.Wel G C	110	E7
Chalfont St Peter .... C St P	172	A3	Henlow	Henlw	10	D8	Pinner	Pnr	175	E1	Westmill	West	40	F3
Cheddington	Ched	80	A8	Hertford	Hert	113	C5	Pirton	Pirt	20	C4	Weston	Wes	24	C1
Chenies	Chen	151	B2	Hertford Heath	Hert H	114	B3	Pitstone	Pit	80	D4	Wheathampstead	Whea	108	C5
Cheshunt	Ches	148	C1	Hertingfordbury	Hertng	112	F5	Potten End	Pot En	123	C7	Whipsnade	Whip	82	A8
Chipperfield	Chipf	152	B8	Hexton	Hex	19	B2	Potters Bar	Pot B	159	D6	Whitwell	Whit	66	E6
Chiswellgreen	Chis	141	A5	High Wych	H Wy	97	B1	Preston	Pres	48	D6	Widford	Widf	95	E4
Cholesbury	Chol	120	C2	Hinxworth	Hin	3	D6	Radlett	Radl	156	B5	Wigginton	Wigg	100	D1
Chorleywood	Chor	164	E5	Hitchin	Hit	34	E8	Redbourn	Red	106	B6	Wilstone	Wils	79	D1
Clavering	Clav	30	E4	Hoddesdon	Hod	135	B5	Reed	Reed	16	F5	Wingrave	Wing	60	C3
Clothall	Clo	24	E4	Holwell	Hol	21	B7	Rickmansworth	Ric	165	D1	Wyddial	Wyd	28	B3
Codicote	Cod	67	E1	Hunsdon	Hun	95	D1	Ridge	Ridge	157	F5				
Colney Heath	Coln H	143	D8	Ickleford	Ick	21	E4	Roydon	Roy	116	C1				
Cottered	Cotrd	39	C7	Kelshall	Kel	15	D5	Royston	Royst	7	C5				

Bengarth Dr. Har HA3 ... 176 D1
Bengeo Inf Sch. Hert ... 92 C1
Bengeo Jun Sch. Hert ... 92 C1
Bengeo Meadows. Hert SG14 ... 92 C1
Bengeo Mews. Hert SG14 ... 92 C1
Bengeo St. Hert SG14 ... 113 C8
Benhooks Ave. Bis St CM23 ... 76 E5
Benhooks Pl. Bis St CM23 ... 76 E5
Benington Cl. Luton LU2 ... 45 E5
Benington Jun Mix Inf Sch. Ben ... 52 D4
Benington Rd. Ast SG2 ... 51 F2
Benington Rd. Ben SG2 ... 52 A7
Bennett Cl. Norwd HA6 ... 174 F3
Bennett Cl. Wel G C AL7 ... 110 F2
Bennett Ct. Letw ... 23 A5
Bennetts Cl. Col H AL4 ... 143 D8
Bennetts End Cl. Heml H HP3 ... 124 F1
Bennetts End Hospl. Heml H ... 124 F1
Bennetts End Rd. Heml H HP3 ... 125 A1
Bennettsgate. Heml H HP3 ... 139 A8
Bennick House. Watf WD1 ... 166 E3
Benningfield Rd. Widf SG12 ... 95 D4
Benningfield. Widf SG12 ... 95 D5
Benskin Rd. Watf WD1 ... 167 A4
Benslow La. Hit SG4 ... 35 A7
Benslow Rise. Hit SG4 ... 35 A8
Benson Cl. Luton LU3 ... 44 F7
Benstede. Stev SG2 ... 69 C8
Bentfield Cty Prim Sch. Sta M ... 59 D8
Bentfield End Cswy. Sta M CM24 ... 59 D7
Bentfield Gdns. Sta M CM24 ... 59 D7
Bentfield Green. Sta M CM24 ... 59 D8
Bentfield Rd. Sta M CM24 ... 59 D7
Bentick Way. Cod SG4 ... 67 F2
Bentley Cl. Bis St CM23 ... 76 F5
Bentley Ct. Luton LU4 ... 63 C8
Bentley Heath La. Pot B EN5 ... 158 F4
Bentley Lodge. Bus WD2 ... 176 E8
Bentley Rd. Hert SG14 ... 112 F7
Bentley Wood High Sch. Stan ... 176 F5
Benton Rd. Sth Ox WD1 ... 175 D5
Bentsley Cl. St Alb AL4 ... 128 C7
Berceau Wlk. Watf WD1 ... 166 E8
Berefield. Heml H HP2 ... 124 D5
Beresford Rd. Luton LU4 ... 45 A1
Beresford Rd. Ric WD3 ... 164 F1
Beresford Rd. St Alb AL1 ... 128 C2
Bericot Way. Wel G C AL7 ... 111 D6
Berkeley Cl. Abb L WD5 ... 153 F8
Berkeley Cl. Bor WD6 ... 170 A4
Berkeley Cl. Hit SG5 ... 34 D8 6
Berkeley Cl. Pot B EN6 ... 158 F7
Berkeley Cl. Stev SG2 ... 69 A8
Berkeley Cl. Ware SG12 ... 93 C2
Berkeley Ct. Cro Gr WD3 ... 166 D4
Berkeley Ct. Harp AL5 ... 86 A2
Berkeley. Letw SG6 ... 23 A4
Berkeley Path. Luton LU2 ... 63 E8 3
Berkeley Sq. Heml H HP2 ... 105 C1
Berkhamsted La. L Berk AL9 ... 132 B3
Berkhamsted Rd. Heml H HP1 ... 123 E5
Berkhamsted Sch. Berk ... 122 C4
Berkhamsted Sch for Girls. Berk ... 122 B3
Berkhamsted Sta. Berk ... 122 C5
Berkley Ave. Ches EN8 ... 162 D5
Berkley Cl. St Alb AL4 ... 128 C7
Berkley Ct. Berk HP4 ... 122 C4
Berkley Pl. Ches EN8 ... 162 D5
Berks Hill. Chor WD3 ... 164 C4
Bernard St. St Alb AL3 ... 127 D4
Bernard's Heath Inf Sch. St Alb ... 127 F5
Berners Dr. St Alb AL1 ... 141 E8
Berners Way. Hod EN10 ... 148 F8
Bernhardt Cres. Stev SG2 ... 51 C6
Berries The. St Alb AL4 ... 128 A7
Berrow Cl. Luton LU2 ... 46 E2 2
Berry Ave. Watf WD2 ... 154 B3
Berry Cl. Ric WD3 ... 165 B2
Berry Grove La. Bus WD2 ... 154 E1
Berry La. Ric WD3 ... 165 A2
Berry Leys. Luton LU3 ... 44 E7
Berry Way. Ric WD3 ... 165 B2
Berryfield. Ched LU7 ... 79 F7
Berrygrove La. Bus WD2 ... 168 A8
Berrymead. Heml H HP2 ... 124 F5
Bertram House. Stev SG1 ... 50 E6 4
Berwick Cl. Ches EN8 ... 163 A5
Berwick Cl. Har HA7 ... 176 F4
Berwick Rd. Bor WD6 ... 156 F1
Besant House. Watf WD2 ... 167 D7 2
Besford Cl. Luton LU2 ... 46 E2 1
Bessemer Cl. Hit SG5 ... 21 E2
Bessemer Dr. Stev SG1 ... 50 B4
Bessemer Rd. Wel G C AL7,AL8 ... 89 E2
Bethune Cl. Luton LU1 ... 63 B6
Bethune Ct. Luton LU1 ... 63 B6
Betjeman Cl. Ches EN7 ... 148 A3
Betjeman Way. Heml H HP1 ... 124 B4
Betony Vale. Royst SG8 ... 7 E5
Bettespol Meadows. Red AL3 ... 106 A6
Betty's La. Tri HP23 ... 100 A4
Bevan Cl. Heml H HP3 ... 124 E1
Bevan House. Watf WD2 ... 167 D7 3
Beverley Cl. Royst SG8 ... 7 B8
Beverley Gdns. Ches EN7 ... 148 A1
Beverley Gdns. St Alb AL4 ... 128 D7
Beverley Gdns. Wel G C AL7 ... 111 C6
Beverley Rd. Luton LU4 ... 44 F1
Beverley Rd. Luton LU4 ... 45 A1
Beverley Rd. Stev SG1 ... 37 B2
Beverly Cl. Hod EN10 ... 134 E2
Bevil Ct. Hod EN11 ... 115 A1
Bewdley Cl. Harp AL5 ... 107 D6
Bewley Cl. Ches EN8 ... 162 D8
Bexhill Rd. Luton LU2 ... 46 D2
Beyers Gdns. Hod EN11 ... 115 A1
Beyers Prospect. Hod EN11 ... 115 A1
Beyers Ride. Hod EN11 ... 115 A1
Bibbs Hall La. Kim SG4 ... 87 E6
Biddenham Turn. Watf WD2 ... 154 C4
Bideford Gdns. Luton LU3 ... 45 D4
Bideford Rd. Enf EN3 ... 162 F1
Bidwell Cl. Letw SG6 ... 23 B5
Biggin Hill. Wyd SG9 ... 28 D7
Biggin La. Hit SG5 ... 34 F7
Bignells Cnr. Pot B EN6 ... 158 B5
Billet La. Berk HP4 ... 122 A6
Billy Lows La. Pot B EN6 ... 159 B8
Bilton Rd. Hit SG4 ... 21 F2
Bilton Way. Enf EN3 ... 162 F1
Bingen Rd. Hit SG5 ... 21 C1
Bingley Rd. Hod EN11 ... 135 C6
Binham Cl. Luton LU2 ... 45 D7
Binyon Cres. Stan HA7 ... 176 F5
Birch Copse. Bri Wd AL2 ... 140 E1
Birch Ct. Norwd HA6 ... 174 C4
Birch Dr. Hat AL10 ... 130 A4
Birch Dr. Map Cr WD3 ... 172 D5
Birch Gn. Heml H HP1 ... 123 F5
Birch Gn. Hertng SG14 ... 112 C4
Birch Gr. Pot B EN6 ... 159 B7
Birch Gr. Welw AL6 ... 89 E8
Birch La. Flau HP3 ... 151 B7
Birch Leys. Heml H HP2 ... 125 C8
Birch Link. Luton LU4 ... 45 C1
Birch Pk. Stan HA3 ... 176 C3
Birch Rd. Nthch HP4 ... 121 D7
Birch Rd. Welw SG3 ... 69 B1
Birch Tree Gr. Bot HP5 ... 136 B1
Birch Tree Wlk. Watf WD1 ... 153 F2
Birch Way. Harp AL5 ... 107 C8
Birch Way. Lon C AL2 ... 142 D4
Birch Wlk. Bor WD6 ... 170 A8
Birchall La. Hertng SG14 ... 111 E4
Birchall Wood. Wel G C AL7 ... 111 C5
Birchalls. Sta M CM24 ... 59 E8
Birchanger C of E Prim Sch. Birhr ... 59 D2
Birchanger Green
Motorway Service Area. Gt Ha ... 77 E7
Birchanger Ind Est. Bis St ... 59 B2
Birchanger La. Birhr CM23 ... 59 D2
Birchen Gr. Luton LU2 ... 45 F3
Bircherley Ct. Hert SG14 ... 113 D6 12
Bircherley Green Ctr The. Hert ... 113 C6 8
Bircherley St. Hert SG14 ... 113 D6
Birches The. Bus WD2 ... 168 C4
Birches The. Cod SG4 ... 89 A8
Birches The. Heml H HP3 ... 137 F8
Birches The. Letw SG6 ... 22 E8
Birchfield Rd. Ches EN8 ... 148 C2
Birchfield Terr. Watf WD1 ... 167 C5
Birchfield. Watf WD1 ... 154 A1
Birchmead Cl. St Alb AL3 ... 127 D6
Birchmead. Watf WD1 ... 153 F1
Birchway. Hat AL10 ... 130 B7
Birchwood Ave. Hat AL10 ... 130 A7
Birchwood. Birhr CM23 ... 59 E2
Birchwood Cl. Hat AL10 ... 130 A7
Birchwood High Sch. Bis St ... 77 C8
Birchwood. Shen WD7 ... 157 A5
Birchwood. Wa Aby EN9 ... 163 E5
Birchwood Way. Chis AL2 ... 141 B3
Bird La. Hare UB9 ... 173 C1
Birdcroft Rd. Wel G C AL8 ... 110 D5
Birdie Way. Hert SG13 ... 114 B7
Birds Cl. Wel G C AL7 ... 111 B4
Birds Hill. Letw SG6 ... 23 A6
Birdsfoot La. Luton LU3 ... 45 B6
Birkbeck Rd. Enf EN2 ... 161 D1
Birkdale Gdns. Sth Ox WD1 ... 175 D7
Birklands La. St Alb AL1 ... 142 B7
Birklands. St Alb AL1 ... 142 B7
Birling Dr. Luton LU2 ... 46 C4
Birnbeck Ct. Barn EN5 ... 171 D5
Birstall Gn. Sth Ox WD1 ... 175 D6
Birtley Croft. Luton LU2 ... 46 E1
Biscot Rd. Luton LU3 ... 45 C2
Bishop Ken Rd. Har HA3 ... 176 F2
Bishop Sq. Hat AL10 ... 129 E5
Bishop Wood Jun Sch. Tri ... 100 A3
Bishop's Ave. Bis St CM23 ... 76 F3
Bishop's Cl. St Alb AL4 ... 128 A7
Bishop's Garth. St Alb AL4 ... 128 A7
Bishop's Hatfield Girls' Sch. Hat ... 130 A5
Bishop's Stortford Bsns Ctr. Bis St ... 77 A6
Bishop's Stortford Coll. Bis St ... 76 E7
Bishop's Stortford Golf Course.
Bis St ... 77 D6
Bishop's Stortford High Sch The.
Bis St ... 76 F4
Bishop's Stortford Sta. Bis St ... 77 A6
Bishops Ave. Bor WD6 ... 169 F4
Bishops Ave. Mo Pk HA6 ... 174 F7
Bishops Cl. Barn EN5 ... 171 D3
Bishops Cl. Hat AL10 ... 129 F5
Bishops' Coll. Ches ... 148 B1
Bishops Field. Ast Cl HP22 ... 99 A4
Bishops Mead. Heml H HP1 ... 124 B1
Bishops Park Way. Bis St CM23 ... 76 F7
Bishops Rd. Tewin AL6 ... 90 E6
Bishops Rise. Hat AL10 ... 129 F1
Bishops Rise. Hat AL10 ... 129 F4
Bishopscote Rd. Luton LU3 ... 45 B3
Biskra. Watf WD1 ... 167 A8
Bisley Cl. Ches EN8 ... 162 D6
Bit The. Wigg HP23 ... 100 D1
Bittern Cl. Stev SG2 ... 51 D2
Bittern Way. Letw SG6 ... 11 E1
Black Boy Wood. Bri Wd AL2 ... 141 A1
Black Cut. St Alb AL1 ... 127 E2
Black Ditch Rd. Wa Aby EN9 ... 163 C3
Black Ditch Way. Wa Aby EN9 ... 163 B3
Black Fan Rd. Wel G C AL7 ... 110 F7
Black Fan Rd. Wel G C AL7 ... 111 B6
Black Lion Ct. Harl CM17 ... 118 C4
Black Lion Hill. Shen WD7 ... 156 F7
Black Swan Ct. Ware SG12 ... 93 D1 1
Black Swan La. Luton LU3 ... 45 A5
Blackberry Mead. Stev SG2 ... 51 D3
Blackbirds La. Radl WD2 ... 155 C5
Blackbury Cl. Pot B EN6 ... 159 C8
Blackbush Spring. Harl CM20 ... 118 A1
Blackbushe. Bis St CM23 ... 59 C1
Blackdale. Ham St EN7 ... 148 A4
Blacketts Wood Dr. Chor WD3 ... 164 B5
Blackford Rd. Sth Ox WD1 ... 175 D5
Blackhorse Cl. Hit SG4 ... 35 A5
Blackhorse La. Hit SG4 ... 35 A5
Blackhorse La. Red AL3 ... 106 A6
Blackhorse La. Ridge AL2 ... 157 F8
Blackhorse Rd. Letw SG6 ... 23 C8
Blackley Cl. Watf WD1 ... 153 F2
Blackmoor La. Watf WD1 ... 166 D4
Blackmore. Letw SG6 ... 23 D3
Blackmore Way. Kim AL4 ... 87 B6
Blacksmith's La. Reed SG8 ... 16 D5
Blacksmith's La. St Alb AL3 ... 127 B3
Blacksmiths Cl. Gt Am SG12 ... 115 A7
Blacksmiths Hill. Ben SG2 ... 52 E4
Blacksmiths Row. Mark AL3 ... 83 E5
Blacksmiths Way. H Wy CM21 ... 97 B1
Blackthorn Cl. St Alb AL4 ... 128 C6
Blackthorn Cl. Watf WD2 ... 154 B7
Blackthorn Dr. Luton LU2 ... 46 C4
Blackthorn Jun Sch. Wel G C ... 111 A5
Blackthorn Rd. Wel G C AL7 ... 111 A5
Blackthorne Cl. Hat AL10 ... 129 F2
Blackwater La. Heml H HP3 ... 125 E1
Blackwell Cl. Har HA3 ... 176 D3
Blackwell Dr. Watf WD1 ... 167 C3
Blackwell Hall La. Lat HP5 ... 150 C6
Blackwell Rd. Kin L WD4 ... 139 A2
Blackwood Ct. Ham St ... 148 A4
Bladon Cl. L Wym SG4 ... 35 F3
Blair Cl. Heml H HP2 ... 105 B1
Blair Cl. Stev SG2 ... 50 F1
Blairhead Dr. Sth Ox WD1 ... 175 B7
Blake Cl. St Alb AL1 ... 142 A8
Blakemere Rd. Wel G C AL8 ... 110 D8
Blakemore End Rd. L Wym SG4 ... 35 D3
Blakeney Dr. Luton LU2 ... 45 C7
Blakeney Ho. Stev SG1 ... 50 A7
Blakeney Rd. Stev SG1 ... 50 A7
Blakes Ct. Saw CM21 ... 97 E2
Blakes Way. Welw AL6 ... 89 C6
Blanche La. Ridge WD6 ... 157 F5
Blandford Ave. Luton LU2 ... 45 D6
Blandford Rd. St Alb AL1 ... 128 A3
Blanes The. Ware SG12 ... 93 C3
Blaydon Rd. Luton LU2 ... 64 A8
Blenheim Cl. Saw CM21 ... 118 C8
Blenheim Cl. Watf WD1 ... 167 D2
Blenheim Cres. Luton LU3 ... 45 C2
Blenheim Ct. Bis St CM23 ... 76 C7
Blenheim Rd. Barn EN5 ... 171 D5
Blenheim Rd. St Alb AL1 ... 127 F4
Blenheim Way. Stev SG2 ... 69 D7
Blenhiem Rd. Abb L WD5 ... 154 A7
Blenkin Cl. St Alb AL3 ... 127 C7
Blind La. Ard SG2 ... 38 F5
Blindman's La. Ches EN8 ... 148 D2
Bloomfield Ave. Luton LU2 ... 46 A1
Bloomfield House. Stev SG1 ... 50 E6 6
Bloomfield Rd. Harp AL5 ... 85 F3
Blossom La. Enf EN2 ... 161 C1
Blue Bridge Rd. Bro Pk AL9 ... 144 E4
Bluebell Cl. Heml H HP1 ... 123 E2
Bluebell Cl. Hert SG13 ... 114 A6
Bluebells. Welw AL6 ... 89 D7
Blueberry Cl. St Alb AL3 ... 127 D7
Bluebridge Ave. Bro Pk AL9 ... 144 F4
Bluecoat Yd. Ware SG12 ... 93 D1
Bluecoats Ave. Hert SG14 ... 113 D6
Bluecoats Ct. Hert SG14 ... 113 D6 15
Bluehouse Hill. St Alb AL3 ... 127 A3
Bluett Rd. Lon C AL2 ... 142 D4
Blundell Cl. St Alb AL3 ... 127 D7
Blundell Rd. Luton LU3 ... 45 A4
Blunesfield. Pot B EN6 ... 159 D8
Blunts La. Bri Wd AL2 ... 140 D5
Blyth Cl. Bor WD6 ... 170 A8
Blyth Cl. Stev SG1 ... 50 A7
Blyth Pl. Luton LU1 ... 63 D6
Blythe Rd. Lo Naz EN11 ... 135 D5
Blythway House. Wel G C AL7 ... 89 F1
Blythway. Wel G C AL7 ... 89 F1
Blythwood Gdns. Sta M CM24 ... 59 D6
Blythwood Rd. Pnr HA5 ... 175 D2
Boardman Cl. Barn EN5 ... 171 E4
Bockings. Walk SG2 ... 38 C1
Bodmin Rd. Luton LU4 ... 44 F3
Bodwell Cl. Heml H HP1 ... 124 A4
Bognor Rd. Bar SG8 ... 18 A8
Bognor Gdns. Sth Ox WD1 ... 175 C5
Bohemia. Heml H HP2 ... 124 E4
Boissy Cl. Coln H AL4 ... 128 E2
Boleyn Cl. Heml H HP2 ... 125 C8
Boleyn Dr. St Alb AL1 ... 127 D1
Bolingbroke Rd. Luton LU1 ... 63 B6
Bolingbrook. St Alb AL4 ... 128 A7
Bolingey Gn. Luton LU2 ... 46 D3
Bolton Rd. Luton LU1 ... 63 F7
Boltons Park
(Royal Veterinary Coll). Pot B ... 145 A2
Bond Ct. Harp AL5 ... 85 F3 4
Bondley Hill Jun Mix Inf Sch. Stev ... 51 C3
Boniface Gdns. Har HA3 ... 176 B3
Boniface Wlk. Har HA3 ... 176 B3
Bonks Hill. Saw CM21 ... 97 D1
Bonney Gr. Ches EN7 ... 148 A1
Bonnick Cl. Luton LU1 ... 63 C6
Booths Cl. Wel G AL9 ... 144 D7
Boreham Holt. Bor WD6 ... 169 F5
Borehamwood Ind Pk. Bor ... 170 D7
Bornedene. Pot B EN6 ... 158 E8
Borodale. Harp AL5 ... 86 A1
Borough Way. Pot B EN6 ... 158 E7
Borrell Cl. Hod EN10 ... 134 F3
Borrowdale Ct. Heml H HP2 ... 124 E6 4
Borton Ave. Henlw SG16 ... 10 B4
Bosanquet Rd. Hod EN11 ... 135 C8
Bosmore Rd. Luton LU3 ... 44 F5
Boswell Dr. Ick SG5 ... 21 E4
Boswell Gdns. Stev SG1 ... 36 D1
Boswick La. Nthch HP4 ... 121 D8
Botley La. Bot HP5 ... 136 A1
Botley Rd. Bot HP5 ... 136 A1
Botley Rd. Heml H HP2 ... 125 B8
Bottom House La. Wigg HP23 ... 101 A1
Bottom La. Sar WD3 ... 152 C4
Bottom Rd. St Le HP23 ... 119 F3
Bough Beech Ct. Enf EN3 ... 162 D2
Boughton Way. L Chal HP6 ... 150 C1
Boulevard Ctr The. Bor ... 170 A6
Boulevard The. Watf WD1 ... 166 D4
Boulevard The. Wel G C AL7 ... 110 F8
Boulton Rd. Stev SG1 ... 37 C2
Bounce The. Heml H HP2 ... 124 D5
Boundary Ct. Wel G C AL7 ... 110 F2
Boundary Dr. Hert SG14 ... 113 D8
Boundary House. Wel G C AL7 ... 110 D3
Boundary La. Wel G C AL7 ... 110 E2
Boundary Rd. Bis St CM23 ... 77 A5
Boundary Rd. St Alb AL1 ... 127 E5
Boundary Way. Heml H HP2 ... 125 C6
Boundary Way. Watf WD2 ... 154 C7
Bounds Field. L Had SG11 ... 75 F8
Bourne Cl. Hod EN10 ... 134 F3
Bourne Cl. Ware SG12 ... 93 D2
Bourne End La. Heml H HP1 ... 123 C1
Bourne End Rd. Mo Pk HA6 ... 174 E6
Bourne Hall. Bus WD2 ... 168 A3
Bourne Honour. Ton SG12 ... 92 E7
Bourne Rd. Berk HP4 ... 121 F5
Bourne Rd. Bus WD2 ... 168 A4
Bourne The. Bis St CM23 ... 77 A8
Bourne The. Bov HP3 ... 137 A4
Bourne The. Ware SG12 ... 93 D2
Bournehall Ave. Bus WD2 ... 168 A4
Bournehall La. Bus WD2 ... 168 A4
Bournehall Rd. Bus WD2 ... 168 A3
Bournehall Sch. Bus ... 168 B4
Bournemouth Rd. Stev SG1 ... 50 B8 3
Bouvier Rd. Enf EN3 ... 162 C1
Bovingdon Cres. Watf WD2 ... 154 D5
Bovingdon Ct. Bov HP3 ... 137 A3
Bovingdon Green La. Bov HP3 ... 136 F3
Bovingdon Inf Sch. Bov ... 137 B4
Bovingdon Jun Mix Sch. Bov ... 137 B4
Bowbrook Vale. Luton LU2 ... 46 F1
Bowcock Wlk. Stev SG1 ... 50 E3
Bower Heath La. Whea AL5 ... 86 C6
Bower's Par. Harp AL5 ... 86 A1
Bowers Way. Harp AL5 ... 86 A1
Bowershott. Letw SG6 ... 23 A4
Bowes Lyon Mews. St Alb AL3 ... 127 D3
Bowgate. St Alb AL1 ... 127 E4
Bowlers Mead. Bun SG9 ... 40 D7
Bowles Gn. Enf EN1 ... 162 B3
Bowling Cl. Bis St CM23 ... 76 F6
Bowling Cl. Harp AL5 ... 107 C7
Bowling Ct. Watf WD1 ... 167 A5
Bowling Gn. Stev SG1 ... 50 C8
Bowling Green La. Bun SG9 ... 40 D8
Bowling Green La. Luton LU2 ... 45 E2
Bowling Rd. Ware SG12 ... 93 E1
Bowman Trad Est. Stev ... 50 B5
Bowmans Ave. Hit SG4 ... 35 B6
Bowmans Cl. Pot B EN6 ... 159 D7
Bowmans Cl. Welw AL6 ... 89 C6
Bowmans Ct. Heml H HP2 ... 124 E5
Bowmans Gn. Watf WD2 ... 154 E3
Bowmansgreen Prim Sch
(Jun Mix & Inf). Lon C ... 142 C4
Bowring Gn. Sth Ox WD1 ... 175 C5
Bowyer's Cl. Hit SG5 ... 21 D1
Bowyers. Heml H HP2 ... 124 D5 6
Box La. Heml H HP3 ... 137 E7
Box La. Hod EN11 ... 134 E6
Boxberry Cl. Stev SG1 ... 50 E6
Boxfield Gn. Stev SG2 ... 51 D8
Boxfield. Wel G C AL7 ... 111 B3
Boxgrove Cl. Luton LU2 ... 46 C5
Boxhill. Heml H HP2 ... 124 D5 3
Boxmoor House Sch. Heml H ... 137 F8
Boxmoor Jun Mix Inf Sch. Heml H ... 124 A2
Boxted Cl. Luton LU4 ... 44 C5
Boxted Rd. Heml H HP1 ... 123 F5
Boxtree La. Har HA3 ... 176 D3
Boxtree Rd. Har HA3 ... 176 D3
Boxwell Rd. Berk HP4 ... 122 B4
Boyce Cl. Bor WD6 ... 169 E8
Boyd Cl. Bis St CM23 ... 77 B8
Boyle Cl. Luton LU2 ... 63 E8
Braceby Cl. Luton LU3 ... 44 F6
Brache Cl. Red AL3 ... 106 A5
Brache Ct. Luton LU1 ... 63 F6
Bracken La. Welw AL6 ... 89 F7
Brackendale Gr. Harp AL5 ... 85 D3
Brackendale Gr. Luton LU3 ... 45 B5
Brackendale. Pot B EN6 ... 159 A6
Brackens The. Heml H HP2 ... 124 D4
Bracklesham Gdns. Luton LU2 ... 46 D3
Bracknedene. Bri Wd AL2 ... 140 F1
Bracknell Pl. Heml H HP2 ... 124 F7
Bradbery. Map Cr WD3 ... 172 D5
Bradbury Cl. Bor WD6 ... 170 B8
Bradden La. Gt Gd HP2 ... 103 E7
Bradford Rd. Chor WD3 ... 164 C2
Bradford St. Hit SG5 ... 34 D7
Bradgate Cl. Cuf EN6 ... 146 D3
Bradgate. Cuf EN6 ... 146 D4
Bradgers Hill Rd. Luton LU2 ... 45 E4
Bradley Comm. Birhr CM23 ... 59 C3
Bradley Rd. Enf EN3 ... 162 E2
Bradley Rd. Luton LU4 ... 44 D4
Bradleys Cnr. Hit SG4 ... 35 C8
Bradman Way. Stev SG1 ... 37 A1
Bradmore Gn. Bro Pk AL9 ... 144 E5
Bradmore La. Bro Pk AL9 ... 144 C5
Bradmore La. Wel G AL9 ... 144 C5
Bradmore Way. Bro Pk AL9 ... 144 E5
Bradshaw Rd. Watf WD2 ... 154 C1
Bradshaws. Hat AL10 ... 129 F1
Bradway. Whit SG4 ... 66 E6
Braemar Cl. Stev SG2 ... 69 B7
Braemar Ct. Bus WD2 ... 168 A3
Braeside Cl. Pnr HA5 ... 176 A3
Bragbury Cl. Stev SG2 ... 69 D7
Bragbury La. Dat SG3 ... 69 D5
Bragmans La. Sar HP5 ... 151 E6
Braham Ct. Hit SG5 ... 34 E7 2
Brain Cl. Hat AL10 ... 130 B6
Braithwaite Ct. Luton LU3 ... 45 D1 1
Brakynbery. Nthch HP4 ... 121 E7
Brallings La. C St P SL9 ... 172 A6
Bramble Cl. Harp AL5 ... 85 F3
Bramble Cl. Luton LU4 ... 44 C4
Bramble Cl. Watf WD2 ... 154 A5
Bramble Rd. Hat AL10 ... 129 D5
Bramble Rd. Luton LU4 ... 44 C4
Bramble Rise. Harl CM20 ... 117 C1
Brambles The. Bis St CM23 ... 76 C6
Brambles The. Ches EN8 ... 162 D8
Brambles The. Royst SG8 ... 7 E5
Brambles The. St Alb AL1 ... 127 D1
Brambles The. Stev SG1 ... 36 D2
Brambles The. Ware SG12 ... 93 C3
Brambles The. Welw AL6 ... 89 E8
Brambling Cl. Watf WD2 ... 167 E5
Brambling Rise. Heml H HP2 ... 124 E6
Bramfield Ct. Hert SG14 ... 113 A7
Bramfield. Hit SG4 ... 35 B6
Bramfield La. Stap SG14 ... 91 F3
Bramfield Pl. Heml H HP2 ... 105 A1
Bramfield Rd. Dat SG3 ... 90 E8
Bramfield Rd. Hert SG14 ... 112 F8
Bramfield. Watf WD2 ... 154 E5
Bramhanger Acre. Luton LU3 ... 44 D7
Bramingham Bsns Pk. Luton ... 45 B8
Bramingham Prim Sch. Luton ... 45 B8
Bramingham Rd. Luton LU3 ... 44 E5
Bramleas. Watf WD1 ... 166 F5
Bramley Cl. Bal SG7 ... 12 F1
Bramley Ct. Watf WD2 ... 154 B8
Bramley Gdns. Sth Ox WD1 ... 175 C5
Bramley House Ct. Enf EN2 ... 161 D2
Bramley Shaw. Wa Aby EN9 ... 163 F6
Brampton Cl. Ches EN7 ... 148 A3
Brampton Cl. Harp AL5 ... 86 D1
Brampton Park Rd. Hit SG5 ... 21 E1
Brampton Rd. Royst SG8 ... 7 F6
Brampton Rd. St Alb AL1 ... 128 A4
Brampton Rd. Sth Ox WD1 ... 175 A7
Brampton Terr. Bor WD6 ... 157 A1
Bramshaw Gdns. Sth Ox WD1 ... 175 D5
Bramshott Cl. Hit SG4 ... 34 F5
Branch Cl. Hat AL10 ... 130 C7
Branch Rd. Pk St AL2 ... 141 D4
Branch Rd. St Alb AL3 ... 127 B4
Brand St. Hit SG5 ... 34 E7
Brandles Close Sch. Bal ... 23 E7
Brandles Rd. Letw SG6 ... 23 A3
Brandon Cl. Ham St EN7 ... 147 F5
Branksome Cl. Heml H HP2 ... 125 A4
Branton Cl. Luton LU2 ... 46 E2
Brantwood Rd. Luton LU1 ... 63 C7
Bray Cl. Bor WD6 ... 170 C8
Bray Lodge. Ches EN8 ... 148 E3
Brayes Manor. Stot SG5 ... 11 F6
Brays Ct. Luton LU2 ... 46 B3
Brays Rd. Luton LU2 ... 46 B3
Braziers End. Chol HP5 ... 120 C1
Braziers Field. Hert SG13 ... 113 F6
Braziers Quay. Bis St CM23 ... 77 A6
Breachwood Green Cty Prim Sch.
Bre Gr ... 47 E1
Bread & Cheese La. Ham St EN7 ... 147 E6
Breadcroft La. Harp AL5 ... 86 B1
Breakmead. Wel G C AL7 ... 111 B4
Breaks Rd. Hat AL10 ... 130 B6
Breakspear Ave. St Alb AL1 ... 127 F2
Breakspear Coll. Abb L ... 139 F1
Breakspear Ct. Abb L WD5 ... 139 F1
Breakspear Hospl. Heml H ... 138 F6
Breakspear Rd N. Hare UB9 ... 173 D1
Breakspear. Stev SG2 ... 51 C3
Breakspear Way. Heml H HP2 ... 125 D4
Breakspeare Cl. Watf WD2 ... 154 B1
Breakspeare Rd. Abb L WD5 ... 153 E8
Brecken Cl. St Alb AL4 ... 128 A7
Brecon Cl. Luton LU1 ... 63 D6
Breeze Terr. Ches EN8 ... 148 D3
Brent Ct. Stev SG1 ... 50 E5
Brent Pl. Barn EN5 ... 171 F4
Brett Pl. Watf WD2 ... 154 A2
Brett Rd. Barn EN5 ... 171 C4
Bretts Mead. Luton LU1 ... 63 C5
Brewery La. Bal SG7 ... 23 E8
Brewery La. Sta M CM24 ... 59 E7
Brewery Rd. Hod EN11 ... 135 A6
Brewhouse Hill. Whea AL4 ... 108 C8
Brewhouse La. Hert SG14 ... 113 C6
Briants Cl. Pnr HA5 ... 175 F1
Briar Cl. Ches EN8 ... 148 C2
Briar Cl. Luton LU2 ... 46 C4
Briar Cl. Pot En HP4 ... 123 A7
Briar Patch La. Letw SG6 ... 22 D3
Briar Rd. St Alb AL4 ... 128 D6
Briar Rd. Watf WD2 ... 154 B4
Briar Way. Berk HP4 ... 122 D3
Briarcliff. Heml H HP1 ... 123 E4
Briardale. Stev SG1 ... 50 E4
Briardale. Ware SG12 ... 93 C3
Briarley Cl. Hod EN10 ... 134 F1
Briars Cl. Hat AL10 ... 130 A5
Briars La. Hat AL10 ... 130 A5
Briars The. Bus WD2 ... 168 E2
Briars The. Ches EN8 ... 162 E8
Briars The. Hert SG13 ... 114 A6
Briars The. Sar WD3 ... 152 A3
Briars Wood. Hat AL10 ... 130 A5
Briarwood Dr. Pnr HA6 ... 175 A1
Briary La. Royst SG8 ... 7 C5
Briary Wood End. Welw AL6 ... 89 F8
Briary Wood La. Welw AL6 ... 89 F8
Brick Kiln La. Hit SG4 ... 34 E5
Brick Knoll Pk. St Alb AL1 ... 128 C2
Brickcroft. Ches EN10 ... 148 E5
Brickenden Ct. Wa Aby EN9 ... 163 F6
Brickendon Ct. Hod EN11 ... 135 A5
Brickendon Golf Course. Bric ... 133 B4
Brickendon La. Bric SG13 ... 133 D6
Bricket Rd. St Alb AL1 ... 127 E3
Bricket Wood Sta. Bri Wd ... 141 A1
Brickfield Ave. Heml H HP3 ... 125 B1
Brickfield Ct. Hat AL10 ... 130 B2
Brickfield. Hat AL10 ... 130 A2
Brickfield La. Edg EN5 ... 170 F3
Brickfields The. Ware SG12 ... 93 B2
Brickkiln Rd. Stev SG1 ... 50 C6
Brickly Rd. Luton LU4 ... 44 C5
Brickmakers La. Heml H HP3 ... 125 B2
Brickwall Cl. A St P AL6 ... 110 A8
Brickyard La. Reed SG8 ... 16 E5
Bride Hall La. A St L AL6 ... 88 A5
Bridewell Cl. Bun SG9 ... 40 E8
Bridge Ct. Berk HP4 ... 122 D4
Bridge Ct. Harp AL5 ... 85 F3 5
Bridge Ct. Radl WD7 ... 156 B4
Bridge End. Bun SG9 ... 40 E8
Bridge Foot. Ware SG12 ... 93 D1
Bridge Pl. Watf WD1 ... 167 D4
Bridge Rd. Abb L WD4 ... 153 C6
Bridge Rd E. Wel G C AL7 ... 110 F6
Bridge Rd. Letw SG6 ... 22 F6
Bridge Rd. Stev SG1 ... 50 C7
Bridge Rd. Wel G C AL8 ... 110 C7
Bridge Rd. Welw SG3 ... 69 A2
Bridge St. Berk HP4 ... 122 D4
Bridge St. Bis St CM23 ... 76 F7
Bridge St. Heml H HP1 ... 124 C2
Bridge St. Hit SG5 ... 34 E6
Bridge St. Knee SG8 ... 2 B8
Bridge St. Luton LU1 ... 63 E8
Bridgefields. Wel G C AL7 ... 110 F7
Bridgefoot. Bun SG9 ... 40 E7

Bridgeford House. Watf WD1 167 B6 5
Bridgegate Bsns Ctr. Wel G C 110 F7
Bridgend Rd. Enf EN1 162 C4
Bridgenhall Rd. Enf EN1 161 F1
Bridger Cl. Watf WD2 154 E6
Bridges Ct. Hert SG14 113 C6
Bridges Rd. Stan HA7 176 F5
Bridgewater Ct. L Gad HP4 102 C8
Bridgewater Hill. Nthch HP4 121 F7
Bridgewater Rd. Berk HP4 122 B5
Bridgewater Sch. Berk 122 A6
Bridgewater Way. Bus WD2 168 B3
Bridgeways. Hod EN11 135 B6
Bridle Cl. Enf EN3 162 F2
Bridle Cl. Hod EN11 115 A2
Bridle Cl. St Alb AL3 127 E5
Bridle La. Ric WD3 165 D6
Bridle Path. Watf WD2 167 B7
Bridle Way. Berk HP4 122 A6
Bridle Way. Gt Am SG12 115 A6
Bridle Way. Hod EN11 115 A1
Bridle Way (N). Hod EN11 115 B2
Bridle Way (S). Hod EN11 115 A1
Bridleway. St Le HP23 119 E5
Bridlington Rd. Sth Ox WD1 175 D7
Brierley Cl. Luton LU2 46 D2
Briery Field. Chor WD3 165 A5
Briery Way. Heml H HP2 125 A4
Brigadier Ave. Enf EN2 161 C1
Brigadier Hill. Enf EN2 161 C1
Brightman Cotts. Luton LU3 45 A7
Brighton Rd. Watf WD2 154 A1
Brighton Way. Stev SG1 50 A8
Brightview Cl. Bri Wd AL2 140 E2
Brightwell Rd. Watf WD1 167 A4
Brill Cl. Luton LU2 46 D2
Brimfield Cl. Luton LU2 46 D2
Brimsdown Ave. Enf EN3 162 E1
Brimstone Wlk. Berk HP4 121 F6
Brinklow Ct. St Alb AL3 141 B8
Brinley Cl. Ches EN8 162 D8
Brinsley Rd. Har HA3 176 D1
Brinsmead. Pk St AL2 141 E4
Briscoe Cl. Hod EN11 134 F8
Briscoe Rd. Hod EN11 134 F8
Bristol Rd. Luton LU3 45 B4
Britannia Ave. Luton LU3 45 B4
Britannia Rd. Ches EN8 162 F5
Britannia. Stand SG11 55 E2
Britannic Bsns Pk. Ches 162 F5
Britannica Works. Wa Aby 163 D5
Brittain Way. Stev SG2 51 B4
Britten Cl. Elst WD6 169 D3
Britton Ave. St Alb AL3 127 D3
Brixham Cl. Stev SG1 50 B7
Brixton Rd. Watf WD2 167 B8
Broad Acre. Bri Wd AL2 140 E1
Broad Acres. Hat AL10 129 F8
Broad Ct. Wel G C AL7 110 E6
Broad Gn. Bay SG13 132 F8
Broad Green Wood. Bay SG13 133 A8
Broad Mead. Luton LU3 45 A3
Broad Oak Ct. Luton LU2 46 D3 2
Broad Oak Way. Stev SG2 50 F1
Broad St. Heml H HP2 124 D4
Broad Wlk. Harl CM20 117 D1
Broad Wlk The. Norwd HA6 174 C1
Broadacres. Luton LU2 45 D6
Broadcroft. Heml H HP2 124 D5 2
Broadcroft. Letw SG6 22 F2
Broadfield. Bis St CM23 58 F2
Broadfield Cl. Muc H SG10 74 E1
Broadfield Ct. Bus WD2 176 E8
Broadfield. Harl CM20 117 E1
Broadfield Inf Sch. Heml H 124 F3
Broadfield Jun Sch. Heml H 124 F3
Broadfield Pl. Wel G C AL8 110 B5
Broadfield Rd. Heml H HP2 124 F3
Broadfield Rd. Welw SG3 69 B1
Broadfield Way. Muc H SG10 74 F1
Broadfields Cty Prim Sch. Harl 117 E1
Broadfields. Gofs O EN7 147 B2
Broadfields. H Wy CM21 97 B1
Broadfields. Har HA2 176 B1
Broadfields. Harp AL5 85 F2
Broadfields La. Watf WD1 167 B1
Broadgate. Wa Aby EN9 163 F7
Broadhall Way. Stev SG2 51 B2
Broadlake Cl. Lon C AL2 142 D4
Broadlands Cl. Ches EN8 162 D5
Broadlawns Ct. Har HA3 176 F2
Broadleaf Ave. Bis St CM23 76 D4
Broadmead Cl. Pnr HA5 175 E3
Broadmead. Hit SG4 35 B5
Broadmead Ind Sch. Luton 63 E5
Broadmeadow Ride. Hit SG4 35 A4
Broadmeads. Ware SG12 93 D1
Broadoak Ave. Enf EN3 162 D4
Broadstone Rd. Harp AL5 107 D7
Broadview. Stev SG1 50 E6
Broadwater Ave. Letw SG6 22 E5
Broadwater. Berk HP4 122 C5
Broadwater Cres. Stev SG2 69 C8
Broadwater Cres. Wel G C AL7 110 D5
Broadwater Dale. Letw SG6 22 E5
Broadwater La. Ast SG2 51 D1
Broadwater. Pot B EN6 145 B1
Broadwater Rd. Wel G C AL7 110 E6
Broadway Ave. Harl CM17 118 B4
Broadway Ct. Letw SG6 22 E3
Broadway. Letw SG6 22 F5
Broadway The. Har HA3 176 F1
Broadway The. Hat AL9 130 C6
Broadway The. Kim AL4 87 B5
Broadway The. Pnr HA5 175 F3
Broadway The. Watf WD1 167 C6
Brocket Ct. Luton LU4 44 D5
Brocket Rd. Hat AL8 110 A3
Brocket Rd. Hod EN11 135 A6
Brocket View. Whea AL4 108 D8
Brockett Cl. Wel G C AL8 110 B6
Brockhurst Cl. Stan HA7 176 F4
Brocklesbury Cl. Watf WD2 167 D7
Brockley Hill. Stan HA7 169 C1
Brockswood La. Wel G C AL8 110 B7
Brockswood Prim Sch. Heml H 105 C1
Brockwell Shott. Walk SG2 38 B1
Brodewater Rd. Bor WD6 170 B7
Brodie Rd. Enf EN2 161 C1
Bromborough Gn. Sth Ox WD1 175 C5
Bromet Cl. Watf WD1 153 F1
Bromet Jun Mix Inf Sch. Watf 167 D2
Bromleigh Cl. Ches EN8 148 E3
Bromley. Lon M HP23 79 A4
Brompton Cl. Luton LU3 44 F8
Bronte Cres. Heml H HP2 105 B1
Bronte Paths. Stev SG2 51 C6
Brook Cotts. Sta M CM24 59 E5
Brook Dr. Radl WD7 155 F6
Brook Dr. Stev SG2 69 B8
Brook End. Saw CM21 97 D2
Brook Field. Ast SG2 51 E2
Brook La. Berk HP4 122 B5
Brook La. Saw CM21 97 D2
Brook Rd. Bor WD6 170 A7
Brook Rd. Saw CM21 97 D1
Brook Rd. Sta M CM24 59 E6
Brook St. Luton LU3 63 D8
Brook St. Stot SG5 11 E6
Brook St. Tri HP23 100 B4
Brook View. Hit SG4 35 C6
Brookbridge La. Dat SG3 69 D2
Brookdene Ave. Watf WD1 167 C1
Brookdene Dr. Norwd HA6 174 F4
Brooke Cl. Bus WD2 168 C2
Brooke Gdns. Bis St CM23 77 C7
Brooke Rd. Royst SG8 7 D8
Brooke Way. Bus WD2 168 C2
Brooker Rd. Wa Aby EN9 163 C5
Brookfield Ctr. Ches 148 D4
Brookfield Cl. Tri HP23 100 B4
Brookfield Gdns. Ches EN8 148 D4
Brookfield Jun Sch. Bor 169 F8
Brookfield La. Ast SG2 51 F3
Brookfield La. Ches EN8 148 B3
Brookfield La E. Ches EN8 148 D3
Brookfield La W. Ches EN8 148 C4
Brookfields. Saw CM21 97 D2
Brookhill. Stev SG2 68 F8
Brookland Inf Sch. Ches 148 E3
Brookland Jun Sch. Ches 148 E3
Brooklands Cl. Luton LU4 44 C6
Brooklands Gdns. Pot B EN6 158 E7
Brookmans Ave. Bro Pk AL9 144 F5
Brookmans Park Cty Prim Sch.
Bro Pk 144 E5
Brookmans Park Sta. Bro Pk 144 E5
Brookmead Cty Prim Sch. Pit 80 E5
Brookmore Park Golf Club. Bro Pk 145 A6
Brooks Ct. Hert SG14 112 F7
Brooksfield. Wel G C AL7 111 B7
Brookshill Ave. Stan HA3 176 E5
Brookshill Dr. Stan HA3 176 D5
Brookshill. Stan HA3 176 D5
Brookside Cl. Barn EN5 171 E3
Brookside Cres. Cuf EN6 146 E4
Brookside Gdns. Enf EN1 162 C2
Brookside. Hat AL10 129 D5
Brookside. Hert SG13 113 E5
Brookside. Hod EN11 135 A6
Brookside. Letw SG6 22 F5
Brookside. Pot B EN6 158 A7
Brookside Rd. Watf WD1 167 B2
Brookside. Wa Aby EN9 163 E7
Brookside. Watf WD2 154 D3
Brookside. Watf WD1 167 B2
Broom Barns Jun Mix Inf Sch. Stev 50 E5
Broom Cl. Ham St EN7 148 A4
Broom Cl. Hat AL10 129 F2
Broom Gr. Kneb SG3 68 F5
Broom Gr. Watf WD1 154 A1
Broom Hill. Heml H HP1 123 E2
Broom Hill. Welw AL6 90 A8
Broom Wlk. Stev SG1 50 E5
Broomer Pl. Ches EN8 148 C2
Broomfield Ave. Ches EN10 148 E5
Broomfield. Chis AL2 141 C4
Broomfield Cl. Welw AL6 89 C4
Broomfield. Harl CM20 118 B3
Broomfield Rd. Welw AL6 89 C4
Broomfield Rise. Abb L WD5 153 D7
Broomhills. Wel G C AL7 111 B7
Broomleys. St Alb AL4 128 D6
Brooms Cl. Wel G C AL8 89 D1
Brooms Rd. Luton LU2 63 F8
Broomstick Hall Rd. Wa Aby EN9 163 E6
Broomstick La. Bot HP5 136 A1
Broughinge Rd. Bor WD6 170 B7
Broughton Ave. Luton LU3 45 C5
Broughton Hill. Letw SG6 23 B6
Broughton Way. Ric WD3 165 A2
Brow The. Watf WD2 154 B6
Brown's Cl. Luton LU4 44 D5
Brown's Rise. St Le HP23 119 F3
Brownfield Way. Kim AL4 87 B6
Brownfields. Wel G C AL7 110 F7
Browning Dr. Hit SG4 35 B8
Browning Rd. Dun LU4 44 A2
Browning Rd. Enf EN2 161 D1
Browning Rd. Harp AL5 86 C2
Brownlow La. Ched LU7 80 A7
Brownlow Rd. Berk HP4 122 C5
Brownlow Rd. Bor WD6 170 A5
Browns Spring. Pot En HP4 123 C7
Brox Dell. Stev SG1 50 E6
Broxbourne Jun Mix Inf Sch. Hod 134 F2
Broxbourne Sch The. Hod 134 E1
Broxbourne Sta. Hod 135 A3
Broxbournebury Sch. Hod 134 E3
Broxley Mead. Luton LU4 44 D5
Bruce Gr. Watf WD2 154 C1
Bruce Rd. Barn EN5 171 E6
Bruce Rd. Har HA3 176 E1
Bruce Way. Ches EN8 162 D6
Brunel Rd. Stev SG2 51 B7
Brunswick Ct. Hod EN11 135 A5
Brunswick Ct. Stev SG1 50 A7
Brunswick St. Luton LU2 63 E8
Brushrise. Watf WD2 154 A3
Brushwood Dr. Chor WD3 164 C5
Brussels Way. Luton LU3 44 D8
Bryan Rd. Bis St CM23 76 F8
Bryanstone Rd. Ches EN8 162 F5
Bryant Cl. Barn EN5 171 F4
Bryant Ct. Harp AL5 86 A3
Bryce Cl. Ware SG12 93 D3
Bryn La. St Alb AL4 128 C1
Bryn Way. St Alb AL4 128 C1
Bsns Ctr E. Letw 23 C6
Bsns Ctr W. Letw 23 C6
Buchanan Ct. Bor WD6 170 C7
Buchanan Ct. Luton LU2 64 B8
Buchanan Dr. Luton LU2 64 B8
Buckettsland La. Shen WD6 157 D2
Buckingham Dr. Luton LU2 46 D2
Buckingham Rd. Bor WD6 170 D5
Buckingham Rd. Tri HP23 99 E3
Buckingham Rd. Watf WD2 154 C2
Buckinghamshire Coll The. L Chal 172 A8
Buckland Rd. Ast Cl HP22 99 A4
Buckland Rise. Pnr HA5 175 D2
Bucklands The. Ric WD3 165 A2
Bucklers Cl. Hod EN10 134 F1
Bucklersbury. Hit SG5 34 E6
Buckley Cl. Luton LU3 44 F7
Bucknalls Cl. Watf WD2 154 E7
Bucknalls Dr. Bri Wd AL2 154 F8
Bucknalls La. Bri Wd WD2 154 E7
Bucknalls La. Watf WD2 154 E7
Bucks Alley. L Berk SG13 132 D4
Bucks Ave. Watf WD1 167 E2
Bucks Hill. Sar WD4 152 C5
Buckthorn Ave. Stev SG1 50 E4
Buckton Rd. Bor WD6 156 F1
Buckwood La. Whip LU6 82 C7
Buckwood Rd. Mark AL3 83 C6
Buddcroft. Wel G C AL7 111 B7
Bude Cres. Stev SG1 50 A7
Bulbourne Cl. Berk HP4 121 F6
Bulbourne Cl. Heml H HP1 124 A2
Bulbourne Rd. Tri HP23 100 B7
Bull La. Buck SG8 27 C8
Bull La. Cotrd SG9 39 C8
Bull La. Whea 108 A6
Bull Plain. Hert SG14 113 D6
Bull Rd. Harp AL5 107 B8
Bull Stag Gn. Hat AL9 130 C7
Bull's Cross. Enf EN2 162 A3
Bullace Cl. Heml H HP1 124 A4
Bullbeggars La. Berk HP4 123 A4
Bullbeggars La. Pot En HP4 123 A4
Bullen's Green La. Coln H AL4 143 E8
Bullfields. Saw CM21 97 E3
Bullhead Rd. Bor WD6 170 C6
Bullock's Hill. Whit SG4 49 B1
Bullock's La. Hert SG13 113 C4
Bullrush Cl. Hat AL10 130 B4
Bulls Cross Ride. Gofs O EN7 162 A5
Bulls La. Bro Pk AL9 144 E7
Bulls La. Wel G AL9 144 E7
Bullsland Gdns. Chor WD3 164 B3
Bullsland La. Chor WD3 164 B2
Bullsmoor Cl. Enf EN8 162 C4
Bullsmoor Gdns. Enf EN8 162 B4
Bullsmoor La. Enf EN1,EN3 162 C4
Bullsmoor Ride. Enf EN8 162 C4
Bullsmoor Sec Sch & Sports Ctr.
Enf 162 C4
Bullsmoor Way. Enf EN8 162 C4
Bullwell Cres. Ches EN8 148 E2
Bulstrode La. Chipf HP3 137 F3
Bulstrode La. Heml H HP3 138 A5
Bulwer Link. Stev SG1 50 E3
Buncefield La. Heml H HP2 125 C5
Bungalows The. Harp AL5 86 C3
Bunkers La. Heml H HP3 139 B7
Bunnsfield. Wel G C AL7 111 C7
Bunstrux. Tri HP23 100 A4
Bunting Rd. Dun LU4 44 A4
Buntingford Rd. Stand SG11 55 D4
Bunyan Cl. Pirt SG5 20 D4
Bunyan Cl. Tri HP23 100 B5
Bunyan Rd. Hit SG5 34 F8
Bunyans Cl. Luton LU3 45 A5
Burbage Cl. Ches EN8 162 F8
Burchell Ct. Bus WD2 168 C2
Burfield Cl. Hat AL10 130 A7
Burfield Ct. Luton LU2 46 D3 1
Burfield Rd. Chor WD3 164 C4
Burford Cl. Luton LU3 31 A1
Burford Gdns. Hod EN11 135 B7
Burford Mews. Hod EN11 135 A7
Burford Pl. Hod EN11 135 A7
Burford St. Hod EN11 135 A7
Burford Way. Hit SG5 21 D2
Burge End La. Pirt SG5 20 C5
Burgess Ct. Bor WD6 156 F1
Burghley Ave. Bis St CM23 76 C7
Burghley Ave. Bor WD6 170 C4
Burghley Cl. Stev SG2 69 A8
Burgoyne Hatch. Harl CM20 118 A1
Burgundy Croft. Wel G C AL7 110 F4
Burhill Gr. Pnr HA5 175 E1
Burleigh Mead. Hat AL9 130 C7
Burleigh Prim Sch. Ches 148 D1
Burleigh Rd. Ches EN8 162 E7
Burleigh Rd. Heml H HP2 125 C2
Burleigh Rd. Hert SG13 114 A7
Burleigh Rd. St Alb AL1 128 B3
Burleigh Way. Cuf EN6 146 E1
Burley House. Abb L WD5 153 F7
Burley. Letw SG6 11 F2
Burley Rd. Bis St CM23 77 A4
Burnell Rise. Letw SG6 22 D5
Burnell Wlk. Letw SG6 22 D5
Burnells Way. Sta M CM24 59 E7
Burnet Cl. Heml H HP3 124 E2
Burnett Ave. Henlw SG16 10 B4
Burnett Sq. Hert SG14 112 F7
Burnham Cl. Dat AL6 90 C6
Burnham Cl. Enf EN1 161 E1
Burnham Green Rd. Dat AL6,SG3 90 D6
Burnham Rd. Luton LU2 46 B2
Burnham Rd. St Alb AL1 128 B3
Burnley Cl. Sth Ox WD1 175 C5
Burns Cl. Hit SG4 35 B8
Burns Cl. Stev SG2 51 C8
Burns Dr. Heml H HP2 105 B1
Burns Rd. Royst SG8 7 D8
Burnsall Pl. Harp AL5 107 C6
Burnside Cl. Hat AL10 130 A8
Burnside. Hert SG14 113 A5
Burnside. Hod EN11 134 F6
Burnside. Saw CM21 97 D2
Burnside. St Alb AL1 128 B1
Burnside Terr. Harl CM17 118 F3
Burnt Cl. Luton LU3 44 F7
Burnt Mill Comp Sch. Harl 117 E2
Burntfarm Ride. Gofs O EN2,EN7 161 B7
Burntmill Cl. Harl CM20 117 C3
Burntmill La. Harl CM20 117 D3
Burr Cl. Lon C AL2 142 E4
Burr St. Luton LU2 63 E8
Burr's Pl. Luton LU1 63 E6
Burrowfield. Wel G C AL7 110 D4
Burrs La. Bark SG8 17 C3
Bursland. Letw SG6 22 D6
Burston Dr. Chis AL2 141 C3
Burton Ave. Watf WD1 167 A5
Burton Cl. Kim AL4 87 C5
Burton La. Gofs O EN7 147 E3
Burtons La. L Chal WD3 164 A4
Burtons Mill. Saw CM21 97 F3
Burvale Ct. Watf WD1 167 B6 3
Burwell Rd. Stev SG2 51 C4
Bury Cotts. Fla AL3 105 E5
Bury End. Pirt SG5 20 D4
Bury Gn. Heml H HP1 124 C4
Bury Gn. Whea AL4 108 C8
Bury Green Rd. Ches EN7 162 A7
Bury Green Rd. Ches EN7 162 A8
Bury Hill Cl. Heml H HP1 124 C4
Bury Hill. Heml H HP1 124 C4
Bury Holme. Hod EN10 148 F8
Bury La. Bram SG14 91 B4
Bury La. Cod SG4 67 F2
Bury La. Dat SG3 69 D3
Bury La. Ric WD3 165 D1
Bury La. Str LU3 31 A5
Bury Mead. Arl SG15 11 A7
Bury Mead Rd. Hit SG5 21 F1
Bury Meadows. Ric WD3 165 D1
Bury Park Rd. Luton LU1 63 C8
Bury Rd. Harl CM17 118 D4
Bury Rd. Hat AL10 130 C6
Bury Rd. Heml H HP1 124 C3
Bury Rise. Heml H HP3 137 D6
Bury The. Cod SG4 67 F2
Burycroft. Wel G C AL8 89 E1
Burydale Jun Sch. Stev 51 B1
Burydell La. Pk St AL2 141 D5
Buryfield Terr. Ware SG12 93 C1
Burymead. Stev SG1 36 C1
Burywick. Harp AL5 107 B5
Bush Hall La. Hat AL9 130 D8
Bush Spring. Bal SG7 13 A1
Bushbarns. Ches EN7 148 A2
Bushby Ave. Hod EN10 134 F1
Bushel Wharf. Tri HP23 100 A6
Bushell Gn. Bus WD2 176 D8
Bushey Cl. Wel G C AL7 111 B5
Bushey Gn. Wel G C AL7 111 B5
Bushey Grove Rd. Watf WD2 167 E5
Bushey Hall Dr. Watf WD2 167 E5
Bushey Hall Golf Course. Bus 167 E6
Bushey Hall Rd. Watf WD2 167 E5
Bushey Hall Sch. Bus 167 F4
Bushey Heath
Jun Mix Inf Prim Sch. Bus 168 D1
Bushey Ley. Wel G C AL7 111 B5
Bushey Manor Jun Sch. Watf 167 E4
Bushey Maternity Hospl. Stan 168 F1
Bushey Meads Sch. Bus 168 C4
Bushey Mill Cres. Watf WD2 154 C3
Bushey Mill La. Bus WD2 167 E8
Bushey Mill La. Watf WD2 154 D1
Bushey & Oxhey Sta. Watf 167 D3
Bushfield Rd. Bov HP3 137 C6
Bushmead Prim Sch. Luton 45 E5
Bushmead Rd. Luton LU2 45 E5
Bushwood Cl. Wel G AL9 144 B8
Bute Sq. Luton LU1 63 E7
Bute St. Luton LU1 63 E7
Butely Rd. Luton LU4 44 B5
Butler's Hall La. H Wy CM23 76 A3
Butlers Dr. Wa Aby EN9 163 C1
Butlin Rd. Luton LU1 63 B7
Butt Field View. St Alb AL1 141 C7
Butterfield Green Rd. Str LU2 46 A6
Butterfield La. St Alb AL1 141 E7
Butterfield Rd. Whea AL4 108 C7
Butterfly La. Radl WD6 169 B7
Buttermere Cl. St Alb AL1 128 B2
Buttersweet Rise. Saw CM21 97 E1
Butterwick Adult Training Ctr.
St Alb 128 D2
Butterwick. Watf WD2 154 E3
Butterworth Path. Luton LU2 63 E8 2
Buttlehide. Map Cr WD3 172 D5
Buttondene Cres. Lo Naz EN10 135 B1
Butts End. Heml H HP1 124 A5
Butts The. Ches EN10 148 F7
Buttsmead. Norwd HA6 174 C3
Buxton Cl. St Alb AL4 128 D6
Buxton Path. Sth Ox WD1 175 C7
Buxton Rd. Luton LU1 63 D7
Buxtons La. Gu M SG8 1 F3
Buzzard Rd. Dun LU4 44 A4
By The Mount. Wel G C AL7 110 D5
By-The-Wood. Sth Ox WD1 175 E8
Byde St. Hert SG14 113 C7
Bye Way The. Har HA3 176 F2
Byers Cl. Pot B EN6 159 C5
Byeway The. Ric WD3 173 E8
Byfield Cl. Dun LU4 44 B1
Byfield. Wel G C AL8 89 E1
Byford House. Barn EN5 171 D5
Bygrave Rd. Bal SG7 12 F1
Bygrave. Stev SG1 36 C2
Bylands Cl. Bis St CM23 76 D6
Byng Dr. Pot B EN6 159 A8
Byng Rd. Barn EN5 171 D6
Byrd Wlk. Bal SG7 23 F7
Byron Ave. Bor WD6 170 A4
Byron Ave. Watf WD2 167 D8
Byron Cl. Ham St EN7 147 F4
Byron Cl. Hit SG4 35 B8
Byron Cl. Stev SG2 51 C7
Byron Ct. Ches EN2 148 B3
Byron Pl. Heml H HP2 105 B1
Byron Rd. Dun LU4 44 B2
Byron Rd. Har HA3 176 F1
Byron Rd. Harp AL5 86 A2
Byron Rd. Royst SG8 7 E8
Byslips Rd. Stu LU6 82 D5
Byslips Rd. Whip LU6 82 D5
Byway The. Pot B EN6 159 A6
Byways. Berk HP4 122 E5
Cabot Cl. Stev SG2 51 A7
Caddington Comm. Mark AL3 83 E8
Caddis Cl. Har HA7 176 F3
Cade Cl. Letw SG6 12 C1
Cades Cl. Luton LU1 63 A6
Cades La. Luton LU1 63 A6
Cadia Cl. Cad LU1 62 E4
Cadmore Ct. Ches EN8 148 D3
Cadmore La. Ches EN8 148 E2
Cadwell Ct. Hit SG4 22 A2
Cadwell La. Hit SG4 22 A2
Caernarvon Cl. Heml H HP2 124 D3
Caernarvon Cl. Stev SG2 69 B7
Caernarvon Ct. Heml H HP2 124 D3
Caesars Rd. Whea AL4 108 E8
Cage Pond Rd. Shen WD7 156 F6
Cairn Way. Har HA7 176 F4
Caishowe Rd. Bor WD6 170 B8
Caister Cl. Stev SG1 36 A1
Calbury Cl. St Alb AL1 128 B2
Caldbeck. Wa Aby EN9 163 D5
Caldecot Ave. Gofs O EN7 147 F2
Caldecot Way. Hod EN10 134 F1
Caldecote Gdns. Bus WD2 168 E2
Caldecote La. Bus WD2 168 F3
Caldecote Rd. Newn SG7 12 E8
Calder Ave. Bro Pk AL9 145 B5
Caldwell Rd. Sth Ox WD1 175 D6
Caleb Cl. Luton LU4 44 F2
Caledon Rd. Lon C AL2 142 D5
Caledonian Ct. Watf WD1 167 B7
California. Bal SG7 12 F1
California La. Bus WD2 168 D1
Callanders The. Bus WD2 168 E1
Callisto Ct. Heml H HP2 124 F6
Callowland Pl. Watf WD2 154 B1
Calnwood Rd. Dun LU4 44 C3
Calton Ave. Hert SG14 112 F7
Calton Ct. Hert SG14 112 F6
Calton House. Hert SG14 112 F6
Calverley Cl. Bis St CM23 76 E4
Calvert Rd. Barn EN5 171 D7
Calverton Rd. Luton LU3 44 F6
Cam Ctr. Hit SG4 22 A3
Cam Sq. Hit SG4 22 A3
Camberley Pl. Harp AL5 107 D6
Camborne Dr. Heml H HP2 124 E7
Cambrian Way. Heml H HP2 124 F6
Cambridge Cl. Ches EN8 148 C2
Cambridge Cotts. Thun SG11 72 E2
Cambridge Cres. Knee SG8 2 A8
Cambridge Dr. Pot B EN6 158 E8
Cambridge Rd. Bar SG8 9 A3
Cambridge Rd. Bar SG8 17 F7
Cambridge Rd. Bark SG8 17 D5
Cambridge Rd. Harl CM20 118 C6
Cambridge Rd. Hit SG4 35 B8
Cambridge Rd. Saw CM21 97 E4
Cambridge Rd. St Alb AL1 128 B2
Cambridge Rd. Sta M CM24 59 E8
Cambridge Rd. Stand SG11 55 C2
Cambridge Rd. Watf WD1 167 C5
Cambridge St. Luton LU1 63 F5
Cambridge Terr. Berk HP4 122 D4
Cameron Ct. Ware SG12 93 D2 8
Cameron Dr. Ches EN8 162 D5
Camfield. Wel G C AL7 110 F2
Camford Way. Luton LU3 44 B8
Camlet Way. St Alb AL3 127 B4
Camp Jun Mix Inf Sch. St Alb 128 B2
Camp Rd. St Alb AL1 128 B2
Camp View Rd. St Alb AL1 128 B2
Campana Ct. Barn EN5 171 D6
Campania Gr. Luton LU3 45 A8
Campbell Cl. Hit SG4 35 B8
Campers Ave. Letw SG6 22 E5
Campers Rd. Letw SG6 22 E5
Campers Wlk. Letw SG6 22 E5
Campfield Rd. Hert SG14 113 B5
Campfield Rd. St Alb AL1 128 A3
Campfield Way. Letw SG6 22 D5
Campine Cl. Ches EN8 148 D3
Campion Cl. Watf WD2 154 A6
Campion Ct. Stev SG1 50 C8
Campion Rd. Heml H HP1 123 E2
Campion Way. Royst SG8 7 E5
Campions Ct. Berk HP4 122 B3
Campions The. Bor WD6 157 A1
Campions The. Sta M CM24 59 E8
Campkin Mead. Stev SG2 51 D3
Camps Hill Jun Mix Inf Sch. Stev 51 B6
Campus Five. Letw 23 C7
Campus The. Wel G C AL8 110 D7
Canada La. Ches EN10 148 E6
Canadas The. Ches EN10 148 E6
Canberra Cl. Knee SG8 2 B5
Canberra Cl. St Alb AL3 127 F7
Canberra Gdns. Luton LU3 45 B6
Candlefield Cl. Heml H HP3 139 A8
Candlefield Rd. Heml H HP3 139 A8
Candlefield Wlk. Heml H HP3 139 A8
Caneland Ct. Wa Aby EN9 163 F5
Canfield. Bis St CM23 76 E8
Cangels Cl. Heml H HP1 124 A1
Canham Cl. Kim SG4 66 D1
Cannix Cl. Stev SG2 51 A2
Cannon House. Hit SG4 34 F6 1
Cannon La. Luton LU2 46 B5
Cannon Rd. Watf WD1 167 C4
Cannon St. St Alb AL3 127 D4
Cannons Cl. Bis St CM23 59 A1
Cannons Cl. Gu M SG8 1 F5
Cannons Cl. Stand SG11 55 D3
Cannons Mead. Sta M CM24 59 D7
Cannons Meadow. Tewin AL6 90 E2
Cannons Mill La. Bis St CM23 59 A1
Canon Brook Golf Club. Harl 117 A1
Canons Cl. Radl WD7 156 B4
Canons Field. Welw AL6 89 E8
Canons Field. Whea AL6 87 D1
Canons Gate. Harl CM20 117 A1
Canons Rd. Ware SG12 93 C2
Canonsfield Ct. Welw AL6 89 E7
Canonsfield Rd. Welw AL6 89 E8
Canopus Way. Mo Pk HA6 175 A6
Cantelowes House. Barn EN5 171 D4
Canterbury Cl. Luton LU3 44 F4
Canterbury Cl. Norwd HA6 174 F4

Canterbury Ct. St Alb AL1 ... 127 F4
Canterbury House. Bor WD6 ... 170 A7
Canterbury Rd. Bor WD6 ... 170 A7
Canterbury Rd. Watf WD1 ... 167 B7
Canterbury Way. Cro Gr WD3 ... 166 C6
Canterbury Way. Stev SG1 ... 36 F2
Cape Rd. St Alb AL1 ... 128 B3
Capel Ct. Alb SG11 ... 57 E2
Capel House. Sth Ox WD1 ... 175 D6
Capel Manor Prim Sch. Enf ... 162 B4
Capel Rd. Enf EN1 ... 162 B3
Capel Rd. Watf WD1 ... 167 E3
Capell Ave. Chor WD3 ... 164 C4
Capell Rd. Chor WD3 ... 164 D4
Capell Way. Chor WD3 ... 164 D4
Capella Rd. Mo Pk HA6 ... 174 F6
Capelvere Wlk. Watf WD1 ... 166 E8
Caponfield. Wel G C AL7 ... 111 B4
Cappell La. Sta Ab SG12 ... 115 D5
Capron Rd. Luton LU4 ... 44 E4
Captains Wlk. Berk HP4 ... 122 D3
Caractacus Cottage View. Watf WD1 ... 167 A3
Caractacus Gn. Watf WD1 ... 166 F3
Caravan La. Ric WD3 ... 165 E2
Carbone Hill. Cuf EN6,SG13 ... 146 D5
Carde Cl. Hert SG14 ... 112 F7
Cardiff Cl. Stev SG2 ... 69 B7
Cardiff Gr. Luton LU1 ... 63 D7
Cardiff Pl. Knee SG8 ... 2 A8
Cardiff Rd. Luton LU1 ... 63 D7
Cardiff Rd. Watf WD1 ... 167 B4
Cardigan Ct. Luton LU1 ... 63 D7
Cardigan St. Luton LU1 ... 63 D7
Cardinal Ave. Bor WD6 ... 170 B5
Cardinal Cl. Ham St EN7 ... 147 F5
Cardinal Ct. Bor WD6 ... 170 B6
Cardinal Gr. St Alb AL3 ... 127 B1
Cardinal Newman Sch. Luton ... 31 C1
Cardy Rd. Heml H HP1 ... 124 B3
Carew Rd. Norwd HA6 ... 174 F4
Careys Croft. Berk HP4 ... 122 A7
Carisbrook Rd. Chis AL2 ... 141 B5
Carisbrooke Ave. Watf WD2 ... 167 D8
Carisbrooke Rd. Harp AL5 ... 86 C2
Carisbrooke Rd. Luton LU4 ... 44 E1
Carleton Rd. Ches EN8 ... 148 E4
Carleton Rise. Welw AL6 ... 89 C6
Carlisle Ave. St Alb AL3 ... 127 D4
Carlton Bank. Harp AL5 ... 86 B1 3
Carlton Cl. Bor WD6 ... 170 D5
Carlton Cl. Luton LU3 ... 45 C2
Carlton Cres. Luton LU3 ... 45 C2
Carlton Ct. Harp AL5 ... 86 B1 1
Carlton Ct. Watf WD1 ... 167 C3
Carlton Rd. Harp AL5 ... 86 B2
Carman Ct. Tri HP23 ... 99 F3
Carmelite Cl. Har HA3 ... 176 C2
Carmelite Rd. Dun LU4 ... 44 A3
Carmelite Rd. Har HA3 ... 176 C1
Carmelite Way. Har HA3 ... 176 C1
Carmelite Wlk. Har HA3 ... 176 C2
Carmen Ct. Bor WD6 ... 156 F1
Carnaby Rd. Hod EN10 ... 134 E3
Carnarvon Rd. Barn EN5 ... 171 E6
Carnegie Dr. St Alb AL3 ... 127 D7
Carnegie Gdns. Luton LU3 ... 45 A8
Caro La. Heml H HP3 ... 125 B1
Carol Cl. Luton LU3 ... 45 B4
Caroline Pl. Watf WD1 ... 167 E3
Caroon Dr. Sar WD3 ... 152 B3
Carpenders Ave. Sth Ox WD1 ... 175 E8
Carpenders Cl. Harp AL5 ... 85 D4
Carpenders Park Sta. Sth Ox ... 175 D7
Carpenter Way. Pot B EN6 ... 159 D6
Carpenters Rd. Enf EN1 ... 162 C3
Carpenters The. Bis St CM23 ... 76 B5
Carpenters Wood Dr. Chor WD3 ... 164 B5
Carrigans. Bis St CM23 ... 76 E8
Carrington Ave. Bor WD6 ... 170 C4
Carrington Cl. Barn EN5 ... 171 A4
Carrington Cl. Bor WD6 ... 170 C4
Carrington Pl. Tri HP23 ... 100 C5
Carrington Sq. Stan HA3 ... 176 C3
Carsdale Cl. Luton LU3 ... 45 A6
Cart Path. Watf WD2 ... 154 C6
Carteret Rd. Luton LU2 ... 46 C1
Carterhatch La. Enf EN1 ... 161 F1
Carters Cl. Arl SG15 ... 11 A7
Carters Cl. Ast SG2 ... 51 D4
Carters La. Hit SG5 ... 34 A6
Carters Leys. Bis St CM23 ... 76 D8
Carters Way. Arl SG15 ... 11 A7
Carters Wlk. Arl SG15 ... 11 A7
Cartersfield Rd. Wa Aby EN9 ... 163 C5
Cartwright Rd. Royst SG8 ... 7 D5
Cartwright Rd. Stev SG1 ... 37 C2
Carve Ley. Wel G C AL7 ... 111 B5
Carvers Croft. Welw SG3 ... 69 B2
Cashio La. Letw SG6 ... 23 A8
Caslon Way. Letw SG6 ... 11 F1
Cassandra Gate. Ches EN8 ... 148 F4
Cassio Coll. Watf ... 154 A1
Cassio Rd. Watf WD1 ... 167 B5
Cassiobridge Rd. Watf WD1 ... 166 E5
Cassiobridge Terr. Cro Gr WD3 ... 166 D4
Cassiobury Dr. Watf WD1 ... 166 F7
Cassiobury Dr. Watf WD1 ... 167 A6
Cassiobury Inf Sch. Watf ... 166 E8
Cassiobury Park Ave. Watf WD1 ... 166 F6
Cassiobury Prim Sch. Watf ... 166 E8
Castano Ct. Abb L WD5 ... 153 E8
Castellane Cl. Har HA7 ... 176 F3 1
Castile Ct. Ches EN8 ... 163 A5
Castle Cl. Bus WD2 ... 168 B3
Castle Cl. Hod EN11 ... 115 C1
Castle Croft Rd. Luton LU1 ... 63 A6
Castle Gate Way. Berk HP4 ... 122 C6
Castle Hill Ave. Berk HP4 ... 122 C5
Castle Hill. Berk HP4 ... 122 C6
Castle Hill Cl. Berk HP4 ... 122 C5
Castle Mead Gdns. Hert SG14 ... 113 C6
Castle Mead. Heml H HP1 ... 124 B1
Castle Mews. Berk HP4 ... 122 D4
Castle Rd. Enf EN3 ... 162 E1
Castle Rd. Hod EN11 ... 115 C1
Castle Rd. St Alb AL1 ... 128 B3
Castle Rise. Whea AL4 ... 86 F2
Castle St. Berk HP4 ... 122 C4
Castle St. Bis St CM23 ... 76 F6
Castle St. Hert SG14 ... 113 C5
Castle St. Luton LU1 ... 63 E6
Castle St. Wing HP22 ... 60 B3
Castle View. Bis St CM23 ... 77 A7 3
Castle Wlk. Sta M CM24 ... 59 E6
Castles Cl. Stot SG5 ... 11 F8
Catalin Ct. Wa Aby EN9 ... 163 D6
Caterham Ct. Wa Aby EN9 ... 163 F5
Catesby Gn. Luton LU3 ... 31 A1
Catham Cl. St Alb AL1 ... 128 B1
Cathedral Ct. St Alb AL3 ... 127 B1
Catherall Rd. Luton LU3 ... 45 B6
Catherine Cl. Heml H HP2 ... 125 B8
Catherine Rd. Enf EN3 ... 162 E3
Catherine St. St Alb AL3 ... 127 D4
Catisfield Rd. Enf EN3 ... 162 E2
Catkin Cl. Heml H HP1 ... 124 B4
Catlin St. Heml H HP3 ... 138 B8
Catsbrook Rd. Luton LU3 ... 45 B6
Catsdell Bottom. Heml H HP3 ... 139 B8
Catsey La. Bus WD2 ... 168 C2
Catsey Wood. Bus WD2 ... 168 C2
Catterick Way. Bor WD6 ... 169 F8
Cattlegate Hill. Nort EN6 ... 160 D7
Cattlegate Rd. Cre H EN2 ... 161 A5
Cattlegate Rd. Nort EN6 ... 160 D6
Cattsdell. Heml H HP2 ... 124 E5
Causeway Cl. Pot B EN6 ... 159 D8
Causeway House. Abb L WD5 ... 153 E8
Causeway The. Bis St CM23 ... 76 F7
Causeway The. Brag SG9 ... 42 D1
Causeway The. Bre P SG9 ... 30 B1
Causeway The. Bun SG9 ... 40 F8
Causeway The. Fur P SG9 ... 43 A4
Causeway The. Knee SG8 ... 2 A5
Causeway The. Pot B EN6 ... 159 D8
Causeway The. Ther SG8 ... 15 F7
Cautherly La. Gt Am SG12 ... 115 A5
Cavalier Cl. Luton LU3 ... 45 A5
Cavalier Ct. Berk HP4 ... 122 C4
Cavalier. Stev SG1 ... 36 B1
Cavan Ct. Hat AL10 ... 130 A4
Cavan Dr. St Alb AL3 ... 127 D8
Cavan Rd. Red AL3 ... 106 A6
Cavell Rd. Ham St EN7 ... 148 A4
Cavell Wlk. Stev SG2 ... 51 C5
Cavendish Cres. Bor WD6 ... 170 A5
Cavendish Ct. Cro Gr WD3 ... 166 D4
Cavendish Rd. Barn EN5 ... 171 C6
Cavendish Rd. Luton LU3 ... 45 B2
Cavendish Rd. Mark AL3 ... 83 D6
Cavendish Rd. St Alb AL1 ... 127 F3
Cavendish Rd. Stev SG1 ... 50 B5
Cavendish Sch The. Heml H ... 124 B4
Cavendish Way. Hat AL10 ... 129 F5
Cawkell Cl. Sta M CM24 ... 59 D7
Cawley Hill Sch. Bor ... 170 A8
Caxton Ct. Enf EN3 ... 162 E4
Caxton Hill. Hert SG13 ... 113 F6
Caxton Rd. Hod EN11 ... 115 B2
Caxton Way. Mo Pk WD1 ... 166 D2
Caxton Way. Stev SG1 ... 50 B4
Cecil Cl. Bis St CM23 ... 77 D7
Cecil Cres. Hat AL10 ... 130 B7
Cecil Ct. Barn EN5 ... 171 D6
Cecil Rd. Bric SG13 ... 113 C3
Cecil Rd. Ches EN8 ... 162 E7
Cecil Rd. Hod EN11 ... 135 C8
Cecil Rd. Pot B EN6 ... 158 B7
Cecil Rd. St Alb AL1 ... 127 F3
Cecil St. Watf WD2 ... 154 B1
Cedar Ave. Ches EN8 ... 162 D6
Cedar Ave. Ick SG5 ... 21 E4
Cedar Cl. Hert SG14 ... 113 B6
Cedar Cl. Pot B EN6 ... 145 A1
Cedar Cl. Saw CM21 ... 97 E1
Cedar Cl. Ware SG12 ... 114 D8
Cedar Cres. Royst SG8 ... 7 B6
Cedar Ct. Bis St CM23 ... 58 F1
Cedar Ct. St Alb AL4 ... 128 D3
Cedar Dr. Pnr HA5 ... 176 A4
Cedar Gn. Hod EN11 ... 135 A5
Cedar Lawn Ave. Barn EN5 ... 171 E4
Cedar Park Rd. Enf EN2 ... 161 C1
Cedar Pk. Bis St CM23 ... 76 D4
Cedar Pl. Norwd HA6 ... 174 C4
Cedar Rd. Berk HP4 ... 122 E3
Cedar Rd. Enf EN2 ... 161 C1
Cedar Rd. Hat AL10 ... 130 A4
Cedar Rd. Watf WD1 ... 167 D3
Cedar Way. Berk HP4 ... 122 D3
Cedar Wlk. Heml H HP3 ... 124 D1
Cedar Wood Dr. Watf WD2 ... 154 B4
Cedars Ave. Ric WD3 ... 165 C1
Cedars Cl. Bor WD6 ... 170 B5
Cedars Cty Prim Sch. Har ... 176 C2
Cedars The. Harp AL5 ... 86 B1
Cedars The. St Alb AL3 ... 127 C5
Cedarwood Dr. St Alb AL4 ... 128 D3
Celandine Dr. Luton LU3 ... 45 A8
Cell Barnes Cl. St Alb AL1 ... 128 B1
Cell Barnes Hospl. St Alb ... 128 C1
Cell Barnes La. St Alb AL1 ... 128 B1
Cemetery Hill. Heml H HP1 ... 124 C2
Cemetery Rd. Bis St CM23 ... 76 F6
Cemmaes Court Rd. Heml H HP1 ... 124 C3
Cemmaes Meadow. Heml H HP1 ... 124 C3
Central App. Letw SG6 ... 22 F6
Central Ave. Ches EN8 ... 162 E6
Central Ave. Henlw SG16 ... 10 B3
Central Ave. Whip LU6 ... 81 E8
Central Dr. St Alb AL4 ... 128 C4
Central Dr. Wel G C AL7 ... 110 F8
Central Rd. Harl CM20 ... 118 A4
Central Way. Norwd HA6 ... 174 E3
Centre Way. Wa Aby EN9 ... 163 C3
Centro. Heml H HP2 ... 125 C5
Century Rd. Hod EN11 ... 135 A7
Century Rd. Ware SG12 ... 93 D2
Cervantes Ct. Norwd HA6 ... 174 F3
Chace Ave. Pot B EN6 ... 159 D7
Chace The. Stev SG2 ... 50 F1
Chad La. Fla AL3 ... 84 C4
Chadwell Ave. Ches EN8 ... 148 C3
Chadwell Cl. Luton LU2 ... 45 F1
Chadwell Rd. Stev SG1 ... 50 B4
Chadwell Rise. Ware SG12 ... 114 C8
Chadwell. Ware SG12 ... 114 C8
Chaffinch La. Watf WD1 ... 166 F2
Chaffinches Gn. Heml H HP3 ... 139 A7
Chagney Cl. Letw SG6 ... 22 E6
Chalet Cl. Berk HP4 ... 121 F4
Chalfont Cl. Heml H HP2 ... 125 B8
Chalfont La. Chor WD3 ... 164 B4
Chalfont La. Map Cr WD3 ... 172 D3
Chalfont Pl. St Alb AL1 ... 127 E3
Chalfont Rd. Map Cr WD3 ... 172 C7
Chalfont Way. Luton LU2 ... 46 D2
Chalfont Wlk. Pnr HA5 ... 175 C1 4
Chalgrove. Wel G C AL7 ... 111 D7
Chalk Dale. Wel G C AL7 ... 111 B7
Chalk Dell Inf Sch. Hert ... 113 C4
Chalk Field. Letw ... 23 C3
Chalk Hill. Gt Of LU2 ... 47 A5
Chalk Hill. Watf WD1 ... 167 E3
Chalk Hills. Bal ... 23 F5
Chalkdell Fields. St Alb AL4 ... 128 A7
Chalkdell Hill. Heml H HP2 ... 124 E3
Chalkdell Path. Hit SG5 ... 34 D8 8
Chalkdown Cl. Luton LU2 ... 45 E6
Chalkdown. Stev SG2 ... 51 D7
Chalks Ave. Saw CM21 ... 97 D3
Challney Cl. Luton LU4 ... 44 D2
Challney High Sch. Luton ... 44 D2
Chalmers Ct. Cro Gr WD3 ... 165 F3
Chalton Rd. Luton LU4 ... 44 C5
Chamberlaines. Harp AL5 ... 85 A5
Chambers La. Ick SG5 ... 21 E4
Chambers' St. Hert SG14 ... 113 C6
Chambersbury La. Heml H HP3 ... 139 A7
Chambersbury Prim Sch. Heml H ... 139 B8
Champions Cl. Bor WD6 ... 157 B2
Champions Gn. Hod EN11 ... 115 B1
Champions Way. Hod EN11 ... 115 A1
Chancellor's Sch. Bro Pk ... 145 A6
Chancellors Rd. Stev SG1 ... 36 D1
Chancery Cl. St Alb AL4 ... 128 D8
Chandler's La. Sar WD3 ... 152 E2
Chandlers Rd. St Alb AL4 ... 128 C6
Chandlers Way. Hert SG14 ... 113 A6
Chandos Cl. L Chal HP6 ... 150 C1
Chandos Rd. Bor WD6 ... 170 A7
Chandos Rd. Luton LU4 ... 44 F1
Chantry Cl. Bis St CM23 ... 76 E8
Chantry Cl. Enf EN2 ... 161 C1
Chantry Cl. Kin L WD4 ... 139 A2
Chantry Ct. Hat AL10 ... 130 A4
Chantry Fst & Mid Sch. Har ... 176 C2
Chantry La. Hat AL10 ... 129 F4
Chantry La. Hat AL10 ... 130 A4
Chantry La. L Wy SG4 ... 36 A3
Chantry La. L Wym SG4 ... 35 F2
Chantry La. Lon C AL2 ... 142 D5
Chantry Pl. Har HA3 ... 176 B2
Chantry Rd. Bis St CM23 ... 76 E8
Chantry Rd. Har HA3 ... 176 B2
Chantry The. Bis St CM23 ... 76 F8
Chantry The. Harl CM20 ... 118 A2
Chaomans. Letw SG6 ... 22 F3
Chapel Cl. L Gad HP4 ... 102 D6
Chapel Cl. Luton LU2 ... 45 C8
Chapel Cl. St Alb AL1 ... 141 D8
Chapel Cotts. Heml H HP2 ... 124 D4
Chapel Croft. Chipf WD4 ... 152 A8
Chapel Crofts. Nthch HP4 ... 121 E6
Chapel End. Bun SG9 ... 40 E7
Chapel End. Hod EN11 ... 135 A5
Chapel End La. Wils HP23 ... 99 C8
Chapel Hill. Sta M CM24 ... 59 E6
Chapel La. Hertng SG14 ... 112 B3
Chapel La. L Had SG11 ... 75 A8
Chapel La. Lon M HP23 ... 79 B4
Chapel Meadow. Tri HP23 ... 100 B6
Chapel Pl. Stot SG5 ... 11 F5
Chapel Rd. Bre Gr SG4 ... 65 E8
Chapel Rd. Fla AL3 ... 84 B2
Chapel Row. Hare UB9 ... 173 C2
Chapel Row. Hit SG5 ... 34 F8 6
Chapel St. Berk HP4 ... 122 D4
Chapel St. Heml H HP2 ... 124 D4
Chapel St. Hin SG7 ... 3 D6
Chapel St. Luton LU1 ... 63 E6
Chapel St. Tri HP23 ... 99 F3
Chapel Viaduct. Luton LU1 ... 63 E7
Chapelfields. Sta Ab SG12 ... 115 D4
Chapman Rd. Stev SG1 ... 36 B1
Chapmans End. Stand SG11 ... 55 D3
Chapmans Yd. Watf WD1 ... 167 C5
Chappell Ct. Ton SG12 ... 92 E7
Chapter House Rd. Dun LU4 ... 44 A3
Chard Dr. Luton LU3 ... 31 B1
Chardins Cl. Heml H HP1 ... 123 F4
Charles St. Berk HP4 ... 122 B4
Charles St. Heml H HP1 ... 124 C2
Charles St. Luton LU2 ... 63 F8
Charles St. Tri HP23 ... 100 A3
Charlesworth Cl. Heml H HP3 ... 124 D1 4
Charlock Way. Watf WD1 ... 166 F3
Charlton Cl. Hod EN11 ... 135 A6
Charlton Mead La. Hod EN11 ... 135 D5
Charlton Rd. Hit SG5 ... 34 D5
Charlton Way. Hod EN11 ... 135 A6
Charlwood Cl. Har HA3 ... 176 E4
Charlwood Rd. Dun LU4 ... 44 B1
Charmbury Rise. Luton LU2 ... 46 A4
Charmouth Ct. St Alb AL1 ... 128 A6
Charmouth Rd. St Alb AL1 ... 128 A5
Charndon Cl. Luton LU3 ... 31 B1
Charnwood Rd. Enf EN1 ... 162 B3
Charter Pl. Watf WD1 ... 167 C6
Chartley Ave. Har HA7 ... 176 F4
Chartridge Cl. Barn EN5 ... 171 A4
Chartridge Cl. Bus WD2 ... 168 C3
Chartridge Way. Heml H HP2 ... 125 C3
Chartwell Cl. Wa Aby EN9 ... 163 E6
Chartwell Ct. Barn EN5 ... 171 E5 8
Chartwell Dr. Luton LU2 ... 45 E3
Chartwell Rd. Norwd HA6 ... 174 F4
Chasden Rd. Heml H HP1 ... 123 F5
Chase Cl. Arl SG15 ... 11 A8
Chase Farm Hospl. Enf ... 161 A1
Chase Hill Rd. Arl SG15 ... 11 A7
Chase St. Luton LU1 ... 63 E6
Chase The. Bis St CM23 ... 76 F6
Chase The. Gofs O EN7 ... 147 B3
Chase The. Gt Am SG12 ... 115 A6
Chase The. Heml H HP2 ... 124 E2
Chase The. Hert SG13 ... 113 F6
Chase The. Radl WD7 ... 155 F4
Chase The. Watf WD1 ... 166 E5
Chase The. Welw AL6 ... 89 F7
Chaseside Cl. Ched LU7 ... 80 A7
Chaseways. Saw CM21 ... 118 C8
Chasten Hill. Letw SG6 ... 22 D7
Chater Inf Sch. Watf ... 167 A5
Chatsworth Cl. Bis St CM23 ... 76 C7
Chatsworth Cl. Bor WD6 ... 170 A6
Chatsworth Ct. St Alb AL1 ... 127 F3
Chatsworth Ct. Stev SG2 ... 50 F1
Chatsworth Rd. Luton LU4 ... 45 B1
Chatteris Cl. Luton LU4 ... 44 D4
Chatterton. Letw SG6 ... 23 C5
Chatton Cl. Luton LU2 ... 46 E2
Chaucer Cl. Berk HP4 ... 121 F5
Chaucer House. Barn EN5 ... 171 D5
Chaucer Rd. Luton LU3 ... 45 C2
Chaucer Rd. Royst SG8 ... 7 C8
Chaucer Way. Hit SG4 ... 35 C7
Chaucer Way. Hod EN11 ... 115 A2
Chaucer Wlk. Heml H HP2 ... 105 B1
Chaul End La. Luton LU4 ... 44 E1
Chaul End Rd. Cad LU1 ... 62 D6
Chaul End Rd. Dun LU1 ... 44 B1
Chaulden House Gdns. Heml H HP1 ... 123 F1
Chaulden Jun & Inf Schs. Heml H ... 123 F2
Chaulden La. Heml H HP1 ... 123 E1
Chaulden Terr. Heml H HP1 ... 123 F2
Chauncey House. Watf WD1 ... 166 E3
Chauncy Ave. Pot B EN6 ... 159 C6
Chauncy Cl. Ware SG12 ... 93 D3
Chauncy Ct. Hert SG14 ... 113 D6 16
Chauncy Gdns. Bal SG7 ... 13 B1
Chauncy House. Stev SG1 ... 50 E6 3
Chauncy Rd. Stev SG1 ... 50 E6
Chauncy Sch The. Ware ... 93 B2
Chaworth Gn. Luton LU4 ... 44 C5
Cheapside. Luton LU1 ... 63 E7
Cheapside Sq. Luton LU1 ... 63 E7
Chedburgh. Wel G C AL7 ... 111 D7
Cheddington Cty Combd Sch. Ched ... 80 A7
Cheddington La. Ched HP23 ... 79 C5
Cheddington La. Lon M HP23 ... 79 C5
Cheddington Rd. Pit LU7 ... 80 C4
Cheffins Rd. Hod EN11 ... 114 F1
Chells La. Stev SG2 ... 51 D7
Chells Way. Stev SG2 ... 51 B6
Chelmsford Rd. Hert SG14 ... 113 B5
Chelsing Rise. Heml H HP2 ... 125 C2
Chelsworth Cl. Luton LU2 ... 46 D1
Chelveston. Wel G C AL7 ... 111 D7
Chelwood Ave. Hat AL10 ... 130 A8
Chelwood Cl. Norwd HA6 ... 174 C3
Chenduit Way. Stan HA7 ... 176 F5
Cheney Rd. Luton LU4 ... 44 C5
Chenies Ave. L Chal HP6 ... 150 D1
Chenies Ct. Heml H HP2 ... 125 B8
Chenies Gr. Bis St CM23 ... 76 D6
Chenies Rd. Chor WD3 ... 164 E6
Chenies Way. Watf WD1 ... 166 E2
Chennells Cl. Hit SG4 ... 22 B2
Chennells. Hat AL10 ... 129 F4
Chennies The. Harp AL5 ... 107 C7
Chepstow Cl. Stev SG1 ... 51 B8
Chepstow. Harp AL5 ... 85 F2
Chequer Ct. Luton LU1 ... 63 F6
Chequer La. Red AL3 ... 106 B4
Chequer St. Luton LU1 ... 63 F6
Chequer St. St Alb AL1 ... 127 D3
Chequers. Bis St CM23 ... 76 C8
Chequers Bridge Rd. Stev SG1 ... 50 C6
Chequers Cl. Bun SG9 ... 40 D8
Chequers Cl. Pit LU7 ... 80 C4
Chequers Cl. Stand SG11 ... 55 D4
Chequers Cl. Stot SG5 ... 12 A6
Chequers Cotts. Pres SG4 ... 48 D6
Chequers Field. Wel G C AL7 ... 110 D3
Chequers. Hat AL9 ... 130 D8
Chequers Hill. Fla AL3 ... 84 C2
Chequers La. Abb L WD5 ... 140 C1
Chequers La. Pit LU7 ... 80 C5
Chequers La. Pres SG4 ... 48 D7
Chequers. Wel G C AL7 ... 110 D3
Chequers Wlk. Wa Aby EN9 ... 163 F6
Cheriton Ct. St Alb AL4 ... 128 D7
Cherry Bank. Heml H HP2 ... 124 D5
Cherry Cl. Kneb SG3 ... 68 F4
Cherry Croft Gdns. Pnr HA5 ... 175 F3 2
Cherry Croft. Wel G C AL8 ... 89 D2
Cherry Dr. Royst SG8 ... 7 E7
Cherry Gdns. Bis St CM23 ... 77 A8
Cherry Gdns. Saw CM21 ... 97 E4
Cherry Gdns. Tri HP23 ... 99 F3
Cherry Hill. Chis AL2 ... 141 A6
Cherry Hill. Har HA3 ... 176 E4
Cherry Hill. Ric WD3 ... 165 B6
Cherry Hollow. Abb L WD5 ... 153 F8
Cherry Orch. Heml H HP1 ... 124 A5
Cherry Rd. Enf EN3 ... 162 C1
Cherry Tree Ave. Lon C AL2 ... 142 D5
Cherry Tree Cl. Arl SG15 ... 11 A4
Cherry Tree Cl. Luton LU2 ... 46 A1
Cherry Tree Gn. Hert SG14 ... 112 F7
Cherry Tree Jun Mix Inf Sch. Watf ... 154 A3
Cherry Tree La. Chol HP23 ... 120 A3
Cherry Tree La. Chor WD3 ... 164 C1
Cherry Tree La. Heml H HP2 ... 125 C7
Cherry Tree La. Whea AL4 ... 87 A2
Cherry Tree Rd. Hod EN11 ... 135 A7
Cherry Tree Rd. Watf WD2 ... 154 B3
Cherry Tree Rise. Walk SG2 ... 38 B1
Cherry Trees. L Ston SG16 ... 10 B3
Cherry Way. Hat AL10 ... 130 A2
Cherry Wlk. Ric WD3 ... 165 C7
Cherrydale. Watf WD1 ... 166 F5
Chertsey Cl. Luton LU2 ... 64 D8
Chertsey Rise. Stev SG2 ... 51 C4
Cherwell Cl. Cro Gr WD3 ... 166 A4
Chesfield Cl. Bis St CM23 ... 76 F5
Chesford Rd. Luton LU2 ... 46 C4
Chesham Ct. Norwd HA6 ... 174 F4
Chesham Prep Sch. Ash Gr ... 136 A4
Chesham Rd. Berk HP4 ... 122 C3
Chesham Rd. Bov HP3 ... 136 E3
Chesham Rd. Wigg HP23 ... 120 E7
Chesham Way. Watf WD1 ... 166 F3
Cheshunt Bonneygrove Inf Sch. Ches ... 148 A1
Cheshunt Bonneygrove Jun Sch. Ches ... 148 A1
Cheshunt Cottage Hospl. Ches ... 148 D2
Cheshunt Ctr The. Ches EN8 ... 148 D3
Cheshunt Gram Sch. Ches ... 148 E1
Cheshunt Sch The. Ches ... 148 C1
Cheshunt Wash. Ches EN8 ... 148 E4
Cheslyn Cl. Luton LU2 ... 46 E2
Chess Cl. Lat HP5 ... 150 D3
Chess Cl. Ric WD3 ... 165 D5
Chess Hill. Ric WD3 ... 165 D5
Chess La. Ric WD3 ... 165 D5
Chess Vale Rise. Cro Gr WD3 ... 165 F3
Chess Way. Chor WD3 ... 165 A6
Chesswood Way. Pnr HA5 ... 175 D1
Chester Ave. Luton LU4 ... 44 E3
Chester Cl. Luton LU4 ... 44 F2
Chester Cl. Pot B EN6 ... 145 B2
Chester Pl. Norwd HA6 ... 174 E3
Chester Rd. Bor WD6 ... 170 D6
Chester Rd. Norwd HA6 ... 174 F3
Chester Rd. Stev SG1 ... 37 A1
Chester Rd. Watf WD1 ... 167 A5
Chesterfield Flats. Barn EN5 ... 171 D4
Chesterfield Rd. Barn EN5 ... 171 D4
Chesterfield Rd. Enf EN3 ... 162 E2
Chesterfield Sch. Enf ... 162 E2
Chesterton Ave. Harp AL5 ... 86 D1
Chestnut Ave. Henlw SG16 ... 10 C3
Chestnut Ave. Luton LU3 ... 44 C8
Chestnut Ave. Norwd HA6 ... 174 F2
Chestnut Ave. Ric WD3 ... 165 A4
Chestnut Ave. Ware SG12 ... 93 F3
Chestnut Cl. Bis St CM23 ... 76 E6
Chestnut Cl. Dagn HP4 ... 81 C5
Chestnut Cl. Hun SG12 ... 95 D1
Chestnut Cl. Pot En HP4 ... 123 B6
Chestnut Ct. Hit SG5 ... 34 D8 4
Chestnut Dr. Berk HP4 ... 122 D3
Chestnut Dr. Har HA3 ... 176 F2
Chestnut Dr. St Alb AL4 ... 128 C5
Chestnut La. Barn N20 ... 171 E1
Chestnut La. Knee SG8 ... 2 B6
Chestnut Rd. Enf EN3 ... 162 E3
Chestnut Rise. Bus WD2 ... 168 B2
Chestnut Wlk. Royst SG8 ... 7 E6
Chestnut Wlk. Stev SG1 ... 36 D1
Chestnut Wlk. Watf WD2 ... 154 A2
Chestnuts The. Cod SG4 ... 67 F2
Chestnuts The. Heml H HP3 ... 137 F7
Chestnuts The. Hert SG13 ... 113 D5
Cheverells Cl. Mark AL3 ... 83 D4
Cheviot Cl. Bus WD2 ... 168 C3
Cheviot Cl. Luton LU3 ... 44 D7
Cheviot Rd. Luton LU3 ... 44 D7
Cheviots. Hat AL10 ... 130 A3
Cheviots. Heml H HP2 ... 124 F6
Cheyne Cl. Pit LU7 ... 80 D4
Cheyne Cl. Ware SG12 ... 93 D3
Cheynes Inf Sch. Luton ... 44 D8
Chicheley Gdns. Har HA3 ... 176 C3
Chichester Way. Watf WD2 ... 154 E6
Chigwell Hurst Ct. Pnr HA5 ... 175 D1
Chilcott Rd. Watf WD2 ... 153 F3
Chilcourt. Royst SG8 ... 7 C6
Childbrook House. Watf WD1 ... 166 E3
Childs Ave. Hare UB9 ... 173 C1
Childwick Ct. Heml H HP3 ... 139 B8
Chilham Cl. Heml H HP2 ... 124 E2
Chiltern Ave. Bus WD2 ... 168 C3
Chiltern Cl. Bor WD6 ... 169 F7
Chiltern Cl. Bus WD2 ... 168 B3
Chiltern Cl. Gofs O EN7 ... 147 B4
Chiltern Cl. Ware SG12 ... 93 D3
Chiltern Ct. St Alb AL4 ... 128 D7
Chiltern Dr. Ric WD3 ... 165 A2
Chiltern Gdns. Luton LU4 ... 44 F3
Chiltern Park Ave. Berk HP4 ... 122 A6
Chiltern Rd. Bal SG7 ... 23 F6
Chiltern Rd. Hit SG4 ... 35 A7
Chiltern Rd. St Alb AL4 ... 128 C7
Chiltern Rd. Wing HP22 ... 60 A3
Chiltern Rise. Luton LU1 ... 63 D6
Chiltern View. Letw SG6 ... 22 D5
Chiltern Way. Tri HP23 ... 100 C5
Chilterns. Hat AL10 ... 130 A2
Chilterns. Heml H HP2 ... 124 E5
Chilterns The. Hit SG4 ... 35 A6
Chilterns The. Ken Co LU6 ... 82 F8
Chilton Ct. Harp AL5 ... 86 B1
Chilton Gn. Wel G C AL7 ... 111 C6
Chilvers Bank. Bal SG7 ... 23 E7
Chilwell Gdns. Sth Ox WD1 ... 175 C6
Chilworth Gate. Hod EN10 ... 134 F1
Chinnery Cl. Enf EN1 ... 161 F1
Chinnery Hill. Bis St CM23 ... 76 F5
Chipperfield Rd. Bov HP3 ... 137 C3
Chipperfield Rd. Heml H HP3 ... 138 C7
Chipperfield Rd. Kin L WD4 ... 138 D2
Chipping Cl. Barn EN5 ... 171 E6
Chippingfield. Harl CM17 ... 118 C3
Chirdland House. Watf WD1 ... 166 E3
Chishill Rd. Bar SG8 ... 9 A2
Chishill Rd. Gt Ch SG8 ... 9 F3
Chishill Windmill. Gt Ch ... 9 C2
Chiswell Ct. Watf WD2 ... 154 C1
Chiswellgreen La. Chis AL2 ... 140 E6
Chobham Ct. Luton LU1 ... 63 F6
Chobham St. Luton LU1 ... 63 F6
Chobham Wlk. Luton LU1 ... 63 E6 5
Cholesbury La. Chol HP23 ... 120 B2
Chorleywood Bottom. Chor WD3 ... 164 D4
Chorleywood Cl. Ric WD3 ... 165 D2
Chorleywood Coll. Chor ... 164 F5
Chorleywood Cty Prim Sch. Chor ... 164 C3
Chorleywood Rd. Ric WD3 ... 165 C4
Chorleywood Sta. Chor ... 164 D5
Chouler Gdns. Stev SG1 ... 36 C2
Chowns The. Harp AL5 ... 107 A5
Christ Church CE Inf Sch. Barn ... 171 D7
Christ Church CE Jun Mix Inf Sch. Chor ... 164 F5
Christ Church Jun Mix & Inf Sch. Ware ... 93 E1
Christ Church La. Barn EN5 ... 171 E7
Christchurch Cl. St Alb AL3 ... 127 D4
Christchurch Cres. Radl WD7 ... 156 A3
Christchurch Rd. Heml H HP2 ... 124 D4

Cow La. Watf WD2 ... 154 C3
Cowards La. Cod SG4 ... 88 F8
Cowbridge. Hert SG14 ... 113 C6
Cowdray Cl. Luton LU2 ... 46 C3
Cowles. Ham St EN7 ... 147 F4
Cowley Hill. Bor WD6 ... 157 B1
Cowlins. Harl CM17 ... 118 D4
Cowper Cres. Hert SG14 ... 92 B1
Cowper Ct. Mark AL3 ... 83 D5
Cowper Ct. Watf WD2 ... 154 A2
Cowper Endowed Prim Sch. Tewin . 90 E2
Cowper Rd. Berk HP4 ... 122 B4
Cowper Rd. Harp AL5 ... 86 C1
Cowper Rd. Heml H HP1 ... 124 B2
Cowper Rd. Mark AL3 ... 83 D5
Cowper Rd. Wel G C AL7 ... 110 F4
Cowper Rise. Mark AL3 ... 83 D5
Cowper St. Luton LU1 ... 63 E5
Cowpers Way. Tewin AL6 ... 90 D5
Cowridge Cres. Luton LU2 ... 64 A8
Cowslip Cl. Royst SG8 ... 7 F5
Cowslip Hill. Letw SG6 ... 22 E7
Cowslips. Wel G C AL7 ... 111 C5
Cox Cl. Shen WD7 ... 156 F7
Cox's Way. Arl SG15 ... 11 A6
Coxfield Cl. Heml H HP2 ... 124 E2
Coyney Gn. Luton LU3 ... 45 C1
Cozens La E. Hod EN10 ... 134 F1
Cozens La W. Hod EN10 ... 134 F1
Cozens Rd. Ware SG12 ... 94 A2
Crab La. Radl WD2 ... 155 B4
Crab Tree La. Pirt SG5 ... 20 D4
Crab Tree Rd. Kneb SG3 ... 68 F4
Crabb's La. Sto P SG9 ... 43 F6
Crabbes Cl. Hit SG5 ... 34 E7
Crabtree Cl. Bus WD2 ... 168 B4
Crabtree Cl. Heml H HP3 ... 124 D1
Crabtree Ct. Heml H HP3 ... 124 E1 1
Crabtree Dell. Letw SG6 ... 23 B3
Crabtree Inf Sch. Harp ... 86 C1
Crabtree La. Harp AL5 ... 107 C8
Crabtree La. Heml H HP3 ... 124 D1
Crabtree Prim Sch. Harp ... 86 C1
Crackley Meadow. Heml H HP2 ... 125 B8
Cradock Rd. Dun LU4 ... 44 B1
Cragg Ave. Radl WD7 ... 155 F3
Cragside. Stev SG2 ... 69 C7
Craig Mount. Radl WD7 ... 156 B4
Craigavon Rd. Heml H HP2 ... 124 F7
Craiglands. St Alb AL4 ... 128 D7
Craigs Wlk. Ches EN8 ... 148 D3
Craigweil Ave. Radl WD7 ... 156 B4
Crakers Mead. Watf WD1 ... 167 B6 4
Cranborne Ave. Hit SG5 ... 34 D6
Cranborne Cl. Bric SG13 ... 113 C3
Cranborne Cl. Pot B EN6 ... 158 E8
Cranborne Cres. Pot B EN6 ... 158 E8
Cranborne Ct. Enf EN3 ... 162 D3
Cranborne Gdns. Wel G C AL7 ... 110 F5
Cranborne Ind Est. Pot B ... 144 E1
Cranborne Par. Pot B EN6 ... 158 D8
Cranborne Prim Sch. Pot B ... 158 F8
Cranborne Rd. Ches EN8 ... 162 D7
Cranborne Rd. Hat AL10 ... 130 B6
Cranborne Rd. Hod EN11 ... 135 C7
Cranborne Rd. Pot B EN6 ... 144 E1
Cranbourne Dr. Harp AL5 ... 107 D6
Cranbourne Dr. Hod EN11 ... 115 C2
Cranbourne Prim Sch The. Hod ... 115 B2
Cranbourne Rd. Norwd HA6 ... 174 F1
Cranbourne. Stev SG1 ... 36 B1
Cranbrook Cl. Ware SG12 ... 93 D3
Cranbrook Dr. Coln H AL4 ... 128 E3
Cranbrook Dr. Luton LU3 ... 44 D8
Crane Mead. Ware SG12 ... 114 E8
Cranefield Dr. Watf WD2 ... 154 E6
Cranes Way. Bor WD6 ... 170 C4
Cranfield Cres. Cuf EN6 ... 146 E2
Cranford Ct. Harp AL5 ... 86 C1
Cranleigh Cl. Ches EN7 ... 148 A3
Cranleigh Gdns. Luton LU3 ... 45 D3
Cranmer Cl. Pot B EN6 ... 145 C1
Cranmer House. Kin L WD4 ... 139 A2
Cranmore Ct. St Alb AL1 ... 127 F4
Cranwell Gdns. Bis St CM23 ... 59 C1
Cravells Rd. Harp AL5 ... 107 C7
Crawford Rd. Hat AL10 ... 130 A7
Crawley Cl. Cad LU1 ... 63 C1
Crawley Dr. Heml H HP2 ... 124 F7
Crawley Gn. Luton LU2 ... 46 B1
Crawley Green Rd. Luton LU1,LU2 . 46 D1
Crawley Rd. Luton LU1 ... 63 D8
Crawley's La. Wigg HP23 ... 120 F7
Creamery Ct. Letw SG6 ... 23 C3
Crecy Gdns. Red AL3 ... 106 A6
Creighton Ave. St Alb AL1 ... 141 D8
Crescent E. Had W EN4 ... 159 C1
Crescent Rd. Bis St CM23 ... 77 A6
Crescent Rd. Heml H HP2 ... 124 D3
Crescent Rd. Luton LU2 ... 63 F8
Crescent Rise. Luton LU2 ... 63 F8
Crescent The. Abb L WD5 ... 139 F1
Crescent The. Ard SG2 ... 38 F2
Crescent The. Bri Wd AL2 ... 141 A1
Crescent The. Cad LU1 ... 62 E3
Crescent The. Cotrd SG9 ... 39 D7
Crescent The. Cro Gr WD3 ... 166 B3
Crescent The. Harl CM17 ... 118 C6
Crescent The. Henlw SG16 ... 10 C4
Crescent The. Hit SG5 ... 21 D1
Crescent The. Letw SG6 ... 23 A5
Crescent The. Mars HP23 ... 80 A1
Crescent The. Pit LU7 ... 80 C4
Crescent The. St Ipp SG4 ... 35 A3
Crescent The. Watf WD1 ... 167 C5
Crescent The. Welw AL6 ... 89 C4
Crescent W. Had W EN4 ... 159 C1
Cress End. Ric WD3 ... 165 A1
Cresset Cl. Gt Am SG12 ... 115 C3
Cresswick. Whit SG4 ... 66 E7
Crest Dr. Enf EN3 ... 162 C1
Crest Pk. Heml H HP2 ... 125 C4
Crest The. Gofs O EN7 ... 147 B4
Crest The. Luton LU3 ... 45 B7
Crest The. Saw CM21 ... 97 D2
Crest The. Ware SG12 ... 93 D3
Crest The. Welw AL6 ... 89 D8
Cresta Cl. Dun LU5 ... 44 A2
Creswick Ct. Wel G C AL7 ... 110 D5
Creswick Jun Mix Inf Sch.
Wel G C ... 110 D3
Crew Curve. Berk HP4 ... 121 F7
Crews Hill. Cer H EN2 ... 160 F5
Crews Hill Sta. Cer H ... 160 F5
Crib St. Ware SG12 ... 93 D2
Cricketer's Rd. Arl SG15 ... 11 A4
Cricketers Cl. St Alb AL3 ... 127 E4
Cricketfield La. Bis St CM23 ... 76 E8
Cringle Ct. Pot B EN6 ... 145 C1
Crispin Field. Pit LU7 ... 80 C4
Croasdaile Rd. Sta M CM24 ... 59 E8
Croasdale Cl. Sta M CM24 ... 59 E8
Crocus Field. Barn EN5 ... 171 F3
Croft Cl. Chipf WD4 ... 138 A1
Croft Ct. Hit SG5 ... 34 E7
Croft End Rd. Chipf WD4 ... 138 A1
Croft Field. Chipf WD4 ... 138 A1
Croft Field. Hat AL10 ... 130 A5
Croft La. Chipf WD4 ... 138 A1
Croft La. Letw SG6 ... 12 B1
Croft Meadow. Chipf WD4 ... 138 A1
Croft Meadows. Ched LU7 ... 80 A7
Croft Rd. Luton LU2 ... 46 B3
Croft Rd. Ware SG12 ... 93 C2
Croft The. Barn EN5 ... 171 E5
Croft The. Chis AL2 ... 141 A6
Croft The. Hod EN10 ... 148 E8
Croft The. Luton LU3 ... 44 D8
Croft The. Wars SG12 ... 94 E4
Croft The. Wel G C AL7 ... 110 F3
Crofters End. Saw CM21 ... 97 E3
Crofters Rd. Mo Pk HA6 ... 174 E6
Crofters. Saw CM21 ... 97 E3
Crofts Path. Heml H HP3 ... 125 B1
Crofts The. Heml H HP3 ... 125 B2
Crofts The. Stot SG5 ... 11 F6
Croftwell. Harp AL5 ... 107 F8
Cromer Cl. L Gad HP4 ... 102 E4
Cromer Cl. L Gad HP4 ... 102 E5
Cromer Rd. Watf WD2 ... 154 C1
Cromer Way. Luton LU2 ... 45 D7
Crompton Rd. Stev SG1 ... 50 A6
Cromwell Ave. Ches EN7 ... 148 B1
Cromwell Cl. Bis St CM23 ... 76 B7
Cromwell Cl. St Alb AL4 ... 128 D8
Cromwell Gn. Letw SG6 ... 23 B8
Cromwell Hill. Luton LU2 ... 45 D1
Cromwell Rd. Bor WD6 ... 169 E8
Cromwell Rd. Ches EN7 ... 148 B3
Cromwell Rd. Hert SG13 ... 114 A7
Cromwell Rd. Letw SG6 ... 23 B8
Cromwell Rd. Luton LU3 ... 45 D1
Cromwell Rd. Stev SG2 ... 51 C5
Cromwell Rd. Ware SG12 ... 93 F2
Cromwell Way. Pirt SG5 ... 20 D4
Crooked Mile. Wa Aby EN9 ... 163 C7
Crookhams. Wel G C AL7 ... 90 A1
Crop Comm. Hat AL10 ... 130 B7
Crosby Cl. Luton LU4 ... 45 A2
Cross La. Harp AL5 ... 107 D5
Cross La. Hert SG14 ... 113 B6
Cross Oak Rd. Berk HP4 ... 122 A4
Cross Rd. Ches EN8 ... 162 E6
Cross Rd. Hert SG14 ... 113 C7
Cross Rd. Watf WD1 ... 167 E3
Cross St. Letw SG6 ... 22 F7
Cross St. Luton LU2 ... 63 E8
Cross St. St Alb AL3 ... 127 D3 2
Cross St. Ware SG12 ... 93 E1
Cross St. Watf WD1 ... 167 C6
Cross Way. Harp AL5 ... 86 C3
Cross Way The. Har HA3 ... 176 E1
Cross Way The. Luton LU1 ... 63 C5
Crossbrook. Hat AL10 ... 129 E4
Crossbrook St. Ches EN8 ... 148 D1
Crossbrook St. Ches EN8 ... 162 D8
Crossett Gn. Heml H HP3 ... 125 C1
Crossfell Rd. Heml H HP3 ... 125 C2
Crossfield Cl. Berk HP4 ... 121 F4
Crossfield Rd. Hod EN11 ... 135 B8
Crossfields. St Alb AL3 ... 141 B8
Crossgates. Stev SG1 ... 50 E5
Crosslands. Cad LU1 ... 62 E3
Crossleys. Letw SG6 ... 11 F2
Crossmead. Watf WD1 ... 167 B3
Crossoaks La. Ridge WD6 ... 157 F5
Crossoaks La. Shen WD6 ... 157 D5
Crosspath The. Radl WD7 ... 156 A4
Crosspaths. Harp AL5 ... 85 C4
Crossway. Pnr HA5 ... 175 B1
Crossway. Wel G C AL8 ... 89 C2
Crossways. Bar SG8 ... 8 F1
Crossways. Berk HP4 ... 121 F3
Crossways. Heml H HP3 ... 125 C3
Crouch Hall Gdns. Red AL3 ... 106 A6
Crouch Hall La. Red AL3 ... 106 A6
Crouch La. Gofs O EN7 ... 147 C4
Crouchfield. Heml H HP1 ... 124 B2
Crouchfield. Hert SG14 ... 92 C1
Crouchfield La. Hert SG14 ... 92 E4
Crow Furlong. Hit SG5 ... 34 D7
Crowborough Path. Sth Ox WD1 .. 175 D6
Crowland Rd. Luton LU2 ... 46 C5
Crown Cl. Sheer CM22 ... 98 C1
Crown La. Reed SG8 ... 16 F5
Crown Lodge. Arl SG15 ... 11 A4
Crown Rd. Bor WD6 ... 170 B8
Crown Rise. Watf WD2 ... 154 D5
Crown St. Red AL3 ... 106 B5
Crown Terr. Bis St CM23 ... 77 A7
Crownfield. Lo Naz EN10 ... 135 A2
Croxdale Rd. Bor WD6 ... 170 A7
Croxley Ctr. Watf ... 166 D4
Croxley Green Sta. Cro Gr ... 166 D4
Croxley Sta. Cro Gr ... 166 B3
Croxley View. Watf WD1 ... 166 E3
Croxton Cl. Luton LU3 ... 45 A7
Crozier Ave. Bis St CM23 ... 76 C8
Crusader Way. Watf WD1 ... 166 F3
Cubbington Cl. Luton LU3 ... 45 A7
Cubitts Cl. Welw AL6 ... 89 F3
Cublands. Hert SG13 ... 114 B6
Cuckmans Dr. Chis AL2 ... 141 A6
Cuckoo's Nest. Luton LU2 ... 64 A7
Cuffley Ave. Watf WD2 ... 154 D5
Cuffley Cl. Luton LU3 ... 44 F4
Cuffley Ct. Heml H HP2 ... 125 C8
Cuffley Hill. Gofs O EN7 ... 147 B2
Cuffley Jun Mix Inf Sch. Cuf ... 146 F1
Cuffley Sta. Cuf ... 146 F2
Cullera Cl. Norwd HA6 ... 174 F4
Cullings Ct. Wa Aby EN9 ... 163 F6
Culver Rd. St Alb AL1 ... 127 E5
Culverden Rd. Sth Ox WD1 ... 175 B7
Culverhouse Rd. Luton LU3 ... 45 C3
Culworth Cl. Cad LU1 ... 62 E3
Cumberland Cl. Abb L WD5 ... 139 E7
Cumberland Cl. Hert SG14 ... 113 C8
Cumberland Ct. Hod EN11 ... 135 A7
Cumberland Ct. St Alb AL3 ... 127 E4
Cumberland Dr. Red AL3 ... 106 B6
Cumberland St. Luton LU1 ... 63 E6
Cumberlow Pl. Heml H HP2 ... 125 C2
Cumcum Hill. Ess AL9 ... 131 E2
Cundalls Rd. Ware SG12 ... 93 E2
Cunningham Ave. Enf EN3 ... 162 E3
Cunningham Ave. St Alb AL1 ... 127 F1
Cunningham Hill Inf Sch. St Alb ... 128 A1
Cunningham Hill Jun Sch. St Alb .. 128 A1
Cunningham Hill Rd. St Alb AL1 ... 128 A1
Cunningham Rd. Ches EN8 ... 148 E4
Cupid Green La. Gt Gd HP2 ... 104 E3
Cupid Green La. Heml H HP2 ... 105 A1
Curlew Cl. Berk HP4 ... 122 C3
Curlew Cl. Letw SG6 ... 11 E1
Curlew Rd. Luton LU2 ... 46 C5
Currie St. Hert SG13 ... 113 E6
Curteys. Harl CM17 ... 118 D5
Curtis Cl. Ric WD3 ... 165 A1
Curtis Rd. Heml H HP3 ... 125 D2
Curtis Way. Berk HP4 ... 122 D3
Curzon Rd. Luton LU3 ... 45 C1
Cussans House. Watf WD1 ... 166 E3
Cussons Cl. Ches EN7 ... 148 A2
Cut Throat Ave. Whip LU6 ... 81 E7
Cutenhoe Rd. Luton LU1 ... 63 E4
Cutforth Rd. Saw CM21 ... 97 E3
Cuthbert Cl. Gofs O EN7 ... 147 F2
Cutlers Gn. Luton LU2 ... 46 F2
Cutmore Dr. Coln H AL4 ... 129 B1
Cutts La. Kim SG4 ... 66 D1
Cuttsfield Terr. Heml H HP1 ... 123 F2
Cuttys La. Stev SG1 ... 50 E5
Cwmbran Ct. Heml H HP2 ... 124 F7
Cygnet Cl. Bor WD6 ... 170 C8
Cygnet Cl. Norwd HA6 ... 174 C4
Cygnet Ct. Bis St CM23 ... 76 F6
Cylers Thicket. Welw AL6 ... 89 C6
Cypress Ave. Cre H EN2 ... 161 A4
Cypress Cl. Wa Aby EN9 ... 163 D5
Cypress Rd. Har HA3 ... 176 D1
Cypress Wlk. Watf WD2 ... 154 B4
Cyrils Way. St Alb AL1 ... 141 D8

Dacorum Coll of F Ed. Heml H ... 124 C4
Dacorum Way. Heml H HP1 ... 124 C3
Dacre Cres. Kim SG4 ... 66 C1
Dacre Gdns. Bor WD6 ... 170 D4
Dacre Gn. Royst SG8 ... 7 F6
Dacre Rd. Hit SG5 ... 35 A8
Dagger La. Elst WD6 ... 169 B4
Daggs Dell Rd. Heml H HP1 ... 123 E5
Dagnall Cty Fst Sch. Dagn ... 81 C5
Dagnall Rd. Gt Gd HP1 ... 103 C5
Dagnall Rd. Whip LU6 ... 81 D8
Dagnalls. Letw SG6 ... 22 F2
Dahlia Cl. Luton LU2 ... 46 B4
Daintrees. Widf SG12 ... 95 E4
Daintry Lodge. Norwd HA6 ... 174 F3
Daisy Ct. Letw CM1 ... 23 A8
Dalby Cl. Dun LU4 ... 44 B3
Dale Ave. Kim AL4 ... 87 B5
Dale Cl. Hit SG4 ... 34 F4
Dale Cl. Pnr HA5 ... 175 B2
Dale Ct. Saw CM21 ... 97 D1
Dale Rd. Luton LU1 ... 63 C7
Dale The. Letw SG6 ... 22 E5
Dale The. Wa Aby EN9 ... 163 E5
Dales Path. Bor WD6 ... 170 D4
Dales Rd. Bor WD6 ... 170 D4
Daleside Dr. Pot B EN6 ... 158 F6
Dalewood. Harp AL5 ... 86 D1
Dalewood. Wel G C AL7 ... 111 D5
Dalkeith Rd. Harp AL5 ... 86 C1
Dallow Jun & Inf Schs. Luton ... 63 C8
Dallow Rd. Luton LU1 ... 63 B8
Dalroad Ind Est. Luton ... 63 B8
Dalton Gdns. Bis St CM23 ... 76 E3
Dalton St. St Alb AL3 ... 127 D4
Dalton Way. Whit SG4 ... 66 E7
Daltry Cl. Stev SG1 ... 36 C2
Daltry Rd. Stev SG1 ... 36 C2
Damask Cl. Wes SG4 ... 37 B8
Damask Gn. Heml H HP1 ... 123 E2
Damask Green Rd. Wes SG4 ... 37 B8
Dame Alice Owen's Sch. Pot B ... 158 E6
Dammersey Cl. Mark AL3 ... 83 F4
Dancers End La. Ast Cl HP23 ... 99 C2
Dancers Hill Rd. Pot B EN5 ... 158 E3
Dancote. Kneb SG3 ... 68 F5
Dane Acres. Bis St CM23 ... 76 D8
Dane Bridge La. Muc H SG10 ... 75 B2
Dane Cl. Harp AL5 ... 86 C4
Dane Cl. Stot SG5 ... 11 F8
Dane Ct. Hert SG13 ... 113 E6
Dane End House. Stev SG1 ... 36 C1
Dane End La. Wes SG4 ... 37 E5
Dane End Rd. Thun SG11 ... 72 E3
Dane House. Bis St CM23 ... 76 D8
Dane O'Coys Rd. Bis St CM23 ... 58 E1
Dane Pk. Bis St CM23 ... 76 D8
Dane Rd. Luton LU3 ... 45 C2
Dane St. Bis St CM23 ... 77 A7
Danebridge Rd. Muc H SG10 ... 75 B2
Danefield Rd. Pirt SG5 ... 20 C4
Danemead. Hod EN11 ... 115 A1
Danes The. Chis AL2 ... 141 C3
Danesbury Hospl. Welw ... 89 C7
Danesbury La. Welw AL6 ... 89 D8
Danesbury Park Caravan Site.
Welw ... 89 D8
Danesbury Park Rd. Welw AL6 ... 89 D8
Danesbury Pk. Hert SG14 ... 113 D7
Danesgate. Stev SG1 ... 50 D4
Danestrete. Stev SG1 ... 50 D5
Daniells. Wel G C AL7 ... 111 A7
Danvers Croft. Tri HP23 ... 100 C5
Danvers Dr. Luton LU3 ... 31 C1
Danziger Way. Bor WD6 ... 170 C8
Darby Dr. Wa Aby EN9 ... 163 C6
Darby Dr. Welw AL6 ... 68 E3
Darcy Cl. Ches EN8 ... 162 E8
Dark La. Ches EN7 ... 148 A1
Dark La. Harp AL5 ... 107 D7
Dark La. San SG9 ... 15 B1
Dark La. Wing HP22 ... 60 C3
Darkes La. Pot B EN6 ... 159 A8
Darley Rd. Bre Gr SG4 ... 47 C2
Darnicle Hill. Ham St EN7 ... 147 A6
Darr's La. Nthch HP4 ... 121 D6
Darrington Rd. Bor WD6 ... 169 E8
Darwin Cl. Heml H HP2 ... 105 B1
Darwin Cl. St Alb AL3 ... 127 E7
Darwin Gdns. Sth Ox WD1 ... 175 C5
Darwin Rd. Stev SG2 ... 51 B6
Dashes The. Harl CM20 ... 117 E1
Datchet Cl. Heml H HP2 ... 125 B8
Datchworth Turn. Heml H HP2 ... 125 C3
Davenham Ave. Mo Pk HA6 ... 174 F5
Daventer Dr. Har HA7 ... 176 F3
Davies St. Hert SG13 ... 113 E6
Davis Cres. Pirt SG5 ... 20 D4
Davis Ct. St Alb AL1 ... 127 E3
Davis' Row. Arl SG15 ... 11 A4
Davison Cl. Ches EN8 ... 148 D3
Davison Dr. Ches EN8 ... 148 D3
Davys Cl. Whea AL4 ... 108 E7
Dawes La. Sar WD3 ... 151 F3
Dawley Ct. Heml H HP2 ... 125 A7
Dawley. Wel G C AL7 ... 89 F1
Dawlish Cl. Stev SG2 ... 69 C7
Dawlish Rd. Luton LU4 ... 44 F3
Dawson Cl. Henlw SG16 ... 10 C5
Day's Cl. Royst SG8 ... 7 C5
Dayemead. Wel G C AL7 ... 111 B3
Days Cl. Hat AL10 ... 129 F5
Days Mead. Hat AL10 ... 129 F5
De Haviland Cl. Hat AL10 ... 129 F6
De Havilland Ct. Shen WD7 ... 156 E7
De Havilland Way. Abb L WD5 ... 153 F7
De Tany Ct. St Alb AL1 ... 127 D2
De Vere Wlk. Watf WD1 ... 166 E7
Deacon Cl. St Alb AL1 ... 141 D7
Deacons Cl. Bor WD6 ... 170 A5
Deacons Cl. Pnr HA5 ... 175 B1
Deacons Ct. Luton LU2 ... 63 D8 8
Deacons Hill. Watf WD1 ... 167 C3
Deacon's Hill Rd. Bor WD6 ... 170 A4
Deacons Hts. Bor WD6 ... 170 A3
Deacons Way. Hit SG5 ... 21 D1
Deaconsfield Rd. Heml H HP3 ... 138 E8
Dead Woman's La. Pres SG4 ... 48 C7
Deadman's Ash La. Sar WD3 ... 152 B3
Deakin Cl. Watf WD1 ... 166 E2
Dean Ct. Watf WD2 ... 154 D6
Dean Field. Bov HP3 ... 137 A4
Dean Moore Cl. St Alb AL1 ... 127 D2
Dean The. Wing HP22 ... 60 B3
Dean's Gdns. St Alb AL4 ... 128 A7
Deans Cl. Abb L WD5 ... 153 D7
Deans Cl. Tri HP23 ... 100 A4
Deans Furlong. Tri HP23 ... 100 A4
Deans Meadow. Dagn HP4 ... 81 C5
Deanscroft. Kneb SG3 ... 68 F5
Deansway. Heml H HP3 ... 138 F8
Deard's End La. Kneb SG3 ... 68 F6
Deards Wood. Kneb SG3 ... 68 F5
Debenham Ct. Barn EN5 ... 171 C4
Debenham Rd. Ham St EN7 ... 148 B4
Dee The. Heml H HP2 ... 124 F8
Deep Denes. Luton LU2 ... 46 A2
Deepdene. Pot B EN6 ... 158 D8
Deeping Cl. Kneb SG3 ... 68 F4
Deer Cl. Hert SG13 ... 113 F6
Deerfield Cl. Ware SG12 ... 93 D2
Deerings The. Harp AL5 ... 107 A4
Deerswood Ave. Hat AL10 ... 130 B3
Deeves Hall La. Ridge WD6 ... 157 E6
Deimos Dr. Heml H HP2 ... 125 A6
Delahay Rise. Berk HP4 ... 122 B6
Delamare Rd. Ches EN8 ... 148 F2
Delamere Rd. Bor WD6 ... 170 B8
Delfcroft. Ware SG12 ... 93 C2
Delfield Cl. Cad LU1 ... 62 E4
Delius Cl. Elst WD6 ... 169 C3
Dell Cl. Harp AL5 ... 86 B3
Dell La. L Hal CM22 ... 98 A8
Dell La. Saw CM22 ... 98 A8
Dell Meadow. Heml H HP3 ... 138 E7
Dell Rd. Enf EN3 ... 162 C1
Dell Rd. Nthch HP4 ... 121 D7
Dell Rd. Watf WD2 ... 154 A2
Dell Rise. Chis AL2 ... 141 B5
Dell Side. Watf WD2 ... 154 A2
Dell Springs. Bun SG9 ... 40 E8
Dell The. Bal ... 23 E6
Dell The. Bric SG13 ... 113 C3
Dell The. Cad LU1 ... 62 E3
Dell The. Luton LU2 ... 46 F1
Dell The. Mark AL3 ... 83 D5
Dell The. Mo Pk HA6 ... 174 E8
Dell The. Pnr HA5 ... 175 D1
Dell The. Radl WD7 ... 156 A4
Dell The. Royst SG8 ... 7 C5
Dell The. St Alb AL1 ... 128 A4
Dell The. Stev SG1 ... 50 E5
Dell The. Welw AL6 ... 90 A4
Dellcot Cl. Luton LU2 ... 46 B4
Dellcott Cl. Wel G C AL8 ... 110 C7
Dellcroft Way. Harp AL5 ... 107 A5
Dellcut Rd. Heml H HP2 ... 125 A5
Dellfield Ave. Berk HP4 ... 122 B6
Dellfield. Berk HP4 ... 122 A6
Dellfield Cl. Radl WD7 ... 155 F4
Dellfield Cl. Watf WD1 ... 167 A7
Dellfield Ct. Harl CM17 ... 118 C4
Dellfield Ct. Luton LU2 ... 46 D2
Dellfield Rd. Hat AL10 ... 130 A5
Dellfield. St Alb AL1 ... 127 F2
Dellfield. Thun SG12 ... 93 D8
Dellmeadow. Abb L WD5 ... 139 E1
Dellors Cl. Barn EN5 ... 171 D4
Dells The. Bis St CM23 ... 76 F7 4
Dells The. Heml H HP3 ... 125 B2
Dellsome La. Col H AL9 ... 143 F8
Dellsome La. Wel G AL9 ... 144 B8
Dellswood Cl. Hert SG13 ... 113 E5
Dellwood Cl. Ric WD3 ... 165 B1
Delmar Ave. Heml H HP2 ... 125 D2
Delmer Ct. Bor WD6 ... 156 F1
Delmerend La. Fla AL3 ... 84 C1
Delphine Cl. Luton LU1 ... 63 A6
Delta Gain. Sth Ox WD1 ... 175 D7
Demontfort Rise. Ware SG12 ... 93 C3
Denbigh High Sch. Luton ... 45 B2
Denbigh High Sch. Luton ... 45 C2
Denbigh Rd. Luton LU3 ... 45 B2
Denby. Letw SG6 ... 23 B4
Dencora Way. Luton LU3 ... 44 B8
Dendridge Cl. Enf EN1 ... 162 B2
Dene La. Ast SG2 ... 51 E2
Dene Rd. Norwd HA6 ... 174 D4
Denes The. Heml H HP3 ... 138 F7
Denewood Cl. Watf WD1 ... 153 F2
Denham Cl. Heml H HP2 ... 125 A8
Denham Cl. Luton LU3 ... 44 E8
Denham La. C St P SL9 ... 172 A2
Denham Way. Bor WD6 ... 170 C8
Denham Way (North Orbital Rd).
Map Cr WD3 ... 172 E4
Denham Way (North Orbital Rd).
Ric WD3 ... 164 E1
Denmark Cl. Luton LU3 ... 44 E8
Denmark Rd. Watf WD1 ... 167 B7
Denny Ave. Wa Aby EN9 ... 163 D5
Denny Ct. Bis St CM23 ... 59 B2
Denny Gate. Ches EN8 ... 148 F4
Denny's La. Berk HP4 ... 121 F3
Densley Cl. Wel G C AL8 ... 110 D8
Denton Cl. Barn EN5 ... 171 C4
Denton Cl. Dun LU4 ... 44 B4
Denton Rd. Stev SG1 ... 50 E4
Dents Cl. Letw SG6 ... 23 C3
Derby Ave. Har HA3 ... 176 D2
Derby House. Pnr HA5 ... 175 D1
Derby Rd. Dun LU4 ... 44 C2
Derby Rd. Lo Naz EN11 ... 135 D4
Derby Rd. Watf WD1 ... 167 C5
Derby Way. Stev SG1 ... 51 B8
Derwent Ave. Luton LU3 ... 45 B7
Derwent Ave. Pnr HA5 ... 175 E4
Derwent Lower Sch. Henlw ... 10 C4
Derwent Rd. Harp AL5 ... 85 C4
Derwent Rd. Heml H HP3 ... 125 C2
Derwent Rd. Henlw SG16 ... 10 B4
Derwent Rd. Luton LU2 ... 64 A8
Desborough Cl. Hert SG14 ... 92 C1
Desborough Dr. Tewin AL6 ... 90 D5
Desborough Rd. Hit SG4 ... 35 C8
Desmond Rd. Watf WD2 ... 153 F3
Deva Cl. St Alb AL3 ... 127 A1
Devereux Dr. Watf WD1 ... 153 E1
Devoils La. Bis St CM23 ... 76 F7
Devon Ct. St Alb AL1 ... 127 E2
Devon Rd. Luton LU2 ... 64 B8
Devon Rd. Watf WD1 ... 167 D8
Devonshire Cl. Stev SG2 ... 69 A8
Devonshire Rd. Harp AL5 ... 86 B1
Devonshire Rd. Pnr HA5 ... 175 F2
Dewars Cl. Welw AL6 ... 89 C6
Dewes Green Rd. Clav CM23 ... 30 F1
Dewgrass Gr. Enf EN8 ... 162 D4
Dewhurst Rd. Ches EN8 ... 148 C2
Dewhurst St Mary Jun Mix Inf Sch.
Ches ... 148 C2
Dewpond Cl. Stev SG1 ... 50 C8
Dewsbury Rd. Luton LU3 ... 45 C6
Dexter Cl. Luton LU3 ... 31 B1
Dexter Rd. Barn EN5 ... 171 D3
Dexter Rd. Hare UB9 ... 173 C1
Diamond Rd. Watf WD2 ... 154 A1
Dickens Cl. St Alb AL3 ... 127 D4
Dickens Ct. Heml H HP2 ... 105 B1
Dicker Mill. Hert SG13 ... 113 D7
Dicker Mill Ind Pk. Hert ... 113 E7
Dicket Mead. Welw AL6 ... 89 C5
Dickins Cl. Ham St EN7 ... 148 A5
Dickinson Ave. Cro Gr WD3 ... 166 A3
Dickinson Sq. Cro Gr WD3 ... 166 A3
Dickson. Ham St EN7 ... 147 F4
Dig Dag Hill. Ham St EN7 ... 147 F4
Digswell Cl. Bor WD6 ... 157 A1
Digswell Hill. Welw AL6 ... 89 B2
Digswell House Mews.
Wel G C AL8 ... 89 D2
Digswell La. Wel G C AL7 ... 89 F2
Digswell Park Rd. Wel G C AL8 ... 89 D3
Digswell Park Rd. Wel G C AL8 ... 89 E3
Digswell Rd. Wel G C AL8 ... 89 E1
Digswell Rise. Wel G C AL8 ... 110 E8
Dimmocks La. Sar WD3 ... 152 B3
Dimsdale Cres. Bis St CM23 ... 77 B6
Dimsdale St. Hert SG14 ... 113 C6
Dinant Link Rd. Hod EN11 ... 135 B7
Dingle Cl. Edg EN5 ... 170 F3
Dinmore. Bov HP3 ... 136 F3
Ditchfield Rd. Hod EN11 ... 115 A1
Ditchling Cl. Luton LU2 ... 46 C3
Ditchmore La. Stev SG1 ... 50 D6
Ditton Gn. Gt Of LU2 ... 46 E3
Divine Saviour RC Jun Mix Inf Sch.
Abb L ... 153 D7
Divot Pl. Hert SG13 ... 114 B7
Dixies Cl. Ashw SG7 ... 4 D3
Dixon Pl. Bun SG9 ... 40 E7
Dixons Hill Cl. Wel G AL9 ... 144 B6
Dixons Hill Rd. Wel G AL9 ... 144 C7
Dobb's Weir Rd.
Lo Naz EN11,CM19 ... 135 D4
Docklands. Pirt SG5 ... 20 D4
Doctor's Commons Rd. Berk HP4 . 122 B4
Dodds La. Fla HP2 ... 104 E1
Dodwood. Wel G C AL7 ... 111 B5
Dog Kennel La. Hat AL10 ... 130 A6
Dog Kennel La. Royst SG8 ... 7 D6
Doggetts Way. St Alb AL1 ... 127 C1
Dognell Gn. Wel G C AL8 ... 110 B7
Dolesbury Dr. Welw AL6 ... 89 E8
Dollis Brook Wlk. Barn EN5 ... 171 E3
Dollis Valley Way. Barn EN5 ... 171 F3
Dolphin Ct. Har HA3 ... 176 E1
Dolphin Sq. Tri HP23 ... 100 A3
Dolphin Way. Bis St CM23 ... 77 A8
Dolphin Yd. Hert SG14 ... 113 D6 2
Dolphin Yd. St Alb AL1 ... 127 D3
Dolphin Yd. Ware SG12 ... 93 D1 6
Doncaster Cl. Stev SG1 ... 51 C8

Doncaster Gn. Sth Ox WD1 .... 175 C5
Donkey La. Tri HP23 .... 99 E2
Donne Cl. Royst SG8 .... 7 C8
Dorant House. St Alb AL3 .... 127 D7
Dorchester Ave. Hod EN11 .... 135 A8
Dorchester Ct. Cro Gr WD3 .... 166 D4
Dorchester Ct. Watf WD3 .... 167 E3
Dordans Rd. Luton LU4 .... 44 F4
Dorel Cl. Luton LU2 .... 45 F2
Dormans Cl. Norwd HA6 .... 174 D3
Dormer Cl. Barn EN5 .... 171 D4
Dormie Cl. St Alb AL3 .... 127 C5
Dorrien's Croft. Berk HP4 .... 121 F7
Dorrington Cl. Luton LU3 .... 45 C1
Dorrofield Cl. Cro Gr WD3 .... 166 D4
Dorset Cl. Berk HP4 .... 121 F5
Dorset Ct. Luton LU1 .... 63 F6
Douglas Ave. Watf WD2 .... 154 E2
Douglas Dr. Stev SG1 .... 51 A8
Douglas House. Ches EN8 .... 148 D3
Douglas Rd. Harp AL5 .... 85 F2
Douglas Rd. Luton LU4 .... 45 A2
Douglas Way. Wel G C AL7 .... 111 C6
Dove Cl. Bis St CM23 .... 76 E3
Dove Cl. Sta M CM24 .... 59 E8
Dove Ct. Hat AL10 .... 130 A3
Dove House La. Ken Co LU6 .... 82 D8
Dove La. Pot B EN6 .... 159 C5
Dove Pk. Chor WD3 .... 164 C4
Dove Pk. Pnr HA5 .... 176 A3
Dovedale Cl. Hare UB9 .... 173 C1
Dovedale. Luton LU2 .... 45 E6
Dovedale. Stev SG2 .... 51 B4
Dovedale. Ware SG12 .... 93 C3
Dovehouse Croft. Harl CM20 .... 118 A2
Dovehouse Hill. Luton LU2 .... 46 B1
Dover Cl. Luton LU3 .... 45 A3
Dover Way. Cro Gr WD3 .... 166 C5
Doverfield. Gofs O EN7 .... 147 C2
Dower Ct. Hit SG4 .... 34 F5 1
Dowland House. Enf EN1 .... 161 F1
Dowling Ct. Heml H HP3 .... 138 D8
Down Edge. Red AL3 .... 105 F5
Down Green La. Whea AL4 .... 108 B7
Downalong. Bus WD2 .... 168 D1
Downedge. St Alb AL3 .... 127 B4
Downer Dr. Sar WD3 .... 152 A3
Downes Rd. St Alb AL4 .... 128 B7
Downfield Cl. Hert H SG13 .... 114 C4
Downfield Jun Mix Inf Sch. Ches .. 162 E8
Downfield Rd. Ches EN8 .... 162 E8
Downfield Rd. Hert H SG13 .... 114 C5
Downfields. Wel G C AL8 .... 110 B4
Downhall Ley. Bun SG9 .... 40 E7
Downings Wood. Map Cr WD3 .... 172 D5
Downlands. Bal SG7 .... 13 A1
Downlands. Luton LU3 .... 44 C7
Downlands. Royst SG8 .... 7 C6
Downlands. Stev SG2 .... 51 D7
Downlands. Wa Aby EN9 .... 163 E5
Downs Rd. Luton LU1 .... 63 C7
Downs The. Hat AL10 .... 130 A3
Downs View. Luton LU4 .... 44 D4
Downsfield. Hat AL10 .... 130 B2
Downside. Heml H HP2 .... 124 E4
Downside Inf Sch. Luton 44 E1
Downside Jun Sch. Luton 44 E1
Downsway Ct. Royst SG8 .... 7 C6
Downton Ct. Luton LU3 .... 63 D8 3
Downview. Dun LU4 .... 44 B2
Dowry Wlk. Watf WD1 .... 153 F1
Drakes Cl. Ches EN8 .... 148 D3
Drakes Dr. Norwd HA6 .... 174 B2
Drakes Dr. St Alb AL1 .... 128 C1
Drakes Dr. St Alb AL1 .... 142 B8
Drakes Dr. Stev SG2 .... 51 B7
Drakes Way. Hat AL10 .... 130 B3
Drapers Mews. Luton LU3 .... 45 C1
Drapers Way. Stev SG1 .... 50 C7
Drayson Cl. Wa Aby EN9 .... 163 E7
Drayton Ave. Pot B EN6 .... 158 E7
Drayton Rd. Bor WD6 .... 170 A5
Drayton Rd. Dun LU4 .... 44 A3
Driftway. Reed SG8 .... 16 E4
Driftway The. Heml H HP2 .... 124 F3
Driftwood Ave. Chis AL2 .... 141 B5
Drive The. Barn EN5 .... 171 E6
Drive The. Gofs O EN7 .... 147 B3
Drive The. Ham St EN8 .... 148 B3
Drive The. Harl CM20 .... 117 E1
Drive The. Harp AL5 .... 86 A1
Drive The. Hert SG14 .... 113 C8
Drive The. Hod EN11 .... 135 A8
Drive The. Kim AL4 .... 87 B7
Drive The. Lon C AL2 .... 142 A5
Drive The. Norwd HA6 .... 174 E2
Drive The. Pot B EN6 .... 158 F7
Drive The. Radl WD7 .... 156 A5
Drive The. Ric WD3 .... 165 C3
Drive The. Saw CM21 .... 97 E2
Drive The. St Alb AL4 .... 128 C1
Drive The. Watf WD1 .... 153 E2
Drive The. Welw AL6 .... 69 A1
Driver's End La. Cod SG4 .... 68 A4
Driveway The. Cuf EN6 .... 146 E3
Driveway The. Heml H HP1 .... 124 B1
Dromey Gdns. Har HA3 .... 176 F3
Drop La. Bri Wd AL2 .... 155 C7
Drovers Way. Bis St CM23 .... 76 C5
Drovers Way. Hat AL10 .... 130 B8
Drovers Way. St Alb AL3 .... 127 D3
Drovewood Cl. Chor WD3 .... 164 B4
Drummond Dr. Har HA7 .... 176 F3
Drummond Ride. Tri HP23 .... 100 A5
Drummonds The. Dun LU4 .... 44 C2
Drury La. Hun SG12 .... 95 E1
Drycroft. Wel G C AL7 .... 110 E2
Dryden Cres. Stev SG2 .... 51 C8
Dryden Rd. Har HA3 .... 176 F2
Drysdale Cl. Norwd HA6 .... 174 E3
Dubbs Knoll Rd. Gu M SG8 .... 1 F5
Dubrae Cl. St Alb AL3 .... 127 A1
Duchess Cl. Bis St CM23 .... 76 C7
Duchy Rd. Had W EN4 .... 159 D1
Duck La. Ben SG2 .... 52 E4
Duck's Hill Rd. Norwd HA6 .... 174 B2
Ducketts La. Muc H SG10 .... 75 D1
Ducketts Mead. Roy CM19 .... 116 B1
Ducketts Wood. Thun SG12 .... 93 E7
Duckling La. Saw CM21 .... 97 E2
Duckmore La. Tri HP23 .... 99 E2
Dudley Ave. Ches EN8 .... 162 D7
Dudley Hill Cl. Welw AL6 .... 89 E8
Dudley St. Luton LU2 .... 63 E8
Dudswell La. Nthch HP4 .... 121 D7
Dugdale Ct. Hit SG5 .... 21 C1
Dugdale Hill La. Pot B EN6 .... 158 E7
Dugdales. Cro Gr WD3 .... 166 A5
Duke St. Hod EN11 .... 135 A7
Duke St. Luton LU2 .... 63 E8
Duke St. Watf WD1 .... 167 C6
Duke's La. Hit SG5 .... 34 F8
Dukes Ave. Whip LU6 .... 81 E8
Dukes Ride. Bis St CM23 .... 76 C8
Dukes Way. Berk HP4 .... 122 A6
Dulwich Way. Cro Gr WD3 .... 166 A4
Dumbarton Ave. Ches EN8 .... 162 D5
Dumfries Cl. Sth Ox WD1 .... 175 A7
Dumfries St. Luton LU1 .... 63 D6
Duncan Cl. Wel G C AL7 .... 110 E5
Duncan Way. Bus WD2 .... 167 F7
Duncombe Cl. Hert SG14 .... 113 C8
Duncombe Cl. Luton LU3 .... 45 C6
Duncombe Rd. Hert SG14 .... 113 C8
Duncombe Rd. Nthch HP4 .... 121 E6
Duncombe Sch Daneshill. Hert 113 C7
Dundale Inf Sch. Tri 100 A5
Dundale Jun Sch. Tri 100 A5
Dundale Rd. Tri HP23 .... 100 A4
Dunhams La. Letw SG6 .... 23 C6
Dunkirks Mews. Hert SG13 .... 113 D4
Dunlin. Letw SG6 .... 11 E1
Dunlin Rd. Heml H HP2 .... 124 E8
Dunmow Ct. Luton LU3 .... 45 D2
Dunmow Rd. Bis St CM23 .... 77 C7
Dunmow Rd. Gt Ha CM22 .... 77 F7
Dunn Cl. Stev SG1 .... 50 E3
Dunnock Cl. Bor WD6 .... 170 A5
Dunny La. Chipf WD4 .... 151 F7
Dunsby Rd. Luton LU3 .... 45 A6
Dunsley Pl. Tri HP23 .... 100 B3
Dunsmore Cl. Bus WD2 .... 168 D3
Dunsmore Rd. Luton LU1 .... 63 C6
Dunsmore Way. Bus WD2 .... 168 D3
Dunstable Cl. Luton LU4 .... 45 A1
Dunstable Ct. Luton LU4 .... 44 F2
Dunstable Pl. Luton LU1 .... 63 D7
Dunstable Rd. Cad LU1 .... 62 C3
Dunstable Rd. Dagn HP4 .... 81 C7
Dunstable Rd. Dun LU4 .... 44 B2
Dunstable Rd. Luton LU4 .... 45 B1
Dunstable Rd. Red AL3 .... 106 A7
Dunstable Rd. Stu LU6 .... 82 B6
Dunstable Rd. Whip LU6 .... 81 C7
Dunstable Road. Whip LU6 .... 82 B6
Dunstable Road Jun Inf Sch. Luton 63 C8
Dunster Cl. Barn EN5 .... 171 D5
Dunster Cl. Hare UB9 .... 173 B2
Dunster Rd. Heml H HP2 .... 105 B1
Dunsters Mead. Wel G C AL7 .... 111 B4
Dunston Hill. Tri HP23 .... 100 A4
Durban Rd E. Watf WD1 .... 167 A5
Durban Rd W. Watf WD1 .... 167 A5
Durbar Rd. Luton LU4 .... 45 B1
Durham Cl. Gt Am SG12 .... 115 B5
Durham Cl. Saw CM21 .... 97 C1
Durham Rd. Bor WD6 .... 170 D6
Durham Rd. Luton LU2 .... 64 A7
Durham Rd. Stev SG1 .... 37 A1
Durler Gdns. Luton LU1 .... 63 D5
Durrant Ct. Har HA3 .... 176 E2
Durrants Dr. Cro Gr WD3 .... 166 C5
Durrants Hill Rd. Heml H HP3 .... 138 D8
Durrants La. Berk HP4 .... 121 F5
Durrants Rd. Berk HP4 .... 121 F5
Dury Rd. Barn EN5 .... 171 F7
Duxford Cl. Luton LU3 .... 45 B7
Duxons Turn. Heml H HP2 .... 125 B4
Dwight Rd. Mo Pk WD1 .... 166 D2
Dyes La. Lan SG1 .... 49 F3
Dyke La. Whea AL4 .... 108 E7
Dylan Cl. Elst WD6 .... 169 D2
Dymoke Gn. St Alb AL4 .... 128 A7
Dymokes Way. Hod EN11 .... 115 A1
Dyrham La. Pot B EN5 .... 158 A3
Dyson Ct. Watf WD1 .... 167 C5
Dysons Cl. Ches EN8 .... 162 D6

Eagle Cl. Dun LU4 .... 44 A4
Eagle Ct. Bal SG13 .... 12 E1
Eagle Ct. Hert SG13 .... 114 B7
Eagle Way. Hat AL10 .... 130 A3
Ealing Cl. Bor WD6 .... 170 D8
Earl St. Watf WD1 .... 167 C6
Earls Cl. Bis St CM23 .... 76 D6
Earls Hill Gdns. Royst SG8 .... 7 C6
Earls La. Ridge WD6 .... 157 F6
Earls Meade. Luton LU2 .... 45 D1
Earlsmead. Letw SG6 .... 22 F3
Easington Rd. Dan En SG12 .... 71 E7
Easingwold Gdns. Luton LU1 .... 62 F8
Easneye (Coll). Sta Ab 115 C7
East Burrowfield. Wel G C AL7 .... 110 D4
East Cl. Chis AL2 .... 141 B6
East Cl. Hit SG4 .... 22 B1
East Cl. Stev SG1 .... 50 F5
East Comm. Harp AL5 .... 107 C7
East Comm. Red AL3 .... 106 A4
East Dr. Coln H AL4 .... 128 F4
East Dr. Lon C AL2 .... 142 B5
East Dr. Mo Pk WD1 .... 174 E8
East Dr. Saw CM21 .... 97 E1
East Dr. Watf WD2 .... 154 B3
East End Way. Pnr HA5 .... 175 F1
East Flint. Heml H HP1 .... 123 F4
East Gate. Harl CM20 .... 117 D1
East Gn. Heml H HP3 .... 139 A6
East Herts Coll of F Ed Annexe.
Ches 162 D8
East Herts Coll of F Ed. Ches 148 F6
East Herts Hospl. Hert 114 A7
East Hill. Luton LU3 .... 45 B6
East La. Abb L WD5 .... 140 A2
East La. Whea AL4 .... 87 D1
East Lodge La. Had W EN2 .... 160 E4
East Mead. Wel G C AL7 .... 111 B3
East Mimms. Heml H HP2 .... 124 E4 4
East Mount. Whea AL4 .... 87 D1
East Pk. Harl CM17 .... 118 C3
East Pk. Saw CM21 .... 97 E1
East Rd. Bis St CM23 .... 77 B7
East Rd. Enf EN3 .... 162 C1
East Rd. Harl CM20 .... 118 B4
East Reach. Stev SG2 .... 51 A2
East Ridgeway. Cuf EN6 .... 146 E3
East Riding. Tewin AL6 .... 90 D5
East St. Heml H HP2 .... 124 D3
East St. Lily LU2 .... 32 D2
East St. Ware SG12 .... 93 D1
East View. Barn EN5 .... 171 F6
East View. Ess AL9 .... 131 F6
East View. St Ipp SG4 .... 35 C2
East Way. Wa Aby EN9 .... 163 D3
East Wlk. Harl CM20 .... 117 D1
Eastbourne Ave. Stev SG1 .... 50 A6
Eastbrook Inf Sch. Heml H 125 A8
Eastbrook Mix Inf Sch. Heml H 125 A8
Eastbrook Rd. Wa Aby EN9 .... 163 E6
Eastbrook Way. Heml H HP2 .... 124 E3
Eastbury Ave. Mo Pk HA6 .... 174 F5
Eastbury Cl. Mo Pk HA6 .... 174 E5
Eastbury Ct. St Alb AL1 .... 127 F4
Eastbury Farm Jun Mix & Inf Sch.
Mo Pk 174 F6
Eastbury Pl. Mo Pk HA6 .... 174 F5
Eastbury Rd. Norwd HA6 .... 174 E4
Eastbury Rd. Watf WD1 .... 167 C3
Eastcheap. Letw SG6 .... 22 F6
Eastcote Dr. Harp AL5 .... 107 D6
Eastcott Cl. Luton LU2 .... 46 D1
Eastern Ave. Ches EN8 .... 162 F6
Eastern Ave. Henlw SG16 .... 10 C3
Eastern Way. Letw SG6 .... 12 A1
Eastfield Ave. Watf WD2 .... 167 D8
Eastfield Cl. Luton LU2 .... 46 C4
Eastfield Ct. St Alb AL4 .... 128 D6
Eastfield Prim Sch. Enf 162 D1
Eastfield Rd. Ches EN8 .... 162 F7
Eastfield Rd. Enf EN3 .... 162 D1
Eastfield Rd. Royst SG8 .... 7 E6
Eastgate. Stev SG1 .... 50 D5
Eastglade. Mo Pk HA6 .... 174 F5
Easthall House. Stev SG1 .... 36 C1
Eastham Cl. Barn EN5 .... 171 F4
Eastholm Gn. Letw SG6 .... 23 A8
Eastholm. Letw SG6 .... 23 A8
Eastlea Ave. Watf WD2 .... 154 E2
Eastman Way. Heml H HP2 .... 125 A6
Eastmoor Ct. Harp AL5 .... 107 C6
Eastmoor Pk. Harp AL5 .... 107 C6
Eastnor. Bov HP3 .... 137 A3
Easton Gdns. Bor WD6 .... 170 E5
Eastor. Wel G C AL7 .... 90 A1
Eastwick Cres. Ric WD3 .... 172 F8
Eastwick Hall La. East CM20 .... 117 A5
Eastwick Rd. East CM20 .... 117 B4
Eastwick Rd. East CM20 .... 117 C4
Eastwick Rd. East CM20 .... 117 E6
Eastwick Row. Heml H HP2 .... 125 A2
Eastwood Ct. Heml H HP2 .... 125 A4
Eaton Gate. Norwd HA6 .... 174 C4
Eaton Green Ct. Luton LU2 .... 64 C8
Eaton Green Rd. Luton LU2 .... 64 C8
Eaton Pl. Luton LU2 .... 46 D1
Eaton Rd. Heml H HP2 .... 125 B6
Eaton Rd. St Alb AL1 .... 128 B3
Eaton Valley Rd. Luton LU2 .... 64 B8
Ebberns Rd. Heml H HP3 .... 138 E8
Ebenezer St. Luton LU1 .... 63 D6
Ebury App. Ric WD3 .... 165 D1
Ebury Cl. Norwd HA6 .... 174 C5
Ebury Rd. Ric WD3 .... 165 D1
Ebury Rd. Watf WD1 .... 167 C6
Echo Hill. Royst SG8 .... 7 C5
Eddy St. Berk HP4 .... 122 A5
Edenhall Cl. Heml H HP2 .... 125 D2
Edens Cl. Bis St CM23 .... 77 B7
Edens Mount. Saw CM21 .... 97 F4
Edgars Ct. Wel G C AL7 .... 110 E5
Edgbaston Dr. Shen WD7 .... 156 E7
Edgcott Cl. Luton LU3 .... 31 B1
Edgecote Cl. Cad LU1 .... 62 E3
Edgehill Gdns. Luton LU3 .... 44 C8
Edgewood Dr. Luton LU2 .... 46 C6
Edgeworth Cl. Stev SG2 .... 51 C1
Edgware Way. Stan HA8 .... 169 D1
Edgwarebury La. Stan WD6,HA8 .. 169 F1
Edinburgh Ave. Ric WD3 .... 165 A2
Edinburgh Cres. Ches EN8 .... 162 E6
Edinburgh Pl. Harl CM20 .... 118 A4
Edinburgh Way. Harl CM20 .... 117 E3
Edison Rd. Stev SG2 .... 51 B6
Edkins Cl. Luton LU2 .... 45 E5
Edlyn Cl. Berk HP4 .... 121 F5
Edmonds Dr. Ast SG2 .... 51 D4
Edmund Beaufort Dr. St Alb AL3 ... 127 E5
Edmunds Rd. Hert SG14 .... 112 F7
Edna Daniels Sch The. St Alb 128 C1
Edridge Cl. Bus WD2 .... 168 C4
Edulf Rd. Bor WD6 .... 170 B8
Edward Amey Cl. Watf WD2 .... 154 C3
Edward Cl. Abb L WD5 .... 153 F7
Edward Cl. St Alb AL1 .... 128 A2
Edward Ct. Heml H HP3 .... 138 D7
Edward Ct. Wa Aby EN9 .... 163 F6
Edward St. Luton LU2 .... 45 F1
Edwards House. Stev SG1 .... 50 E6 5
Edwick Ct. Ches EN8 .... 148 D2
Edwin Ware Ct. Pnr HA5 .... 175 C1 2
Edwinstree Sch. Bun 40 D8
Edwyn Cl. Barn EN5 .... 171 D3
Egdon Dr. Luton LU2 .... 45 D6
Egerton Rd. Berk HP4 .... 122 B6
Egerton-Rothesay Sch. Berk 121 E4
Eight Acres. Tri HP23 .... 100 A4
Eighth Ave. Luton LU3 .... 44 D7
Eisenberg Cl. Bal SG7 .... 13 B1
Elaine Gdns. Cad LU1 .... 63 A1
Elbow La. Hert H SG13 .... 134 B7
Elbow La. Stev SG2 .... 51 B1
Eldefield. Letw SG6 .... 22 D7
Elder Ct. Bus WD2 .... 176 E8
Elder Rd. Ware SG12 .... 93 F3
Elder Way. Stev SG1 .... 50 E3
Elderbeck Cl. Ches EN7 .... 148 A2
Elderberry Cl. Luton LU2 .... 46 B4
Elderberry Dr. Hit SG4 .... 35 A4
Elderberry Way. Watf WD2 .... 154 B4
Elderfield. Harl CM17 .... 118 D3
Eldon Ave. Bor WD6 .... 170 B7
Eldon Rd. Dun LU4 .... 44 C1
Eldon Rd. Lo Naz EN11 .... 135 D4
Eleanor Ave. St Alb AL3 .... 127 D5
Eleanor Cross Rd. Ches EN8 .... 162 F5
Eleanor Gdns. Barn EN5 .... 171 D4
Eleanor Rd. Ches EN8 .... 162 E6
Eleanor Rd. Hert SG14 .... 113 C7
Eleanor Way. Ches EN8 .... 162 F5
Elfrida Rd. Watf WD1 .... 167 C4
Elgar Cl. Elst WD6 .... 169 D2
Elgar Path. Luton LU2 .... 63 E8 1
Elgin Dr. Norwd HA6 .... 174 E3
Elgin House. Hit SG4 .... 35 A6
Elgin Rd. Ches EN8 .... 148 C1
Elgin Rd. Hod EN10 .... 148 F8
Elgood Ave. Norwd HA6 .... 175 A3
Eliot Rd. Royst SG8 .... 7 D8
Eliot Rd. Stev SG2 .... 51 C6
Elizabeth Cl. Barn EN5 .... 171 D6
Elizabeth Cl. Lo Naz EN9 .... 149 D8
Elizabeth Cl. Wel G C AL7 .... 111 C6
Elizabeth Ct. St Alb AL4 .... 128 D6
Elizabeth Ct. Watf WD1 .... 153 F1
Elizabeth Dr. Tri HP23 .... 100 B6
Elizabeth House. Wel G C AL7 .... 111 C6
Elizabeth Rd. Bis St CM23 .... 76 E5
Elizabeth St. Luton LU1 .... 63 D6
Elizabeth Way. Harl CM19, CM20 . 117 B2
Ella Ct. Luton LU2 .... 45 F1
Ellen Cl. Heml H HP2 .... 124 F4
Ellenborough Cl. Bis St CM23 .... 76 D5
Ellenbrook Cres. Hat AL10 .... 129 D5
Ellenbrook La. Hat AL10 .... 129 D4
Ellenhall Cl. Luton LU3 .... 45 C1
Ellerdine Cl. Luton LU3 .... 45 B4
Ellesborough Cl. Sth Ox WD1 .... 175 C5
Ellesfield. Welw AL6 .... 89 B5
Ellesmere Gr. Barn EN5 .... 171 F4
Ellesmere Rd. Berk HP4 .... 122 A4
Ellice. Letw SG6 .... 23 B4
Ellingham Cl. Heml H HP2 .... 125 A5
Ellingham Rd. Heml H HP2 .... 124 F4
Elliott Cl. Wel G C AL7 .... 110 D3
Ellis Ave. Stev SG1 .... 50 E8
Elliswick Rd. Harp AL5 .... 86 B2
Ellwood Gdns. Watf WD2 .... 154 C5
Elm Ave. Cad LU1 .... 62 E3
Elm Ave. Watf WD1 .... 167 E2
Elm Cl. Wa Aby EN9 .... 163 D5
Elm Dr. Ches EN8 .... 148 E3
Elm Dr. Hat AL10 .... 130 A4
Elm Dr. St Alb AL4 .... 128 C3
Elm Gdns. Enf EN2 .... 161 D1
Elm Gdns. Wel G C AL8 .... 110 B6
Elm Gn. Heml H HP1 .... 123 E5
Elm Gr. Berk HP4 .... 122 C4
Elm Gr. Bis St CM23 .... 77 B7
Elm Gr. Watf WD2 .... 154 A2
Elm Hatch. Pnr HA5 .... 175 F3
Elm Park Rd. Pnr HA5 .... 175 D1
Elm Pk. Bal SG7 .... 23 F8
Elm Rd. Barn EN5 .... 171 F5
Elm Rd. Bis St CM23 .... 76 F8
Elm Terr. Har HA3 .... 176 D2
Elm Tree Wlk. Chor WD3 .... 164 F5
Elm Tree Wlk. Tri HP23 .... 100 A5
Elm Way. Ric WD3 .... 165 B1
Elm Wlk. Radl WD7 .... 155 F3
Elm Wlk. Royst SG8 .... 7 F7
Elm Wlk. Stev SG2 .... 51 B3
Elmbank Ave. Barn EN5 .... 171 C5
Elmbridge. Harl CM17 .... 118 F3
Elmbrook Dr. Bis St CM23 .... 76 E3
Elmcote Way. Cro Gr WD3 .... 165 F3
Elmfield Cl. Pot B EN6 .... 158 E6
Elmfield Ct. Luton LU2 .... 46 A1
Elmfield Rd. Pot B EN6 .... 158 E6
Elmhurst Cl. Bis St CM23 .... 76 E7
Elmhurst. Hod EN10 .... 135 A4
Elmhurst Rd. Enf EN3 .... 162 C2
Elmoor Ave. Welw AL6 .... 89 B5
Elmoor Cl. Welw AL6 .... 89 B4
Elmore Rd. Enf EN3 .... 162 D1
Elmore Rd. Luton LU2 .... 46 A1
Elmroyd Ave. Pot B EN6 .... 158 F6
Elmroyd Cl. Pot B EN6 .... 158 F6
Elms Cl. L Wym SG4 .... 35 E3
Elms Rd. Har HA3 .... 176 E3
Elms Rd. Ware SG12 .... 94 A2
Elms The. Cod SG4 .... 67 F2
Elms The. Hert SG13 .... 114 A6
Elmscroft Gdns. Pot B EN6 .... 158 F7
Elmside. Ken Co LU6 .... 82 E8
Elmside Wlk. Hit SG5 .... 34 E7
Elmtree Ave. Gt Of LU2 .... 46 E3
Elmwood Ave. Bal SG7 .... 23 F7
Elmwood Ave. Bor WD6 .... 170 B5
Elmwood Cres. Luton LU2 .... 45 E3
Elmwood Ct. Bal SG7 .... 23 F8
Elmwood. Saw CM21 .... 97 F1
Elmwood. Wel G C AL8 .... 110 B5
Elsinge Rd. Enf EN1 .... 162 C3
Elstree Hill N. Elst WD6 .... 169 D4
Elstree Hill S. Elst WD6 .... 169 D2
Elstree Pk. Bor WD6 .... 170 D3
Elstree Rd. Bus WD2 .... 168 E2
Elstree Rd. Elst WD6 .... 169 A3
Elstree Rd. Heml H HP2 .... 105 A1
Elstree Sta. Bor 170 A5
Elstree Way. Bor WD6 .... 170 C7
Elstree Way. Bor WD6 .... 170 E6
Elton Ave. Barn EN5 .... 171 F4
Elton Ct. Hert SG14 .... 113 C7
Elton Rd. Hert SG14 .... 113 C7
Elton Way. Bus WD2 .... 168 B7
Elvaston Ct. Barn EN5 .... 171 C4
Elveden Cl. Luton LU2 .... 45 E6
Elvington Gdns. Luton LU3 .... 31 B1
Ely Cl. Hat AL10 .... 129 F6
Ely Cl. Stev SG1 .... 37 B2
Ely Gdns. Bor WD6 .... 170 D4
Ely Rd. St Alb AL1 .... 128 B2
Ely Way. Luton LU4 .... 44 D4
Embleton Rd. Sth Ox WD1 .... 175 A7
Emerald Ct. Bor WD6 .... 156 F1
Emerald Rd. Dun LU4 .... 44 A2
Emerton Ct. Nthch HP4 .... 121 E7
Emerton Garth. Nthch HP4 .... 121 E7
Emma Rothschild Ct. Tri HP23 .... 100 A5
Emma's Cres. Gt Am SG12 .... 115 B4
Emmanuel Lodge. Ches EN8 .... 148 C1
Emmanuel Rd. Norwd HA6 .... 174 F3
Emmer Gn. Luton LU2 .... 46 F2
Emperor Cl. Nthch HP4 .... 121 F7
Emperors Gate. Stev SG2 .... 51 D8
Empire Ctr. Watf 167 C8
Empress Rd. Luton LU3 .... 44 E4
Endeavour Rd. Ches EN8 .... 148 E4
Enderby Rd. Luton LU3 .... 45 C6
Enderley Cl. Har HA3 .... 176 E2
Enderley Rd. Har HA3 .... 176 E2
Endersby Rd. Barn EN5 .... 171 C4
Endymion Ct. Hat AL10 .... 130 C6
Endymion Rd. Hat AL10 .... 130 C6
Enfield Chase Lower Sch. Enf 161 E1
Enfield Lock Sta. Enf 162 E2
Englefield. Luton LU2 .... 45 F3
Englehurst. Harp AL5 .... 86 D1
Enid Cl. Bri Wd AL2 .... 154 F8
Enjakes Cl. Stev SG2 .... 69 B7
Ennerdale Cl. St Alb AL1 .... 128 B1
Ennis Cl. Harp AL5 .... 107 D6
Ennismore Cl. Letw SG6 .... 23 C3
Ennismore Gn. Luton LU2 .... 46 F1
Enslow Cl. Cad LU1 .... 62 E3
Enterprise Ctr. Luton 63 F8
Enterprise Ctr The. Stev 50 B8
Enterprise Way. Luton LU3 .... 45 B8
Epping Gn. Heml H HP2 .... 125 B8
Epping House Sch. L Berk 132 C2
Epping Way. Luton LU3 .... 44 C8
Epsom Ct. Ric WD3 .... 165 B1
Ereswell Rd. Luton LU3 .... 45 A7
Erin Cl. Luton LU4 .... 45 A2
Erin Ct. Luton LU4 .... 45 A2
Ermine Cl. Ches EN7 .... 162 B8
Ermine Cl. Royst SG8 .... 7 D8
Ermine Cl. St Alb AL3 .... 127 A2
Ermine Ct. Bun SG9 .... 40 E8
Ermine Point Bsns Pk. Ware 93 B3
Ermine St. Thun SG12 .... 93 D7
Escarpment Ave. Whip LU6 .... 81 D8
Escot Way. Barn EN5 .... 171 C4
Esdaile La. Hod EN11 .... 135 A5
Eskdale Ct. Heml H HP2 .... 124 E6 3
Eskdale. Lon C AL2 .... 142 F4
Eskdale. Luton LU4 .... 44 C5
Essendon Gdns. Wel G C AL7 .... 110 F6
Essendon Hill. Ess AL9 .... 131 E6
Essendon Jun Mix Inf Sch. 131 F6
Essex Cl. Luton LU1 .... 63 F6
Essex Ct. Luton LU1 .... 63 E6 4
Essex La. Abb L WD4 .... 153 D6
Essex Mead. Heml H HP2 .... 105 A1
Essex Rd. Bor WD6 .... 170 A6
Essex Rd. Hod EN11 .... 135 B7
Essex Rd. Hod EN11 .... 135 C6
Essex Rd. Stev SG1 .... 50 B8
Essex Rd. Watf WD1 .... 167 B7
Essex St. St Alb AL1 .... 127 E4
Estcourt Rd. Watf WD1 .... 167 C6
Ethelred Cl. Wel G C AL7 .... 110 F5
Etna Rd. St Alb AL3 .... 127 D4
Etonbury Sch. Arl 11 C7
Europa Rd. Heml H HP2 .... 124 F6
Euston Ave. Watf WD1 .... 166 F4
Evan's Cl. Cro Gr WD3 .... 166 A4
Evans Ave. Watf WD2 .... 153 F4
Evans Gr. St Alb AL4 .... 128 C7
Evedon Cl. Luton LU3 .... 44 F6
Evelyn Dr. Pnr HA5 .... 175 D3
Evelyn Rd. Dun LU5 .... 44 A2
Everard Cl. St Alb AL1 .... 127 D1
Everest Cl. Arl SG15 .... 11 B5
Everest Way. Heml H HP2 .... 125 A3
Everett Cl. Bus WD2 .... 168 E1
Everett Ct. Radl WD7 .... 156 A5
Evergreen Cl. Welw SG3 .... 69 A2
Evergreen Rd. Ware SG12 .... 93 F3
Evergreen Way. Luton LU3 .... 45 A8
Everlasting La. St Alb AL3 .... 127 C5
Eversley Lodge. Hod EN11 .... 135 A6
Evron Pl. Hert SG14 .... 113 D6 4
Exchange Rd. Stev SG1 .... 50 F5
Exchange Rd. Watf WD1 .... 167 B5
Executive Park Ind Est. St Alb 128 B3
Exeter Cl. Stev SG1 .... 37 B2
Exeter Cl. Watf WD1 .... 167 C7
Explorer Dr. Watf WD1 .... 166 F3
Exton Ave. Luton LU2 .... 46 A1
Eynsford Ct. Hit SG4 .... 34 F6
Eywood Rd. St Alb AL1 .... 127 C1

Faggots Cl. Radl WD7 .... 156 C4
Fair Cl. Bus WD2 .... 168 B2
Fair Oak Dr. Luton LU2 .... 45 F3
Fair View. Pot B EN6 .... 145 B2
Fairacre Ct. Norwd HA6 .... 174 E3
Fairacre. Heml H HP3 .... 138 F7
Fairacres Cl. Pot B EN6 .... 158 F6
Fairburn Cl. Bor WD6 .... 170 A8
Faircross Way. St Alb AL1 .... 128 A5
Fairfax Ave. Luton LU3 .... 44 D7
Fairfax Rd. Hert SG13 .... 113 F7
Fairfield Ave. Sth Ox WD1 .... 175 D7
Fairfield. Bun SG9 .... 40 F6
Fairfield Cl. Harp AL5 .... 86 D1
Fairfield Cl. Hat AL10 .... 130 C8
Fairfield Cl. Radl WD7 .... 155 E2
Fairfield Dr. Ches EN10 .... 148 F7
Fairfield Hospl. Stot 11 C3
Fairfield Prim Sch. Radl 155 E3
Fairfield Rd. Hod EN11 .... 135 A8
Fairfield Way. Hit SG4 .... 35 D8
Fairfield Wlk. Ches EN8 .... 148 E3
Fairfields Prim Sch. Ham St 148 A4
Fairfolds. Watf WD2 .... 154 E4
Fairford Ave. Luton LU2 .... 45 E4
Fairgreen Rd. Cad LU1 .... 62 F3
Fairhaven Cres. Sth Ox WD1 .... 175 A7
Fairhaven. Pk St AL2 .... 141 D4
Fairhill. Heml H HP3 .... 138 F7
Fairlands Inf Sch. Stev 50 D6
Fairlands Jun Sch. Stev 50 D6
Fairlands Way. Stev SG1 .... 51 A7
Fairlawns. Pnr WD1 .... 175 D1
Fairlawns. Watf WD1 .... 153 F1

Fairley Way. Ches EN7 148 B3
Fairmead Ave. Harp AL5 107 C8
Fairseat Cl. Bus WD2 176 E8
Fairthorn Cl. Tri HP23 99 E3
Fairview Dr. Watf WD1 153 E3
Fairview Rd. Stev SG1 50 B7
Fairway Ave. Bor WD6 170 B7
Fairway. Bis St CM23 77 C6
Fairway Cl. Chis AL2 141 C4
Fairway Cl. Harp AL5 107 A5
Fairway. Heml H HP3 138 F7
Fairway House. Bor WD6 170 B6
Fairway. Saw CM21 97 F2
Fairway The. Abb L WD5 153 D7
Fairway The. Mo Pk HA6 174 E6
Fairway. Ware SG12 114 C8
Fairways. Ches EN8 148 D5
Faithfield. Watf WD2 167 E3
Falcon Cl. Hat AL10 130 A3
Falcon Cl. Norwd HA6 174 D3
Falcon Cl. Saw CM21 97 C1
Falcon Cl. Stev SG2 51 D2
Falcon Ct. Ware SG12 93 C3 2
Falcon Ridge. Berk HP4 122 C3
Falcon Way. Watf WD2 154 E5
Falcon Way. Wel G C AL7 110 E8
Falconer Rd. Bus WD2 168 A3
Falconer St. Bis St CM23 76 C5
Falconers Field. Harp AL5 85 E3
Falconers Pk. Saw CM21 97 D1
Falconers Rd. Luton LU2 64 C1
Falkirk Gdns. Sth Ox WD1 175 D5
Falkland Rd. Barn EN5 171 E7
Fallow Rise. Hert SG13 113 F6
Fallowfield Cl. Hare UB9 173 C2
Fallowfield. Luton LU3 45 C4
Fallowfield. Stev SG2 51 C3
Fallowfield. Wel G C AL7 89 F1
Fallowfield Wlk. Heml H HP1 124 A6
Fallows Gn. Harp AL5 86 B3
Falstaff Gdns. St Alb AL1 141 C8
Falstone Gn. Luton LU2 46 E1
Fanhams Hall Rd. Ware SG12 93 F3
Fanhams Rd. Ware SG12 93 E2
Fanshaw Ct. Hert SG14 113 C7
Fanshawe Cres. Ware SG12 93 C2
Fanshawe St. Hert SG14 113 B7
Fanshaws La. Bric SG13 133 C5
Fantail La. Tri HP23 99 F4
Far End. Hat AL10 130 B2
Faraday Cl. Watf WD1 166 D3
Faraday Rd. Stev SG2 51 B6
Faringdon Rd. Dun LU4 44 C3
Faringford Cl. Pot B EN6 159 D8
Farland Rd. Heml H HP2 125 B3
Farley Ct. Luton LU1 63 C5
Farley Farm Rd. Luton LU1 63 B5
Farley Hill. Luton LU1 63 C5
Farley Jun Sch. Luton 63 C6
Farley Lodge. Luton LU1 63 D5
Farm Ave. Harp AL5 85 D4
Farm Cl. Barn EN5 171 C4
Farm Cl. Bor WD6 156 E1
Farm Cl. Ches EN8 148 C1
Farm Cl. Cuf EN6 146 E4
Farm Cl. Hert SG14 113 A6
Farm Cl. Letw SG6 12 A1
Farm Cl. Roy CM19 116 B1
Farm Cl. Stev SG1 50 E4
Farm Cl. Wel G C AL8 110 C6
Farm Gn. Luton LU1 63 C5
Farm Hill Rd. Wa Aby EN9 163 D6
Farm La. Ric WD3 165 C6
Farm La. Stand SG11 73 A8
Farm Pl. Berk HP4 121 F5
Farm Rd. L Chal WD3 164 A5
Farm Rd. Norwd HA6 174 C5
Farm Rd. Nwml E LU1 85 B7
Farm Rd. St Alb AL1 128 B4
Farm Way. Bus WD2 168 B5
Farm Way. Mo Pk HA6 174 F6
Farmbrook. Luton LU2 45 D7
Farmers Cl. Watf WD2 154 B6
Farmhouse Cl. Ches EN10 148 F6
Farmhouse La. Heml H HP2 125 A5
Farmstead Rd. Har HA3 176 D1
Farnham C of E Prim Sch. Far 58 D6
Farnham Cl. Bov HP3 137 A3
Farnham Cl. Saw CM21 97 C1
Farnham Rd. Bis St CM23 58 F3
Farquhar St. Hert SG14 113 C7
Farr's La. Nwml E LU2 65 A1
Farraline Rd. Watf WD1 167 B5
Farrant Way. Bor WD6 169 E8
Farrer Top. Mark AL3 83 E5
Farriday Cl. St Alb AL3 127 E7
Farriers Cl. Bal SG7 12 E1
Farriers Cl. Cod SG4 67 F1
Farriers End. Ches EN10 148 F5
Farriers. Gt Am SG12 115 A6
Farriers Way. Bor WD6 170 D4
Farringford Cl. Chis AL2 141 B5
Farrow Cl. Luton LU3 31 C1
Farthing Dr. Letw SG6 23 C3
Farthings The. Heml H HP1 124 B3
Faulkner Ct. St Alb AL1 127 E5
Faverolle Gn. Ches EN8 148 D3
Faversham Cl. Tri HP23 100 A4
Fawbert & Barnard's
Jun Mix & Inf Sch. Harl 118 C3
Fawbert & Bernard Inf Sch The.
Saw 97 E2
Fawcett Rd. Stev SG2 51 B7
Fawkon Wlk. Hod EN11 135 A6
Fawn Ct. Hat AL9 130 C7
Fay Gn. Abb L WD5 153 D6
Fayerfield. Pot B EN6 159 D8
Fayland Cotts. Gt Ho SG9 41 E7
Feacey Down. Heml H HP1 124 B5
Fearney Mead. Ric WD3 165 A1
Fearnhill Sch. Letw 22 C5
Fearnley Rd. Wel G C AL8 110 C5
Fearnley St. Watf WD1 167 B5
Feather Dell. Hat AL10 130 A5
Featherbed La. Heml H HP3 138 B7
Featherston Rd. Stev SG2 51 C3
Featherstone Gdns. Bor WD6 170 C5
Federal Way. Watf WD2 167 C8
Felbrigg Cl. Luton LU2 46 F2
Felden Cl. Watf WD2 154 D5
Felden Dr. Heml H HP3 138 A7
Felden La. Heml H HP3 138 A7
Feldon Cl. Pnr HA5 175 E3
Felix Ave. Luton LU2 46 A2
Fellowes La. Col H AL4 143 E8
Fellowes Way. Stev SG2 51 A2
Fells Cl. Hit SG5 34 F8
Felmersham Ct. Luton LU1 63 B7
Felmersham Rd. Luton LU1 63 A7
Felmongers. Harl CM20 118 B2
Felstead Cl. Luton LU2 45 F3
Felstead Rd. Ches EN8 162 E7
Felstead Way. Luton LU2 45 F3
Felton Cl. Bor WD6 156 E1
Felton Cl. Ches EN10 148 F6
Felton Cl. Luton LU2 46 D1
Fen End. Stot SG5 11 F8
Fennycroft Rd. Heml H HP1 124 A6
Fensom's Alley. Heml H HP2 124 D4
Fensom's Cl. Heml H HP2 124 D4
Fenwick Cl. Luton LU3 45 B5
Fermor Cres. Luton LU2 46 C1
Fern Cl. Hod EN10 148 F8
Fern Dells. Hat AL10 129 F4
Fern Dr. Heml H HP3 124 E2
Fern Gr. Wel G C AL8 89 D2
Fern Way. Watf WD2 154 B4
Ferndale. Muc H SG10 74 F2
Ferndale Rd. Enf EN3 162 E2
Ferndale Rd. Luton LU1 63 B7
Ferndene. Bri Wd AL2 154 F8
Ferndown Cl. Pnr HA5 175 E3
Ferndown. Pnr HA6 175 A1
Ferndown Rd. Sth Ox WD1 175 C6
Fernecroft. St Alb AL1 141 D8
Fernheath. Luton LU3 31 A1
Fernhills. Abb L WD4 153 D6
Fernleigh Ct. Har HA2 176 B1
Fernleys. St Alb AL4 128 C5
Ferns Cl. Enf EN3 162 E3
Fernville La. Heml H HP2 124 D3
Ferny Hill. Had W EN4 159 F1
Ferrars Cl. Dun LU4 44 B1
Ferrars Inf Sch. Dun 44 B3
Ferrars Jun Sch. Dun 44 B3
Ferrers La. Whea 108 B5
Ferrier Rd. Stev SG2 51 C6
Ferryhills Cl. Sth Ox WD1 175 C7
Feryngs Cl. Harl CM17 118 D4
Fesants Croft. Harl CM20 118 B3
Fetherstone Cl. Pot B EN6 159 D7
Fiddle Bridge La. Hat AL10 129 F6
Fiddlebridge Ind Ctr. Hat 129 F6
Fidler Pl. Bus WD2 168 B3
Field Cl. Harp AL5 107 D7
Field Cl. St Alb AL4 128 A7
Field Cres. Royst SG8 7 F7
Field End Cl. Luton LU2 46 C4
Field End Cl. Watf WD1 167 E2
Field End Cl. Wigg HP23 100 D1
Field Fare Gn. Dun LU4 44 A5
Field House Ct. Harp AL5 86 A2
Field Inf Sch. Watf 167 C4
Field La. Letw SG6 22 F4
Field Rd. Heml H HP2 125 A3
Field Rd. Watf WD1 167 E3
Field View. Barn EN5 171 B5
Field View Rd. Pot B EN6 159 A6
Field View Rise. Bri Wd AL2 140 E2
Field Way. Bov HP3 137 A4
Field Way. Hod EN11 115 C2
Field Way. Ric WD3 165 B1
Field's Ct. Pot B EN6 159 D6
Fielder Ctr (Univ of Herts). Hat 129 D8
Fieldfare. Letw SG6 11 E1
Fieldfare. Stev SG2 51 D3
Fieldfares. Lon C AL2 142 D4
Fieldgate House. Stev SG1 50 F5
Fieldgate Rd. Luton LU4 44 D2
Fieldings Rd. Ches EN8 148 F3
Fields End La. Heml H HP1 123 E5
Fields End. Tri HP23 100 A6
Fieldway. Berk HP4 122 E2
Fieldway. Gt Am SG12 115 B4
Fieldway. Wigg HP23 100 D1
Fifth Ave. Letw SG6 23 C6
Fifth Ave. Watf WD2 154 D4
Fifth Ave. Harl CM20 117 D2
Figtree Hill. Heml H HP2 124 D4
Filey Cl. Stev SG1 50 A7
Filmer Rd. Luton LU4 44 E4
Finch Cl. Dun LU4 44 A4
Finch Cl. Hat AL10 130 A3
Finch La. Bus WD2 168 A5
Finch Rd. Berk HP4 122 A4
Finchdale. Heml H HP1 124 A3
Finche's End. Walk SG2 52 B8
Finches The. Hert SG13 114 B6
Finches The. Hit SG4 35 A7
Finley Rd. Harp AL5 86 D3
Finsbury Ct. Ches EN8 162 E5
Finsbury Rd. Luton LU4 44 D5
Finucane Rise. Bus WD2 176 C8
Finway Ct. Watf WD1 166 F4
Finway. Luton LU1 63 A8
Finway Rd. Heml H HP2 125 B7
Fir Cl. Stev SG2 50 F1
Fir Tree Cl. Heml H HP3 125 B2
Fir Tree Ct. Bor WD6 169 F5
Fir Tree Hill. Sar WD3 153 A2
Firbank Dr. Watf WD1 167 E2
Firbank Rd. St Alb AL3 127 F7
Firbank Trad Est. Luton 63 A8
Fire Station Alley. Barn EN5 171 E7
Firecrest. Letw SG6 11 E1
Firlands. Bis St CM23 76 E6
Firlands House. Bis St CM23 76 E6
Firs Cl. Hat AL10 130 B4
Firs Cl. Hit SG5 34 D8
Firs Dr. Kim AL4 87 C5
Firs Jun Sch The. Bis St 76 E6
Firs La. Pot B EN6 159 B6
Firs The. Ham St EN7 147 E4
Firs The. Harp AL5 86 D2
Firs The. St Alb AL1 142 B7
Firs The. Wel G C AL8 89 C2
Firs The. Wigg HP23 100 D1
Firs Wlk. Norwd HA6 174 D4
Firs Wlk. Tewin AL6 90 E5
Firs Wood Cl. Nort EN6 159 F7
First Ave. Watf WD2 154 D4
First Ave. Harl CM20 117 E2
Firway Cl. Welw AL6 89 F7
Firway. Welw AL6 89 F7
Firwood Ave. Coln H AL4 128 E3
Fish Farm St. Red AL3 106 B5
Fish Hill. Royst SG8 7 D6
Fish St. Red AL3 106 B5
Fisher Cl. Kin L WD4 139 A2
Fisher Rd. Har HA3 176 F1
Fisher's Green Rd. Stev SG1 50 B8
Fisher's Ind Est. Watf 167 C4
Fishers Cl. Ches EN8 163 A5
Fishers Cl. Stand SG11 55 D3
Fishers Gn. Stev SG1 36 A1
Fishers Mead. Stand SG11 55 D3
Fishery Cotts. Heml H HP1 124 A1
Fishery Rd. Heml H HP1 124 A1
Fishponds Rd. Hit SG5 34 E8
Fishpool St. St Alb AL3 127 C3
Fitzjohn Ave. Barn EN5 171 F5
Fitzroy Ave. Luton LU3 45 B3
Fitzwarin Cl. Luton LU3 44 E8
Fitzwilliam Ct. Harl CM17 118 E4
Five Acres Ave. Bri Wd AL2 140 F2
Five Acres. Kin L WD4 138 F2
Five Acres. Lon C AL2 142 D6
Five Acres. Sta M CM24 59 E8
Five Oaks. Cad LU1 62 F4
Five Oaks. Hat AL10 130 B2
Five Oaks Sch. Cad 62 F3
Five Oaks Sch. Hat 130 A3
Five Springs Ct. Luton LU3 44 E6
Five Springs. Luton LU3 44 E6
Five Springs Sch. Luton 44 F7
Flags The. Heml H HP2 125 B3
Flagstaff Rd. Wa Aby EN9 163 B6
Flamstead End Inf Sch. Ham St 148 A4
Flamstead End Jun Sch. Ham St 148 A4
Flamstead End Rd. Ches EN8 148 B3
Flamstead Jun Mix Inf Sch. Fla 84 B1
Flamsteadbury La. Red AL3 106 A4
Flash La. Cre H EN2 161 C3
Flatfield Rd. Heml H HP3 125 A1
Flaunden Bottom. Flau HP5 150 E4
Flaunden Bottom. Lat HP5 150 E4
Flaunden Hill. Flau HP3 151 A6
Flaunden La. Bov HP3 137 D3
Flavian Cl. St Alb AL3 126 F1
Flax Mews. Mark AL3 83 E5
Flecker Cl. Stan HA7 176 F5
Fleet The. Royst SG8 7 C6
Fleetville Inf Sch. St Alb 128 B3
Fleetville Jun Mix Sch. St Alb 128 A3
Fleetwood Cres. Stev SG1 50 B7
Fleetwood. Letw SG6 23 B4
Fleetwood Way. Sth Ox WD1 175 C6
Fleming Cl. Ham St EN7 148 A5
Fleming Cres. Hert SG14 113 A6
Fletcher Way. Heml H HP2 124 D6
Flete House. Watf WD1 166 E3
Flexley Wood. Wel G C AL7 90 A1
Flinders Ct. St Alb AL1 128 A1
Flinders Cl. Stev SG2 51 D5
Flint Cl. Luton LU3 44 E7
Flint Copse. Red AL3 106 C6
Flint Rd. Letw SG6 23 C8
Flint Way. St Alb AL3 127 C7
Flora Gr. St Alb AL1 127 F2
Floral Dr. Lon C AL2 142 D5
Florence Ave. Luton LU3 44 D6
Florence Cl. Watf WD2 154 A4
Florence St. Hit SG5 34 F8
Florence Wlk. Bis St CM23 76 F8
Flowers Ind Est. Luton 63 E6 6
Flowers Way. Luton LU1 63 F7
Flowton Gr. Harp AL5 107 A7
Fold Croft. Harl CM20 117 A1
Foldingshott. Dat SG3 69 D3
Follett Dr. Abb L WD5 153 F8
Folly Ave. St Alb AL3 127 D4
Folly Cl. Hit SG4 35 A5
Folly Cl. Radl WD7 155 F3
Folly Fields. Whea AL4 87 B2
Folly La. Cad LU1 62 E4
Folly La. St Alb AL3 127 C4
Folly Pathway. Radl WD7 155 F3
Folly The. Bun SG9 40 D7
Folly The. Hert SG14 113 D6
Folly View. Gt Am SG12 115 B4
Fontmell Cl. St Alb AL3 127 E5
Fontwell Cl. Har HA3 176 E3
Football Cl. Bal SG7 12 E1
Forbes Ave. Pot B EN6 159 D7
Ford Cl. Bus WD2 168 C5
Ford Hill. L Had SG11 75 B8
Ford St. Brag SG11 55 E6
Fordham Cl. Ashw SG7 4 D4
Fordham Rd. Royst SG8 7 E5
Fordwich Cl. Hert SG14 113 A6
Fordwich Hill. Hert SG14 113 A6
Fordwich Rd. Wel G C AL8 110 C5
Fordwich Rise. Hert SG14 113 A6
Fore St. Harl CM17 118 C4
Fore St. Hat AL9 130 C6
Fore St. Hert SG14 113 D6
Fore St. Wes SG4 24 B1
Forebury Ave. Saw CM21 97 F2
Forebury Cres. Saw CM21 97 F2
Forebury The. Saw CM21 97 F2
Forefield. Chis AL2 141 A4
Forelands Pl. Saw CM21 97 E2
Forest Ave. Heml H HP3 124 D1 5
Forest Rd. Ches EN8 148 D2
Forest Rd. Enf EN3 162 E3
Forest Rd. Watf WD2 154 B6
Forest Row. Stev SG2 50 F1
Forest Wlk. Bus WD2 167 F8
Foresters Cl. Ham St EN7 147 E4
Foresthall Rd. Sta M CM24 59 E4
Forge Cl. Chipf WD4 152 A8
Forge Cl. Hit SG5 34 F8 5
Forge Cotts. Ess AL9 131 E6
Forge End. Chis AL2 141 A5
Forge La. Norwd HA6 174 E3
Forge La. Welw AL6 89 C5
Forres Cl. Hod EN11 135 A8
Forres Jun Mix & Inf Sch. Hod 115 B1
Forrest Cres. Luton LU2 46 A3
Forresters Dr. Wel G C AL7 111 C5
Fortnums Acre. Har HA7 176 F4
Fortuna Cl. Stev SG1 51 C8
Fortune La. Elst WD6 169 D3
Forty Hill C of E Sch. Enf 162 A2
Forty Hill. Enf EN2 161 F1
Fosman Cl. Hit SG5 34 D8 7
Foster Cl. Stev SG1 36 D1
Foster Dr. Hit SG4 35 A5
Foster Rd. Heml H HP1 124 B1
Foston Cl. Luton LU3 44 F6
Fotherley Rd. Ric WD3 172 F8
Foulds Jun Mix Inf Sch. Barn 171 D6
Founceley Ave. Dan En SG12 71 F8
Fountain Pl. Wa Aby EN9 163 C5
Fountains Rd. Luton LU3 45 D3
Four Acres. Stev SG1 50 D7
Four Acres. Wel G C AL7 110 F4
Four Acres The. Sheer CM21 98 A2
Four Limes. Whea AL4 108 D8
Four Swannes Jun Mix Inf Sch.
Ches 162 E6
Four Tubs The. Bus WD2 168 D2
Fouracres. Letw SG6 23 A3
Fouracres Dr. Heml H HP3 124 F1
Fouracres Wlk. Heml H HP3 124 F1
Fourth Ave. Harl CM20 117 C1
Fourth Ave. Letw SG6 23 C7
Fourth Ave. Luton LU3 44 D7
Fourth Ave. Watf WD2 154 D4
Fourways Market. Wel G AL9 144 C7
Fovant Cl. Harp AL5 107 C6
Fovant. Stev SG1 36 B1
Fowley Cl. Ches EN8 162 F5
Fowlmere Rd. Gt Ch SG8 9 F8
Fox Cl. Bus WD2 168 B5
Fox Cl. Elst WD6 169 D3
Fox Cl. Wigg HP23 100 D1
Fox Cnr. Gu M SG8 1 F5
Fox La. Ther SG8 15 F7
Fox Rd. Stev SG1 50 E4
Fox Rd. Wigg HP23 100 C2
Fox's La. Bro Pk AL9 144 F7
Foxbury Cl. Luton LU2 45 D6
Foxcroft. St Alb AL1 128 A1
Foxdell Inf Sch. Luton 63 A8
Foxdell Jun Sch. Luton 62 E8
Foxdell. Norwd HA6 174 D4
Foxdells. Hertng SG14 112 C3
Foxdells La. Bis St CM23 58 F2
Foxes Cl. Hert SG13 114 B6
Foxes Dr. Ches EN7 148 A2
Foxfield Cl. Norwd HA6 174 F4
Foxfield. Stev SG2 51 C3
Foxglove Bank. Royst SG8 7 F5
Foxglove Cl. Bis St CM23 76 C6
Foxglove Cl. Hat AL10 130 B4
Foxglove Way. Welw AL6 89 E8
Foxgloves The. Heml H HP1 123 E2
Foxgrove Path. Sth Ox WD1 175 D5
Foxhill. Gu M SG8 1 F5
Foxhill. Luton LU2 45 E5
Foxhill Rd. Gu M SG8 1 F5
Foxhill. Watf WD2 154 A3
Foxholes Ave. Hert SG13 113 F6
Foxhollows. Hat AL10 130 B7
Foxlands Cl. Watf WD2 154 A5
Foxley Dr. Bis St CM23 77 B8
Foxley Gr. Welw AL6 89 F4
Foxleys. Sth Ox WD1 175 E7
Foxton Rd. Hod EN11 135 A6
Foxtree House. Watf WD2 154 E3
Frampton Rd. Pot B EN6 145 C1
Frampton St. Hert SG14 113 D6
Francis Ave. St Alb AL3 127 D6
Francis Bacon Sch. St Alb 142 B8
Francis Cl. Hit SG4 35 A5
Francis Cl. Stot SG5 11 E6
Francis Combe Sch. Watf 154 C7
Francis Rd. Hin SG7 3 C6
Francis Rd. Ware SG12 93 D2
Francis Rd. Watf WD1 167 B5
Francis St. Luton LU1 63 D8
Frank Martin Ct. Ches EN7 148 B1
Frankland Cl. Cro Gr WD3 166 A2
Frankland Rd. Cro Gr WD3 166 B3
Franklin Ave. Ches EN7 148 B1
Franklin Cl. Coln H AL4 129 E1
Franklin Cl. Heml H HP3 138 E8
Franklin Ct. Pirt SG5 20 D4
Franklin Gdns. Hit SG4 22 B1
Franklin Rd. Watf WD1 167 B7
Franklin's Rd. Stev SG1 50 C8
Franks Cl. Henlw SG16 10 B5
Franshams Dr. Bus WD2 176 D8
Fraser Rd. Ches EN8 148 E3
Fred Millard Ct. Stev SG1 50 E5
Frederick St. Luton LU2 45 E1
Frederick St Pas. Luton LU2 45 E1
Freeman Ave. Luton LU3 45 B8
Freemans Cl. Hit SG5 21 D1
Freewaters Cl. Ick SG5 21 E4
Freman Dr. Bun SG9 40 D8
French Horn La. Hat AL10 130 B6
French Row. St Alb AL3 127 D3 4
French's Cl. Gt Am SG12 115 B4
Frensham Dr. Hit SG4 22 C2
Frensham. Ham St EN7 148 A4
Freshwater Cl. Luton LU3 44 F7
Freshwaters. Harl CM20 117 E1
Fretherne Rd. Wel G C AL8 110 D6
Friars Cl. Luton LU1 63 B5
Friars Field. Nthch HP4 121 E7
Friars Rd. Brag SG11 56 A7
Friars Rd. Wes SG4 24 B1
Friars Way. Bus WD2 167 F8
Friars Way. Kin L WD4 139 A1
Friars Way. Luton LU1 63 B5
Friars Wlk. Tri HP23 100 A4
Friars Wood. Bis St CM23 77 C8
Friarscroft. Hod EN10 135 A3
Friday Furlong. Hit SG5 34 C8
Friedberg Ave. Bis St CM23 76 D4
Friendless La. Fla AL3 83 E3
Friends Ave. Ches EN8 162 D7
Friesian Cl. Dun LU4 44 A3
Frimley Rd. Heml H HP1 123 E4
Fringewood Cl. Norwd HA6 174 B2
Frinton Cl. Sth Ox WD1 175 B8
Friston Gn. Luton LU2 46 D1
Frithsden Copse. Pot En HP4 122 F8
Frithwood Ave. Norwd HA6 174 F4
Frithwood Prim Sch. Norwd 174 F4
Frobisher Dr. Stev SG2 51 B7
Frobisher Rd. St Alb AL1 128 C1
Frobisher Way. Hat AL10 129 D8
Froghall La. Walk SG2 38 B1
Frogmoor Ct. Ric WD3 173 D8
Frogmoor La. Ric WD3 173 D8
Frogmore Hill. Ast SG14 70 B7
Frogmore House. Stev SG1 36 C1
Frogmore. Pk St AL2 141 E4
Frogmore Rd. Heml H HP3 138 D8
Frogmore St. Tri HP23 100 A3
Frogs Hall La. Dan En SG11 53 F3
Frome Cl. Luton LU4 44 E4
Frome Sq. Heml H HP2 125 A8
Front St. Cad LU1 63 C1
Front The. Pot En HP4 123 B7
Frowick Cl. Wel G AL9 144 B8
Frowyke Cres. Ridge EN6 158 A7
Fry Rd. Stev SG2 51 C5
Fryth Mead. St Alb AL3 127 B4
Fulbeck Way. Har HA2 176 C1
Fulbourne Cl. Luton LU4 44 E2
Fulford Gr. Sth Ox WD1 175 B8
Fuller Ct. Bis St CM23 77 A7 1
Fuller Gdns. Watf WD2 154 B2
Fuller Rd. Watf WD2 154 B2
Fuller Way. Cro Gr WD3 166 A4
Fullers Ct. Letw SG6 22 F7
Fulling Mill La. Welw AL6 89 B6
Fulmar Cres. Heml H HP1 124 A3
Fulmore Cl. Harp AL5 86 D4
Fulton Cl. Stev SG1 50 C5
Fulton Cres. Bis St CM23 77 C8
Fulton Ct. Bor WD6 156 F1
Furham Field. Pnr HA5 176 A3
Furlay Cl. Letw SG6 22 D7
Furlong Way. Gt Am SG12 115 A7
Furlongs. Heml H HP1 124 A4
Furneux Pelham Jun Mix Inf Sch.
Fur P 43 A4
Furrowfield. Hat AL10 130 B7
Furrows The. Luton LU3 45 B7
Furse Ave. St Alb AL4 128 A7
Furtherfield. Abb L WD5 153 E7
Furtherground. Heml H HP2 124 E2 1
Furze Cl. Luton LU2 45 D7
Furze Cl. Sth Ox WD1 175 C5
Furze Gr. Royst SG8 7 E5
Furze Rd. Heml H HP1 123 E2
Furze View. Chor WD3 164 C4
Furzebushes La. Chis AL2 140 F6
Furzedown Ct. Harp AL5 86 B1 10
Furzedown. Stev SG2 51 B4
Furzefield. Ches EN8 148 B3
Furzefield Ct. Pot B EN6 158 E8
Furzefield Ctr The. Pot B 158 D8
Furzefield Rd. Wel G C AL7 110 E4
Furzehill Mid Sch. Bor 170 A5
Furzehill Par. Bor WD6 170 A6
Furzehill Rd. Bor WD6 170 B5
Furzen Cres. Hat AL10 129 F2

Gable Cl. Abb L WD5 153 E7
Gable Cl. Pnr HA5 176 A3
Gables Ave. Bor WD6 169 F6
Gables The. Saw CM21 97 E2
Gaddesden Cres. Watf WD2 154 E5
Gaddesden Gr. Wel G C AL7 111 B6
Gaddesden La. Gt Gd AL3 105 C4
Gaddesden Row CP Sch. Gt Gd 104 B6
Gaddesden Row. Gt Gd HP2 104 C6
Gade Ave. Watf WD1 166 E5
Gade Bank. Cro Gr WD1 166 D5
Gade Cl. Heml H HP1 124 B6
Gade Cl. Watf WD1 166 E5
Gade Side. Watf WD1 153 E4
Gade Valley Cl. Kin L WD4 139 A3
Gade Valley Cotts. Gt Gd HP1 103 D4
Gade Valley Jun Mix Inf Sch.
Heml H 124 B4
Gade View Gdns. Abb L WD4 153 C7
Gade View Rd. Heml H HP3 138 D7
Gadebridge Ct. Heml H HP1 124 C4
Gadebridge La. Heml H HP1 124 B5
Gadebridge La. Heml H HP1 124 C5
Gadebridge Rd. Heml H HP1 124 B4
Gadeview. Heml H HP1 124 C3
Gadswell Cl. Watf WD2 154 E3
Gage Cl. Royst SG8 7 D7
Gainsborough Ave. St Alb AL1 127 F4
Gainsford Cres. Hit SG4 22 C2
Gainswood. Wel G C AL7 110 E5
Gall End La. Sta M CM24 59 F7
Galleria The. Hat 129 F5
Galley Gn. Hod SG13 115 A2
Galley Hill. Heml H HP1 124 B6
Galley La. Barn EN5 171 B7
Galley La. Bor EN5 171 B7
Galleyhill Rd. Wa Aby EN9 163 E8
Galliard Cl. Luton LU3 45 B4
Galloway Cl. Bis St CM23 76 F8
Galloway Cl. Ches EN10 148 F5
Galloway Rd. Bis St CM23 58 F1
Gallows Hill. Abb L WD4 153 C7
Gallows Hill La. Abb L WD5 153 D8
Galston Rd. Luton LU3 44 D8
Gammons La. Watf WD1,WD2 154 A2
Gamnel Terr. Tri HP23 100 B7
Ganders Ash. Watf WD2 154 A6
Gandhi Ct. Watf WD2 167 D7 1
Gangies Hill. H Wy CM21 97 A4
Gant Ct. Wa Aby EN9 163 F5
Ganton Wlk. Sth Ox WD1 175 E6
Ganymede Pl. Heml H HP2 124 F6
Gaping La. Hit SG5 34 D7
Garden Ave. Hat AL10 130 A2
Garden Cl. Barn EN5 171 C5
Garden Cl. Harp AL5 107 A5
Garden Cl. Royst SG8 7 E7
Garden Cl. St Alb AL1 128 B4
Garden Cl. Watf WD1 166 F7
Garden Cl. Welw SG3 69 B2
Garden Ct. Whea AL4 87 D1
Garden Field. Ast SG2 51 E2
Garden Field La. Berk HP4 122 F2

Garden Fields Jun Mix Inf Sch. St Alb 127 D6
Garden La. Royst SG8 7 D5
Garden Rd. Abb L WD5 153 E8
Garden Rd. Bun SG9 40 E8
Garden Rd. Welw SG3 69 B2
Garden Row. Hit SG5 34 F8 6
Garden Terr. Sac SG12 92 E4
Garden Terrace Rd. Harl CM17 118 C4
Garden Wlk. Royst SG8 7 E7
Garden Wlk. Stev SG1 50 E5
Gardenia Ave. Luton LU3 45 A4
Gardens The. Bal SG7 23 E8
Gardens The. Bro Pk AL9 144 E4
Gardens The. Henlw SG16 10 D8
Gardens The. Stot SG5 11 E6
Gardens The. Watf WD1 166 F7
Gardiners La. Ashw SG7 4 D4
Gareth Ct. Bor WD6 156 F1
Garfield Ct. Luton LU2 46 D3 3
Garfield St. Watf WD2 154 B1
Garland Cl. Heml H HP2 124 D4
Garland Rd. Ware SG12 93 E1
Garnault Rd. Enf EN1 161 F1
Garner Dr. Ches EN10 148 E5
Garnett Cl. Watf WD2 154 D3
Garnett Dr. Bri Wd AL2 140 F2
Garrard Way. Whea AL4 108 D8
Garratts Rd. Bus WD2 168 C2
Garretts Mead. Luton LU2 46 B3
Garrison Ct. Hit SG4 34 F7 2
Garrowsfield. Barn EN5 171 F4
Garsmouth Way. Watf WD2 154 D3
Garston Cres. Watf WD2 154 C5
Garston Dr. Watf WD2 154 C5
Garston Inf Sch. Watf 154 D4
Garston La. Watf WD2 154 D5
Garston Manor Medical Rehabilitation Ctr. Abb L 154 C8
Garston Manor Sch. Watf 154 C7
Garston Park Par. Watf WD2 154 D5
Garston Sta. Watf 154 D4
Garth Rd. Letw SG6 22 E3
Garth The. Abb L WD5 153 D6
Garthland Dr. Barn EN5 171 C4
Gartlet Rd. Watf WD1 167 C6
Gas La. Bark SG8 17 C3
Gascoyne Cecil Prim Sch. Hat 130 A7
Gascoyne Cl. Pot B EN6 158 A7
Gascoyne Way. Hert SG13,SG14 113 D5
Gate Cl. Bor WD6 170 C8
Gate Cotts. Chor WD3 164 D5
Gate End. Norwd HA6 175 A3
Gatecroft. Heml H HP3 124 F1 1
Gatecroft. Heml H HP3 139 A8
Gatehill Gdns. Luton LU3 31 B1
Gatehill Rd. Norwd HA6 175 A3
Gates Way. Stev SG1 50 C6
Gatesbury Way. Stand SG11 55 D3
Gatesdene Cl. L Gad HP4 102 C8
Gateshead Rd. Bor WD6 170 A8
Gateway Cl. Norwd HA6 174 C4
Gatwick Cl. Bis St CM23 59 B1
Gauldie Way. Stand SG11 55 D2
Gaumont App. Watf WD1 167 B6
Gaunts Way. Letw SG6 12 A1
Gaveston Dr. Berk HP4 122 B6
Gayland Ave. Luton LU2 64 B8
Gayton Cl. Luton LU3 45 B4
Gaywood Ave. Ches EN8 148 D1
Gazelda Ind Est. Watf 167 D4
Geddes Rd. Bus WD2 168 C5
Geddings Rd. Hod EN11 135 B6
Generals Wlk The. Enf EN3 162 E2
Gentle Ct. Bal SG7 23 E8
Gentlemens Field. Ware SG12 93 B3
George Gn. L Hal CM22 77 B1
George La. Royst SG8 7 D6
George Leighton Ct. Stev SG2 51 B4
George St. Berk HP4 122 D4
George St. Heml H HP2 124 D4
George St. Hert SG14 113 C6
George St. Luton LU1 63 E7
George St. Mark AL3 83 E5
George St. St Alb AL3 127 D3
George St W. Luton LU1 63 E7
George St. Watf WD1 167 C5
George Street Sch. Heml H 124 D4
George V Ave. Pnr HA5 175 F1
George V Way. Sar WD3 152 B3
George's Wood Rd. Bro Pk AL9 145 B5
Georges Mead. Elst WD6 169 E3
Georgewood Rd. Heml H HP3 139 A7
Georgina Ct. Arl SG15 11 A3
Gerard Ave. Bis St CM23 76 E4
Gernon Rd. Letw SG6 22 F5
Gernon Wlk. Letw SG6 22 F5
Gew's Cnr. Ches EN8 148 D2
Gew's Corner Prim Sch. Ches 148 E2
Ghlbert Way. Berk HP4 122 A4
Giant Tree Hill. Bus WD2 168 D1
Gibbons Cl. Bor WD6 169 E8
Gibbons Cl. Sand AL4 108 C1
Gibbons Way. Kneb SG3 68 F5
Gibbs Cl. Ches EN8 148 D2
Gibbs Couch. Sth Ox WD1 175 D7
Gibbs Field. Bis St CM23 76 D5
Gibraltar Lodge. Harp AL5 86 D3
Gibson Cl. Hit SG4 35 B7
Gidian Ct. Pk St AL2 141 D4
Gifford's La. Dan E SG11 54 A2
Gilbert Rd. Hare UB9 173 D1
Gilbert St. Enf EN3 162 C2
Gilbert's Hill. St Le HP23 119 E3
Gilbey Ave. Bis St CM23 77 B6
Gilbey Cres. Sta M CM24 59 E8
Gilden Cl. Harl CM17 118 E4
Gilden Way. Harl CM17 118 D4
Gilder Cl. Luton LU3 45 A8
Gilderdale. Luton LU4 44 B6
Gilders. Saw CM21 97 D2
Giles Cl. Sand AL4 108 C1
Giles Inf Sch The. Stev 37 A1
Giles Jun Sch The. Stev 37 A1
Gillam St. Luton 63 E8
Gillan Gn. Bus WD2 176 C8
Gillian Ave. St Alb AL1 141 C7
Gilliat's Gn. Chor WD3 164 D5
Gilliflower House. Hod EN11 135 A5
Gillings Ct. Barn EN5 171 E5
Gillison Cl. Letw SG6 23 B5
Gills Hill. Radl WD7 155 F4
Gills Hill Inf Sch. Radl 155 F4
Gills Hill La. Radl WD7 155 F3
Gills Hollow. Radl WD7 155 F3
Gilmour Cl. Enf EN2 162 A4
Gilpin Gn. Harp AL5 86 C1
Gilpin Rd. Ware SG12 114 E8
Gilpin's Gallop. Gt Am SG12 115 B4
Gilpin's Ride. Berk HP4 122 E5
Gilsland. Wa Aby EN9 163 E4
Ginns Rd. Sto P SG9 43 D6
Gippeswyck Cl. Pnr HA5 175 D2
Gipsy La. Bis St CM23 59 C4
Gipsy La. Kneb SG3 68 E4
Gipsy La. Luton LU1 64 A6
Gipsy La. Sta M CM23 59 C4
Girdle Rd. Hit SG4 22 A2
Girons Cl. Hit SG4 35 B7
Girtin Rd. Bus WD2 168 C5
Girton Ct. Ches EN8 148 E1
Girton Way. Cro Gr WD3 166 C4
Glade The. Bal SG7 23 E7
Glade The. Letw SG6 22 F3
Glade The. Wel G C AL8 110 C8
Glades The. Heml H HP1 123 E4
Gladeside. St Alb AL4 128 D6
Gladeway The. Wa Aby EN9 163 D6
Gladsmuir Rd. Barn EN5 171 E7
Gladstone Ave. Luton LU1 63 C7
Gladstone Ct. Stev SG2 69 A8
Gladstone Pl. Barn EN5 171 D5
Gladstone Rd. Dan En SG12 71 F8
Gladstone Rd. Hod EN11 135 B7
Gladstone Rd. Ware SG12 93 C2
Gladstone Rd. Watf WD1 167 C6
Glamis Cl. Ches EN7 148 A2
Glamis Cl. Heml H HP2 105 B1
Glean Wlk. Hat AL10 130 A2 3
Gleave Cl. St Alb AL1 128 B4
Glebe Ave. Arl SG15 11 A7
Glebe Cl. Ess AL9 131 F6
Glebe Cl. Heml H HP3 138 E7
Glebe Cl. Hert SG14 113 D8
Glebe Cl. Pit LU7 80 D5
Glebe Cl. Wat St SG14 70 D3
Glebe Cotts. Ess AL9 131 F6
Glebe Ct. Bis St CM23 77 B8
Glebe Ct. Hat AL10 130 C6
Glebe Ct. Wat St SG14 70 E3
Glebe House. Ess AL9 131 F6
Glebe La. Barn EN5 171 A3
Glebe Rd. Hert SG14 113 D8
Glebe Rd. Letw SG6 23 B8
Glebe Rd. Welw AL6 89 B5
Glebe The. Kin L WD4 139 A2
Glebe The. Stev SG2 51 B6
Glebe The. Watf WD2 154 D6
Glebelands. Harl CM20 117 F3
Gleed Ave. Bus WD2 176 D8
Glemsford Cl. Luton LU4 44 B6
Glemsford Dr. Harp AL5 86 D2
Glen Chess. Ric 165 C6
Glen Faba Rd. Lo Naz CM19 135 F6
Glen The. Cad LU1 62 E3
Glen The. Heml H HP2 124 F8
Glen The. Heml H HP2 125 A8
Glen The. Norwd HA6 174 D3
Glen Way. Watf WD1 153 E1
Glenblower Ct. St Alb AL4 128 D3
Glencoe Rd. Bus WD2 168 A3
Glencourse Gn. Sth Ox WD1 175 D6
Glendale. Heml H HP1 124 B3
Glendale Wlk. Ches EN8 148 E1
Gleneagles Cl. Sth Ox WD1 175 D6
Gleneagles Dr. Luton LU2 45 E6
Glenester Cl. Hod EN11 115 B1
Glenferrie Rd. St Alb AL1 128 A3
Glenfield Ct. Hert SG14 112 F7
Glenfield Rd. Luton LU3 45 C6
Glengall Pl. St Alb AL1 141 E8
Glenhaven Ave. Bor WD6 170 A6
Glenlyn Ave. St Alb AL1 128 B2
Glenmire Terr. Sta Ab SG12 115 D4
Glenmore Gdns. Abb L WD5 154 A7
Glenshee Cl. Norwd HA6 174 C4
Glenview Gdns. Heml H HP1 124 B3
Glenview Rd. Heml H HP1 124 B3
Glenville Ave. Enf EN2 161 D1
Glenwood Cl. Stev SG2 51 C2
Glenwood. Hod EN10 134 F4
Glenwood. Wel G C AL7 111 D5
Glevum Cl. St Alb AL3 126 F1
Globe Cl. Harp AL5 86 B1
Globe Cres. Far CM23 58 D6
Globe Ct. Hert SG14 113 C8
Gloucester Ave. Ches EN8 162 E6
Gloucester Cl. Stev SG1 36 D1
Gloucester Rd. Enf EN2 161 C1
Gloucester Rd. Luton LU1 63 F6
Glover Cl. Ham St EN7 147 F4
Glovers Cl. Hert SG13 113 C4
Glynde The. Stev SG2 69 B8
Goat La. Enf EN1 161 F1
Gobions Way. Bro Pk EN6 145 B3
Goblins Gn. Wel G C AL7 110 D5
Goddard End. Stev SG2 69 C8
Goddards Cl. L Berk SG13 132 C4
Gode Tower. Heml H HP3 138 F6
Godfrey Cl. Stev SG2 51 B3
Godfreys Cl. Luton LU1 63 B6
Godfreys Ct. Luton LU1 63 D1
Godfries Cl. Tewin AL6 90 E3
Godsafe. Harl CM17 118 E4
Godwin Cl. Wa Aby EN9 163 C1
Goff's La. Gofs O EN7 147 E2
Goff's Oak Ave. Gofs O EN7 147 C3
Goffs Cres. Gofs O EN7 147 C2
Goffs La. Ches EN7 148 A2
Goffs Oak Jun Mix Inf Sch. Gofs O 147 B3
Goffs Sch. Ches 148 A2
Gold Crest Cl. Dun LU4 44 A5
Golda Cl. Barn EN5 171 D3
Goldcrest Way. Bus WD2 168 C1
Goldcroft. Heml H HP3 125 A1
Golden Dell. Wel G C AL7 110 F2
Goldfield Inf Sch. Tri 99 F3
Goldfield Rd. Tri HP23 99 F3
Goldfinch Way. Bor WD6 170 A5
Goldings. Bis St CM23 77 B8
Goldings Cres. Hat AL10 130 B6
Goldings House. Hat AL10 130 B6
Goldings La. Stap SG14 92 A2
Goldington Cl. Hod EN11 114 F1
Goldon. Letw SG6 23 C4
Goldstone Cl. Ware SG12 93 D2
Golf Cl. Bus WD2 167 D6
Golf Club Rd. Bro Pk AL9 145 A6
Golf Ride. Cre H EN2 161 A4
Gombards. St Alb AL3 127 D4
Gomer Cl. Cod SG4 67 E2
Gonville Ave. Cro Gr WD3 166 B3
Gonville Cres. Stev SG2 51 C2
Goodey Meade. Ben SG2 52 F2
Goodliffe Pk. Bis St 59 B2
Goodrich Cl. Watf WD2 154 A4
Goodwin Ct. Ches EN8 148 E3
Goodwin House. Watf WD1 166 E3
Goodwin Stile. Bis St CM23 76 D5
Goodwins Mead. Ched LU7 80 A7
Goodwood Ave. Enf EN3 162 C2
Goodwood Ave. Watf WD2 153 E3
Goodwood Cl. Hod EN11 135 A7
Goodwood Par. Watf WD1 153 E3
Goodwood Path. Bor WD6 170 A7
Goodwood Rd. Royst SG8 7 F6
Goodyers Ave. Radl WD7 155 F5
Goose Acre. Bot HP5 136 A1
Goose Acre. Ched LU7 80 A7
Goose La. Hat H CM22 98 E7
Gooseacre. Wel G C AL7 110 F4
Gooseberry Hill. Luton LU3 45 B7
Goosecroft. Heml H HP1 123 F4
Goral Mead. Ric WD3 165 D1
Gordian Way. Stev SG2 37 C1
Gordon Ave. Har HA7 176 F4
Gordon Cl. St Alb AL1 128 B2
Gordon House. St Alb AL1 128 B2
Gordon Rd. Ches EN8 163 A5
Gordon St. Luton LU1 63 D7
Gordon Way. Barn EN5 171 F5
Gore La. Stand SG11 73 D3
Gorelands La. C St P HP8 172 A7
Gorham Dr. St Alb AL1 141 E8
Gorle Cl. Watf WD2 154 A4
Gorleston Cl. Stev SG1 36 A1
Gorse Cl. Hat AL10 129 F2
Gorse Cnr. St Alb AL3 127 D5
Gorselands. Harp AL5 107 C7
Gorst Cl. Letw SG6 22 E5
Gosford House. Watf WD1 166 E3
Gosforth La. Sth Ox WD1 175 B7
Gosforth Path. Sth Ox WD1 175 A7
Goshawk Cl. Dun LU4 44 A4
Goslett Ct. Bus WD2 168 A4
Gosling Ave. Gt Of SG5 33 C2
Gosling Sports Pk. Wel G C 110 C4
Gosmore Ley Cl. Hit SG4 34 F3
Gosmore Rd. Hit SG4 34 F5
Gosmore. Stev SG1 36 C2
Gossamers The. Watf WD2 154 E4
Gossoms End. Berk HP4 122 B4
Gossoms Ryde. Berk HP4 122 A5
Gothic Mede Lower Sch. Arl 11 A5
Gothic Way. Arl SG15 11 B5
Gould Cl. Wel G AL9 144 B7
Government Row. Enf EN3 163 A2
Gower Field. Pot B EN6 158 A7
Gower Rd. Royst SG8 7 C7
Gowers The. Harl CM20 118 B2
Grace Cl. Bor WD6 170 D8
Grace Gdns. Bis St CM23 76 F4
Grace Way. Stev SG1 50 E7
Graces Maltings. Tri HP23 100 A3
Graemesdyke Rd. Berk HP4 122 A3
Graham Ave. Hod EN10 134 E2
Graham Cl. St Alb AL1 127 D1
Graham Gdns. Luton LU3 45 C4
Graham Rd. Har HA3 176 E1
Grailands. Bis St CM23 76 D8
Grammar School Wlk. Hit SG5 34 E7
Grampian Way. Luton LU3 44 C8
Granaries The. Wa Aby EN9 163 E5
Granary Cl. Whea AL4 108 D8
Granary Ct. Saw CM21 97 E2
Granary La. Harp AL5 86 C1
Granary The. Roy CM19 116 B1
Granby Ave. Harp AL5 86 D2
Granby Rd. Luton LU4 44 D2
Granby Rd. Stev SG1 36 C2
Grandfield Ave. Watf WD1 167 A8
Grange Ave. Barn N20 171 E2
Grange Ave. Luton LU4 44 D5
Grange Bottom. Royst SG8 7 E5
Grange Cl. Heml H HP2 125 A2
Grange Cl. Hert SG14 113 B6
Grange Cl. Hit SG4 35 A4
Grange Cl. Mark AL3 83 D6
Grange Court Rd. Harp AL5 107 C6
Grange Ct. Hert SG14 113 C7
Grange Ct. Wa Aby EN9 163 C5
Grange Dr. Stot SG5 11 E5
Grange Gdns. Ware SG12 114 E8
Grange Hill. Welw AL6 89 C6
Grange Jun Mix Sch The. Letw 12 A2
Grange La. Radl WD2 168 D8
Grange Pk. Bis St CM23 58 F1
Grange Rd. Bis St CM23 77 A7
Grange Rd. Bor WD6 169 F4
Grange Rd. Letw SG6 22 F8
Grange Rd. Pit LU7 80 D5
Grange Rd. Tri HP23 100 C5
Grange Rd. Watf WD2 167 F4
Grange Rd. Wils HP23 79 D1
Grange Rise. Cod SG4 67 F1
Grange St. St Alb AL3 127 D4
Grange The. Abb L WD5 153 E6
Grange The. Bis St CM23 58 F1
Grange The. Hod EN11 135 A5
Grange The. Ric WD3 165 A2
Grange Wlk. Bis St CM23 77 A7
Grangedale Cl. Norwd HA6 174 E2
Grangeside. Bis St CM23 59 A2
Grangewood Inf Sch. Ches 148 D1
Grangewood. Pot B EN6 145 B1
Gransden Cl. Luton LU3 45 A7
Grant Gdns. Harp AL5 86 B2
Grantham Cl. Royst SG8 7 B8
Grantham Gdns. Ware SG12 93 E2
Grantham Gn. Bor WD6 170 C4
Grantham Rd. Luton LU4 45 B1
Granville Ct. St Alb AL1 127 F3
Granville Dene. Bov HP3 137 A4
Granville Gdns. Hod EN11 115 A2
Granville Rd. Barn EN5 171 D6
Granville Rd. Hit SG4 22 C1
Granville Rd. Luton LU1 63 B8
Granville Rd. St Alb AL1 127 F3
Granville Rd. Watf WD1 167 C5
Grasmere Ave. Harp AL5 86 C1
Grasmere Ave. Luton LU3 45 B7
Grasmere Cl. Heml H HP3 125 B1
Grasmere Cl. Watf WD2 154 B7
Grasmere Rd. Luton LU3 45 C7
Grasmere Rd. St Alb AL1 128 B1
Grasmere Rd. Ware SG12 93 E3
Grass Meadows. Stev SG2 51 D7
Grass Warren. Tewin AL6 90 E1
Grassington Cl. Bri Wd AL2 141 A1
Grassy Cl. Heml H HP1 124 A4
Grave Inf Sch The. Harp 107 D7
Grave Jun Sch The. Harp 107 D7
Gravel Dr. Ast Cl HP23 99 B3
Gravel La. Heml H HP1 124 A3
Gravel Path. Berk HP4 122 E5
Gravel Path. Heml H HP1 124 A3
Graveley Ave. Bor WD6 170 C4
Graveley Cl. Stev SG1 36 C2
Graveley Dell. Wel G C AL7 111 B5
Graveley La. Gt Wy SG4 36 B5
Graveley Rd. Gra SG4 36 B3
Graveley Rd. Gt Wy SG4 35 F6
Gravelhill Terr. Heml H HP1 124 A2
Gravelly La. Brag SG11 55 F8
Gravely Ct. Heml H HP2 125 C2
Gray's La. Hit SG5 34 D7
Grayling Ct. Nthch HP4 121 F6
Graylings The. Abb L WD5 153 D6
Grays Cl. Royst SG8 7 C8
Grays Ct. Bis St CM23 76 E8
Graysfield. Wel G C AL7 111 A3
Grazings The. Heml H HP2 124 F5
Greasy Cl. Abb L WD5 153 F8
Great Braitch La. Hat AL10 109 F1
Great Break. Wel G C AL7 111 B5
Great Brookmead Sch. Bor 156 F1
Great Cambridge Rd. Ches EN8 148 D4
Great Cambridge Rd. Enf EN1 162 C6
Great Conduit. Wel G C AL7 111 C7
Great Dell. Wel G C AL8 89 D1
Great Elms Rd. Heml H HP3 138 F7
Great Gaddesden Prim Sch. Gt Gd 103 D3
Great Ganett. Wel G C AL7 111 C4
Great Gn. Pirt SG5 20 D4
Great Gr. Bus WD2 168 B5
Great Hadham Golf Club. Muc H 75 D4
Great Hadham Rd. Bis St CM23 76 C6
Great Heart. Heml H HP2 124 E5
Great Heath. Hat AL10 130 B8
Great Innings N. Wat St SG14 70 D4
Great Innings S. Wat St SG14 70 D3
Great Lawne. Dat SG3 69 D2
Great Ley. Wel G C AL7 110 E4
Great Meadow. Lo Naz EN10 135 A1
Great Molewood. Hert SG14 92 B1
Great North Rd. Barn EN5 171 E6
Great North Rd. Bro Pk AL9,EN6 145 B5
Great North Rd.Hat AL8 110 A4
Great North Rd. Hat AL9 130 C5
Great North Rd. Newn SG7 12 D4
Great North Rd. Stot SG5 3 A2
Great North Rd. Wel G C AL8 110 A7
Great North Rd. Welw AL6 89 E7
Great Palmers. Heml H HP2 124 F8
Great Pk. Kin L WD4 139 A1
Great Plumtree. Harl CM20 117 F2
Great Rd. Heml H HP2 124 F4
Great Slades. Pot B EN6 158 F6
Great Sturgess Rd. Heml H HP1 123 F3
Great Whites Rd. Heml H HP3 124 F1
Great Wood Ctry Pk. Cuf 146 B5
Greatfield Cl. Harp AL5 85 C4
Greatham Rd. Watf WD2 167 D6
Green Acres. Lily LU2 32 D2
Green Acres. Stev SG2 51 C1
Green Acres. Wel G C AL7 110 F3
Green Bushes. Luton LU4 44 D6
Green Cl. Bro Pk AL9 144 E5
Green Cl. Ches EN8 162 E8
Green Cl. Luton LU4 44 C5
Green Cl. Stev SG2 50 F2
Green Croft. Hat AL10 130 A8
Green Ct. Luton LU4 44 B5
Green Dell Way. Heml H HP3 125 C3
Green Drift. Royst SG8 7 C7
Green Edge. Watf WD2 154 A4
Green End Gdns. Heml H HP1 124 A2
Green End La. Heml H HP1 123 F3
Green End Rd. Heml H HP1 124 A2
Green End. Welw AL6 89 B4
Green Hill Cl. Brag SG11 55 F7
Green La. Ashw SG7 4 E5
Green La. Bov HP3 137 A3
Green La. Brag SG11 55 F7
Green La. Cro Gr WD3 165 F4
Green La. Heml H HP2 125 D4
Green La. Hit SG4 22 B1
Green La. Ken Co LU6 82 E8
Green La. Lat HP5 150 C6
Green La. Letw SG6 23 C8
Green La. Lo Naz EN10 149 B8
Green La. Luton LU2 46 C4
Green La. Mark AL3 83 F5
Green La. Norwd HA6 174 E3
Green La. Pit LU7 80 E5
Green La. St Alb AL1 142 A7
Green La. St Alb AL3 127 D7
Green La. Watf WD1 167 C2
Green La. Wel G C AL7 111 D5
Green Lane Cl. Harp AL5 107 E8
Green Lanes. Hat AL10 109 F2
Green Lanes Sch. Hat 109 F1
Green Leys Cotts. Stand SG11 55 F1
Green Meadow. Pot B EN6 145 A1
Green Oaks. Luton LU2 45 F3
Green Path. Ast Cl HP22 99 D4
Green St. Chor WD3 164 C5
Green St. Royst SG8 7 D8
Green St. Shen WD7 157 A3
Green St. Stev SG1 50 C7
Green The. Bis St CM23 76 F4
Green The. Ched LU7 80 A7
Green The. Ches EN8 148 C3
Green The. Cod SG4 67 F1
Green The. Kim SG4 65 C3
Green The. Kim SG4 66 D1
Green The. Kneb SG3 68 C5
Green The. Luton LU4 44 C5
Green The. Newn SG7 12 E7
Green The. Pit LU7 80 D4
Green The. Royst SG8 7 D6
Green The. Sar WD3 152 A3
Green The. Stot SG5 11 F7
Green The. Ware SG12 93 D3
Green The. Wel G C AL7 111 A4
Green The. Welw AL6 89 B5
Green Vale. Wel G C AL7 111 A5
Green View Cl. Bov HP3 137 A2
Green Way Gdns. Har HA3 176 E1
Green Way The. Har HA3 176 E2
Greenacre Cl. Barn EN5 158 F1
Greenacres. Bus WD2 176 D8
Greenacres. Heml H HP2 125 D2
Greenacres. Pit LU7 80 C4
Greenall Cl. Ches EN8 148 E1
Greenbank. Ches EN8 148 B3
Greenbank Rd. Watf WD1 153 D3
Greenbury Cl. Bar SG8 8 F1
Greenbury Cl. Chor WD3 164 C5
Greencoates. Hert SG13 113 E5
Greene Field Rd. Berk HP4 122 C4
Greene Wlk. Berk HP4 122 D3
Greenfield Ave. Ick SG5 21 D4
Greenfield Ave. Sth Ox WD1 175 E8
Greenfield. Hat AL9 130 D8
Greenfield La. Ick SG5 21 E4
Greenfield Rd. Stev SG1 50 E7
Greenfield. Royst SG8 7 B7
Greenfield St. Wa Aby EN9 163 C5
Greenfield. Wel G C AL8 89 D1
Greenfields. Cuf EN6 146 E1
Greenfields Jun Mix Inf Sch. Sth Ox 175 C5
Greenfields. Sta M CM24 59 E7
Greengate. Luton LU3 44 C8
Greenheys Cl. Norwd HA6 174 E2
Greenhill Ave. Luton LU2 45 E3
Greenhill Cres. Watf WD1 166 E3
Greenhill Ct. Heml H HP1 124 B2
Greenhill Pk. Bis St CM23 76 D5
Greenhills Cl. Ric WD3 165 B4
Greenhills. Ware SG12 93 C3
Greenland Rd. Barn EN5 171 C3
Greenlands. Bor NW7 170 D3
Greenlane Ind Est. Letw 23 C7
Greenriggs. Luton LU2 46 F2
Greenside. Bor WD6 157 A1
Greenside Sch. Stev 51 B2
Greensleeves Cl. St Alb AL4 128 C2
Greenstead. Saw CM21 97 E1
Greensward. Bus WD2 168 B3
Greenway. Berk HP4 122 A4
Greenway. Bis St CM23 77 C6
Greenway Cty Prim Sch. Berk 121 F4
Greenway. Harp AL5 107 E8
Greenway. Heml H HP2 125 B3
Greenway. Letw SG6 23 A2
Greenway. Pnr HA5 175 B1
Greenway The. Enf EN3 162 D4
Greenway The. Pot B EN6 159 A6
Greenway The. Ric WD3 165 A2
Greenway The. Tri HP23 99 F5
Greenway. Walk SG2 52 B8
Greenways. Abb L WD5 153 E7
Greenways. Bun SG9 40 D8
Greenways. Gofs O EN7 147 B2
Greenways. Hert SG14 113 B6
Greenways. Luton LU2 46 B5
Greenways. Stev SG1 50 E6
Greenwood Ave. Ches EN7 162 B8
Greenwood Cl. Ches EN7 162 B8
Greenwood Dr. Watf WD2 154 B5
Greenwood Park L Ctr. Chis 141 B6
Greenyard. Wa Aby EN9 163 C6
Greer Rd. Har HA3 176 C2
Gregories Cl. Luton LU3 45 D1
Gregory Ave. Pot B EN6 159 C6
Gregson Cl. Bor WD6 170 C8
Grenadier Cl. St Alb AL4 128 C2
Grenadine Cl. Ham St EN7 147 F4
Grenadine Way. Tri HP23 100 A5
Greneway Sch The. Royst 7 E7
Grenville Ave. Hod EN10 134 F2
Grenville Cl. Ches EN8 162 D7
Grenville Ct. Chor WD3 164 C5
Gresford Cl. St Alb AL4 128 D3
Gresham Cl. Luton LU2 64 D8
Gresham Ct. Berk HP4 122 B3
Gresley Cl. Wel G C AL8 110 E8
Gresley Ct. Enf EN1 162 C4
Gresley Ct. Pot B EN6 145 C1
Gresley Way. Stev SG2 51 D5
Greville Cl. Wel G AL9 144 C7
Grey House The. Watf WD1 167 A7
Greycaine Rd. Watf WD2 154 D2
Greydells Rd. Stev SG1 50 E6
Greyfriars La. Harp AL5 107 A7
Greyfriars. Ware SG12 93 B3
Greyhound La. Pot B EN6 158 A6
Greystoke Cl. Berk HP4 122 A3
Griffiths Way. St Alb AL1 127 C1
Grimaldi Ave. Luton LU3 45 A3
Grimsdyke Cres. Barn EN5 171 C6
Grimsdyke Fst & Mid Sch. Pnr 175 F4
Grimsdyke Lodge. St Alb AL1 128 A3
Grimsdyke Rd. Pnr HA5 175 E3
Grimsdyke Rd. Wigg HP23 100 D1
Grimston Rd. St Alb AL1 127 F2
Grimstone Rd. L Wym SG4 35 E4
Grimthorpe Cl. St Alb AL3 127 D6
Grindcobbe Cl. St Alb AL1 141 D8
Grinstead La. L Hal CM22 98 C6
Groom Rd. Ches EN10 148 F5
Grooms Cotts. Bot HP5 136 B1
Groomsby Dr. Pit LU7 80 E5
Grosvenor Ave. Abb L WD4 139 C3

Grosvenor Cl. Bis St CM23 76 D4
Grosvenor Cl. Cro Gr WD3 166 D4
Grosvenor House. Bis St CM23 77 B8
Grosvenor Rd. Bal SG7 12 F1
Grosvenor Rd. Bor WD6 170 B6
Grosvenor Rd. Hod EN10 134 F3
Grosvenor Rd. Luton LU3 45 B5
Grosvenor Rd. Mo Pk HA6 174 F5
Grosvenor Rd. St Alb AL1 127 E2
Grosvenor Rd W. Bal SG7 12 F1
Grosvenor Rd. Watf WD1 167 C6
Grosvenor Terr. Heml H HP1 124 A2
Grotto The. Ware SG12 114 D8
Ground La. Hat AL10 130 B7
Grove Ave. Harp AL5 107 D7
Grove Cotts. Bus WD2 168 A3
Grove Cres. Cro Gr WD3 166 A5
Grove Ct. Barn EN5 171 F6
Grove Ct. Wa Aby EN9 163 B6
Grove End. Luton LU1 63 B5
Grove Farm Pk. Mo Pk HA6 174 D5
Grove Gdns. Enf EN3 162 D1
Grove Gdns. Tri HP23 100 B5
Grove Hall Rd. Watf WD2 167 E5
Grove Hill. Sta M CM24 59 E7
Grove House. Bus WD2 167 F3
Grove House. Ches EN7 148 B1
Grove La. Ash Gr HP5 136 B5
Grove Lea. Hat AL10 130 A2
Grove Mead. Hat AL10 129 F5
Grove Meadow. Wel G C AL7 111 C6
Grove Mill La. Sar WD1 153 C1
Grove Park Rd. Cad LU1 63 B3
Grove Path. Ches EN7 162 A8
Grove Pk. Tri HP23 100 C5
Grove Pl. Bis St CM23 76 F7
Grove Pl. Wel G AL9 144 C7
Grove Rd. Bor WD6 170 A8
Grove Rd. Cad LU1 63 B2
Grove Rd. Harp AL5 107 D7
Grove Rd. Heml H HP1 124 A1
Grove Rd. Hit SG4,SG5 21 F1
Grove Rd. Luton LU1 63 D7
Grove Rd. Norwd HA6 174 D5
Grove Rd. Ric WD3 173 A8
Grove Rd. St Alb AL1 127 D2
Grove Rd. Stev SG1 50 D7
Grove Rd. Tri HP23 100 C5
Grove Rd W. Enf EN3 162 C2
Grove Rd. Ware SG12 93 F2
Grove Road Inf Sch. Tri 100 C5
Grove Road Jun Sch. Tri 100 C5
Grove The. Bro Pk AL9 145 A4
Grove The. Gt Ha CM22 77 F4
Grove The. L Had SG11 75 E7
Grove The. Lat HP5 150 D3
Grove The. Luton LU1 63 B5
Grove The. Pot B EN6 159 C7
Grove The. Radl WD7 156 A5
Grove The. Tri HP23 100 C5
Grove Way. Chor WD3 164 B4
Grove Wlk. Hert SG14 113 C8
Grovebury Gdns. Chis AL2 141 C4
Grovedale Cl. Ches EN7 147 F1
Groveland Way. Stot SG5 12 A5
Grovelands Ave. Hit SG4 22 C2
Grovelands. Chis AL2 141 B4
Grovelands. Heml H AL2 125 C5
Grover Cl. Heml H HP2 124 D4
Grover Rd. Watf WD1 167 D3
Grovewood Cl. Chor WD3 164 C4
Grubbs La. Hat AL9 145 C8
Grubs La. Hat AL9 131 A1
Guardian Ind Est. Luton 63 C8
Guernsey Cl. Dun LU4 44 A3
Guernsey House. Enf EN3 162 D1
Guessens Ct. Wel G C AL8 110 C6
Guessens Gr. Wel G C AL8 110 C6
Guessens Rd. Wel G C AL8 110 C6
Guessens Wlk. Wel G C AL8 110 C7
Guilden Morden Sch. Gu M 1 F5
Guildford Rd. St Alb AL1 128 B2
Guildford St. Luton LU1 63 E7
Guilfords The. Harl CM17 118 D5
Guinevere Gdns. Ches EN8 162 E8
Gulland Cl. Bus WD2 168 C4
Gullbrook. Heml H HP1 124 A3
Gullet Wood Rd. Watf WD2 154 A4
Gulphs The. Hert SG13 113 D5
Gun La. Kneb SG3 68 F4
Gun Meadow Ave. Kneb SG3 69 A4
Gun Rd. Kneb SG3 69 A4
Gun Road Gdns. Kneb SG3 68 F4
Gunnels Wood Ind Est. Stev 50 D3
Gunnels Wood Rd. Stev SG1 50 B5
Gurney Court Rd. St Alb AL1 127 F5
Gurney's La. Hol SG5 21 B7
Gwent Cl. Watf WD2 154 D5
Gwynfa Cl. Welw AL6 89 D7
Gwynne Cl. Tri HP23 100 A5
Gwynns Wlk. Hert SG13 113 E6
Gyfford Wlk. Ches EN7 162 B8
Gypsy Cl. Gt Am SG12 114 F4
Gypsy La. Abb L WD4 153 D5
Gypsy La. Gt Am SG12 114 F4
Gypsy La. Hat AL7 110 F1
Haberdashers' Aske's Sch The. Radl 169 B6
Hackforth Cl. Barn EN5 171 B4
Hackney Cl. Bor WD6 170 D4
Haddon Cl. Bor WD6 170 A6
Haddon Cl. Heml H HP3 125 A2
Haddon Cl. Stev SG2 69 C7
Haddon Ct. Harp AL5 86 B1
Haddon Rd. Chor WD3 164 C4
Haddon Rd. Luton LU2 63 F8
Hadham Rd. Bis St CM23 76 D8
Hadham Rd. L Had SG11 57 F1
Hadham Rd. Stand SG11 55 F1
Hadleigh Ct. Hod EN10 134 F1
Hadleigh Ct. Whea AL5 107 E6
Hadleigh. Letw SG6 23 B4
Hadley Bourne (St Martha's Convent Sch). Barn 171 F8
Hadley Cl. Bor WD6 169 F3
Hadley Ct. Luton LU3 45 D1 3
Hadley Gn. Barn EN5 171 F7
Hadley Gn W. Barn EN5 171 F7
Hadley Gr. Barn EN5 171 E7
Hadley Green Rd. Barn EN5 171 F7
Hadley Highstone. Barn EN5 171 F8
Hadley Rd. Had W EN2,EN4 160 D1
Hadley Ridge. Barn EN5 171 F6
Hadley Wood Jun Mix Inf Sch. Had W 159 C1
Hadlow Down Cl. Luton LU3 45 A5
Hadrain Cl. St Alb AL3 127 A1
Hadrian Way. Letw SG7 23 D7
Hadrians Wlk. Stev SG1 51 C8
Hadwell Cl. Stev SG2 51 A3
Hagdell Rd. Luton LU1 63 C5
Hagden La. Watf WD1 167 A4
Haggerston Rd. Bor WD6 156 E1
Hagsdell Rd. Hert SG13 113 D5
Haig Cl. St Alb AL1 128 B2
Haig House. St Alb AL1 128 B2
Hailey Ave. Hod EN11 115 A2
Hailey Hall Sch. Hod 114 F2
Hailey La. Hert H SG13 114 E2
Hailey La. Hod SG13 114 E2
Haileybury Coll. Hert H 114 D2
Haines Way. Watf WD2 154 A5
Haldens House. Wel G C 3 AL7 89 F1
Haldens. Wel G C AL7 89 F1
Hale La. St Le HP22 119 A3
Hale Rd. Hert SG13 113 D5
Hales Meadow. Harp AL5 86 A2
Hales Park Cl. Heml H HP2 125 C4
Hales Pk. Heml H HP2 125 C4
Haleswood Rd. Heml H HP2 125 B4
Half Acres. Bis St CM23 76 F8
Half Moon La. Cad LU1 63 C1
Half Moon Meadow. Heml H HP2 125 C8
Half Moon Mews. St Alb AL1 127 D3 5
Halfacre La. Gt Ho SG9 29 A1
Halfhide La. Ches EN8 148 D5
Halfhides. Wa Aby EN9 163 D6
Halfway Ave. Luton LU4 44 D1
Halifax Rd. Chor WD3 164 C2
Halifax Way. Wel G C AL7 111 E6
Hall Cl. Ric WD3 165 A1
Hall Cotts. Gt Ho SG9 29 A1
Hall Dr. Hare UB9 173 C2
Hall Gdns. Col H AL4 143 D8
Hall Gr. Wel G C AL7 111 B4
Hall Heath Cl. St Alb AL1 128 B5
Hall La. Gt Ch SG8 9 F2
Hall La. Gt Ho SG9 29 A1
Hall La. Kim SG4 87 C8
Hall La. Welw SG3 69 A2
Hall Mead. Letw SG6 22 D6
Hall Park Gate. Berk HP4 122 E3
Hall Park Hill. Berk HP4 122 E3
Hall Pk. Berk HP4 122 E3
Hall Place Cl. St Alb AL1 127 E4
Hall Place Gdns. St Alb AL1 127 E4
Hall Rd. Heml H HP2 125 B5
Hallam Cl. Watf WD1 167 C7
Hallam Gdns. Pnr HA5 175 E3
Halland Way. Norwd HA6 174 D4
Halleys Ridge. Hert SG14 113 A5
Halling Hill. Harl CM20 117 F2
Hallingbury Cl. L Hal CM22 77 B1
Hallingbury Rd. Bis St CM23 77 B4
Hallingbury Rd. Gt Ha CM22 77 B4
Hallingbury Rd. L Hal CM21 98 A4
Hallmores. Hod EN10 135 A4
Hallowell Rd. Norwd HA6 174 E3
Hallowes Cres. Sth Ox WD1 175 A7
Halls Cl. Welw AL6 89 C4
Hallside Rd. Enf EN1 161 F1
Hallwicks Rd. Luton LU2 46 B3
Hallworth Dr. Stot SG5 11 E6
Hallworth House. Stot SG5 11 E6
Halsey Dr. Hit SG4 35 B7
Halsey Pk. Lon C AL2 142 F4
Halsey Pl. Watf WD2 154 B1
Halsey Rd. Watf WD1 167 B6
Halstead Hill. Gofs O EN7 147 E1
Haltere Cl. Bor WD6 170 D4
Haltside. Hat AL10 129 E4
Halwick Cl. Heml H HP1 124 B1
Halyard Cl. Luton LU3 45 B6
Halyard High Sch. Dun 44 A3
Hamberlins La. Nthch HP4 121 C7
Hamble Ct. Watf WD1 167 A5
Hambridge Way. Pirt SG5 20 D4
Hambro Cl. Nwml E LU2 85 F7
Hamburgh Ct. Ches EN8 148 D3
Hamels Dr. Hert SG13 114 B7
Hamer Cl. Bov HP3 137 A3
Hamilton Ave. Hod EN11 135 A8
Hamilton Cl. Bri Wd AL2 155 A8
Hamilton Cl. Ridge EN6 158 A6
Hamilton Ct. Hat AL10 130 B3 3
Hamilton Mead. Bov HP3 137 A4
Hamilton Rd. Abb L WD4 153 C6
Hamilton Rd. Berk HP4 122 B4
Hamilton Rd. St Alb AL1 128 A4
Hamilton Rd. Sth Ox WD1 175 B7
Hamilton St. Watf WD1 167 C4
Hamlet The. Pot En HP4 123 A7
Hammarskjold Rd. Harl CM20 117 D2
Hammer La. Heml H HP2 124 F4
Hammers Gate. Chis AL2 141 A5
Hammond Cl. Ham St EN7 147 F5
Hammond Cl. Stev SG1 50 D6
Hammond Ct. Cad LU1 63 C1
Hammond Jun Mix Inf Sch The. Heml H 124 F6
Hammonds La. Sand AL4 109 B3
Hammondstreet Rd. Ham St EN7 147 D5
Hammondswick. Harp AL5 106 F4
Hamonte. Letw SG6 23 C4
Hampden Cl. Letw SG6 23 B8
Hampden Cres. Ches EN7 162 B8
Hampden Hill Cl. Ware SG12 93 F2
Hampden Hill. Ware SG12 93 F2
Hampden. Kim SG4 66 C1
Hampden Pl. Lon C AL2 141 E2
Hampden Rd. Har HA3 176 C1
Hampden Rd. Hit SG4 22 C1
Hampden Way. Watf WD1 153 E3
Hampermill La. Watf WD1 167 A1
Hampton Cl. Stev SG2 69 C7
Hampton Gdns. Saw CM21 118 C7
Hampton Rd. Luton LU4 63 B8
Hamstel Rd. Harl CM20 117 C1
Hanaper Dr. Bar SG8 8 F2
Hanbury Cl. Ches EN8 148 E2
Hanbury Cl. Ware SG12 93 D1
Hanbury Cotts. Ess AL9 131 E6
Hanbury Dr. Thun SG12 93 C6
Hanbury Mews. Thun SG12 93 C5
Hancock Ct. Bor WD6 170 C8
Hancock Dr. Luton LU2 45 E5
Hancroft Rd. Heml H HP3 124 F1
Hand La. Saw CM21 97 C1
Handa Cl. Heml H HP3 139 B8
Handcross Rd. Luton LU2 46 D2
Handside Cl. Wel G C AL8 110 C6
Handside Gn. Wel G C AL8 110 C7
Handside La. Wel G C AL8 110 C6
Handsworth Cl. Sth Ox WD1 175 A7
Hangar Ruding. Sth Ox WD1 175 F7
Hanger Cl. Heml H HP1 124 B2
Hanger's Wood Sch. Sth Ox 175 B7
Hangmans La. Welw AL6 89 F8
Hanover Cl. Stev SG2 50 F1
Hanover Ct. Cro Gr WD3 166 A4
Hanover Ct. Luton LU4 44 D5
Hanover Gdns. Abb L WD5 139 F1
Hanover Gn. Heml H HP1 124 A1
Hanover Wlk. Hat AL10 129 F2
Hanscombe End Rd. Shil SG5 19 D7
Hanselin Cl. Stan HA7 176 F5
Hanswick Cl. Luton LU2 46 B2
Hanworth Cl. Luton LU2 45 D7
Hanyards End. Cuf EN6 146 E3
Hanyards La. Cuf EN6 146 D3
Happy Valley Ind Pk. Kin L 139 B2
Harbell Cl. Hert SG13 114 B6
Harborne Cl. Sth Ox WD1 175 C5
Harbury Dell. Luton LU3 45 B7
Harcourt Rd. Bus WD2 168 C4
Harcourt Rd. Tri HP23 100 C4
Harcourt St. Luton LU1 63 E5
Harding Cl. Luton LU3 44 E7
Harding Cl. Red AL3 106 B5
Harding Cl. Watf WD2 154 C6
Harding Par. Harp AL5 86 B1
Hardings. Wel G C AL7 111 C7
Hardingstone Ct. Ches EN8 162 F5
Hardwick Cl. Stev SG2 69 C7
Hardwick Gn. Luton LU3 45 B7
Hardwick Pl. Lon C AL2 142 D4
Hardy Cl. Barn EN5 171 E4
Hardy Cl. Hit SG4 35 C7
Hardy Dr. Royst SG8 7 D8
Hardy Rd. Heml H HP2 124 F4
Hare Cres. Watf WD2 154 A7
Hare La. Hat AL10 130 B3
Hare Street Rd. Bun SG9 41 C8
Harebell. Wel G C AL7 110 E3
Harebreaks The. Watf WD2 154 A2
Harefield Ct. Luton LU1 62 F8
Harefield. Harl CM20 118 A1
Harefield Hospl. Hare 173 C3
Harefield Inf Sch. Hare 173 C2
Harefield Jun Sch. Hare 173 C2
Harefield Pl. St Alb AL4 128 D6
Harefield Rd. Luton LU1 62 F8
Harefield Rd. Ric WD3 173 D7
Harefield. Stev SG2 51 C3
Harepark Cl. Heml H HP1 123 F4
Harewood Rd. Sth Ox WD1 175 B7
Harewood. Ric WD3 165 C4
Harford Dr. Watf WD1 166 E8
Harforde Ct. Hert 114 A6
Hargrave Cl. Sta M CM24 59 E8
Hargreaves Ave. Ches EN7 162 B8
Hargreaves Cl. Ches EN7 162 B8
Hargreaves Rd. Royst SG8 7 D5
Harkett Cl. Har HA3 176 F1
Harkness. Ches EN8 148 B2
Harkness Ct. Hit SG4 22 B1
Harkness Way. Hit SG4 22 C2
Harlequin The. Watf WD1 167 C5
Harlesden Rd. St Alb AL1 128 A3
Harlestone Cl. Luton LU3 31 A1
Harley Ct. St Alb AL4 128 D7
Harlings The. Hert H SG13 114 C2
Harlow Coll. Harl 117 E1
Harlow Ct. Heml H HP2 125 A7
Harlow Mill Sta. Harl 118 C5
Harlow Rd. Roy CM19 116 C1
Harlow Rd. Saw CM21 118 C8
Harlow Sport Ctr. Harl 117 D2
Harlow The Spinney Cty Jun & Inf Sch. Harl 118 A1
Harlow Town Sta. Harl 117 D3
Harlowbury Cty Prim Sch. Harl 118 D4
Harlton Ct. Wa Aby EN9 163 F5
Harmer Dell. Welw AL6 89 F4
Harmer Green La. Welw AL6 90 B5
Harmony Cl. Hat AL10 130 A7
Harmsworth Way. Barn N20 171 F1
Harness Way. St Alb AL4 128 D6
Harold Cres. Wa Aby EN9 163 C7
Harpenden Central Sta. Harp 86 B1
Harpenden Hospl. Harp 86 A4
Harpenden La. Red AL3 106 B6
Harpenden Memorial Hospl. Harp 86 B2
Harpenden Rd. Whea AL4 108 B8
Harpenden Rise. Harp AL5 85 F3
Harper Ct. Stev SG1 50 F5
Harper La. Lon C WD7,AL2 156 B8
Harperbury Hospl. Lon C 156 C8
Harps Hill. Mark AL3 83 E5
Harpsfield Broadway. Hat AL10 129 F6
Harptree Way. St Alb AL1 128 A5
Harriet Way. Bus WD2 168 D2
Harrington Ct. Bis St CM23 77 A7
Harrington Ct. Hert H SG13 114 C3
Harris La. Gt Of SG5 33 D2
Harris La. Shen WD7 157 A6
Harris Rd. Watf WD2 154 A4
Harris's La. Ware SG12 93 C1
Harrison Cl. Hit SG4 34 F7
Harrison Cl. Norwd HA6 174 C4
Harrison Wlk. Ches EN8 148 D1
Harrisons. Birhr CM23 59 D2
Harrogate Rd. Sth Ox WD1 175 C7 2
Harrow Coll of F Ed. Pnr 176 A3
Harrow Ct. Stev SG1 50 E5
Harrow View. Har HA2 176 C1
Harrow Way. Sth Ox WD1 175 E6
Harrow Weald Pk. Stan HA3 176 D4
Harrow Weald Sixth Form Coll. Stan 176 E4
Harrow Yd. Tri HP23 100 A3
Harrowden Ct. Luton LU2 64 C8
Harrowden Rd. Luton LU2 64 C8
Harrowdene. Stev SG2 51 C4
Harry Scott Ct. Luton LU4 44 C6
Hart Hill Dr. Luton LU2 63 F8
Hart Hill Jun & Inf Sch. Luton 63 F8
Hart Hill La. Luton LU2 63 F8
Hart La. Luton LU2 46 A1
Hart Lodge. Barn EN5 171 E6
Hart Rd. Harl CM17 118 C6
Hart Rd. St Alb AL1 127 D2
Hart Wlk. Luton LU2 46 A1
Hartfield Ave. Bor WD6 170 A4
Hartfield Cl. Bor WD6 170 A4
Hartfield Ct. Ware SG12 93 D2 6
Hartforde Rd. Bor WD6 170 B8
Harthall La. Abb L WD4,WD5 139 D4
Hartham La. Hert SG14 113 D6
Hartland Rd. Ches EN8 148 D1
Hartley Rd. Luton LU2 63 F8
Hartmoor Mews. Enf EN3 162 D2
Harts Cl. Bus WD2 168 A8
Hartsbourne Ave. Bus WD2 176 D8
Hartsbourne Cl. Bus WD2 176 D8
Hartsbourne Country Club. Bus 176 C8
Hartsbourne Jun Mix Inf Sch. Bus 176 D8
Hartsbourne Rd. Bus WD2 176 D8
Hartsbourne Way. Heml H HP2 125 C2
Hartsfield Jun Mix Inf Sch. Bal 12 F1
Hartsfield Rd. Luton LU2 46 B2
Hartspring La. Bus WD2 168 A8
Hartswood Gn. Bus WD2 176 D8
Hartwell Gdns. Harp AL5 85 E1
Hartwood. Luton LU2 63 F8
Harvest Cl. Dun LU4 44 A3
Harvest Ct. St Alb AL4 128 D7
Harvest Ct. Welw AL6 89 E7
Harvest End. Watf WD2 154 D3
Harvest Mead. Hat AL10 130 B7
Harvest Rd. Bus WD2 168 B5
Harvey Rd. Cro Gr WD3 166 A3
Harvey Rd. Lon C AL2 142 C5
Harvey Rd. Stev SG2 51 B6
Harvey Road Jun Mid Inf Sch. Cro Gr 166 A3
Harvey's Hill. Luton LU2 45 F5
Harveyfields. Wa Aby EN9 163 C5
Harveys Cotts. L Had SG11 75 F8
Harwood Cl. Tewin AL6 90 E2
Harwood Cl. Wel G C AL8 89 E2
Harwood Hill Jun Mix Inf Sch. Wel G C 89 E2
Harwood Hill. Wel G C AL8 89 E1
Harwoods Rd. Watf WD1 167 A5
Hasedines Rd. Heml H HP1 124 A4
Haseldine Meadows. Hat AL10 129 F4
Haseldine Rd. Lon C AL2 142 D5
Haselfoot. Letw SG6 22 E6
Hasketon Dr. Luton LU4 44 B6
Haslemere. Bis St CM23 77 A4
Haslemere Ind Est. Wel G C 110 F7
Haslewood Ave. Hod EN11 135 A6
Haslewood Jun Sch. Hod 135 A6
Haslingden Cl. Harp AL5 85 D3
Hassobury Waterside Sch. Far 58 F7
Haste Hill Golf Course. Norwd 174 E1
Hastings Cl. Stev SG1 50 A8
Hastings St. Luton LU1 63 D6
Hastings Way. Cro Gr WD3 166 C5
Hastings Way. Watf WD2 167 E5
Hastoe La. Tri HP23 100 A2
Hatch End High Sch. Har 176 B2
Hatch End Sta. Pnr 176 A3
Hatch Gn. L Hal CM22 98 B8
Hatch La. Wes SG4 24 A3
Hatching Green Cl. Harp AL5 107 A6
Hatfield Aerodrome. Hat 129 D6
Hatfield Ave. Hat AL10 129 E8
Hatfield Bsns Ctr. Hat 129 E8
Hatfield Cres. Heml H HP2 124 F7
Hatfield Rd. Coln H AL4 128 C3
Hatfield Rd. Ess SG14 111 E1
Hatfield Rd. Hertng SG14 112 B4
Hatfield Rd. Pot B EN6 159 C8
Hatfield Rd. St Alb AL1,AL4 128 C3
Hatfield Rd. Watf WD2 167 B8
Hatfield Sch. Wel Gr 130 B1
Hatfield Sta. Hat 130 C6
Hatfield Tunnel. Hat AL10 129 F6
Hathaway Cl. Dun LU4 44 B2
Hathaway Ct. Coln H AL4 128 E3
Hatherleigh Gdns. Pot B EN6 159 D7
Hatters La. Watf WD1 166 D3
Hatters Way. Luton LU1,LU4 63 B8
Hatton Rd. Ches EN8 148 D2
Havelock Rd. Kin L WD4 138 F3
Havelock Rd. Luton LU2 45 E1
Havelock Rise. Luton LU2 45 E1
Haven Cl. Hat AL10 129 F6
Havenfield. Chipf WD4 152 B8
Havercroft Cl. St Alb AL3 127 C1
Haverdale. Luton LU4 44 C4
Havers Inf Sch The. Bis St 76 E5
Havers La. Bis St CM23 76 F5
Havers Par. Bis St CM23 76 F5
Haward Rd. Hod EN11 135 C8
Hawbush Cl. Welw AL6 89 B4
Hawbush Rise. Welw AL6 89 B5
Hawes Cl. Norwd HA6 174 F3
Hawes La. Wa Aby EN9 163 C1
Haweswater Dr. Watf WD2 154 C6
Hawfield Gdns. Pk St AL2 141 D5
Hawkesworth Cl. Norwd HA6 174 E3
Hawkfield. Letw SG6 22 E8
Hawkfields. Luton LU2 46 E6
Hawkins Cl. Bor WD6 170 C7
Hawkins Hall La. Dat SG3 69 E2
Hawkshead Ct. Ches EN8 162 F5
Hawkshead La. Bro Pk AL9 144 D3
Hawkshead Rd. Pot B EN6 145 B2
Hawkshill Dr. Heml H HP3 137 F8
Hawkshill. St Alb AL1 128 A2
Hawksmead Cl. Enf EN3 162 D3
Hawksmoor. Shen WD7 157 A6
Hawkwell Dr. Tri HP23 100 C4
Hawridge & Cholesbury C of E Combined Sch. Chol 120 E2
Hawridge La. Choi HP5 120 F1
Hawridge Vale. Chol HP5 120 F1
Hawsley Rd. Harp AL5 107 A4
Hawthorn Ave. Luton LU2 46 B4
Hawthorn Cl. Abb L WD5 154 A7
Hawthorn Cl. Harp AL5 107 D7
Hawthorn Cl. Hert SG14 113 A7
Hawthorn Cl. Hit SG5 34 E6
Hawthorn Cl. Royst SG8 7 F7
Hawthorn Cl. Watf WD1 153 F1
Hawthorn Cres. Cad LU1 62 E3
Hawthorn Gr. Enf EN2 161 D1
Hawthorn Hill. Letw SG6 22 F7
Hawthorn La. Heml H HP1 123 F4
Hawthorn Rd. Hod EN11 135 B8
Hawthorn Rise. Bis St CM23 76 F3
Hawthorn Way. Chis AL2 141 A7
Hawthorn Way. Royst SG8 7 F7
Hawthorne Ave. Ches EN7 162 B8
Hawthorne Cl. Ches EN7 162 B8
Hawthorne Ct. Pnr HA6 175 A1
Hawthorne Rd. Radl WD7 156 A5
Hawthornes. Hat AL10 129 F3
Hawthorns The. Berk HP4 122 A5
Hawthorns The. Heml H HP3 137 F7
Hawthorns The. Map Cr WD3 172 D5
Hawthorns The. Stev SG1 51 A4
Hawthorns The. Ware SG12 93 C3
Hawthorns. Wel G C AL8 110 D8
Hawtrees. Radl WD7 155 F4
Hay Cl. Bor WD6 170 C7
Hay La. Harp AL5 86 A1
Haybourn Mead. Heml H HP1 124 B2
Haycroft. Bis St CM23 77 C7
Haycroft Rd. Stev SG1 50 E7
Haydock Rd. Royst SG8 7 F6
Haydon Hill House. Bus WD2 167 F2
Haydon Rd. Watf WD1 167 E3
Hayes Cl. Luton LU2 46 C5
Hayes Wlk. Ches EN10 148 F6
Hayfield Cl. Bus WD2 168 B5
Hayfield. Stev SG2 51 D7
Haygarth. Kneb SG3 69 A4
Hayhurst Rd. Dun LU4 44 B1
Hayley Bell Gdns. Bis St CM23 76 F3
Hayley Comm. Stev SG2 51 C3
Hayling Dr. Luton LU2 46 D3
Hayling Rd. Sth Ox WD1 175 B8
Haymeads La. Bis St CM23 77 C6
Haymeads. Wel G C AL8 89 E1
Haymoor. Letw SG6 22 F7
Haynes Cl. Wel G C AL7 111 A5
Haynes Mead. Berk HP4 122 A6
Haysman Cl. Letw SG6 23 B7
Hayton Cl. Luton LU3 31 B2
Haywood Cl. Pnr HA5 175 D1
Haywood Ct. Wa Aby EN9 163 F5
Haywood La. Ther SG8 16 A6
Haywood Pk. Chor WD3 164 F4
Haywoods Dr. Heml H HP3 137 F8
Haywoods La. Royst SG8 7 E7
Hazel Cl. Ham St EN7 147 E5
Hazel Cl. Welw AL6 89 E3
Hazel Ct. Hit SG4 35 A7
Hazel Gdns. Sheer CM21 97 F1
Hazel Gr. Hat AL10 129 F2
Hazel Gr. Stot SG5 11 E5
Hazel Gr. Watf WD2 154 B4
Hazel Gr. Wel G C AL7 111 C7
Hazel Mead. Barn EN5 171 B4
Hazel Rd. Berk HP4 122 D3
Hazel Rd. Chis AL2 141 B3
Hazel Tree Rd. Watf WD2 154 B3
Hazelbury Ave. Abb L WD5 153 C7
Hazelbury Cres. Luton LU1 63 C8
Hazelcroft. Pnr HA5 176 B4
Hazeldell Link. Heml H HP1 123 E2
Hazeldell Rd. Heml H HP1 123 F2
Hazeldell. Wat St SG14 70 D3
Hazeldene. Ches EN8 162 E7
Hazelend Rd. Bis St CM23 59 B4
Hazelgrove Prim Sch. Hat 129 F2
Hazelmere Rd. St Alb AL4 128 C6
Hazelmere Rd. Stev SG2 69 A8
Hazels The. Tewin AL6 90 E2
Hazelwood Cl. Hit SG5 34 F8
Hazelwood Cl. Luton LU2 46 B4
Hazelwood Dr. Pnr HA5 175 B1
Hazelwood Dr. St Alb AL4 128 C4
Hazelwood Inf Sch. Abb L 153 E8
Hazelwood La. Abb L WD5 153 D7
Hazelwood Rd. Cro Gr WD3 166 C3
Hazely. Tri HP23 100 C4
Heacham Cl. Dun LU4 44 B4
Headingley Cl. Ham St EN7 147 F5
Headingley Cl. Shen WD7 156 E7
Headingley Cl. Stev SG1 50 E8
Headstone La. Har HA2,HA3 176 B2
Headstone Lane Sta. Har 176 B2
Healey Rd. Watf WD1 166 F3
Health Farm La. St Alb AL3 127 E5
Healy Ct. Barn EN5 171 D3
Heath Ave. Royst SG8 7 C6
Heath Ave. St Alb AL3 127 D5
Heath Brow. Heml H HP1 124 C1
Heath Cl. Harp AL5 107 C7
Heath Cl. Heml H HP1 124 C2
Heath Cl. Luton LU1 63 B6
Heath Cl. Pot B EN6 145 B1
Heath Dr. Pot B EN6 145 A1
Heath Dr. Ware SG12 93 D3
Heath Farm Ct. Sar WD1 153 D2
Heath Hall. Bal 23 F7
Heath Hill. Cod SG4 67 D1
Heath La. Cod SG4 67 E1
Heath La. Heml H HP1 124 C2
Heath La. Hert SG13 114 C2
Heath Lodge. Bus WD2 168 D1
Heath Mount Sch. Wat St 71 B2
Heath Rd. Bre Gr SG4 47 D1
Heath Rd. Pot B EN6 145 B1
Heath Rd. St Alb AL1 127 E5
Heath Rd. Watf WD1 167 E2
Heath Rd. Welw AL6 68 F1
Heath Row. Bis St CM23 59 B1
Heath The. Bre Gr SG4 47 D2
Heath The. Radl WD7 156 A6
Heathbourne Rd. Stan WD2,HA7 168 F1

King Edward's Rd. Ware SG12 93 E2
King George Ave. Bus WD2 168 B3
King George Cl. Stev SG1 50 E6
King George Rd. Wa Aby EN9 163 C5
King George Rd. Ware SG12 93 E2
King George's Way. Whit SG4 66 E6
King Georges Ave. Watf WD1 166 E5
King Georges Cl. Hit SG5 21 D1
King Harold Sch. Wa Aby 163 E6
King Harry La. St Alb AL3 127 B1
King Harry St. Heml H HP2 124 D2
King Henry's Mews. Enf EN3 163 A2
King James Ave. Cuf EN6 146 E2
King James Way. Royst SG8 7 D6
King St. Bis St CM23 76 F7
King St. Luton LU1 63 E7
King St. Mark AL3 83 E5
King St. Tri HP23 100 A3
King St. Watf WD1 167 C5
King Street Mews. Bis St CM23 76 F7 1
King's Cotts. Bis St CM23 77 A6
King's La. Chipf WD4 152 B8
King's Mews. Heml H HP2 124 D4 3
King's Rd. Ches EN8 162 E5
King's Rd. Hert SG13 114 A7
King's Rd. Hit SG5 34 F8
King's Rd. Lon C AL2 142 C5
King's Rd. St Alb AL3 127 C3
King's Walden Rd. Gt Of SG5 33 D2
King's Wlk. Royst SG8 7 D5
Kingfisher Cl. Gt Am SG12 115 C3
Kingfisher Cl. Har HA3 176 F3
Kingfisher Cl. Norwd HA6 174 B2
Kingfisher Cl. Whea AL4 87 D1
Kingfisher Lure. Kin L WD4 139 B2
Kingfisher Lure. Ric WD3 165 B5
Kingfisher Rise. Stev SG2 51 D2
Kingfisher Way. Bis St CM23 77 A7
Kingham Rd. Wars SG12 94 E5
Kinghamway. Luton LU2 45 E1
Kings Ave. Heml H HP3 138 F7
Kings Ave. Watf WD1 167 A5
Kings Cl. Chipf WD4 152 B8
Kings Cl. Norwd HA6 174 F4
Kings Cl. Watf WD1 167 C5
Kings Ct. Berk HP4 122 C5
Kings Ct. Bis St CM23 77 A8
Kings Farm Rd. Chor WD3 164 D3
Kings Field Cotts. Abb L WD5 153 F8
Kings Hedges. Hit SG5 34 C8
Kings Langley Jun Sch. Kin L 138 F3
Kings Langley Sch. Kin L 138 E3
Kings Langley Sta. Kin L 139 B1
Kings Meadow. Kin L WD4 139 A3
Kings Oak. Cro Gr WD3 166 A5
Kings Park Ind Est. Kin L 139 B2
Kings Rd. Barn EN5 171 C6
Kings Rd. Berk HP4 122 B3
Kings Walden Rise. Stev SG2 51 C8
Kingsbridge Rd. Bis St CM23 77 A8
Kingsbury Ave. St Alb AL3 127 C4
Kingsbury Water Mill Mus. St Alb 127 B4
Kingscroft. Wel G C AL7 111 B7
Kingsdale House. Welw AL6 89 B3
Kingsdale Rd. Berk HP4 122 A3
Kingsdown Ave. Luton LU2 45 D5
Kingsdown. Hit SG4 35 B6
Kingsfield Ct. Watf WD1 167 D2
Kingsfield Dr. Enf EN3 162 D4
Kingsfield. Hod EN11 135 A8
Kingsfield Rd. Dan En SG12 71 E8
Kingsfield Rd. Watf WD1 167 D3
Kingsfield Way. Enf EN3 162 D4
Kingsgate. St Alb AL3 127 B1
Kingshill Ave. St Alb AL4 128 B6
Kingshill Ct. Barn EN5 171 E5 6
Kingshill Inf Sch. Ware 93 D3
Kingshill Way. Berk HP4 122 B2
Kingshott Sch. Hit 35 B5
Kingsland Ct. Luton LU1 63 F6
Kingsland Rd. Heml H HP1 124 A1
Kingsland Rd. Luton LU1 63 F6
Kingsland Way. Ashw SG7 4 D4
Kingsley Ave. Bor WD6 169 F7
Kingsley Ave. Ches EN8 148 C2
Kingsley Ct. Wel G C AL7 110 F2
Kingsley Rd. Luton LU3 45 A5
Kingsley Wlk. Tri HP23 100 A4
Kingsmead. Ches EN8 148 D3
Kingsmead. Cuf EN6 146 E3
Kingsmead Nursery Sch. Hert 114 A7
Kingsmead Rd. Bis St CM23 77 A8
Kingsmead. Saw CM21 97 E1
Kingsmead. St Alb AL4 128 D6
Kingsmill Ct. Hat AL10 130 B3 1
Kingston Pl. Har HA3 176 F3
Kingston Rd. Luton LU2 45 F1
Kingston Vale. Royst SG8 7 E5
Kingsway. Cuf EN6 146 E1
Kingsway Gdns. Stot SG5 11 E7
Kingsway Ind Est. Luton 63 A8
Kingsway Inf Sch. Watf 154 A5
Kingsway Jun Sch. Watf 154 A5
Kingsway. Luton LU1,LU4 45 A1
Kingsway North Orbital Rd. Watf WD2 154 B5
Kingsway. Royst SG8 7 C8
Kingsway. Stot SG5 11 F7
Kingsway. Ware SG12 93 D3
Kingswell Ride. Cuf EN6 146 E1
Kingswood Ave. Hit SG4 35 D8
Kingswood Rd. Watf WD2 154 B5
Kingwell Rd. Had W EN4 159 D1
Kinross Cres. Luton LU3 44 D8
Kinsbourne Cl. Harp AL5 85 C4
Kinsbourne Cres. Harp AL5 85 D4
Kinsbourne Green La. Harp AL5 85 B3
Kipling Cl. Hit SG4 35 C7
Kipling Gr. Heml H HP2 105 B1
Kipling Pl. Stan HA7 176 F4
Kipling Rd. Royst SG8 2 E1
Kipling The. Luton LU3 45 B6
Kipling Way. Harp AL5 86 B1
Kirby Cl. Norwd HA6 174 F4
Kirby Dr. Luton LU3 45 A8
Kirkcaldy Gn. Sth Ox WD1 175 C7 1
Kirkdale Ct. Luton LU1 63 E6 3
Kirkdale Rd. Harp AL5 86 A2
Kirklands. Wel G C AL8 89 D2
Kirkwick Ave. Harp AL5 86 A1
Kit's La. Wal SG7 25 C8
Kitchener Cl. St Alb AL1 128 B2
Kitching La. St Ipp SG4 49 F5
Kitching La. Stev SG1 50 A5
Kite Field. Nthch HP4 121 E7
Kite Way. Letw SG6 22 E8
Kitsbury Rd. Berk HP4 122 B4
Kitsbury Terr. Berk HP4 122 B4
Kitson Way. Harl CM20 117 C1
Kitswell Rd. Radl WD7 156 A6
Kitswell Way. Radl WD7 155 F6
Kitt's End Rd. Pot B EN5 158 E2
Knap Cl. Letw SG6 23 D8
Knebworth Ct. Bis St CM23 76 D6
Knebworth Ctry Pk. Kneb 68 C7
Knebworth Jun & Mix Inf Sch. Kneb 69 A5
Knebworth Path. Bor WD6 170 D5
Knebworth Sta. Kneb 68 F5
Kneesworth House Hospl. Knee 2 C5
Kneesworth Rd. Meld SG8 2 F8
Kneesworth St. Royst SG8 7 C6
Knella Gn. Wel G C AL7 111 A6
Knella Road Workshops. Wel G C 111 A6
Knight St. Saw CM21 97 E2
Knight's Ct. Saw CM21 97 E2
Knights Cl. Bis St CM23 76 C8
Knights Cl. Bun SG9 40 E6
Knights Ct. Bus WD2 168 D1
Knights Ct. Stand SG11 55 F1
Knights Field. Luton LU2 45 D1
Knights Orch. Heml H HP1 123 F5
Knights Orch. St Alb AL3 127 C3
Knights Templar Sch The. Bal 23 E8
Knights Templars Gn. Stev SG2 51 C8
Knightsbridge Way. Heml H HP2 124 E4
Knightsfield. Wel G C AL8 89 D2
Knoll Cres. Norwd HA6 174 F2
Knoll Gn. Heml H HP2 124 E5
Knoll Rise. Luton LU2 45 E4
Knoll The. Hert SG13 114 B7
Knolles Cres. Wel G AL9 144 B7
Knolls Cl. Wing HP22 60 B3
Knowl Piece. Hit SG4 22 A3
Knowl Pk. Elst WD6 169 E4
Knowl Way. Bor WD6 169 F4
Knowle Dr. Harp AL5 107 D7
Knowle. Stev SG1 36 B1
Knowle The. Hod EN11 135 A5
Knutsford Ave. Watf WD2 154 D1
Knutsford Jun Mix Inf Sch. Watf 154 D1
Koh-I-Noor Ave. Bus WD2 168 A3
Kristiansand Way. Letw SG6 23 C8
Kymswell Rd. Stev SG2 51 C3
Kynance Cl. Luton LU2 46 A2
Kynaston Cl. Har HA3 176 D3
Kynaston Wood. Har HA3 176 D3
Kyrkeby. Letw SG6 23 C4
Kytes Dr. Watf WD2 154 D6

Laburnum Cl. Ches EN8 162 D8
Laburnum Cl. Luton LU3 45 C7
Laburnum Gr. Chis AL2 141 B6
Laburnum Gr. Luton LU3 45 B7
Laburnum Rd. Hod EN11 135 B8
Lachbury Cl. Luton LU1 63 A6
Lackmore Rd. Enf EN1 162 C4
Lacre Way. Letw SG6 23 C7
Ladbrooke Cl. Pot B EN6 159 A7
Ladbrooke Dr. Pot B EN6 159 A7
Ladbrooks Prim Sch. Pot B 159 B7
Ladies Gr. St Alb AL3 127 C5
Lady Gr. Wel G C AL7 110 E2
Lady Spencer's Gr. St Alb AL1 127 C2
Lady Zia Wernher Sch The. Luton 46 B3
Lady's Cl. Watf WD1 167 C5
Ladyhill. Luton LU4 44 B6
Ladymeadow. Kin L HP3 138 D4
Ladyshot. Harl CM20 118 A1
Ladysmith Rd. Har HA3 176 E1
Ladysmith Rd. Pit LU7 80 E5
Ladysmith Rd. St Alb AL3 127 D4
Ladywalk. Map Cr WD3 172 E6
Ladywell Prospect. Sheer CM21 98 A1
Ladywood Cl. Ric WD3 165 C6
Ladywood Rd. Hert SG14 112 F6
Laidon Sq. Heml H HP2 124 D7
Lake Dr. Bus WD2 176 D8
Lake Rd. Lo Naz EN9 135 E2
Lake The. Bus WD2 168 D1
Lake View. Pot B EN6 159 C6
Lake Villas. Fur P SG9 43 B4
Lakeland Cl. Stan HA3 176 D4
Lakeside. Bor WD6 170 A4
Lakeside Pl. Lon C AL2 142 D4
Lakeside Rd. Ches EN8 148 C3
Lakeside Sch. Wel G C 110 B4
Lakeside. Tri HP23 100 A5
Lalleford Rd. Luton LU2 46 D1
Lamb Cl. Hat AL10 130 B4
Lamb Cl. Watf WD2 154 C5
Lamb Ct. Whea AL4 108 E7
Lamb La. Red AL3 106 B5
Lamb Meadow. Arl SG15 11 A3
Lambert Ct. Watf WD2 167 D5
Lambourn Chase. Radl WD7 155 F3
Lambourn Gdns. Harp AL5 85 F3
Lambs Cl. Cuf EN6 146 F2
Lambs Cl. Dun LU5 44 A1
Lambs Gdns. Widf SG12 95 D4
Lambton Ave. Ches EN8 162 D6
Lamer La. Whea AL4 87 D3
Lamers Rd. Luton LU2 46 B2
Lammas Mead. Hit SG5 21 E2
Lammas Path. Stev SG2 51 B4
Lammas Rd. Ched LU7 80 A7
Lammas Rd. Wat St SG14 70 D4
Lammas Rd. Watf WD1 167 C4
Lammas Way. Letw SG6 22 F8
Lammasmead. Hod EN10 148 F8
Lamorna Cl. Luton LU3 44 F6
Lamorna Cl. Radl WD7 156 B5
Lampits. Hod EN11 135 B6
Lamsey Rd. Heml H HP3 124 D1
Lancaster Ave. Had W EN4 159 D1
Lancaster Ave. Hit SG5 34 E8
Lancaster Ave. Luton LU2 45 C8
Lancaster Cl. Stev SG1 36 E2
Lancaster Dr. Bov HP3 136 F4
Lancaster Rd. Hit SG5 34 E8
Lancaster Rd. St Alb AL1 127 F5
Lancaster Way. Abb L WD5 153 F8
Lancaster Way. Bis St CM23 76 C8
Lancaster Way. Wel G C AL6 89 C3
Lancing Rd. Luton LU2 46 D3
Lancing Way. Cro Gr WD3 166 B4
Landau Way. Ches EN10 148 F5
Landford Cl. Ric WD3 173 E8
Landmead Rd. Ches EN8 148 E2
Lands' End. Elst WD6 169 D3
Lane End. Berk HP4 121 F4
Lane End. Hat AL10 129 F2
Lane Gdns. Bus WD2 168 E2
Lanefield Wlk. Wel G C AL8 110 C6
Lanercost Cl. Welw AL6 90 A7
Langbridge Cl. Hit SG4 35 A4
Langdale Ave. Harp AL5 86 D2
Langdale Ct. Heml H HP2 124 E6 2
Langdale Gdns. Enf EN3 162 D4
Langdon St. Tri HP23 100 A3
Langfield Cl. Lo Naz EN9 135 E1
Langford Dr. Luton LU2 46 A3
Langham Cl. Luton LU2 45 D7
Langham Cl. St Alb AL4 128 D8
Langholme. Bus WD2 168 C1
Langland Ct. Norwd HA6 174 E3
Langland Dr. Pnr HA5 175 E3
Langley Ave. Heml H HP3 138 F8
Langley Cres. Kin L WD4 139 A1
Langley Cres. St Alb AL3 127 C5
Langley Gr. Sand AL4 108 C2
Langley Hill Cl. Kin L WD4 139 A2
Langley Hill. Kin L WD4 138 F2
Langley La. Abb L WD5 153 F7
Langley La. Lan SG4 49 E2
Langley Lodge La. Kin L WD4 153 A8
Langley Rd. Abb L WD5 153 F8
Langley Rd. Chipf WD4 138 B1
Langley Rd. Watf WD1 167 A8
Langley Row. Barn EN5 171 F8
Langley St. Luton LU1 63 E6
Langley Warf. Abb L 139 A4
Langley Way. Watf WD1 166 F8
Langleybury La. Abb L WD4 153 B4
Langleybury Sch. Abb L 153 B5
Langmead Dr. Bus WD2 168 D1
Langthorne Ave. Stev SG1 50 E6
Langton Gr. Norwd HA6 174 C5
Langton House. Hod EN11 134 F6
Langton Rd. Har HA3 176 C3
Langton Rd. Hod EN11 134 F6
Langwood Gdns. Watf WD1 167 A8
Lankester Rd. Royst SG8 7 C5
Lannock Hill. Wes SG4 23 E1
Lannock Jun Mix Inf Sch. Letw 23 C4
Lannock. Letw SG6 23 D4
Lanrick Copse. Berk HP4 122 E5
Lansdowne Cl. Watf WD2 154 D4
Lansdowne Ct. Hod EN10 135 A3
Lansdowne Rd. Luton LU3 45 D1
Lanterns La. Stev SG2 51 D5
Lanthony Ct. Arl SG15 11 A4
Laporte Way. Luton LU4 44 F1
Laporte Way. Luton LU4 45 A1
Lapwing Cl. Heml H HP2 124 E6
Lapwing Dell. Letw SG6 23 B3
Lapwing Rd. Dun LU4 44 A4
Lapwing Rise. Stev SG2 51 D3
Larch Ave. Bri Wd AL2 140 E1
Larch Ave. Hit SG4 35 A4
Larch Cl. Ham St EN7 147 E4
Larch La. Welw AL6 89 F8
Larch Rise. Berk HP4 122 A5
Larches Ave. Enf EN1 162 C4
Larches The. Luton LU2 45 D1
Larches The. Norwd HA6 174 C4
Larches The. Nthch HP4 121 D5
Larches The. St Alb AL4 128 D7
Larches The. Ware SG12 93 C4
Larches The. Watf WD2 167 E4
Larchwood. Bis St CM23 76 D5
Lark Rise. Hat AL10 130 A3
Larke Way. Luton LU4 44 C5
Larken Cl. Bus WD2 168 C1
Larken Dr. Bus WD2 168 C1
Larkens Cl. Stand SG11 55 D3
Larkins Cl. Bal SG7 12 F1
Larkinson. Stev SG1 50 C7
Larks Ridge. Chis AL2 141 A4
Larksfield. Ware SG12 93 E3
Larkspur Cl. Bis St CM23 76 D6
Larkspur Cl. Heml H HP1 123 E4
Larkspur Gdns. Luton LU4 44 F2
Larksway. Bis St CM23 76 C6
Larkswood Rise. St Alb AL4 128 C8
Larmans Rd. Enf EN3 162 D3
Larsen Dr. Wa Aby EN9 163 D5
Larwood Gr. Stev SG1 51 A8
Latchmore Bank. L Hal CM22 77 B1
Latchmore Cl. Hit SG4 34 F5
Latimer Cl. Heml H HP2 125 B8
Latimer Cl. Pnr HA5 175 C2
Latimer Cl. Watf WD1 166 E2
Latimer Ct. Ches EN8 162 F5
Latimer Gdns. Pnr HA5 175 C2
Latimer Gdns. Wel G C AL7 111 B6
Latimer Rd. L Chal HP6 150 C2
Latimer Rd. Luton LU1 63 E6
Latium Cl. St Alb AL1 127 D2
Lattimore Rd. St Alb AL1 127 E3
Lattimore Rd. Whea AL4 108 C8
Latton Hall Cl. Harl CM20 118 A1
Lauderdale Rd. Abb L WD4 153 C6
Laughton Ct. Bor WD6 170 D7
Laundry La. Lo Naz EN9 149 E6
Launton Cl. Luton LU3 31 B1
Laurance Haines Inf & Jun Sch The. Watf 167 A3
Laureate Way. Heml H HP1 124 B5
Laurel Ave. Pot B EN6 158 F7
Laurel Cl. Heml H HP2 124 F6
Laurel Fields. Pot B EN6 158 F8
Laurel Mews. Bal SG7 12 F1
Laurel Pk. Har HA3 176 F3
Laurel Rd. St Alb AL1 127 F3
Laurel Way. Ick SG5 21 E3
Laureldene. Muc H SG10 74 F1
Laurels Cl. St Alb AL3 141 B8
Laurels The. Ham St EN7 147 E5
Laurels The. Pot En HP4 123 C6
Laurino Pl. Bus WD2 176 C8
Lavender Cl. Ham St EN7 147 F4
Lavender Cl. Luton LU2 45 E7
Lavender Ct. Bal SG7 12 E1
Lavender Gdns. Enf EN2 161 B1
Lavender Gdns. Har HA3 176 E4
Lavender Rd. Enf EN2 161 D1
Lavender Sch. Enf 161 E1
Lavender Way. Hit SG5 34 D7
Lavender Wlk. Heml H HP2 124 D5
Lavinia Ave. Watf WD2 154 D5
Lavrock La. Cro Gr WD3 165 F2
Law Hall La. Whit SG4 66 A8
Lawford Ave. Chor WD3 164 C3
Lawford Cl. Chor WD3 164 C3
Lawford Cl. Luton LU1 63 C7
Lawn Ave. Kim SG4 66 C1
Lawn Gdns. Luton LU1 63 D6
Lawn La. Heml H HP3 138 D8
Lawn The. Harl CM20 118 B3
Lawn Vale. Pnr HA5 175 E1
Lawns Cl. Gt Of SG5 33 C2
Lawns Ct. Royst SG8 7 D5
Lawns Dr The. Hod EN10 134 F2
Lawns The. Har HA5 176 B3
Lawns The. Heml H HP1 123 E4
Lawns The. St Alb AL3 127 C4
Lawns The. Stev SG2 51 D4
Lawns The. Wel G C AL8 89 D1
Lawrance Gdns. Ches EN8 148 D3
Lawrance Rd. St Alb AL3 127 C7
Lawrence Ave. Gt Am SG12 115 C3
Lawrence Ave. Letw SG6 23 A4
Lawrence Ave. Saw CM21 97 E4
Lawrence Ave. Stev SG1 50 E7
Lawrence Cl. Hert SG14 112 E7
Lawrence End Rd. Bre Gr LU2 65 D4
Lawrence Moorings. Sheer CM21 97 F1
Lawrie Ct. Har HA3 176 F3
Laxton Cl. Luton LU2 46 E1
Laxton Gdns. Bal SG7 24 A7
Lay Brook. St Alb AL4 128 A7
Layard Rd. Enf EN1 161 F1
Layham Dr. Luton LU2 46 D1
Layhill. Heml H HP2 124 D5
Layston Fst Sch. Bun 40 F8
Layston Meadow. Bun SG9 40 F6
Layston Pk. Royst SG8 7 D5
Lea Bank Ct. Luton LU3 44 E6
Lea Bank. Luton LU3 44 E6
Lea Bushes. Watf WD2 154 E4
Lea Cl. Bis St CM23 59 B1
Lea Cl. Bus WD2 168 B4
Lea Farm Jun Mix Sch. Watf 154 D4
Lea Gr. Bis St CM23 59 B1
Lea Manor High Sch. Luton 44 F8
Lea Manor Recn Ctr. Luton 44 F8
Lea Mount. Gofs O EN7 147 E3
Lea Rd. Ches EN8 163 A5
Lea Rd. Harp AL5 86 B3
Lea Rd. Hod EN11 135 C8
Lea Rd. Luton LU1 63 F7
Lea Rd. Watf WD2 154 B1
Lea Wlk. Harp AL5 86 C4
Leacroft. Harp AL5 86 D3
Leaders Cl. Wing HP22 60 B3
Leaf Cl. Norwd HA6 174 D3
Leafield. Luton LU3 44 F4
Leaford Cres. Watf WD2 153 F2
Leaford Ct. Watf WD2 153 F3
Leaforis Rd. Ches EN7 148 A3
Leafy La. Ast Cl HP23 99 E1
Leagrave High St. Dun LU4 44 B3
Leagrave Inf Sch. Luton 44 C4
Leagrave Jun Mix Sch. Luton 44 C4
Leagrave Rd. Luton LU3,LU4 45 B2
Leagrave Sta. Luton 44 E5
Leahoe Gdns. Hert SG13 113 C5
Lealands High Sch. Luton 44 C8
Leamington Rd. Luton LU3 45 A7
Leander Gdns. Watf WD2 154 B2
Leas The. Bal SG7 23 E7
Leas The. Bus WD2 167 F7
Leas The. Heml H HP3 139 A7
Leaside Ct. Harp AL5 86 C3
Leaside. Heml H HP2 125 C2
Leaside Wlk. Ware SG12 93 D1 5
Leat Cl. Saw CM21 97 F3
Leathersellers Cl. Barn EN5 171 E6
Leathwaite Cl. Luton LU3 44 F6
Leaves Spring. Stev SG2 51 A2
Leavesden Green Sch. Watf 154 A5
Leavesden Green Jun Mix Sch. Watf 154 A5
Leavesden Hospl. Abb L 154 A8
Leavesden Rd. Watf WD2 154 B1
Leaview. Wa Aby EN9 163 B6
Lebanon Cl. Watf WD1 153 D3
Lectern La. St Alb AL1 141 E7
Leda Ave. Enf EN3 162 D1
Ledgemore La. Gt Gd HP2 103 F5
Ledwell Rd. Cad LU1 62 F3
Lee Cl. Gt Am SG12 115 C4
Lee Cl. Hert SG13 113 C4
Lee Farm Cl. Bot HP5 136 A1
Lee Road Ind Pk. Ches 163 A5
Leeches Way. Ched LU7 80 A7
Leecroft Rd. Barn EN5 171 E5
Leefe Way. Cuf EN6 146 D3
Leeming Rd. Bor WD6 169 F8
Lees Ave. Norwd HA6 174 F2
Leeside. Barn EN5 171 E3
Leeside. Pot B EN6 159 D7
Leete Pl. Royst SG8 7 D7
Leggatts Campus The. Watf 154 A3
Leggatts Cl. Watf WD2 153 F3
Leggatts Rise. Watf WD2 154 A4
Leggatts Way. Watf WD2 154 A3
Leggatts Wood Ave. Watf WD2 154 B3
Leggett Gr. Stev SG1 50 E8
Leggfield Terr. Heml H HP1 123 F3
Leghorn Cres. Dun LU4 44 A3
Legions Way. Bis St CM23 77 A8
Leicester Rd. Luton LU4 44 E1
Leigh Comm. Wel G C AL7 110 F4
Leigh Ct. Bor WD6 170 D7
Leigh Rodd. Sth Ox WD1 175 F7
Leighton Buzzard Rd. Gt Gd HP1 103 E2
Leighton Buzzard Rd. Heml H HP1 124 C5
Leighton Ct. Ches LU6 148 D2
Leighton Rd. Har HA3 176 D1
Leighton Rd. Wing HP22 60 C3
Lemon Field Dr. Watf WD2 154 E6
Lemsford Ct. Bor WD6 170 C5
Lemsford La. Wel G C AL8 110 B4
Lemsford Rd. Hat AL10 130 A6
Lemsford Rd. St Alb AL1 127 F4
Lemsford Springs (Nature Reserve). Hat 110 A5
Lemsford Village. Hat AL8 109 F5
Lennon Ct. Luton LU1 63 D7
Lennox Gn. Luton LU2 46 F2
Lensbury Cl. Ches EN8 148 E3
Leonard's Cl. Welw AL6 89 E8
Lesbury Cl. Luton LU2 46 E1
Leslie Cl. Stev SG2 51 C2
Letchfield. Bot HP5 150 B8
Letchmore Cl. Stev SG1 50 D6
Letchmore Rd. Radl WD7 156 A3
Letchmore Rd. Stev SG1 50 D7
Letchmore Road Inf Sch. Stev 50 D7
Letchworth Bsns & Ret Pk. Letw 23 C6
Letchworth Cl. Sth Ox WD1 175 D5
Letchworth Gate. Letw SG6 23 B4
Letchworth La. Letw SG6 22 F3
Letchworth Rd. Bal SG7 23 D7
Letchworth Rd. Letw SG6 23 D7
Letchworth Rd. Luton LU3 45 A4
Letter Box Row. Hit SG4 34 F3
Leven Cl. Ches EN8 162 D6
Leven Cl. Sth Ox WD1 175 D5
Leven Dr. Ches EN8 162 D6
Leven Way. Heml H HP2 124 D7
Levenage La. Widf SG12 95 E3
Leventhorpe Sch The. Saw 97 E4
Leveret Cl. Watf WD2 154 A5
Leverstock Green Jun Mix Inf Sch. Heml H 125 D2
Leverstock Green Rd. Heml H HP2,HP3 125 B3
Leverstock Green Rd. Heml H HP2,HP3 125 C2
Leverstock Green Way. Heml H HP2,HP3 125 C3
Leverton Cty Prim & Inf Sch The. Wa Aby 163 F5
Leverton Way. Wa Aby EN9 163 C6
Lewes Way. Cro Gr WD3 166 C5
Lewis Cl. Hare UB9 173 C1
Lewsey Park Ct. Dun LU4 44 A4
Lewsey Rd. Dun LU4 44 B2
Lexington Cl. Bor WD6 169 F6
Lexington Ct. Pot B EN6 158 D8
Lexington Way. Barn EN5 171 D5
Ley House. Wel G C AL7 111 C6
Ley Park Inf Sch. Hod 134 F1
Ley Park Jun Sch. Hod 134 F1
Ley Wlk. Wel G C AL7 111 C6
Leyburne Cl. Men LU7 61 C8
Leyburne Rd. Luton LU3 45 B6
Leycroft Way. Harp AL5 107 E7
Leyden House (Adult Training Ctr). Stev 50 D2
Leyden Rd. Stev SG1 50 D2
Leygreen Cl. Luton LU2 64 A8
Leyhill Dr. Luton LU1 63 B4
Leyland Ave. St Alb AL1 127 D1
Leyland Cl. Ches EN8 148 C2
Leys Ave. Letw SG6 22 F6
Leys Cl. Hare UB9 173 D2
Leys Rd. Heml H HP3 124 F1
Leys The. St Alb AL4 128 D6
Leys The. Tri HP23 100 B4
Leysdown. Wel G C AL7 111 D6
Leyton Gn. Harp AL5 86 A1
Leyton Rd. Harp AL5 86 A1
Library Rd. Luton LU1 63 E7
Lichfield Rd. Norwd HA6 175 A1
Lichfield Way. Hod EN10 134 F1
Liddel Cl. Luton LU3 45 B3
Lidgate Cl. Luton LU4 44 B6
Lighthorne Rise. Luton LU3 45 A7
Lilac Ave. Enf EN1 162 C3
Lilac Cl. Ches EN7 162 B8
Lilac Gr. Luton LU3 44 C8
Lilac Rd. Hod EN11 135 B8
Lilac Way. Harp AL5 107 D6
Lilley Bottom. Bre Gr SG5 47 C5
Lilley Bottom. Gt Of SG4 47 C5
Lilley Bottom Rd. Bre Gr SG4 48 B1
Lilley Bottom Rd. Whit SG4 48 B1
Lilley CE Jun Mix Inf Sch. Lily 32 D2
Lilleyhoo La. Lily LU2 32 F2
Lilliard Cl. Hod EN11 115 B2
Limberlost The. Welw AL6 89 B7
Limbrick Rd. Harp AL5 107 C6
Limbury Rd. Luton LU3 44 F6
Lime Ave. Dun LU4 44 C3
Lime Ave. Kim AL4 87 B7
Lime Cl. Ast SG2 51 D4
Lime Cl. Ware SG12 93 E2
Lime Cl. Watf WD1 167 D2
Lime Gr. Barn N20 171 F1
Lime Gr. Royst SG8 7 E8
Lime Tree Pl. St Alb AL1 127 E2
Lime Tree Wlk. Bus WD2 176 E8
Lime Tree Wlk. Enf EN2 161 C1
Lime Tree Wlk. Ric WD3 165 B4
Lime Walk Prim Sch. Heml H 124 F1
Lime Wlk. Heml H HP3 124 F1
Limedene Cl. Pnr HA5 175 D2
Limekiln La. Bal SG7 23 F7
Limekiln La. Sta M CM24 59 C5
Limes Cres. Bis St CM23 77 A7
Limes Ct. Hod EN11 135 A6
Limes Rd. Ches EN8 162 E7
Limes The. Arl SG15 11 A8
Limes The. Hit SG5 34 D6
Limes The. St Alb AL1 127 E5
Limes The. Wel G C AL7 111 A4
Limetree Ave. Nwml E LU1 85 A7
Limetree Ct. Pnr HA5 176 A3
Linacres. Luton LU4 44 D4
Linbridge Way. Luton LU2 46 E2
Linces Way. Wel G C AL7 111 B4
Lincoln Cl. Bis St CM23 76 D5
Lincoln Cl. Wel G C AL7 111 D6
Lincoln Ct. Berk HP4 122 B4

Prince St. Watf WD1 167 C6
Prince Way. Luton LU2 64 D8
Prince's St. Stot SG5 11 F7
Princes Ave. Enf EN3 162 E4
Princes Ave. Watf WD1 167 A5
Princes Cl. Berk HP4 122 A6
Princes Ct. Bis St CM23 76 C7
Princes Gate. Bis St CM23 76 C7
Princes Gate. Harl 117 E3
Princes Mews. Royst SG8 7 C6
Princes St. Ware SG12 93 D2
Princess Alexandra Hospl. Harl 117 B1
Princess Helena Coll. Pres 48 E6
Princess St. Luton LU1 63 D7
Printers Way. Harl CM20 118 A5
Priors Cl. Hert H SG13 114 B3
Priors Ct. Sheer CM21 98 A2
Priors Hill. Pirt SG5 20 C4
Priors Wood Rd. Hert H SG13 114 C3
Priory Cl. Barn N20 171 F2
Priory Cl. Ches EN8 148 E7
Priory Cl. Hod EN11 135 A5
Priory Cl. Royst SG8 7 E6
Priory Cl. Stan HA7 176 F7
Priory Ct. Berk HP4 122 C4
Priory Ct. Bis St CM23 76 F7
Priory Ct. Bus WD2 168 C1
Priory Ct. Hert SG14 113 C6 11
Priory Ct. Hit 34 F5
Priory Ct. St Alb AL1 127 E2
Priory Dell. Stev SG1 50 F5
Priory Dr. Sta M CM24 59 E5
Priory Dr. Stan HA7 176 F7
Priory End. Hit SG4 34 F5
Priory Gate. Ches EN8 148 F4
Priory Gdns. Berk HP4 122 C4
Priory Gdns. Luton LU2 45 D4
Priory La. Gt Wy SG4 35 F4
Priory La. Royst SG8 7 D6
Priory Orch. Fla AL3 84 B2
Priory Rd. Harl CM17 118 C5
Priory Sch The. Hit 21 E2
Priory St. Hert SG14 113 D6
Priory St. Ware SG12 93 C1
Priory View. Bus WD2 168 E2
Priory View. L Wym SG4 35 E4
Priory Way. Hit SG4 34 F4
Priory Wharf. Hert SG14 113 C6 10
Priory Wlk. St Alb AL1 141 E8
Proctor Way. Luton LU2 64 C7
Proctors Way. Bis St CM23 77 A4
Progress Way. Luton LU4 44 B7
Progression Ctr. Heml H 125 A6
Prospect La. Harp AL5 107 A4
Prospect Pl. Welw AL6 89 C5
Prospect Rd. Ches EN8 148 C2
Prospect Rd. St Alb AL1 127 D1
Protea Way. Letw SG6 23 B6
Providence Gr. Stev SG1 50 E8
Providence Way. Bal SG7 23 F7
Provost Way. Luton LU2 64 C8
Prowse Ave. Bus WD2 176 C8
Pryor Cl. Abb L WD5 153 F7
Pryor Rd. Bal SG7 23 F6
Pryor Way. Letw SG6 23 D5
Pryors Cl. Bis St CM23 77 A6
Puddephat's La. Fla AL3 104 D7
Pudding La. Bar SG8 9 A1
Pudding La. Heml H HP1 124 A5
Pudgell The. Gt Ch SG8 9 E2
Pullar Memorial Jun Mix & Inf Sch. Thun 72 E2
Puller Rd. Barn EN5 171 E7
Puller Rd. Heml H HP1 124 A2
Pulleys Cl. Heml H HP1 123 F4
Pulleys La. Heml H HP1 123 F4
Pulter's Way. Hit SG4 35 A6
Pump Hill. Bre P SG9 30 A2
Punch Bowl La. Red AL3 126 B8
Purbrock Ave. Watf WD2 154 C3
Purcell Cl. Dat AL6 90 E6
Purcell Cl. Radl WD6 169 D8
Purcell Ct. Stev SG1 50 C8
Purkiss Rd. Bric SG13 113 C3
Purley Ctr. Luton 44 E7
Purlings Rd. Bus WD2 168 B4
Pursley Gdns. Bor WD6 157 A1
Purway Cl. Luton LU3 44 E8
Purwell La. Hit SG4 35 C8
Purwell Sch (Jun Mix & Inf). Hit 35 D8
Putney Rd. Enf EN3 162 D3
Puttenham Cl. Sth Ox WD1 175 D8
Putteridge High Sch. Luton 46 C5
Putteridge Inf Sch. Luton 46 C5
Putteridge Prim Sch. Luton 46 C5
Putteridge Rd. Luton LU2 46 C4
Putteridge Rec Ctr. Luton 46 C5
Putterills The. Harp AL5 86 A1
Putters Croft. Heml H HP2 124 F8
Puttocks Cl. Wel G AL9 144 C8
Puttocks Dr. Wel G AL9 144 C8
Pye Cnr. East CM20 117 D5
Pyghtle Ct. Luton LU1 63 A7
Pyghtle The. Bun SG9 40 D7
Pyghtle The. Luton LU1 63 A7
Pyms Cl. Letw SG6 23 B8
Pynchbek. Bis St CM23 76 E3
Pynchon Paddocks. L Hal CM22 98 D7
Pytchley Cl. Luton LU2 45 E5

Quadrangle The. Wel G C AL8 110 C7
Quadrant The. Letw SG6 22 F6
Quadrant The. Royst SG8 7 C8
Quadrant The. St Alb AL4 128 B6
Quadrant The. Stev SG1 50 D4
Quaker La. Wa Aby EN9 163 C5
Quaker Rd. Ware SG12 93 E3
Quakers La. Pot B EN6 159 B8
Quantock Cl. Luton LU3 45 B8
Quantock Cl. St Alb AL4 128 C7
Quantock Rise. Luton LU3 31 B1
Quantocks. Heml H HP2 124 F6
Quartermass Cl. Heml H HP1 124 A4
Quartermass Rd. Heml H HP1 124 A4
Queen Anne's Cl. Stot SG5 11 F5
Queen Elizabeth Ct. Barn EN5 171 F5
Queen Elizabeth II Hospl. Wel G C 111 A2
Queen Elizabeth's Boys Sch. Barn 171 D6
Queen Elizabeth's Girls Gram Sch. Barn 171 F5
Queen Hoo La. Tewin AL6 90 F6
Queen Mary's Ave. Watf WD1 166 E5
Queen St. Chipf WD4 152 A7
Queen St. Hit SG4,SG5 34 F7
Queen St. Pit LU7 80 D4
Queen St. St Alb AL3 127 C3
Queen St. Stot SG5 12 A6
Queen St. Tri HP23 100 A3
Queen Victoria Memorial Hospl. Welw 89 B4
Queen's Cl. Saw CM21 97 F4
Queen's Ct. Asp SG9 40 D5
Queen's Ct. Hert SG13 113 D5
Queen's Ct. St Alb AL1 128 B3
Queen's Dr. Ches EN8 163 A5
Queen's Dr The. Ric WD3 165 A3
Queen's Pl. Watf WD1 167 C6
Queen's Rd. Ches EN8 162 E6
Queen's Rd. Harp AL5 107 B7
Queen's Rd. Hert SG13 113 D5
Queen's Rd. Watf WD1 167 C6
Queen's Sq The. Heml H HP2 124 F4
Queens Ave. Watf WD1 166 F4
Queens Cl. Luton LU1 63 F6
Queens Cl. Sta M CM24 59 E8
Queens Cres. Bis St CM23 76 E5
Queens Cres. St Alb AL4 128 B6
Queens Dr. Abb L WD5 153 F7
Queens Rd. Barn EN5 171 D6
Queens Rd. Berk HP4 122 A5
Queens Rd. Royst SG8 7 D7
Queens Rd. Ware SG12 93 F2
Queens Sch. Bus 167 F6
Queens Way. Ches EN8 162 F5
Queens Way. Shen WD7 156 E7
Queensgate Ctr. Harl 117 F4
Queenside Dr. Hit SG5 34 D8
Queensway. Hat AL10 130 B6
Queensway. Heml H HP1,HP2 124 E4
Queensway. Royst SG8 7 D7
Queensway. Stev SG1 50 D5
Queenswood Cres. Watf WD2 154 A6
Queenswood Dr. Hit SG4 22 C1
Queenswood Sch. Bro Pk 145 D3
Quendell Wlk. Heml H HP2 124 E3
Quendon Dr. Wa Aby EN9 163 D6
Quickbeams. Wel G C AL7 90 A1
Quickley La. Chor WD3 164 C3
Quickley Rise. Chor WD3 164 C3
Quickly Brow. Chor WD3 164 B3
Quickmoor La. Sar WD4 152 C6
Quickswood. Luton LU3 45 A7
Quickwood Cl. Ric WD3 165 A3
Quills. Letw SG6 23 D4
Quilter Cl. Luton LU3 44 F4
Quinces Croft. Heml H HP1 124 A5
Quincey Rd. Ware SG12 93 C4
Quinn Ct. Brag SG11 55 F7
Quinn Way. Letw SG6 23 C5
Quinta Dr. Barn EN5 171 C4
Quinton Way. Wa Aby EN9 163 C4

Raans Rd. L Chal HP6 150 A1
Raban Cl. Stev SG2 51 C1
Rabley Heath Rd. Cod AL6 68 B2
Radburn Sch (Jun Mix & Inf). Letw 23 C5
Radburn Way. Letw SG6 23 C4
Radcliffe Rd. Hit SG5 35 A8
Radlett La. Shen WD7 156 D6
Radlett Nursery & Inf Sch. Radl 156 B3
Radlett Park Rd. Radl WD7 156 A5
Radlett Rd. Lon C AL2 141 E2
Radlett Rd. Radl WD2 155 C1
Radlett Rd. Watf WD1,WD2 167 D7
Radnor Ct. Har HA3 176 F2
Radstone Pl. Luton LU2 46 E1 3
Radwell La. Letw SG7 12 C4
Raebarn Gdns. Barn EN5 171 B4
Raffin Cl. Dat SG3 69 E3
Raffin Green La. Dat SG3 69 F4
Raffin Pk. Dat SG3 69 E3
Ragged Hall La. Chis AL2 140 E7
Raglan Ave. Ches EN8 162 D5
Raglan Gdns. Watf WD1 167 B1
Raglan House. Berk HP4 122 A4
Rags La. Ham St EN7 147 E4
Railway Pl. Hert SG13 113 E6
Railway Rd. Ches EN8 162 F6
Railway St. Hert SG13,SG14 113 D6
Railway Terr. Abb L WD4 139 A4
Rainbow Cl. Red AL3 105 F6
Rainbow Ct. Watf WD1 167 C3
Rainer Cl. Ches EN8 148 D2
Rainsford Rd. Sta M CM24 59 E8
Raleigh Cres. Stev SG2 51 B8
Raleigh Gr. Luton LU4 44 D1
Rally The. Arl SG15 11 A7
Ralph Sadleir Mid Sch. Stand 55 E3
Ralston Way. Sth Ox WD1 175 D8
Ram Gorse. Harl CM20 117 B2
Ramblers Way. Wel G C AL7 111 C5
Rambling Way. Pot En HP4 123 C6
Ramerick Gdns. Arl SG15 11 A2
Ramney Dr. Enf EN3 162 E2
Ramparts The. St Alb AL3 127 B2
Ramridge Jun Sch. Luton 46 B2
Ramridge Rd. Luton LU2 46 A2
Ramsay Cl. Hod EN10 134 E2
Ramsbury Rd. St Alb AL1 127 E2
Ramsdell. Stev SG1 50 F5
Ramsey Cl. Bro Pk AL9 145 D4
Ramsey Cl. St Alb AL1 128 A1
Ramsey Lodge Ct. St Alb AL1 127 E4
Ramson Rise. Heml H HP1 123 E4
Rand's Cl. Hol SG5 21 B7
Rand's Meadow. Hol SG5 21 B7
Randalls Ride. Heml H HP2 124 E5
Randals Hill. Stev SG2 51 C3
Randon Cl. Har HA2 176 B1
Ranelagh Rd. Heml H HP2 125 B3
Raneleigh Wlk. Harp AL5 107 D6
Ranock Cl. Luton LU3 44 D8
Ranskill Rd. Bor WD6 170 A8
Ransom Cl. Hit SG4 34 F4
Rant Meadow. Heml H HP3 125 A1
Rant Meadow. Heml H HP3 125 A2
Ranworth Ave. Hod EN11 115 B2
Ranworth Ave. Stev SG2 69 C7
Ranworth Cl. Heml H HP3 124 D1 2
Raphael Cl. Shen WD7 156 E7
Raphael Dr. Watf WD2 167 D7
Rasehill Cl. Ric WD3 165 C4
Rathlin. Heml H HP3 139 B8
Ratty's La. Hod EN11 135 D6
Raven Cl. Ric WD3 165 D2
Raven Ct. Hat AL10 130 A4
Ravenbank Rd. Luton LU2 46 C5
Ravenfield Rd. Wel G C AL7 110 F6
Ravenhill Way. Dun LU4 44 B4
Ravens La. Berk HP4 122 D4
Ravens Wharf. Berk HP4 122 D4
Ravenscroft. Harp AL5 107 D6
Ravenscroft Pk. Barn EN5 171 D5
Ravenscroft Sch. Barn 171 F2
Ravenscroft. Watf WD2 154 E4
Ravensdell. Heml H HP1 123 F4
Ravensthorpe. Luton LU2 46 B4
Ravenswood Pk. Norwd HA6 175 A4
Rawdon Dr. Hod EN11 135 A5
Ray's Hill. Chol HP5 120 C2
Rayburn Rd. Heml H HP1 124 A5
Raydon Rd. Ches EN8 162 D7
Rayfield. Wel G C AL8 89 D1
Rayleigh House. Abb L WD5 153 F7
Raymer Cl. St Alb AL1 127 E4
Raymond Cl. Abb L WD5 153 D7
Raymonds Cl. Wel G C AL7 110 E4
Raymonds Plain. Wel G C AL7 110 E4
Raynham Cl. Bis St CM23 77 C8
Raynham Rd. Bis St CM23 77 B8
Raynham St. Hert SG13 113 E6
Raynham Way. Luton LU2 46 D1
Raynsford Rd. Ware SG12 93 E1
Raynton Rd. Enf EN3 162 D2
Readings The. Chor WD3 164 F6
Recreation Ground. Sta M CM24 59 E6
Rectory Cl. Bis St CM23 76 D3
Rectory Cl. Ess AL9 131 F6
Rectory Cl. Hun SG12 116 D8
Rectory Gdns. Hat AL10 130 B5
Rectory La. Berk HP4 122 C4
Rectory La. Far CM23 58 D6
Rectory La. Kin L WD4 139 A3
Rectory La. Lily LU2 32 D2
Rectory La. Ric WD3 165 D1
Rectory La. Shen WD7,AL2 157 B7
Rectory La. Stev SG1 36 D1
Rectory La. Wat St SG14 70 D3
Rectory La. Welw SG3 69 C2
Rectory Rd. Ric WD3 165 D2
Rectory Rd. Wel G C AL8 89 B1
Rectory Wood. Harl CM20 117 C1
Red House Cl. Ware SG12 114 E8
Red Lion Cotts. Gt Of SG5 33 D2
Red Lion Ct. Bis St CM23 77 A7
Red Lion La. Heml H HP3 139 A5
Red Lion La. Sar WD3 152 A4
Red Lodge. Bor WD6 169 F6
Red Lodge Gdns. Berk HP4 122 A3
Red Rails. Luton LU1 63 C5
Red Rd. Bor WD6 169 F6
Redan Rd. Ware SG12 93 E3
Redbourn Ind Est. Red 106 B5
Redbourn Inf Sch. Red 106 A6
Redbourn Jun Sch. Red 106 A6
Redbourn La. Harp AL5 106 E6
Redbourn Rd. Heml H HP2 125 A6
Redbourn Rd. Heml H HP2 125 B8
Redbourn Rd. St Alb AL3 126 E7
Redbournbury La. Red AL3 106 D2
Redcar Dr. Stev SG1 50 A6
Redding House. Watf WD1 166 E3
Redding La. Red AL3 105 F8
Reddings Ave. Bus WD2 168 B4
Reddings Cty Prim Sch The. Heml H 125 A1
Reddings. Heml H HP3 125 A1
Reddings The. Bor WD6 169 F6
Reddings. Wel G C AL8 110 C7
Redfern Ct. Luton LU1 63 A6
Redferns Cl. Luton LU1 63 A6
Redgrave Gdns. Luton LU3 44 F7
Redhall Cl. Hat AL10 129 F1
Redhall Dr. Hat AL10 129 F1
Redhall La. Coln H AL4 129 E1
Redhall La. Sar WD3 165 E8
Redheath Cl. Watf WD2 153 F4
Redhill Rd. Hit SG5 34 D8
Redhoods Way E. Letw SG6 22 E7
Redhoods Way W. Letw SG6 22 E6
Redlands Rd. Enf EN3 162 E1
Redmire Cl. Luton LU4 44 B6
Redricks La. Saw CM21 118 B7
Redvers Cl. Bis St CM23 59 A2
Redwell Ct. Ches EN8 162 F5
Redwood Cl. Sth Ox WD1 175 D6
Redwood Dr. Heml H HP3 124 E1
Redwood Dr. Luton LU3 44 C8
Redwood Rise. Bor WD6 157 B2
Redwood Way. Barn EN5 171 D4
Redwoods. Hert AL8 113 C7
Redwoods. Wel G C AL8 89 D3
Reed Cl. Lon C AL2 142 E4
Reed Jun Mix Inf Sch. Reed 16 E5
Reed Pl. Harp AL5 85 F3 1
Reedham Cl. Bri Wd AL2 141 A2
Reedings Jun Sch. Saw 97 E3
Reedings Way. Saw CM21 97 F4
Reeds Cres. Watf WD1 167 C7
Reeds The. Wel G C AL7 110 D5
Reedsdale. Luton LU2 46 F2
Reeves Ave. Luton LU3 45 B4
Reeves Pightle. Gt Ch SG8 9 F3
Regal Cl. Stand SG11 55 E2
Regal Ct. Hit SG5 34 F8 4
Regal Way. Watf WD2 154 C1
Regency Cl. Bis St CM23 76 E7
Regency Heights. Heml H HP2 124 D3
Regent Cl. Kin L WD4 139 A3
Regent Cl. St Alb AL4 128 C7
Regent Cl. Wel G C AL7 110 E5
Regent Ct. Stot SG5 11 F7
Regent Gate. Ches EN8 162 F6
Regent St. Luton LU1 63 E7
Regent St. Stot SG5 11 F7
Regent St. Watf WD2 154 B1
Regents Cl. Radl WD7 156 A5
Regina Cl. Barn EN5 171 D6
Reginald Rd. Norwd HA6 174 F3
Reginald St. Luton LU2 45 E1
Rendlesham Ave. Radl WD7 155 F2
Rendlesham Cl. Ware SG12 93 B2
Rendlesham Rd. Enf EN2 161 B1
Rendlesham Way. Chor WD3 164 C3
Rennison Cl. Ham St EN7 147 F4
Renshaw Cl. Luton LU2 46 E2
Repton Cl. Luton LU3 44 F6
Repton Gn. St Alb AL3 127 D6
Repton Way. Cro Gr WD3 166 A4
Reson Way. Heml H HP1 124 B2
Reston Cl. Bor WD6 157 B1
Retford Cl. Bor WD6 157 A1
Retreat The. Abb L WD5 153 C8
Revels Cl. Hert SG14 113 D8
Revels Rd. Hert SG14 113 D8
Reynard Copse. Bis St CM23 58 F1
Reynard Way. Hert SG13 114 B6
Reynard's Way. Bri Wd AL2 140 F2
Reynards Rd. Welw AL6 89 C7
Reynolds Cl. Heml H HP1 124 A4
Reynolds Cres. Sand AL4 128 B8
Reynolds. Letw SG6 11 F1
Rhee Spring. Bal SG7 13 B1
Rhodes Ave. Bis St CM23 76 F5
Rhodes Memorial Mus & Commonwealth Ctr. Bis St 77 A6
Rhodes Way. Watf WD2 167 D8
Rib Cl. Stand SG11 55 E2
Rib Vale. Hert SG14 92 D1
Ribbledale. Lon C AL2 142 F4
Ribblesdale. Heml H HP2 124 E6
Ribocon Way. Luton LU4 44 B7
Ribston Cl. Shen WD7 156 D6
Rice Cl. Heml H HP2 124 F4
Richard Ct. Barn EN5 171 E6
Richard Hale Sch. Hert 113 D5
Richard Stagg Cl. St Alb AL1 128 C1
Richard Whittington Jun Mix Inf Sch. Bis St 76 E4
Richards Cl. Bus WD2 168 D2
Richards Cl. Luton LU1 63 B6
Richards Ct. Luton LU1 63 B6
Richardson Cl. Lon C AL2 142 E4
Richardson Pl. Coln H AL4 129 B1
Richfield Rd. Bus WD2 168 C2
Richmond Cl. Bis St CM23 76 C7
Richmond Cl. Ches EN8 148 C2
Richmond Cl. Ware SG12 93 B3
Richmond Ct. Hat AL10 130 B3 4
Richmond Ct. Hod EN10 134 F3
Richmond Ct. Luton LU2 45 F1
Richmond Ct. Pot B EN6 159 C8
Richmond Dr. Watf WD1 166 E7
Richmond Gdns. Har HA3 176 F3
Richmond Gn. Abb L WD5 139 F4
Richmond Hill. Luton LU2 45 F2
Richmond Hill Sch. Luton 45 E2
Richmond Rd. Pot B EN6 159 C8
Richmond Way. Cro Gr WD3 166 C5
Richmond Wlk. St Alb AL4 128 D7
Rickfield Cl. Hat AL10 130 A3
Rickmansworth La. C St P SL9 172 A5
Rickmansworth Park Jun Mix Inf Sch. Ric 165 E2
Rickmansworth Rd. Chor WD3 164 F5
Rickmansworth Rd. Cro Gr WD1 166 E5
Rickmansworth Rd. Hare UB9 173 D3
Rickmansworth Rd. Norwd HA5 174 D3
Rickmansworth Rd. Pnr HA5 175 C1
Rickmansworth Rd. Watf WD1 166 E5
Rickmansworth Rd. Watf WD1 167 B6
Rickmansworth Sch. Cro Gr 165 F3
Rickmansworth Sta. Ric 165 D2
Rickyard Cl. Luton LU2 46 B3
Rickyard Meadow. Red AL3 106 A5
Rickyard The. Ashw SG7 4 D4
Rickyard The. Letw SG7 12 C1
Riddell Gdns. Bal SG7 23 F8
Riddy Hill Cl. Hit SG4 35 A6
Riddy La. Hit SG4 35 A6
Riddy La. Luton LU3 45 C5
Riddy The. Cod SG4 88 F8
Ridge Ave. Harp AL5 85 E4
Ridge Ave. Letw SG6 23 A6
Ridge Ct. Luton LU2 46 A1
Ridge La. Watf WD1 153 F2
Ridge Lea. Heml H HP1 123 F2
Ridge Rd. Letw SG6 23 A6
Ridge St. Watf WD2 154 B1
Ridge The. Barn EN5 171 F4
Ridge The. Letw SG6 23 A6
Ridge The. Norwd HA6 174 F3
Ridge View. Tri HP23 100 C5
Ridge Way. Ric WD3 165 B2
Ridgedown. Red AL3 106 A5
Ridgefield. Watf WD1 153 E2
Ridgehurst Ave. Watf WD2 153 F5
Ridgeview Cl. Barn EN5 171 D3
Ridgeway. Berk HP4 121 F4
Ridgeway Cl. Heml H HP3 138 F5
Ridgeway Ct. Pnr HA5 176 A3
Ridgeway. Harp AL5 85 E4
Ridgeway. Ken Co LU6 82 E8
Ridgeway. L Had SG11 57 B1
Ridgeway. Stev SG1 50 F5
Ridgeway The. Cod SG4 67 F1
Ridgeway The. Cuf EN6 146 A4
Ridgeway The. Had W EN2,EN4 160 D3
Ridgeway The. Hert SG14 112 F7
Ridgeway The. Hit SG5 34 D6
Ridgeway The. Radl WD7 155 F2
Ridgeway The. St Alb AL4 128 C7
Ridgeway The. Ware SG12 93 C3
Ridgeway The. Watf WD1 153 E2
Ridgeway. Wel G C AL7 111 B6
Ridgewood Dr. Harp AL5 85 E4
Ridgewood Gdns. Harp AL5 85 E4
Ridgmont Rd. St Alb AL1 127 E2
Ridgway Rd. Luton LU2 45 F1
Ridings The. Bis St CM23 76 D4
Ridings The. Hert SG14 113 A5
Ridings The. Lat HP5 150 D3
Ridings The. Luton LU3 45 C1
Ridings The. Mark AL3 83 E6
Ridings The. Stev SG2 51 B3
Ridler Rd. Enf EN1 161 E1
Ridlins End. Stev SG2 51 C2
Rigery La. Stand SG11 72 F6
Riley Rd. Enf EN3 162 C1
Ringshall Dr. L Gad HP4 102 C8
Ringshall Rd. Dagn HP4 81 B3
Ringtale Pl. Bal SG7 13 B1
Ringway Rd. Chis AL2 141 C4
Ringwood Rd. Luton LU2 45 D6
Ripley Rd. Dun LU4 44 C1
Ripley Rd. Enf EN2 161 C1
Ripley Way. Ches EN7 148 B1
Ripley Way. Heml H HP1 123 E4
Ripon Rd. Stev SG1 37 A2
Ripon Way. Bor WD6 170 D4
Ripon Way. St Alb AL4 128 D7
Rise Cotts. Hun SG12 95 D2
Rise The. Bal SG7 23 E7
Rise The. Bor WD6 169 F4
Rise The. Pk St AL2 141 D6
Risedale Cl. Heml H HP3 138 E8
Risedale Hill. Heml H HP3 138 E8
Risedale Rd. Heml H HP3 138 E8
Rising Hill Cl. Norwd HA6 174 C4
Risingholme Cl. Bus WD2 168 B2
Risingholme Cl. Har HA3 176 E2
Risingholme Rd. Har HA3 176 E1
Ritcroft Cl. Heml H HP3 125 B2
Ritcroft Dr. Heml H HP3 125 B2
Ritcroft St. Heml H HP3 125 B2
Ritz Ct. Pot B EN6 159 A8
Rivenhall End. Wel G C AL7 111 C6
River Ave. Hod EN11 135 B7
River Cl. Ches EN8 163 A5
River Ct. Ick SG5 21 F4
River Ct. Sac SG14 92 E4
River Gn. Bun SG9 40 E8
River Hill. Fla AL3 84 B2
River Mead. Hit SG5 21 C2
River Meads. Gt Am SG12 115 C4
River Park Ind Est. Berk 122 A5
River Pk. Heml H HP1 124 A1
River St. Ware SG12 93 E1
River View. Wel G C AL7 89 F2
River Way. Harl CM20 118 A5
River Way. Harl CM20 118 C6
River Way. Luton LU3 44 E5
Riverfield La. Saw CM21 97 E3
Riverford Cl. Harp AL5 86 B4
Rivermill Adult Education Ctr. Harl 117 C2
Rivermill Ct. Royst SG8 7 C7
Rivermill. Harl CM20 117 C2
Rivers Hospl The. Saw 97 C1
Riversend Rd. Heml H HP3 138 C8
Rivershill. Wat St SG14 70 E3
Riverside Ave. Lo Naz EN10 135 A1
Riverside. Bis St CM23 76 F7
Riverside. Bun SG9 40 E7
Riverside Cl. Kin L WD4 139 B2
Riverside Cl. St Alb AL1 127 E1
Riverside Cotts. Gt Am SG12 115 C4
Riverside Ct. Saw CM17 118 C6
Riverside Ct. St Alb AL1 127 E1
Riverside Dr. Ric WD3 165 D1
Riverside Gdns. Berk HP4 122 A5
Riverside Mews. Ware SG12 93 D1 7
Riverside Path. Ches EN8 148 C2
Riverside Rd. Luton LU3 45 A5
Riverside Rd. St Alb AL1 127 E2
Riverside Rd. Watf WD1 167 B3
Riverside. Welw AL6 89 B5
Riverside Wlk. Bis St CM23 76 F7
Riversmead. Hod EN11 135 A5
Riversmeet. Hert SG14 113 B5
Rivett Cl. Bal SG7 13 A1
Roan Wlk. Royst SG8 7 E6
Roaring Meg Ret & Leisure Pk. Stev 50 D3
Robbery Bottom La. Welw AL6 90 A8
Robbs Cl. Heml H HP1 124 A5
Robe End. Heml H HP1 123 F5
Robert Allen Ct. Luton LU1 63 E6 1
Robert Ave. St Alb AL1 141 C7
Robert Cl. Pot B EN6 158 E6
Robert Humbert House. Letw SG6 23 A5
Robert Saunders Ct. Letw SG6 22 E4
Robert Tebbutt Ct. Hit SG5 34 E6
Robert Wallace Cl. Bis St CM23 58 F1
Roberts La. C St P SL9 172 B5
Roberts Rd. Watf WD1 167 C4
Roberts Way. Hat AL10 129 F3
Roberts Wood Dr. C St P SL9 172 A5
Robertson Cl. Ches EN10 148 E5
Robeson Way. Bor WD6 170 C8
Robin Cl. Gt Am SG12 115 C3
Robin Hill. Berk HP4 122 C3
Robin Hood Dr. Bus WD2 167 F8
Robin Hood Dr. Har HA3 176 F3
Robin Hood La. Hat AL10 130 A6
Robin Hood Meadow. Heml H HP2 124 F8
Robin Mead. Wel G C AL7 90 A1
Robin Way. Cuf EN6 146 E3
Robina Cl. Norwd HA6 174 F2
Robins Nest Hill. L Berk SG13 132 C6
Robins Rd. Heml H HP3 125 A1
Robins Way. Hat AL10 129 F2
Robinsfield. Heml H HP1 124 A3
Robinson Ave. Gofs O EN7 147 B3
Robinson Cl. Bis St CM23 76 F5
Robinson Cres. Bus WD2 168 C1
Robinsway. Wa Aby EN9 163 E5
Robinswood. Luton LU2 45 E5
Robsons Cl. Ches EN8 148 C2
Rochdale Ct. Luton LU1 63 E6 2
Rochester Ave. Luton LU2 46 C4
Rochester Dr. Watf WD2 154 C4
Rochester Way. Cro Gr WD3 166 B5
Rochester Way. Royst SG8 7 D8
Rochford Ave. Wa Aby EN9 163 D5
Rochford Cl. Ches EN10 148 E5
Rochford Dr. Luton LU2 46 E2
Rochford Rd. Bis St CM23 59 C1
Rock Rd. Royst SG8 7 C8
Rockfield Ave. Ware SG12 93 D3
Rockingham Way. Stev SG1 50 E4
Rockleigh. Hert SG14 113 C6
Rockley Rd. Luton LU1 63 A7
Rockliffe Ave. Kin L WD4 139 A1
Rockways. Edg EN5 170 F3
Rodeheath. Luton LU4 44 D3

Swallows The. Wel G C AL7 89 F2
Swan And Pike Rd. Enf EN3 163 A1
Swan Ct. Bis St CM23 76 F6
Swan La. Gu M SG8 1 F4
Swan Mead. Dun LU4 44 B4
Swan St. Ashw SG7 4 D4
Swanells Wood. Stu LU6 82 C4
Swanfield Rd. Ches EN8 162 E6
Swangley's La. Kneb SG3 69 B4
Swanhill. Wel G C AL7 90 A1
Swanland Rd. Pot B EN6 144 B3
Swanland Rd. Wel G EN6 144 B3
Swanley Bar La. Bro Pk EN6 145 B3
Swanley Cres. Bro Pk EN6 145 B2
Swanley Ct. Watf WD2 154 C2
Swans Cl. Coln H AL4 128 E2
Swans Ct. Ches EN8 162 E5
Swanstand. Letw SG6 23 D4
Swanston Grange. Dun LU4 44 B2
Swanston Path. Sth Ox WD1 175 C7
Swasedale Rd. Luton LU3 45 A6
Sweet Briar. Wel G C AL7 111 A5
Sweetbriar Cl. Heml H HP1 124 A6
Sweyns Mead. Stev SG2 51 C7
Swift Cl. Gt Am SG12 115 C3
Swift Cl. Letw SG6 22 E8
Swift Cl. Royst SG8 2 D1
Swiftfields. Wel G C AL7 111 A7
Swifts Green Cl. Luton LU2 46 B5
Swifts Green Rd. Luton LU2 46 B5
Swinburne Ave. Hit SG5 21 C1
Swinburne Cl. Royst SG8 2 D1
Swing Gate La. Berk HP4 122 D2
Swing Gate Sch. Berk 122 D3
Swingate. Stev SG1 50 D5
Swinnell Cl. Knee SG8 2 B5
Swiss Ave. Watf WD1 166 E6
Swiss Cl. Watf WD1 166 E6
Sworders Yd. Bis St CM23 76 F7 2
Sycamore Ave. Hat AL10 130 A4
Sycamore Cl. Bus WD2 167 E7
Sycamore Cl. Ham St EN7 147 F4
Sycamore Cl. Hit SG4 35 A4
Sycamore Cl. Watf WD2 154 B4
Sycamore Dr. Pk St AL2 141 D4
Sycamore Dr. Tri HP23 100 B4
Sycamore Rd. Cro Gr WD3 166 D4
Sycamore Rise. Berk HP4 122 D3
Sycamores The. Bis St CM23 77 B6
Sycamores The. Heml H HP3 137 F8
Sycamores The. Radl WD7 156 B5
Sycamores The. St Alb AL1 127 D2
Sydney Rd. Watf WD1 166 F4
Sylam Cl. Luton LU3 44 E7
Sylvan Cl. Heml H HP3 125 A2
Sylvan Way. Wel G C AL7 111 C5
Sylvandale. Wel G C AL7 111 C5
Sylvia Ave. Pnr HA5 175 F4
Symonds Green La. Stev SG1 50 A6
Symonds Green Rd. Stev SG1 50 A7
Symonds Rd. Hit SG5 34 D8

Tabbs Cl. Letw SG6 23 B7
Tacitus Cl. Stev SG1 51 C8
Takeley Cl. Wa Aby EN9 163 D6
Talbot Ave. Watf WD1 167 E2
Talbot Ct. Heml H HP3 124 D1
Talbot Rd. Har HA3 176 F1
Talbot Rd. Hat AL10 130 A8
Talbot Rd. Luton LU2 45 F2
Talbot Rd. Ric WD3 165 E1
Talbot St. Hert SG13 113 E6
Talbot St. Hit SG5 34 C8
Talbot Way. Letw SG6 12 B1
Tall Trees. Hit SG4 35 A4
Tall Trees. Royst SG8 7 E6
Tallack Cl. Har HA3 176 E3
Tallents Cres. Harp AL5 86 D3
Tallents Farm (Research Farm).
Kim 86 F8
Tallis Way. Bor WD6 169 E8
Tamar Gn. Heml H HP2 124 F8
Tamarisk Cl. St Alb AL3 127 D7
Tameton Cl. Luton LU2 46 F2
Tamworth Rd. Hert SG13 113 F7
Tancred Rd. Luton LU2 46 A4
Tanfield Cl. Ham St EN7 148 A4
Tanfield Gn. Luton LU2 46 E1
Tanglewood Cl. Stan HA7 176 E8
Tanglewood. Welw AL6 90 A7
Tanners Cl. St Alb AL3 127 C4
Tanners Cres. Hert SG13 113 C4
Tanners Hill. Abb L WD5 154 A8
Tanners Way. Hun SG12 116 C8
Tanners Wood Cl. Abb L WD5 153 E7
Tanners Wood Ct. Abb L WD5 153 E7
Tanners Wood Jun Mix Inf Sch.
Abb L 153 E7
Tanners Wood La. Abb L WD5 153 E7
Tannery Cl. Royst SG8 7 C6
Tannery Drift. Royst SG8 7 C6
Tannery Drift Sch. Royst 7 C6
Tannery The. Bun SG9 40 E7
Tannery Yd. Whit SG4 66 F6
Tannsfield Dr. Heml H HP2 124 F5 1
Tannsmore Cl. Heml H HP2 124 F5 2
Tansycroft. Wel G C AL7 111 B7
Tanworth Cl. Norwd HA6 174 C4
Tanworth Gdns. Pnr HA5 175 C1
Tany's Dell Cty Prim Sch. Harl 118 A3
Tany's Dell. Harl CM20 118 A3
Tanyard La. Cod SG4 88 B8
Tapster St. Barn EN5 171 F6
Taransay. Heml H HP3 125 B1
Tarpan Way. Ches EN10 148 F6
Tarrant Dr. Harp AL5 107 D7
Tarrant. Stev SG1 36 B1
Tasmin Cl. Norwd HA6 174 F2
Tassell Hall. Red AL3 105 F6
Tatlers La. Ast SG2 51 E4
Tatsfield Ave. Lo Naz EN9 149 D8
Tattershall Dr. Heml H HP2 105 B1
Tattle Hill. Bram SG14 91 E2
Tattlers Hill. Wing HP22 60 B3
Tauber Cl. Bor WD6 169 F5
Taunton Rd. Luton LU2 46 B1
Taverners. Heml H HP2 124 E5
Taverners Way. Hod EN11 135 A6
Tavistock Ave. St Alb AL1 141 D8
Tavistock Cl. Pot B EN6 159 D8
Tavistock Cl. St Alb AL1 141 D8
Tavistock Cres. Luton LU1 63 E5
Tavistock Rd. Watf WD2 167 D8
Tavistock St. Luton LU1 63 E6
Taylor Cl. St Alb AL4 128 A8
Taylor St. Luton LU2 63 F8
Taylor Trad Est. Hert 114 B7
Taylor's Hill. Hit SG4 34 F6
Taylor's La. Barn EN5 171 F8
Taylor's Rd. Stot SG5 3 A1
Taylor's Rd. Stot SG5 11 F8
Taylors Ave. Hod EN11 135 A5
Taywood Cl. Stev SG2 51 B2
Teal Dr. Norwd HA6 174 C3
Teal House. Watf WD2 154 E3
Teasdale Cl. Royst SG8 2 D1
Teasel Cl. Royst SG8 7 E5
Tedder Ave. Henlw SG16 10 C5
Tedder Rd. Heml H HP2 125 A4
Tee Side. Hert SG13 114 B7
Teesdale. Heml H HP2 124 E6
Teesdale. Luton LU4 44 C5
Telford Ave. Stev SG2 51 B6
Telford Cl. Watf WD2 154 D4
Telford Ct. Hat AL10 129 F3
Telford Ct. St Alb AL1 127 E2
Telford Rd. Lon C AL2 142 C4
Telford Way. Luton LU1 63 D8
Telmere Ind Est. Luton 63 E6 11
Telscombe Way. Luton LU2 46 C3
Temperance St. St Alb AL3 127 C3
Tempest Ave. Pot B EN6 159 D7
Templar Ave. Bal SG7 23 F6
Templars Dr. Stan HA3 176 D4
Templars La. Pres SG4 48 D6
Temple Bank. Harl CM20 118 B5
Temple Cl. Ches EN7 162 A8
Temple Cl. Luton LU2 45 E5
Temple Cl. Pres SG5 34 B4
Temple Cl. Watf WD1 166 F7
Temple Ct. Bal SG7 23 F6
Temple Ct. Hert SG14 92 D1
Temple Ct. Pot B EN6 158 D8
Temple Fields. Hert SG14 92 D1
Temple Gdns. Letw SG6 23 C8
Temple Gdns. Mo Pk WD3 174 B6
Temple La. Ton SG12 92 F8
Temple Mead. Heml H HP2 124 D5
Temple Mead. Roy CM19 116 B1
Temple View. St Alb AL3 127 C5
Templefields Ent Ctr. Harl 118 A3
Templepan La. Sar WD3 152 E2
Templewood Sch. Wel G C 110 D8
Templewood. Wel G C AL8 89 D1
Tempsford Ave. Bor WD6 170 D5
Tempsford. Wel G C AL7 111 D6
Temsford Cl. Har HA2 176 C1
Tenby Dr. Luton LU4 44 F3
Tene The. Bal SG7 23 F8
Tennand Cl. Ham St EN7 147 F5
Tennison Ave. Bor WD6 170 B4
Tennyson Ave. Hit SG4 35 C7
Tennyson Ave. Wa Aby EN9 163 E5
Tennyson Cl. Royst SG8 2 E1
Tennyson Rd. Chis AL2 141 B5
Tennyson Rd. Harp AL5 86 A2
Tennyson Rd. Luton LU1 63 E5
Tennyson Road Prim Sch. Luton 63 E5
Tenterfield House. Welw AL6 89 C4
Tenth Ave. Luton LU3 44 C7
Tenzing Gr. Luton LU1 63 C6
Tenzing Rd. Heml H HP2 125 A3
Teresa Gdns. Ches EN8 162 D5
Terminus St. Harl CM20 117 D1
Terrace Gdns. Watf WD1 167 B7
Terrace The. Ess AL9 131 E6
Terrace The. Red AL3 106 A5
Terrace The. Tri HP23 100 A3
Tethys Rd. Heml H HP2 124 F6
Tewin Cl. St Alb AL4 128 C7
Tewin Cl. Tewin AL6 90 C5
Tewin Ct. Wel G C AL7 110 F7
Tewin Hill. Tewin AL6 90 F5
Tewin Rd. Heml H HP2 125 C3
Tewin Rd. Wel G C AL7 110 F7
Tewin Water Sch. Tewin 90 B2
Thackeray Cl. Royst SG8 2 D1
Thames Ave. Heml H HP2 124 F8
Thames Ct. Luton LU3 45 B3
Thamesdale. Lon C AL2 142 F4
Thatchers Croft. Heml H HP2 124 E7
Thatchers End. Hit SG4 35 D8
Thaxted Cl. Luton LU2 46 F2
Thaxted Way. Wa Aby EN9 163 D6
Thaynesfield. Pot B EN6 159 D8
Theabald's Grove Sta. Ches 162 D7
Thelby Cl. Luton LU3 44 F6
Thele Ave. Sta Ab SG12 115 D4
Thelusson Ct. Radl WD7 156 A3
Theobald Cres. Har HA3 176 C2
Theobald St. Bor WD6 169 F7
Theobald St. Radl WD7 156 D2
Theobald's La. Ches EN8 162 B7
Theobald's La. Ches EN8 162 C7
Theobald's Rd. Cuf EN6 146 F1
Theobalds Cl. Cuf EN6 146 F1
Theobalds Park Coll. Ches 162 A6
Theobalds Park Rd. Cre H EN2 161 B3
Therfield Fst Sch. Ther 15 F7
Therfield Rd. St Alb AL3 127 D6
Thetford Gdns. Luton LU2 45 E6
Thieves' La. Hert SG14 112 F7
Third Ave. Letw SG6 23 C7
Third Ave. Luton LU3 44 D7
Third Ave. Watf WD2 154 D4
Thirlestane. St Alb AL1 127 F4
Thirlestone Rd. Luton LU4 44 D1
Thirlmere Dr. St Alb AL1 128 B1
Thirlmere Gdns. Norwd HA6 174 C4
Thirsk Rd. Bor WD6 157 A1
Thirston Path. Bor WD6 170 A7
Thistle Cl. Heml H HP1 123 E2
Thistle Gr. Wel G C AL7 111 C3
Thistle Rd. Luton LU1 63 F7
Thistlecroft. Heml H HP1 124 B2
Thistles The. Heml H HP1 124 B4
Thistley La. St Ipp SG4 34 F1
Thomas Alleyne Sch The. Stev 50 C8
Thomas Ct. Berk HP4 121 F5
Thomas Heskin Ct. Bis St CM23 77 A7 5
Thomas Rochford Way. Ches EN8 148 F4
Thomas Tallis Cty Inf Sch The.
Wa Aby 163 F6
Thomas Watson Cottage Homes The.
Barn EN5 171 E4
Thompson Way. Ric WD3 165 A1
Thompsons Cl. Harp AL5 86 A1
Thorley Ctr The. Bis St 76 D4
Thorley High. Bis St CM23 76 F2
Thorley Hill. Bis St CM23 76 F5
Thorley Hill Prim Sch. Bis St 76 F4
Thorley La. Bis St CM23 76 C4
Thorley Park Rd. Bis St CM23 76 F4
Thorn Ave. Bus WD2 168 C1
Thorn Gr. Bis St CM23 77 B6
Thorn Tree Dr. Tri HP23 99 F4
Thornage Cl. Luton LU2 45 D7
Thornbera Cl. Bis St CM23 76 F4
Thornbera Gdns. Bis St CM23 76 F4
Thornbera Rd. Bis St CM23 76 F4
Thornbury Cl. Hod EN11 115 B2
Thornbury Cl. Stev SG2 69 A8
Thornbury Gdns. Bor WD6 170 C5
Thornbury. Harp AL5 86 D1
Thorncroft. Heml H HP3 125 B1
Thorndyke Ct. Pnr HA5 175 F3
Thorne Grove Jun Mix Inf Sch.
Bis St 77 B6
Thornfield Rd. Bis St CM23 76 E8
Thornhill Rd. Luton LU4 44 F2
Thornhill Rd. Mo Pk HA6 174 C6
Thornton Gr. Pnr HA5 176 A4
Thornton Rd. Barn EN5 171 E6
Thornton Rd. Pot B EN6 145 C1
Thornton St. Hert SG14 113 D6
Thornton St. St Alb AL3 127 C4
Thorntondale. Luton LU4 44 C5
Thorpe Cres. Watf WD1 167 C2
Thorpe Rd. St Alb AL1 127 D2
Thorpefield Cl. St Alb AL4 128 D6
Thrales Cl. Luton LU3 44 E7
Three Cherrytrees La.
Heml H HP2 125 B7
Three Close La. Berk HP4 122 C4
Three Corners. Heml H HP3 125 A1
Three Crosses. Pirt SG5 20 D4
Three Houses La. Kneb SG4 67 D5
Three Stiles. Ben SG2 52 E4
Thremhall Ave. Birhr CM23 77 F8
Thricknells Cl. Luton LU3 44 E7
Thrift Farm La. Bor WD6 170 C7
Thristers Cl. Letw SG6 23 B3
Throcking La. Cotrd SG9 27 C1
Thrums. Watf WD2 154 B2
Thrush Ave. Hat AL10 130 A3
Thrush Gn. Ric WD3 165 C2
Thrush La. Cuf EN6 146 F3
Thumbswood Inf Sch. Wel G C 111 A5
Thumbswood. Wel G C AL7 111 A3
Thumpers. Heml H HP2 124 E5
Thunder Hall. Ware SG12 93 D2 1
Thundercourt. Ware SG12 93 D2
Thundridge Cl. Wel G C AL7 111 B5
Thurgood Rd. Hod EN11 135 A8
Thurlow Cl. Stev SG1 36 D2
Thurnall Ave. Royst SG8 7 D5
Thurnall Cl. Bal SG7 23 F8
Tibbles Cl. Watf WD2 154 E4
Tibbs Hill Rd. Abb L WD5 139 F1
Tiberius Rd. Luton LU3 44 F6
Tichborne. Map Cr WD3 172 D5
Tile Kiln Cl. Heml H HP3 125 B2
Tile Kiln Cres. Heml H HP3 125 B2
Tile Kiln La. Heml H HP3 125 B2
Tilecroft. Wel G C AL8 89 D1
Tilehouse Cl. Bor WD6 169 F6
Tilehouse La. Map Cr UB9 172 E2
Tilehouse St. Hit SG5 34 E6
Tilgate. Luton LU2 46 D3
Tillers Link. Stev SG2 51 A2
Tillotson Rd. Har HA3 176 B3
Tilsworth Wlk. St Alb AL4 128 C8
Timber Orch. Stap SG14 92 A2
Timber Ridge. Ric WD3 165 D5
Timbercroft. Wel G C AL7 89 F1
Timbers Ct. Harp AL5 85 F2
Times Cl. Hit SG5 21 D2
Timplings Row. Heml H HP1 124 B5
Timworth Cl. Luton LU2 46 D1
Tingeys Cl. Red AL3 106 A5
Tinkers La. Wigg HP23 121 A6
Tinsley Cl. Luton LU1 63 B5
Tintagel Cl. Heml H HP2 124 D8
Tintagel Cl. Luton LU3 45 B4
Tintern Cl. Harp AL5 85 C4
Tintern Cl. Stev SG2 69 A7
Tinwell Mews. Bor WD6 170 D4
Tippendell La. Chis AL2 141 C5
Tippet Ct. Stev SG1 50 D3
Titan Ct. Luton LU4 44 F1
Titan Rd. Heml H HP2 124 F6
Titchfield Rd. Enf EN3 162 E2
Tithe Barn Cl. St Alb AL1 141 C8
Tithe Cl. Cod SG4 67 F1
Titian Ave. Bus WD2 168 E2
Titmus Cl. Stev SG1 50 E6
Tiverton Ct. Whea AL5 107 E6
Tiverton Rd. Nort EN6 159 E8
Toddington Rd. Luton LU4 44 C6
Toland Cl. Dun LU4 44 C1
Tolcarne Dr. Pnr HA5 175 A1
Tollgate Cl. Chor WD3 164 F5
Tollgate Rd. Col H AL4 143 E7
Tollgate Rd. Enf EN3 162 D4
Tollgate Rd. Wel G AL4 144 A6
Tollpit End. Heml H HP1 124 A6
Tolmers Ave. Cuf EN6 146 E3
Tolmers Gdns. Cuf EN6 146 F2
Tolmers Mews. New St SG13 146 E6
Tolmers Rd. Cuf EN6 146 E3
Tolpits Cl. Watf WD1 166 F4
Tolpits La. Watf WD1 166 E2
Tom's Hill. Sar WD3 152 E3
Tom's La. Abb L WD4,WD5 139 D3
Tomkins Cl. Bor WD6 169 E8
Toms Croft. Heml H HP2 124 E2
Toms Field. Hat AL10 129 E4
Toms Hill Rd. Ald HP23 101 D5
Tonwell Jun Mix Inf Sch. Ton 92 E7
Tooke Cl. Pnr HA5 175 E2
Toorack Rd. Har HA3 176 D1
Tooveys Mill Cl. Kin L WD4 139 A2
Topstreet Way. Harp AL5 107 C8
Torquay Cres. Stev SG1 50 B7
Torquay Dr. Luton LU4 44 D4
Torridge Wlk. Heml H HP2 124 F8 2
Torrington Dr. Pot B EN6 159 D7
Torrington Rd. Berk HP4 122 B4
Tortoiseshell Way. Berk HP4 121 F6
Torwood Cl. Berk HP4 121 F4
Torworth Rd. Bor WD6 157 A1
Tot La. Birhr CM23 59 D4
Totteridge Comm. Barn N20 171 D1
Totteridge Pk. Barn N20 171 C1
Totteridge Rd. Enf EN3 162 D2
Totteridge Village. Barn N20 171 F1
Totton Mews. Red AL3 106 B5
Totts La. Walk SG2 38 C1
Toulmin Dr. St Alb AL3 127 C7
Tovey Ave. Hod EN11 135 A8
Tovey Cl. Lo Naz EN9 149 F8
Tovey Cl. Lon C AL2 142 D5
Tower Cl. Berk HP4 122 A3
Tower Cl. Knee SG8 2 A5
Tower Cl. L Wym SG4 35 F3
Tower Ct. Luton LU2 46 A1 2
Tower Ctr. Hod 135 A7
Tower Hill. Chipf HP3,WD4 137 F1
Tower Hill La. Sand AL4 108 F4
Tower Hill. Muc H SG10 74 F2
Tower Rd. Cod SG4 67 F2
Tower Rd. Luton LU2 64 A8
Tower Rd. Ware SG12 93 F2
Tower Sch. Ware 93 E3
Tower St. Hert SG14 113 C8
Tower Way. Luton LU2 64 A8
Towers Rd. Heml H HP2 124 E4
Towers Rd. Pnr HA5 175 E2
Towers Rd. Stev SG1 50 D4
Towers The. Stev SG1 50 D4
Town Ctr. Hat AL10 130 A6
Town Farm. Ched LU7 80 A7
Town Farm Cres. Stand SG11 55 F2
Town Farm. Whea AL4 108 D8
Town Fields. Hat AL10 130 A6
Town La. Ben SG2 52 E4
Town Mead Rd. Wa Aby EN9 163 C5
Town Sq. Stev SG1 50 D5
Towne Rd. Royst SG8 7 D5
Townfield. Ric WD3 165 C2
Townley. Letw SG6 23 D4
Townsend Ave. St Alb AL1 127 E4
Townsend C of E Sch. St Alb 127 C8
Townsend Cl. Bark SG8 17 C3
Townsend Cl. Harp AL5 85 F1
Townsend Dr. St Alb AL3 127 D5
Townsend. Heml H HP2 124 D5
Townsend La. Harp AL5 85 E1
Townsend Rd. Harp AL5 86 A2
Townsend Way. Norwd HA6 175 A3
Townshend St. Hert SG13 113 E6
Townsley Cl. Luton LU1 63 E6
Tracey Ct. Luton LU1 63 E6 10
Trafalgar Ave. Hod EN10 134 F2
Trafford Cl. Shen WD7 156 E7
Trafford Cl. Stev SG1 36 E1
Traherne Cl. Hit SG4 34 F5 2
Trajan Gate. Walk SG2 37 D1
Trapstyle Rd. Hert SG12 93 A2
Travellers Cl. Wel G AL9 144 C8
Travellers La. Hat AL9,AL10 130 B2
Travellers La. Wel Gr AL9 130 C1
Treacle La. Rus SG9 25 F3
Treacy Cl. Bus WD2 176 C8
Trebellan Dr. Heml H HP2 124 F4
Tree Cl. Heml H HP3 125 B1
Tree Ct. Elst WD6 169 D3
Treehanger Cl. Tri HP23 100 B4
Treetops Cl. Norwd HA6 174 D5
Trefoil Cl. Dun LU4 44 A4
Trefusis Wlk. Watf WD1 166 E8
Tregelles Rd. Hod EN11 135 A8
Tremaine Gr. Heml H HP2 124 E7
Trent Cl. Shen WD7 156 E7
Trent Cl. Stev SG1 50 E8
Trent Rd. Luton LU3 45 B4
Tresco Rd. Berk HP4 121 F5
Trescott Cl. Luton LU2 46 E2
Tresilion Sq. Heml H HP2 125 A8
Treslian Sq. Heml H HP2 124 F8 1
Trevalga Way. Heml H HP2 124 E7
Trevellance Way. Watf WD2 154 D6
Trevelyan Way. Berk HP4 122 B6
Trevero Ct. Ches EN8 162 E6
Trevor Cl. Har HA3 176 F3
Trevor Rd. Hit SG4 35 A8
Trevose Way. Sth Ox WD1 175 C7
Trewenna Dr. Pot B EN6 159 D7
Triangle The. Hit SG4 34 F6
Trident Ave. Hat AL10 129 E6
Trident Ind Est. Hod 135 C7
Trident Rd. Watf WD2 153 F5
Triggs Way. Gt Of LU2 46 E3
Trimley Cl. Luton LU4 44 B5
Trinder Rd. Barn EN5 171 C4
Tring Ford Rd. Wils HP23 100 A7
Tring Hill. Ast Cl HP23 99 C3
Tring Rd. Lon M HP23 79 C3
Tring Rd. Nthch HP4 121 D7
Tring Rd. Wing HP22 60 C1
Tring Sch. Tri 100 B4
Tring Sta. Ald 101 A5
Trinity Cl. Bis St CM23 76 F6
Trinity Cl. Norwd HA6 174 E4
Trinity Ct. Hert SG14 113 C8
Trinity Gr. Hert SG14 113 C8
Trinity Hall Cl. Watf WD2 167 C6
Trinity La. Ches EN8 162 E7
Trinity Mews. Heml H HP2 125 D2
Trinity Pl. Stev SG1 50 D6
Trinity Rd. Hert H SG13 114 C3
Trinity Rd. Luton LU3 45 B4
Trinity Rd. Stev SG1 50 C6
Trinity Rd. Stot SG5 11 F7
Trinity Rd. Ware SG12 93 E2
Trinity St. Bis St CM23 76 F6
Trinity Way. Bis St CM23 76 F6
Trinity Wlk. Hert H SG13 114 C3
Tristram Rd. Hit SG4 22 B2
Triton Way. Heml H HP2 124 F5
Trojan Terr. Saw CM21 97 E3
Troon Gdns. Luton LU2 45 E6
Trooper Rd. Ald HP23 101 C5
Trotter's Gap. Sta Ab SG12 115 E4
Trotters Bottom. Pot B EN5 158 B2
Trotts Hill Jun & Inf Sch. Stev 36 F1
Trout Rise. Ric WD3 165 B6
Troutstream Way. Ric WD3 165 B5
Trouvere Pk. Heml H HP1 124 B5
Trowbridge Gdns. Luton LU2 45 E3
Trowley Bottom. Fla AL3 105 B8
Trowley Hill Rd. Fla AL3 84 B1
Trowley Rise. Abb L WD5 153 F8
Truemans Rd. Hit SG5 21 D2
Trumper Rd. Stev SG1 36 F1
Trumpington Dr. St Alb AL1 141 D8
Trundlers Way. Bus WD2 168 E1
Truro Gdns. Luton LU3 45 C5
Trust Rd. Ches EN8 162 E5
Tucker St. Watf WD1 167 C4
Tucker's Row. Bis St CM23 76 F6
Tudor Ave. Ches EN7 162 B8
Tudor Ave. Watf WD2 154 D2
Tudor Cl. Ches EN7 162 B8
Tudor Cl. Hat AL10 129 F2
Tudor Cl. Hun SG12 116 D8
Tudor Cl. Stev SG1 36 C1
Tudor Cres. Enf EN2 161 C1
Tudor Ct. Bor WD6 169 E7
Tudor Ct. Hit SG5 34 D6
Tudor Ct. Knee SG8 2 B4
Tudor Ct. Ric WD3 165 A1
Tudor Ct. Saw CM21 97 E3
Tudor Dr. Watf WD2 154 D2
Tudor Jun Mix Inf Sch. Heml H 124 E1
Tudor Manor Gdns. Watf WD2 154 D7
Tudor Par. Ric WD3 165 A2
Tudor Rd. Har HA3 176 D1
Tudor Rd. Luton LU3 45 B2
Tudor Rd. Pnr HA5 175 C1
Tudor Rd. St Alb AL3 127 E7
Tudor Rd. Welw AL6 89 B3
Tudor Rd. Whea AL4 108 E8
Tudor Rise. Hod EN10 134 E2
Tudor Way. Hert SG14 113 A7
Tudor Way. Ric WD3 165 A2
Tudor Way. Wa Aby EN9 163 D6
Tudor Wlk. Watf WD2 154 D2
Tuffnells Way. Harp AL5 85 D4
Tunfield Rd. Hod EN11 115 B1
Tunnel Wood Cl. Watf WD1 153 F2
Tunnel Wood Rd. Watf WD1 153 F2
Tunnmeade. Harl CM20 118 A1
Turf La. Gra SG4 36 B4
Turkey St. Enf EN1,EN3 162 C2
Turkey Street Sta. Enf 162 C2
Turmore Dale. Wel G C AL8 110 C5
Turn Braemar. Heml H HP2 105 B1
Turnberry Ct. Sth Ox WD1 175 C7
Turnberry Dr. Bri Wd AL2 140 E1
Turner Cl. Stev SG1 36 C2
Turner Rd. Bus WD2 168 C5
Turners Cl. Bram SG14 91 C4
Turners Cl. Harp AL5 86 C4
Turners Ct. Ches EN8 162 D8
Turners Hill. Ches EN8 148 D1
Turners Hill. Heml H HP2 124 E2
Turners Orch. Chor WD3 164 D4
Turners Rd N. Luton LU2 46 A2
Turners Rd S. Luton LU2 46 A2
Turnford Sch. Ches 148 E3
Turnford Villas. Ches EN10 148 F5
Turnpike Dr. Luton LU3 31 C1
Turnpike Gn. Heml H HP2 124 F7
Turnpike La. Ick SG5 21 E3
Turnstones The. Watf WD2 154 E3
Turpin's Ride. Royst SG8 7 D5
Turpin's Rise. Stev SG2 50 F1
Turpin's Way. Bal SG7 23 F7
Turpins Chase. Welw AL6 89 F7
Turpins Cl. Hert SG14 112 F6
Turpins Ride. Welw AL6 89 F7
Tuxford Cl. Bor WD6 156 E1
Tweed Cl. Berk HP4 122 B5
Twelve Acres. Wel G C AL7 110 E4
Twelve Leys. Wing HP22 60 B3
Twickenham Gdns. Har HA3 176 E3
Twigden Ct. Luton LU3 44 E5
Twinwoods. Stev SG1 50 F4
Twist The. Wigg HP23 100 D2
Twitchell The. Bal SG7 23 F8
Two Acres. Wel G C AL7 110 F3
Two Beeches. Heml H HP2 124 F8
Two Dells La. Ash Gr HP5 136 A4
Two Oaks Dr. Welw AL6 90 C6
Two Waters Jun Mix Inf Sch.
Heml H 138 D6
Two Waters Rd. Heml H HP3 124 C1
Two Waters Rd. Heml H HP3 138 D8
Twyford Bsns Ctr The. Bis St 77 A5
Twyford Bury La. Bis St CM22 77 A4
Twyford Cl. Bis St CM23 77 A5
Twyford Dr. Luton LU2 46 D1
Twyford Gdns. Bis St CM23 76 F4
Twyford Rd. Bis St CM23 77 A5
Twyford Rd. St Alb AL4 128 D7
Tye End. Stev SG2 69 B8
Tyfield Cl. Ches EN8 148 C1
Tylers Cl. Kin L WD4 138 F3
Tylers Cswy. New St SG13 132 C1
Tylers. Harp AL5 86 D1
Tylers Hill Rd. Bot HP5 150 A8
Tylers Mead. Luton LU2 45 E5
Tylers Way. Radl WD2 168 E4
Tylers Wood. Welw AL6 90 C6
Tylersfield. Abb L WD5 154 A8
Tynedale. Lon C AL2 142 F4
Tynemouth Dr. Enf EN1 162 A1
Typleden Cl. Heml H HP2 124 D5
Tysoe Ave. Enf EN3 162 F2
Tythe Rd. Luton LU4 44 C6
Tyttenhanger Gn. Coln H AL1 142 E8

Uckfield Rd. Enf EN3 162 D2
Ufford Cl. Har HA3 176 B3
Ufford Rd. Har HA3 176 B3
Ullswater Rd. Heml H HP3 125 C1

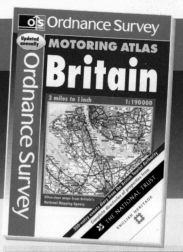

STREET ATLASES
ORDER FORM

The Street Atlases are available from all good bookshops or by mail order direct from the publisher. Orders can be made in the following ways. **By phone** Ring our special Credit Card Hotline on **01933 443863** during office hours (9am to 5pm) or leave a message on the answering machine, quoting your full credit card number plus expiry date and your full name and address. **By post or fax** Fill out the order form below (you may photocopy it) and post it to: **Philip's Direct, 27 Sanders Road, Wellingborough, Northants NN8 4NL** or fax it to: **01933 443849**. Before placing an order by post, by fax or on the answering machine, please telephone to check availability and prices.

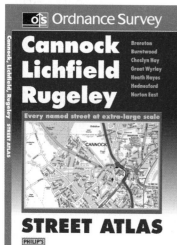

COLOUR LOCAL ATLASES

	PAPERBACK	
	Quantity @ £3.50 each	£ Total
CANNOCK, LICHFIELD, RUGELEY	☐ 0 540 07625 2 ➤	☐
DERBY AND BELPER	☐ 0 540 07608 2 ➤	☐
NORTHWICH, WINSFORD, MIDDLEWICH	☐ 0 540 07589 2 ➤	☐
PEAK DISTRICT TOWNS	☐ 0 540 07609 0 ➤	☐
STAFFORD, STONE, UTTOXETER	☐ 0 540 07626 0 ➤	☐
WARRINGTON, WIDNES, RUNCORN	☐ 0 540 07588 4 ➤	☐

COLOUR REGIONAL ATLASES

	HARDBACK	SPIRAL	POCKET	
	Quantity @ £10.99 each	Quantity @ £8.99 each	Quantity @ £4.99 each	£ Total
MERSEYSIDE	☐ 0 540 06480 7	☐ 0 540 06481 5	☐ 0 540 06482 3 ➤	☐
	Quantity @ £12.99 each	Quantity @ £8.99 each	Quantity @ £5.99 each	£ Total
BERKSHIRE	☐ 0 540 06170 0	☐ 0 540 06172 7	☐ 0 540 06173 5 ➤	☐
	Quantity @ £12.99 each	Quantity @ £9.99 each	Quantity @ £4.99 each	£ Total
DURHAM	☐ 0 540 06365 7	☐ 0 540 06366 5	☐ 0 540 06367 3 ➤	☐
EAST KENT	☐ 0 540 07483 7	☐ 0 540 07276 1	☐ 0 540 07287 7 ➤	☐
WEST KENT	☐ 0 540 07366 0	☐ 0 540 07367 9	☐ 0 540 07369 5 ➤	☐
	Quantity @ £12.99 each	Quantity @ £9.99 each	Quantity @ £5.50 each	£ Total
GREATER MANCHESTER	☐ 0 540 06485 8	☐ 0 540 06486 6	☐ 0 540 06487 4 ➤	☐
TYNE AND WEAR	☐ 0 540 06370 3	☐ 0 540 06371 1	☐ 0 540 06372 X ➤	☐
	Quantity @ £12.99 each	Quantity @ £9.99 each	Quantity @ £5.99 each	£ Total
BIRMINGHAM & WEST MIDLANDS	☐ 0 540 07603 1	☐ 0 540 07604 X	☐ 0 540 07605 8 ➤	☐
BUCKINGHAMSHIRE	☐ 0 540 07466 7	☐ 0 540 07467 5	☐ 0 540 07468 3 ➤	☐
CHESHIRE	☐ 0 540 07507 8	☐ 0 540 07508 6	☐ 0 540 07509 4 ➤	☐
DERBYSHIRE	☐ 0 540 07531 0	☐ 0 540 07532 9	☐ 0 540 07533 7 ➤	☐
EDINBURGH & East Central Scotland	☐ 0 540 07653 8	☐ 0 540 07654 6	☐ 0 540 07656 2 ➤	☐
NORTH ESSEX	☐ 0 540 07289 3	☐ 0 540 07290 7	☐ 0 540 07292 3 ➤	☐

STREET ATLASES ORDER FORM

COLOUR REGIONAL ATLASES

	HARDBACK Quantity @ £12.99 each	SPIRAL Quantity @ £9.99 each	POCKET Quantity @ £5.99 each	£ Total
SOUTH ESSEX	☐ 0 540 07294 X	☐ 0 540 07295 8	☐ 0 540 07297 4	➤ ☐
GLASGOW & West Central Scotland	☐ 0 540 07648 1	☐ 0 540 07649 X	☐ 0 540 07651 1	➤ ☐
NORTH HAMPSHIRE	☐ 0 540 07471 3	☐ 0 540 07472 1	☐ 0 540 07473 X	➤ ☐
SOUTH HAMPSHIRE	☐ 0 540 07476 4	☐ 0 540 07477 2	☐ 0 540 07478 0	➤ ☐
HERTFORDSHIRE	☐ 0 540 06174 3	☐ 0 540 06175 1	☐ 0 540 06176 X	➤ ☐
OXFORDSHIRE	☐ 0 540 07512 4	☐ 0 540 07513 2	☐ 0 540 07514 0	➤ ☐
SURREY	☐ 0 540 06435 1	☐ 0 540 06436 X	☐ 0 540 06438 6	➤ ☐
EAST SUSSEX	☐ 0 540 07306 7	☐ 0 540 07307 5	☐ 0 540 07312 1	➤ ☐
WEST SUSSEX	☐ 0 540 07319 9	☐ 0 540 07323 7	☐ 0 540 07327 X	➤ ☐
WARWICKSHIRE	☐ 0 540 07560 4	☐ 0 540 07561 2	☐ 0 540 07562 0	➤ ☐
SOUTH YORKSHIRE	—	☐ 0 540 07667 8	☐ 0 540 07669 4	➤ ☐
WEST YORKSHIRE	☐ 0 540 07671 6	☐ 0 540 07672 4	☐ 0 540 07674 0	➤ ☐

	Quantity @ £14.99 each	Quantity @ £9.99 each	Quantity @ £5.99 each	£ Total
LANCASHIRE	☐ 0 540 06440 8	☐ 0 540 06441 6	☐ 0 540 06443 2	➤ ☐
NOTTINGHAMSHIRE	☐ 0 540 07541 8	☐ 0 540 07542 6	☐ 0 540 07543 4	➤ ☐
STAFFORDSHIRE	☐ 0 540 07549 3	☐ 0 540 07550 7	☐ 0 540 07551 5	➤ ☐

BLACK AND WHITE REGIONAL ATLASES

	HARDBACK Quantity @ £11.99 each	SOFTBACK Quantity @ £8.99 each	POCKET Quantity @ £3.99 each	£ Total
BRISTOL AND AVON	☐ 0 540 06140 9	☐ 0 540 06141 7	☐ 0 540 06142 5	➤ ☐

	Quantity @ £12.99 each	Quantity @ £9.99 each	Quantity @ £4.99 each	£ Total
CARDIFF, SWANSEA & GLAMORGAN	☐ 0 540 06186 7	☐ 0 540 06187 5	☐ 0 540 06207 3	➤ ☐

Post to: Philip's Direct, 27 Sanders Road, Wellingborough, Northants NN8 4NL

◆ Free postage and packing

◆ All available titles will normally be dispatched within 5 working days of receipt of order but please allow up to 28 days for delivery

☐ Please tick this box if you do not wish your name to be used by other carefully selected organisations that may wish to send you information about other products and services

Registered Office: 2-4 Heron Quays, London E14 4JP

Registered in England number: 3597451

I enclose a cheque / postal order, for a **total** of ☐
made payable to **Octopus Publishing Group Ltd,** or please debit my

☐ Mastercard ☐ American Express ☐ Visa

account by ☐

ACCOUNT NO
☐☐☐☐ ☐☐☐☐ ☐☐☐☐ ☐☐☐☐

Expiry date ☐☐ ☐☐

Signature...

Name...

Address...

....

....POSTCODE.........................

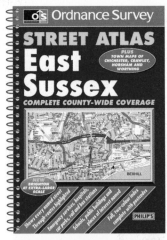

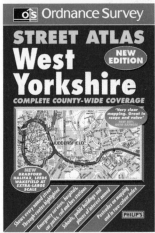

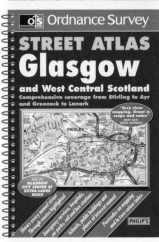